Agent-Based Simulation of Organizational Behavior

Davide Secchi • Martin Neumann
Editors

Agent-Based Simulation of Organizational Behavior

New Frontiers of Social Science Research

Springer

Editors
Davide Secchi
COMAC Research Cluster
Department of Language
and Communication
University of Southern Denmark
Slagelse, Denmark

Martin Neumann
Institute for information systems
Koblenz University
Koblenz, Germany

The Editors gratefully acknowledge the support of the Society for the Study of Artificial Intelligence and Simulation of Behavior (AISB) in developing this volume.

ISBN 978-3-319-18152-3 ISBN 978-3-319-18153-0 (eBook)
DOI 10.1007/978-3-319-18153-0

Library of Congress Control Number: 2015945340

Springer Cham Heidelberg New York Dordrecht London

Printed on acid-free paper

Springer International Publishing AG Switzerland is part of Springer Science+Business Media (www.springer.com)

Preface

This book is the product of a workshop on *Modelling Organisational Behaviour and Social Agency*, hosted by Bournemouth University, January 27–28, 2014, and sponsored by the Society for the Study of Artificial Intelligence and the Simulation of Behavior (AISB). The event sought to examine the applications, structure, how-to, potentials, and philosophical and theoretical underpinnings of agent-based models (ABM) as they apply to organizational behavior and social agency. We had one day and a half of paper sessions, with social and networking activities. Participants came from seven countries, including the UK, Germany, Denmark, Estonia, Lithuania, Canada, and Italy.

The workshop was extremely valuable and all who participated agreed that it delivered more than promised. We spent two interesting days sharing ideas, establishing fruitful research relationships, and learning a lot from each other. This was an attempt to see how ABM can be used to enhance social sciences and, in particular, the study of social agency and organizational behavior. The fruits of that workshop are now collected in this book. The discussions of the two days enabled true cross-disciplinary fertilization and inspired us to start and progress with the idea of this volume. We are extremely pleased that some of the spirit of those two days is now reflected into this book.

Both editors of this volume share a keen interest in computational and mathematical simulation models. Martin is more experienced in ABM and comes from a more sociological background, while Davide came in contact with ABM simulation in 2010 and conducts his work on organizational behavior. Besides ABM and despite (or because) we come from different disciplinary backgrounds, we found ourselves very much aligned on two points, at least. First, we are both interested in understanding distributed cognitive processes and believe that ABM provides a very powerful frame to study them. Second, we both agree that cross-disciplinary efforts are extremely important for the advancement of science, despite contemporary academia does not seem to value or encourage them.

A few words should be spent to describe the process we used to collect and edit this project. After the workshop, we invited participants to submit full papers based on their presentation. All presenters but two agreed to submit their work. We then asked every author to review two chapters in a single-blind peer-review process. This means that reviewers knew who the authors of the two chapters were, but the authors did not know who reviewed their work. We collected reviewers' reports and had another round of reviews; for a few chapters a third round was necessary. As it usually happens when articles fall under an academic niche (such as ABM), we experienced a phenomenon of self-selection so that all chapters submitted were rigorous and up to a good academic standard. The review process improved them all and we are extremely happy with each and every contribution of this volume.

Of course, we could not have done this without the help of the many people who supported us. First and foremost, we wish to thank all the authors for their time, enduring support, and bright contributions. We were thrilled by the high standards of the chapters and especially of the reviews we received. Mutual respect increased reviewers' engagement to address common intellectual puzzles. Sometimes we do not see such detailed, clear, and intellectually challenging reviews from top journals! We really appreciated all of their dedication to this project; indeed, thank you very much. Among everyone, Stephen Cowley deserves a special thanks from us. He originally created the contact between the two of us and has been a true inspiration, constructive critic, and friend to both of us. We know this book could have not been done without you: Thanks a ton! We also wish to thank Yasemin Erden from AISB, who believed in our project and supported our workshop and the book project.

Nick Philipson and Nitza Jones-Sepulveda from Springer New York showed an incredible level of enthusiasm for our project since the very beginning. Their support, both professional and personal, remains unmatched compared to other publication experiences. It is so good to work with you that we wish we could only publish books! Seriously, you need to know that you do a great job. Thank you so very much.

Davide's wife Claudia also deserves a special mention in this book. Her patience, loving care, and understanding for a husband who works for too many weekends can only be reciprocated with Davide's endless love.

Finally, we have enjoyed working with each other very much and we hope to continue working on ABM and other related projects. We hope you will be pleased by what follows as much as we have enjoyed working together and with all the authors.

Have a pleasant read.

Slagelse, Denmark — Davide Secchi
Koblenz, Germany — Martin Neumann

Contents

Chapter 1
Exploring the New Frontier: Computational Studies of Organizational Behavior

Martin Neumann and Davide Secchi

Abstract This chapter introduces the book *Agent-Based Simulation of Organizational Behavior* presenting the idea of agent-based modeling as a "new frontier" for organizational research. After providing some indications of the challenge of bringing together cross-disciplinary and specialization tensions, the chapter suggests that *autonomy*, *sociality*, and *cross-validation* make this technique particularly suited to analyze organizational behavior research. An overview of the book follows with a short summary of the four parts of the book and each and every chapter. This introduction concludes with a map of what this new research frontier is about, covering both methodological and theoretical grounds.

Keywords Specialization • Cross-disciplinary research • Autonomy • Sociality • Cross-validation

1.1 A Misleading Divide: Cross-Disciplinary Fertilization vs. Specialization

Organizational behavior is, broadly speaking, the study of how individuals think, interact, and act in formal social structures. It is also the study of how organizations develop, maintain, and evolve elements of these social structures that transcend individuals and nevertheless affect their behavior. Research covered by the discipline has a broad scope, and its frontiers are open and not sharply defined (Heath & Sitkin, 2001). As an area of research, organizational behavior is claimed to be part of management and, at the same time, part of applied psychology

---

M. Neumann
Institute for Information Systems in Business and Public Administration, University of Koblenz, Koblenz, Germany
e-mail: maneumann@uni-koblenz.de

D. Secchi (✉)
Research Cluster for Cognition, Management and Communication (COMAC), Center for Human Interactivity (CHI), Department of Language and Communication, University of Southern Denmark, Slagelse, Denmark
e-mail: secchi@sdu.dk

D. Secchi, M. Neumann (eds.), *Agent-Based Simulation of Organizational Behavior*, DOI 10.1007/978-3-319-18153-0_1

(of industrial psychology in particular), as well as organizational sociology and organizational economics. To include all of its disciplinary belongings, we may call it *organization research* for the purpose of this introduction. Most of the mainstream journals address micro rather than macro aspects of the discipline and are especially targeted by psychologists and management scholars. Journals dealing with macro organizational research are instead targeted by sociologists and economists. The inherent multidisciplinary core of this area of study affects it in at least two directions. On the one hand, there is a wide interest in cognitive, social, psychological, and economic aspects of human behavior in organizations that runs deep in most of social science. This means that this area of study can be thought of as a center to which most disciplines look at with interest. On the other hand, this interest is segmented and, despite the potential for mutual understanding, scientific progress is seldom shared between scholars from different disciplines.

These two aspects press organizational scholars towards two opposite directions. The nature of the topic urges scholars to look outside of their comfort zone and to other disciplines to better understand and expand their research. The other pressure is that of trying to clarify what makes what they do "special" and "unique" as opposed to other disciplines. This is, for example, a reason why some discuss about routines (Pentland & Rueter, 1994) and some others about tacit knowledge (Foss, 2003; Nelson & Winter, 1982), and some indicate diffusion through popularity as bandwagon (Fiol & O'Connor, 2003) and some others as herding behavior (Banerjee, 1992). The quest for hyper-specialization is also something academics need to face in today's research environment. The irony is that the advancement of scientific knowledge needs both—cross-disciplinary fertilization and specialization—at the same time. This has been the case in many occasions in the history of organization studies. For example, in the 1990s, what we called the "cognitive revolution" (Walsh, 1995) came from a significant and growing body of organization research borrowing concepts, theories, practices, and approaches from cognitive science. Or, we can look at the wave of innovation and renewed attention to macro and societal elements as brought in the discipline by neo-institutionalism (Powell & DiMaggio, 1991). More recently, social semiotics brought new insights into the way of looking at the visual dimensions of organizing and the organization (Meyer, Höllerer, Jancsary, & van Leeuwen, 2013). How to reconcile these two scientific needs is an important challenge that organizational research currently faces.

We are not claiming that the reconciliation between cross-disciplinary fertilization and specialization is an issue for organizational research only, when it is probably one of the current challenges of many disciplines in the social sciences. Instead, we are suggesting that it is particularly relevant to organizational research, given its multidisciplinary core. Although there is no easy way to deal with this challenge, we believe that technological innovation and methodological developments may be of some help.

Agent-based modeling (ABM) and simulation can be brought in to reconcile these two directions. The idea of using computer simulation to study organizational research is not at all new. One of the most remarkable contributions to the literature is that of Cohen, March, and Olsen (1972) featuring a "garbage can" model of decision making. If one ever needed to understand how insightful computer simulations can be or what kind of contribution they can offer to the scientific enterprise, the "garbage can" model clearly serves as a paradigmatic example. Although we have countless examples of further simulation studies in this field, this particular method of inquiry has not taken off over the past decades. ABM shows potentials to change the point of reference for computer simulation in organizational research as well as in other disciplines. This presents ABM as a game changer and as something that could serve as a mediation to facilitate cross-disciplinary research without compromising specialization.

This book is an attempt to show exactly this use of ABM. On the one hand, agent-based simulation allows for abstractions that can be interpreted from multiple disciplinary angles. In fact, the same model may be used to observe an organizational phenomenon from different perspectives. Hence, it is a tool for cross-disciplinary fertilization. Chapters in this book may look particularly heterogeneous at first sight but they are extremely coherent, when we have in mind that ABM makes abstractions more understandable by others. We are not indicating that this particular technique serves the same scope declared by systems theorists around the 1950s—i.e., unifying science on a similar conceptual and formal language (that of mathematics). In the case of ABM, the reference is more specific and we are stating that modeling could serve as a mediation of meaning as well as scientific development. While systems theory was an attempt of *unification* by referring to mathematics as the meta-language for all sciences, ABM provides a means for *diversification* since it enables to integrate diverse disciplines in the study of a single object. Of course, interpretation and action are in the eye of the observer; it is each one of us who should make a decision on whether to use ABM with this particular objective in mind or not.

On the other hand, this particular simulation technique allows for abstractions not to lose key elements of discipline-specific elements. A model of organizational bandwagon (Secchi & Gullekson, 2012), for example, can be used as a way of studying for social ties although it is modeled as a tool to understand and analyze social cognitive dynamics. The specifics of cognitive dynamics are embedded in the modeling effort and make the way agents interact based on organizational cognitive "rules." Another example can be taken from this book and is that of team dynamics (Thomsen, 2015; *this volume*), where the author develops the model on the basis of cognitive altruistic interactions—based on a socio-cognitive mechanism called "docility" (Simon, 1993)—thus giving the model a very specific organizational cognitive dimension. However, results of the model are also particularly useful if someone wants to analyze social interactions and industry-specific (i.e., health) socio-cognitive team dynamics. In short, with ABM there are aspects specific to a particular discipline that do not obscure the potentials for cross-disciplinary fertilization.

The book we are presenting aims to show how ABM can function as a tool to develop organizational research further. Looking at other disciplines to move forward has brought innovation and fresh debates into the field. This is clearly a new frontier for organizational research that some have started to pioneer (e.g., Knudsen & Srikanth, 2014; Miller & Lin, 2010). However, only a handful of scholars

(Fioretti, 2013; Miller, 2015; Secchi, 2015) have attempted to clearly indicate why the use of ABM could bring important advancements to the field. This is where the book stands.

Before summarizing the contents of the book and indicating how the chapters can be read as a coherent mix, we succinctly review some of the features of agent-based modeling and simulation.

1.2 The Impact of Agent-Based Modeling for Studying Organizational Behavior

Agent-based simulation methods allow for studying social behavior in the lab. In fact, simulation technology consists of software objects, called "agents," which operate due to some internal and interaction rules. These rules define the agents as *autonomous* and, for example, typical operations may include target tracking; that is, agents have goals which they aim to realize by certain actions. This is denoted as *pro-activity.* Moreover, these objects (i.e., the agents) operate in a simulated environment. They react to stimuli from the environment and, for this reason, they are denoted as *reactive.* The environment typically includes other agents to which they react, but also other simulated objects that may mimic a social environment. This is denoted as *sociality* (Woolridge, 2009). This is, on a very technical level, a description of key features of the technology.

The analogy to human social interaction is striking and this is why agent-based simulation provides a lab for social science. Agent-based simulation allows observing the effects of agents' social interactions in a controlled manner, as if the researcher is running a social experiment in a lab. This provides insights into the micro–macro link: how macro properties are generated through the agents' interaction and how these emergent properties foster individual agents' attitudes which, in turn, influence behavior (Squazzoni, Jager, & Edmonds, 2014). This has been denoted as *cross-validation*, as the system allows observing how behavioral rules specified on the microlevel generate statistical signatures on the macro level. Of course, the levels of analysis can be more than the two we are simplistically referring to here (i.e., micro and macro) but many. For example, some simulations define meso-levels and these levels may be considered as mediums between the other levels below and above. Clearly, ABM allow for complex representations of the adaptive social systems they are modeling, with the relation between macro and micro being "filtered" by other level(s) (Neumann & Cowley, 2015; *this volume*). In addition, levels can be compared to empirical evidence of different types, i.e., with detailed microlevel data of interpretative, qualitative research and statistical macro data of social surveys (Moss & Edmonds, 2005). Obviously, software agents are not a replication of human actors and always behave according to rather simplified rules. However, this feature makes agents a lab for studying specific effects of defined rules. In the following, we highlight three characteristics that are particularly interesting for studying organizational behavior by the means of agent-based simulation.

First, simply running a simulation implies investigating social dynamics. While seemingly being a trivial fact, this is crucial for the investigation of social change and, in particular, the mechanisms driving change. Obviously, it is a central objective of organizational science to get insights into how change can happen.

Second, the fact that individual software objects follow their internal rules enables the implementation of different internal rules, which open to the representation of individual heterogeneity rather than investigating "representative" actors as typical of neoclassic accounts. In contrast to more classic accounts, ABM is not bounded to represent the multiplicity of human actors by just one actor model. In contrast, ABM enables to explicitly take diversity into account. Some of the agents in a simulation may follow different rules and these agents may interact within the same environment where a diversity of rules is implemented on different sets of agents. Simulation then allows for investigating the effects of the heterogeneity of the agents on a collective object of investigation, such as an organization or the whole society. For instance, this allows for investigating benefits and pitfalls of multicultural society such as the pioneering work of Schelling's segregation model (Schelling, 1971) or Axelrod's model of the dissemination of culture (Axelrod, 1997). In this volume, this can be represented by Thomsen in a chapter that investigates the effects of heterogeneity on organizational performance (Thomsen, 2015; *this volume*). This makes it possible to represent the dynamics of the social meso-level of networks which are of particular relevance for the study of organizational behavior.

This goes along with a *third* characteristic, namely that it is a characteristic feature of social relations that actors are socially embedded (Granovetter, 1985). Social embeddedness can be characterized by actors which, while not simply imitating each other, nevertheless influence each other. This is usually lost in traditional representative statistical samples that are based on an assumption of independent sampling of units from a population and are therefore inapt to study interactions among individuals.[1] This is not to say that a given sample cannot be represented—for what is worth, some models can represent the entire system or population! (e.g., Heckbert, 2013)—but that other elements of the system, specifically interactions, are more relevant in an ABM simulation. Namely, the features of agents being reactive and socially oriented represent exactly this characteristic of the embeddedness of human social actors. This is decisive for a comprehension of actors operating not as more or less rational actors who make decisions based on individual preferences, but as actors operating in a normative and institutional setting. This refers to the micro–macro link: modeling how interactions of socially embedded agents generate structural properties which, in turn, influence individual

[1]Not all samples in organizational behavior have these characteristics; in fact, especially in organizational team research, observations are not independent and this violation led to the adoption of particular techniques called "multilevel regression analysis."

behavior (Conte, Andrighetto, & Campenni, 2014). It is this institutional embedding that has been highlighted by the neo-institutionalist turn in organizational studies as decisive for a comprehension of organizational behavior (Scott, 2001). Thus ABM fills exactly the gap to take into account the inherent cross-disciplinary nature of organizational studies by providing a methodology for studying how agents contribute to an institutional setting and how they are subject to the influence of this institutional setting, at the same time.

Finally, the point mentioned above on cross-validation is also particularly relevant for organization research. Although there are limited examples and a clear methodology is yet to come, using ABM in combination to qualitative and/or quantitative empirical research is probably one of the most intriguing aspects of this technique. Not only ABM can replicate a particular quantitative set of data (Janssen & Ostrom, 2006), and then analyze emergent properties of agents and the system on a "what-if" basis, but it can also be used to "test" (in a loose sense) the theory that comes out of qualitative data (Neumann, 2015). This latter approach is used already by agent-based modelers and has revealed to be very rich in terms of insights gathered and knowledge advancement. A clear methodology as of how to isolate parameters out of qualitative data is yet to come (see Edmonds, 2015 for a collection of steps in that direction) although some of the existing models may serve as a guide. Moreover, ABM can be used to support empirical data collection, where qualitative data provides useful information to create a simulation model that is then tested and compared to quantitative data. This is, to some extent, a way to "close the circle" where three methods can be used together. ABM is a tool that can also advance methodology in organizational behavior, covering the existing gap between qualitative and quantitative research.

1.2.1 A Novel Approach: Interaction and Cognition

Following the diagnosis written above, it should be expected that ABM is a key methodological tool for organizational research. So far this is not the case and one of the objectives of this book is that of contributing to a change. However, first of all, the diagnosis calls for an examination of the question of what kind of research can be expected by agent-based methodologies. It is long known in philosophy of science that the epistemological status of simulation methodologies remains ambiguous. For instance, simulation has been described by a case study (in this case: biological simulation) as experimenting on theories (Dowling, 1999). This brings us to the question whether we can expect empirical or theoretical research from this methodology. Obviously, a number of different approaches exist in agent-based social simulation. Broadly speaking two approaches can be distinguished and are briefly reviewed in the following.

One approach is summarized by the so-called KISS principle: Keep It Simple, Stupid. This approach favors simple models for thought experiments that disclose the implications of key theoretical assumptions. The objective is theoretical research (e.g., Epstein & Axtell, 1996; Hegselmann & Krause, 2002). The other approach stands in contrast and has been summarized by a so-called KIDS principle: Keep It Descriptive, Stupid. This is data-driven empirical research which typically includes any type of evidence, from qualitative narratives to quantitative statistics. This approach is often used in applied research, including stakeholder participation in a participatory research design (e.g., Moss & Edmonds, 2005). The divide between more descriptive and abstract modeling has also been subject of the special issue published in *Computational and Mathematical Organization Theory* (Coen, 2009) and also in another special issue of the *Journal of Artificial Societies and Social Simulation* (Edmonds, 2015).

In summary, a multitude of approaches exist, balancing between theoretical and empirical research. Nevertheless, they have in common that there is no strict separation between a logic of discovery and a logic of justification. While it is possible to test significance of simulation results (Lorscheid, 2012), in the first instance ABM does not follow the research design of hypothesis testing. The particular strength of this type of research design is different. This brings us to an *epistemological* thesis: As Fioretti (2015) argues in detail in this volume, experimenting with different agent rules and settings of interaction offers a methodological tool for creative exploration rather than merely testing of hypotheses. ABM allows exploring possible worlds for a systematic search for unsought discoveries. This is what Bardone (2015; *this volume*) describes as forward-looking exploration rather than backward-looking explanatory accounts. It should be clear that we are referring to the scientific use and interpretation of the simulation, not to its modeling accuracy. In fact, it is important that the simulated lab experiments with ABM are structured so that their results are consistent over repeated runs. Traditional statistical techniques can be used (e.g., power analysis, convergence) to make sure that the simulation is not showing random results but consistent patterns, given the specified parameters. There is one aspect pertaining to the way results are obtained and another that relates to the way results are interpreted. Clearly, the latter aspect is more relevant here.

In this volume this particular feature of using ABM as a forward-looking and creative exploratory tool is approached from a variety of angles. However, all the individual chapters have in common a certain theoretical perspective, discussed after each chapter is summarized.

1.3 Overview of the Volume

This volume counts 15 chapters, excluding this one. Chapters are distributed in four distinct parts that group contributions based on similarity of the topic.

Part I includes suggestive contributions from two authorities in the fields of computer simulation, Guido Fioretti, and distributed cognition, Stephen Cowley. This is the part entitled *Perspectives* and is an attempt to answer a few questions such as the following: What are the challenges that we face when individual-oriented simulation (e.g., micro organizational behavior) is addressed? Why is ABM the most suitable technique to deal with cognition? What are the "secular" issues that ABM may help reframe? How is the relation between the agent and the system shaped?

Fioretti's Chap. 2 on emergent organizations sets out the methodological frame of the book. He argues that rather than simply being a tool for hypothesis testing, ABM provides a methodology for creative exploration of hypotheses, stimulating scientific imagination. He shows the potential of this methodology for organizational studies with two examples of the "garbage can" model and the NK model, before outlining possible pathways for future research. Fioretti suggests that organizational evolution in particular can be understood by using novel concepts from evolutionary theory such as punctuated equilibria or exaptation and that unsupervised neural networks provide unexplored options for studying organizations.

Cowley makes use of ABM to pursue a distributed view of language and cognition in Chap. 3. Rather than reducing cognition to the mind and language of symbols exchanged between minds as it happens in a representationalist view, embedding in interlacing time scales enables agents to self-configure. This is demonstrated at an agent-based model of vowel shift. The model shows how speech patterns shift based on density of interaction. Thus no hypotheses about cognitive learning mechanisms are needed, as assumed by prior language science. Measurable differences need not covary with underlying "lower level" entities. This view of cognition as a distributed and diachronic activity sets a theoretical pace for this volume by outlining a phenomenology of interaction and cognition.

Modeling Organizational Behavior is the title of Part II. A particular emphasis on routines and prosocial attitudes is featured under this theme. Some of the topics in this section deal with questions such as (a) how a clear categorization of routines may lead to a significantly different modeling activity; (b) processes of organizational coevolution to match routines and learning activities; (c) the use of ABM to understand how much disorganization an organization can tolerate; (d) the limits and power of cooperation; and (e) the conditions for the emergence of docility and its impact on teams.

In Chap. 4, Herath, Secchi D., and Homberg present an ABM to test the advantages and disadvantages of disorganization over organization. The simulation is inspired by the "garbage can" model but differs from it in that it compares hierarchical vs. non-hierarchical organizations, includes a function to define simulated employee motivation, and sets targets for the agents. Preliminary results from the simulation suggest that disorganization (or "messiness," as it can also be evocatively called) seems not to be as disruptive as organizational scholars have always thought. The authors suggest that determining its workable level in an organization may be a practical challenge worth enquiring.

Chapter 5 by Kahl and Meyer is dedicated to routines in organizational behavior and it addresses a question at the core of the problem of how to model organizational coevolution by providing an overview of the various meanings of routines in relation to related concepts such as habits, norms, or institutions. The chapter focuses on the question of whether routines are constitutive of behavior or cognition and how these aspects are related. Furthermore, it is applied to the methodology of ABM of organizational routines. The models considered apply evolutionary theory or the concept of a transactive memory. This concept describes a process of distributed cognition, namely what an individual agent can know about others' skills.

Jesi and Mollona are the authors of Chap. 6. They analyze the conditions under which knowledge-based economies see the emergence of cooperation between co-workers in companies where there is no top-down hierarchical control. Building on social exchange theory a P2P ABM is presented and it examines how reciprocal communication between team members is likely to emerge in a way that fosters the exchange of information. Individual agents are arranged in a network and play a prisoner's dilemma game in which they act prosocially or practice free riding. Agents can be rewarded or fired by the firm. Findings indicate that freedom to select co-workers and intraorganizational plasticity is an advantage for companies' performance in case of uncertainty.

In Chap. 7, Breslin, Romano, and Percival present a simulation of organizational coevolution and they provide a critical discussion of evolutionary concepts for modeling organizational behavior. While it is argued that key concepts can be derived from a generalized Darwinian model of evolution, it is emphasized that it is important for a transfer of evolutionary concepts to define and identify the units of analysis. The classic point of view that regards routines as entities of selection is criticized for not representing how routines work in everyday practice. Moving from entities to practices changes the units of analysis. A key framework for simulation is outlined and it enables investigating path-dependent coevolution of interaction. Moreover, it is argued that using this model will elucidate managers about complex possible futures.

The following Chap. 8 by Thomsen presents an ABM of medical teams dealing with a decision-making process. Thomsen utilizes the theoretical framework of human docility to characterize agents in the model. This concept is the attitude to lean on information coming from social channels to make decisions. Findings from the model indicate that teams with moderate levels of docility outperform teams with level of docility that are lower or higher than average. This indicates that coordination among individuals in a team works best when individuals have mutual understanding. Findings may also be related to the composition of the team and to the role played by each individual in their respective position. The chapter is particularly relevant in that it sheds light on how docility may work in a team. As far as our knowledge is concerned, this is the first time the point is approached from a theoretical angle.

The final chapter of this part is Chap. 9 and Secchi D. provides another contribution on individual docility. He presents a simulation model where he tests the boundary conditions for the emergence of docility. His idea is to take the original idea, add an active side—i.e., individuals not only gather information from social channels (passive docility) but also provide information to social channels (active docility) while they make decisions—and test what causes docility to either prosper or disappear in an organization. Findings indicate that lower costs of prosocial behavior and increased social interactions allow docility to prevail over other cognitive strategies.

Part III addresses *Philosophical and Methodological Perspectives*. There is a need to understand the epistemological foundations of computer simulation at a deeper level. This is done with a discussion of ABM as epistemic tools for chance seeking, i.e., tools for hypothesizing out of ignorance (abduction). The book also provides interesting insights into social and asocial agency and ethical implications of (software) agents in (human) society, potentiality and actuality of ABM, and proto-ethical behavior of simulated agents. Under the methodology perspective, the book challenges the ideas of collective consciousness, and it introduces a model on neuro-dynamic waves and individual alignments. It also proposes an analytical approach to ABM, showing results from an equation-based model that, under particular circumstances, may be set to behave in a way similar to ABM.

Bardone's Chap. 10 dives into philosophy foundations of science. Discussing the concept of abduction in the process of hypothesis generation, the chapter argues that this perspective is not sufficient to account for the process of intervention in scientific inquiry. Abduction is backward looking, seeking for a possible explanation of a given fact. This is denoted as explanatory hypothesis formulation. In contrast, scientific intervention is forward looking, exploring possible worlds. In this context systematic *chance seeking* enables exploring unsought discoveries. Taking into account Fioretti's insight about simulation as methodology for creative exploration it becomes evident that Bardone's epistemology of chance seeking describes the advantages of the simulation technique as methodologically sound.

Chapter 11 by Thürmel applies a philosophical perspective on socio-technical systems, in which technical systems are not merely tools but interaction partners. This raises legal issues of the responsibility of technical systems. To examine this question a distinction between potentiality and actuality is drawn. This allows for the construction of a multidimensional framework of agency ranging from passive entities, such as a hammer, to proactive entities, such as an autopilot or automatic bid agents. This framework is applied for assessing issues of responsibility in human-computer interaction. The concept of as-if intentionality is suggested to assess proto-ethical agency in computer-mediated environments.

Chapter 12 by Plikynas and Raudys refers back to Cowley's conceptual outline of a theory of social agency in Chap. 3. They write on nonlocal field like interactions and propose a novel approach to model agents' interaction. Rather than perceiving interaction as an exchange of cognitive "packages" between individuals, individuals are perceived as nodes in a cognitive field. From this perspective, interaction can be described as a nonlocal social phenomenon. Inspired by brain imaging studies in cognitive neuroscience, the oscillation-based multi-agent system (OSIMAS) described in the chapter describes an agent as a coherent system of oscillations distributed among a field. This is implemented in two ways in a simulation model: in a model inspired by phonons and by quantum mechanical wave functions.

Final chapter of Part III is Chap. 13 by Seri. This chapter provides an overview of analytical approximations of solutions for long-term behavior of individual-based models that describe processes of the spreading of an infection. These are well-known and typical examples in the field of ABM. For instance the core principles of these processes are used to model diffusion of information or rumors.

This is modeled mathematically as a Markov chain process. Analytical mathematics provides different solution concepts than simulation modeling and, for this reason, cross-fertilization of analytical and simulation approaches is extremely useful. The chapter introduces readers to the state of the art of this research field which has not been very much explored so far.

Finally, Part IV is on *Macro Aspects of Organizational Behavior* including conflict and cooperation. Criminal organizations present very particular modeling challenges although some of these challenges can be useful to detect and analyze counterproductive behaviors in regular (noncriminal) organizations as well. The book introduces problems and advantages of using ABM to model covert organizations, such as the Italian mafia. The match of macro and micro perspectives could all fit into a distributed/systemic cognitive modeling of agents. A model of cooperation and conflict in the case of controversies over water in developing countries is also presented. ABM offer dramatic advantages over the game-theoretical approaches usually employed in that field although the number and complexity of agents and parameters are a significant constraint. Finally, the use of a model of open innovation networks inspired on an NK landscape model that focuses on the role of intermediaries is discussed. The model highlights that the structure of the network and the way the intermediary is employed affect the final outcome, with some counterintuitive results.

Neumann and Cowley use the example of the Sicilian Mafia to outline the concept of diachronic cognition for a future socio-cognitive science in Chap. 14. They show that both within the criminal organization and in the relation between the organizations and its cultural environment slow processes of a cultural ecosystem give rise to self-maintaining practices that sustain the Mafia. They suggest a framework of an ABM for studying how these time scales are interwoven.

Chapter 15 by Paladini applies ABM to studying nontraditional conflicts about environmental security. The "dam" development project at the Mekong River has provoked controversies for decades. Conflicts involve numerous issues such as threats to the environment and ethnic minorities, and various state and non-state actors. For this reason a complex approach is identified as appropriate and ABM is the final choice. Some modeling concepts are examined to derive key decisions about which components need to be included in a model and first conclusions about the effectiveness of a simulation study are derived.

Secchi E. is the author of Chap. 16 where he presents an ABM of open innovation where an independent firm looks for cooperation. The firms in this model are of two types: innovation seekers and innovation providers. The choice each firm has to make is whether to produce in-house or look for partnerships. In the model, another key role is played by intermediaries between the two types of firms. Findings show that the market is more efficient when intermediaries play a role in the system.

1.4 Mapping the New Frontier

The four sections of this book indicate some of the areas organizational research can benefit from the use of ABM. The two initial chapters set the general feel for how the frontier is shaped and where its borders are located. In fact, both Fioretti and Cowley provide a clear indication of the depth and breadth of the use of ABM, setting the ground for what the other chapters of the book cover. In this section of the introduction, we first outline more clearly what constitutes the common ground for the following chapters and then draw a map of what we have called the "new frontier."

1.4.1 Building a Common Ground

As already stated above, one of the aspects that ABM clearly contributes to analyze is concerned with micro-aspects of human thinking and interaction. A number of chapters deal with team reasoning and, more broadly, collective reasoning. D. Secchi's chapter on "Boundary Conditions for the Emergence of 'Docility' in Organizations," Thomsen's chapter "Exploring Aspects of Coordination by Mutual Adjustment in Fluid Teams," the chapter on the "Simulation of the Effects of Disorganization" by Herath et al., Jesi and Mollona's chapter describing a "P2P-like Simulation Model," or E. Secchi's chapter on "Open Innovation Networks" all describe simulation studies of the effects and performance of coordination and interaction activities. Typically, effects are measured by effective goal achievements, may it be the making of innovations in firm networks or the impact of disorganization. Achieving goals can be described as a proactive manipulation of the environment. If we consider cognition as an effective reaction to environmental triggers as well as a proactive manipulation of the environment, then these chapters can be interpreted as a description of a cognitive activity. Moreover, this activity is not limited to an individual agent but rather an activity distributed throughout the team or the other individuals of the social community. For example, D. Secchi as well as Thomson explicitly refer to Herbert Simons's concept of docility and, implicitly, to that of bounded rationality and distributed cognition. Thus one result of the collective effort of this volume is that docility turns out to be one of the core concepts for exploring how individuals mutually adjust to each other in concerted activity. It can be expected that future research will reveal further insights into this aspect.

A different aspect of collective reasoning can be found in the chapters exploring elements of evolutionary theory, such as Breslin et al.'s "Conceptualizing and Modeling Multi-Level Organizational Co-Evolution," Fioretti's "Emergent Organizations," and the chapter "Modelling Social Agency Using Diachronic Cognition: Learning from the Mafia" by Neumann and Cowley. While the chapters on team reasoning and performance focus on rather immediate results which can be achieved in short time, these chapters explore long-term change. Breslin et al. as well as Fioretti provide an outline of new frontiers of how concepts of evolutionary theory apply to organizational behavior. The key concept for theories of organizational evolution is the notion of routines, which is studied in detail in the chapter of Kahl and Meyer on "Constructing Agent-Based Models of Organizational Routines." The concept of diachronic cognition outlined by Neumann and Cowley in the chapter goes even beyond the application of the Darwinian model by showing how cultural and organizational coevolution entails interlacing time scales of evolutionary dynamics.

A common frame for all these approaches is set out in Cowley's key chapter "Cognition Beyond the Body." Rather than being a representation within the inner mind of an individual, cognition is described as an activity, and in particular as a collective effort. As Thürmel demonstrates in the chapter on "Social and Asocial Agency in Agent-Based Modeling," socially distributed cognition goes beyond human collectives. Rather human-computer interaction has to be considered as a novel cognitive system, posing novel challenges. Perhaps the most radical concept of this social agency is outlined in the field concept of agency outlined by Plikynas et al. in the chapter on "Non-Local Field like Interactions." Making use of ABM, Plikynas et al. unfold a radical distributed theory of agency.

It is striking that all chapters explore and go beyond a wide range of disciplines such as organizational and management studies, psychology, sociology, as well as cognitive or political science and even philosophy. In particular, Seri's chapter on "Analytical Approaches to Agent-Based Models" reveals that the ABM perspective may become so radical to "contaminate" traditional analytical approaches to the point that they can be made to produce agent-oriented results. This underscores the inherently multidisciplinary scope of organizational studies as outlined in the beginning. However, the chapters are not simply an additive sequence of different disciplines, but rather proving that ABM provides a possible methodology for disciplinary integration. For instance, agents can be equipped with psychological theory for realizing managerial goals. From a different angle human-computer interaction in socio-technical systems, as described in Thürmel's chapter, clearly raises novel ethical issues that the twenty-first century is confronted with. Thus, the use of software agents in the information age also poses new questions and problems. It is our hope that the synthesis of these chapters convinces the reader that ABM offers potentials to meet the double-sided challenge of cross-disciplinary fertilization on the one hand and disciplinary specialization on the other hand. In conclusion, as Fioretti argues from a methodological and Bardone from a philosophical perspective, ABM provides a tool and a challenge for exploring new frontiers in social science research. It is the chapter by Bardone on "Intervening via Chance-Seeking" that indicates an interesting perspective that seems immediately taken by Paladini in her "Water Controversies Between Conflict and Cooperation" where the ABM is used as a heuristics tool to manipulate in order to derive explanatory hypotheses on a practical issue.

1.4.2 Drawing the Map

One of the achievements of this book is to make clear that ABM makes cross-disciplinary fertilization a viable option for scholars. In fact, we believe that the common ground that these chapters outline is a practical declaration of how cross-disciplinary research may result in mutual enrichment of diverse contributions. On the other hand, ABM preserves the specialized domain of the discipline. Again, we believe that this is apparent from the chapters included in this volume. More evidence on how ABM contributes to look at this dichotomy differently is offered by considering systems theory.

As already mentioned, systems theory's legacy was that of unifying science with the means of mathematics. This is not what ABM scholars aim since this technique is unlike mathematics and the common scientific enterprise does not mean theoretical homogeneity. An example may clarify this point. Cognition, as intended from management or psychology, may be integrated in the design of an agent whereas interaction rules may rely on sociology and the analysis of the simulation results may inform economics. Nevertheless, while taking into account the advancement of knowledge as it distributes over diverse scientific disciplines, the study of the model enables to focus on objectives that are specific to a single discipline. While focusing on these specialized objectives, results are informed by cross-disciplinary fertilization. Once again, we believe that the balance of these two aspects of scientific enquiry is novel and maps part of what we label a new frontier. It is worth noting that cross-disciplinary work is beneficial to organizational behavior and, at the same time, it contributes to develop the other disciplines too. In short, it is a two-way process where there is giving and taking rather than passive assimilation of concepts. ABM makes this extremely apparent.

Methodological innovation is also linked to ABM and contributes to identify the new frontier of scientific research in organizational behavior. Some of the chapters indicate novel philosophical and epistemological grounds for this innovative technique. This introduction chapter has attempted to present ABM as a potential *trait d'union* between qualitative and quantitative empirical research. This element constitutes new ground in unmapped territory and for this reason it is likely that new methods are much needed in this exploration. This volume starts the exploration but more research is needed.

The new frontier is also defined by a slightly more complex understanding of the individual. In fact, in agent-based simulations the individual is usually portrayed as a social being instead of the social environment being reflected in some configuration of the self. We believe that this approach brings distributed cognition in the picture in that nothing can be understood if it is not embedded in a social environment. Hence, cognition is intended as proactively manipulating and deliberately using triggers from the environment. We may reframe this as the relation between interaction and cognition being two sides of the same coin.

In summary, there are three elements of the new frontier for social science research that emerge from this book. A first line of scientific exploration is that of the balance between cross-disciplinary fertilization and specialization; a second is that of pursuing methodological innovations that fit the overlap of qualitative, quantitative, and simulation methods. A third area of exploration is the challenge of redefining the "self" in an individual who is more socialized and cognitively embodied, embedded, enacted, and extended.

References

Axelrod, R. (1997). The dissemination of culture: A model with local convergence and global polarization. *Journal of Conflict Resolution, 41*(2), 203–226.

Banerjee, A. V. (1992). A simple model of herd behavior. *Quarterly Journal of Economics, 3*, 797–817.

Bardone, E. (2015). Intervening via chance seeking. In D. Secchi & M. Neumann (Eds.), *Agent-based simulation of organizational behavior: New frontiers of social science research*. New York: Springer.

Coen, C. (2009). Simple but not simpler. Introduction CMOT special issue—simple or realistic. *Computational and Mathematical Organization Theory, 15*, 1–4.

Cohen, M. D., March, J. G., & Olsen, H. P. (1972). A garbage can model of organizational choice. *Administrative Science Quarterly, 17*, 1–25.

Conte, R., Andrighetto, G., & Campenni, M. (2014). *Minding norms. Mechanisms and dynamics of social order in agent societies*. Oxford: Oxford University Press.

Dowling, D. (1999). Experimenting on theories. *Science in Context, 12*(2), 261–273.

Edmonds, B. (2015). Introduction to JASSS special issue—Using qualitative evidence to inform the specification of agent-based models. *Journal of Artificial Societies and Social Simulation, 18*(1), 18.

Epstein, J., & Axtell, R. (1996). *Growing artificial societies. Social Science from the bottom-up*. Washington DC: Brookings Institution Press.

Fiol, C. M., & O'Connor, E. J. (2003). Waking up! Mindfulness in the face of bandwagon. *Academy of Management Review, 28*(1), 54–70.

Fioretti, G. (2013). Agent-based simulation models in organization science. *Organizational Research Methods, 16*(2), 227–242.

Fioretti, G. (2015). Emergent organizations. In D. Secchi & M. Neumann (Eds.), *Agent-based simulation of organizational behavior: New frontiers of social science research*. New York: Springer.

Foss, N. J. (2003). Bounded rationality in the economics of organizations: 'Much cited and little used'. *Journal of Economic Psychology, 24*, 245–264.

Granovetter, M. (1985). Economic action and social structure – The problem of embeddedness. *American Journal of Sociology, 91*(3), 481–510.

Heath, C., & Sitkin, S. B. (2001). Big-B versus Big-O: What is organizational about organizational behavior? *Journal of Organizational Behavior, 22*(1), 43–58.

Heckbert, S. (2013). MayaSim: An agent-based model of the ancient Maya social-ecological system. *Journal of Artificial Societies and Social Simulation, 16*(4), 11.

Hegselmann, R., & Krause, U. (2002). Opinion dynamics and bounded confidence: Models, analysis and simulation. *Journal of Artificial Societies and Social Simulation, 5*(3), 2.

Janssen, M. A., & Ostrom, E. (2006). Empirically based, agent-based models. *Ecology and Society, 11*(2), 37.

Knudsen, T., & Srikanth, K. (2014). Coordinated exploration: Organizing joint search by multiple specialists to overcome mutual confusion and joint myopia. *Administrative Science Quarterly, 59*, 409–441.

Lorscheid, I. (2012). Opening the 'black box' of simulations: Increased transparency and effective communication through the systematic design of experiments. *Computational and Mathematical Organization Theory, 18*(1), 22–62.

Meyer, R. E., Höllerer, A. M., Jancsary, D., & van Leeuwen, T. (2013). The visual dimension in organizing, organization, and organization research: Core ideas, current developments, and promising avenues. *Academy of Management Annals, 7*(1), 489–555.

Miller, K. D. (2015). Agent-based modeling and organization studies: A critical realist perspective. *Organization Studies, 36*(2), 175–196.

Miller, K. D., & Lin, S.-J. (2010). Different truths in different worlds. *Organization Science, 21*(1), 97–114.

Moss, S., & Edmonds, B. (2005). Sociology and simulation: Statistical and qualitative cross-validation.*American Journal of Sociology, 110*(4), 1095–1131.

Nelson, R., & Winter, S. (1982). *An evolutionary theory of economic change* (1st ed.). Cambridge, MA: Belknap Press.

Neumann, M. (2015). Grounded simulation. *Journal of Artificial Societies and Social Simulation, 18*(1), 9.

Neumann, M., & Cowley, S. (2015). Modelling social agency using diachronic cognition: Learning from the Mafia. In D. Secchi & M. Neumann (Eds.), *Agent-based simulation of organizational behavior: New frontiers of social science research.* New York: Springer.

Pentland, B. T., & Rueter, H. H. (1994). Organizational routines as grammars of action. *Administrative Science Quarterly, 39*, 484–510.

Powell, W. W., & DiMaggio, P. J. (Eds.). (1991). *The new institutionalism in organizational analysis*. Chicago, IL: Chicago University Press.

Schelling, T. C. (1971). Dynamic models of segregation. *Journal of Mathematical Sociology, 1*, 143–186.

Scott, R. (2001). *Institutions and organizations*. Thousand Oaks, CA: Sage.

Secchi, D. (2015). A case for agent-based model in organizational behavior and team research. *Team Performance Management, 21*(1/2), 37–50.

Secchi, D., Gullekson, N. (2012). The social and cognitive forces behind bandwagon processes: Models of organizational bandwagon. In European Academy of Management Annual Conference. Rotterdam, Netherlands.

Simon, H. A. (1993). Altruism and economics. *American Economic Review, 83*(2), 156–161.

Squazzoni, F., Jager, W., & Edmonds, B. (2014). Social simulation in the social sciences: A brief overview. *Social Science Computer Review, 32*(3), 279–294.

Thomsen, S. E. (2015). How docility impacts team efficiency. An agent-based modeling approach. In D. Secchi & M. Neumann (Eds.), *Agent-based simulation of organizational behavior: New frontiers of social science research.* New York: Springer.

Walsh, J. P. (1995). Managerial and organizational cognition: Notes from a trip down memory lane. *Organization Science, 6*(3), 280–321.

Woolridge, M. (2009). *An introduction to multi-agent systems* (2nd ed.). New York: Wiley.

Part I
Perspectives

Chapter 2
Emergent Organizations

Guido Fioretti

Abstract This chapter overviews existing applications of agent-based modeling (ABMg) in organization science, pointing to possible cross-contaminations of these research fields. The reviewed applications include the garbage can model of organizational choice, the usage of cellular automata and of the NK model in order to investigate various problems of organizational interdependencies, and realistic agent-based models of agile productive plants. Possible future applications may include employing unsupervised neural networks in applied research on organizational routines, as well as employing sophisticated models of organizational evolution in order to understand such neglected features as punctuated equilibria and exaptation. Given the scope of the research agendas that ABMg can provide, it is quite surprising that this tool has been largely ignored by organization science hitherto. One possible explanation is that ABMg, which presents itself as a computational technique, inadvertently conceives its very nature of a tool for the exploration of novel research hypotheses. It is eventually perceived by non-practitioners as one more statistical technique for the validation of given hypotheses, and possibly a needlessly complex one.

Keywords Garbage can model • Organizational interdependencies • Agile manufacturing • Organizational routines • Organizational ecologies

2.1 Introduction

Once upon a time, computers used to make computations. As pieces of hard wares, computers are machines that carry out logical operations specified by the sequences of instructions they are fed with. These input sequences are *computer programs*, or *computer code*. For instance, the left side of Fig. 2.1 illustrates a sequence of instructions taking the absolute value of a number.

G. Fioretti (✉)
Department of Management Science, University of Bologna,
Via Capo di Lucca 34, 40126 Bologna, Italy
e-mail: guido.fioretti@unibo.it

D. Secchi, M. Neumann (eds.), *Agent-Based Simulation of Organizational Behavior*, DOI 10.1007/978-3-319-18153-0_2

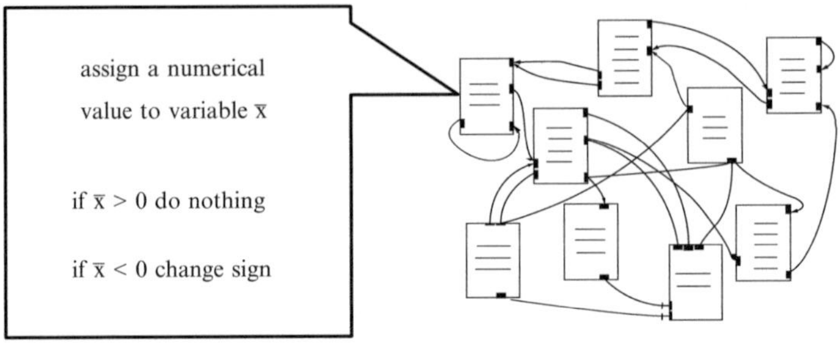

Fig. 2.1 *Left*, a sequence of instructions taking the absolute value of a number. *Right*, objects entailing sequences of instructions and interacting with one another

However, with growing computing power and growing user needs, computer programs grew larger and larger. Programmers started to split long sequences of computer code into small chunks that would be linked to one another, called "objects." This technology for writing computer code has been called *object-oriented* programming. It is illustrated on the right side of Fig. 2.1. The previous technology, consisting of writing one single, possibly long piece of code, has come to be known as *procedural programming*.

Obviously, by splitting a huge program into semi-independent components, its tasks could be handled more easily. However, another implication proved even more important, i.e., that these "objects" must communicate with one another in order to make the whole system work. Some objects would ask other objects for information, which they would deliver (or not) depending on the programs that each object was running. A network of relations would emerge from the behavior of single objects. A huge number of possibilities would arise out of this combinatorial explosion. The set of interacting objects would constitute an *artificial environment*, or *artificial world*, so complex that even its author would be surprised by its outcomes. In the end, object-oriented programming suggested new ways of conceiving computer simulations.

In applications of object-oriented programming, "objects" may represent actors in the real world. Objects can reproduce the behavior of single decision makers, social groups, or institutions, and these artificial actors may interact with one another in their virtual reality pretty much as real actors do. It is out of this mapping between software "objects" and real-life actors that the concept of "autonomous agent" has been conceived (Drogoul, Vanbergue, & Meurisse, 2003), as well as the expression "agent-based models" (ABMs). Agent-based modeling (ABMg) gave rise to new fields of research, such as artificial life and artificial chemistry, as well as to the burgeoning industry of videogames (settlers in a virgin land, astronauts in space, or monsters in fairy tales are autonomous agents who interact in a virtual reality). Essentially, ABMs construct a virtual reality where artificial actors interact, eventually repeating certain interactions along recurring patterns that constitute a sort of collective decision making.

It is fair to remark that the relationship between ABMg and object-oriented programming is not strictly one to one. It is in principle conceivable, though practically difficult, to encode autonomous agents by means of procedural programming, and some early models actually did (Allen & McGlade, 1987). Furthermore, ABMs in a sense generalized a family of models where independent entities would interact with one another, such as the cellular automata (CA), the artificial neural networks (ANNs), and the NK model that will be mentioned later in this chapter. These models may be called connectionist models (Farmer, 1990), and may be understood as ABMs whose agents are particularly simple. These models existed well before object-oriented programming was developed and today's complex ABMs could be conceived. Their existence favored the acceptance and understanding of ABMs by researchers who had already developed a similar modeling philosophy. In some cases, object-oriented code was eventually written for some of these models (Vidgen & Padget, 2009).

Today, ABMg has reached a level of awareness where nearly any scientific discipline has at least a few practicing specialists, and a healthy curiosity surrounds this tool. Moreover, even non-practicing scientists are acquainted with videogames, and this makes it relatively easy for agent-based modelers to explain what they do. "Figure out a videogame where you have consumers, voters, banks, firms and politicians interacting in social space instead of settlers creating a civilization on virgin land," a social scientist may say. One would expect that, in most disciplines, scientists have a clear idea of what ABMs are and what they can do, as well as what they cannot do.

Unfortunately, reality is simply opposite. In particular, misunderstandings among social scientists call for serious concern. Typically, social scientists who do not make use of ABMg associate the word "model" to the sets of equations employed by statistical estimation techniques. Thus, they eventually understand ABMg as one more quantitative technique. Consequently, those social scientists who are skeptical about quantitative techniques stay away from ABMg simply because it is computational. Conversely, those social scientists who employ quantitative techniques may be perplexed at the lack of ready-made rules for building and employing ABMs.

Both attitudes are misplaced, for ABMg is not a tool for hypotheses testing. It is rather a tool for exploring the consequences of hypotheses by means of complex conceptual experiments, which may eventually suggest novel research hypotheses in their turn, and so forth. Model building turns into an opportunity for generalizing empirical observations or conceiving new theories, and the very process of constructing a model is in general just as important as the outputs that the model yields (Epstein, 1999; Gross & Strand, 2000). Thus, to scientists who focus on testing hypotheses that have been formulated by their peers, ABMg is simply useless. By contrast, ABMg is extremely useful for epistemologically sophisticated social scientists who creatively engage in hypotheses formulation. However, insofar these scientists are allergic to techniques of any sort, ABMg has little future.

Paradoxically, ABMg is rejected or ignored precisely by those social scientists who would most benefit from it. In particular organization science (OS), a discipline where ABMg is still unknown to most practitioners, would greatly benefit from ABMg. OS is concerned, among else, about structures of interactions between human beings, stable patterns in human relations, routines, social networks, and, more in general, the relationship between organizational behavior and individual behavior. In its turn, ABMg is concerned with complex behavior emerging out of the interaction of simple components, evolution of networks of relations between agents, and, more in general, generating aggregate behavior out of interactions. OS and ABMg have, in principle, a large area of overlap.

In particular, I envisage a role for ABMg in OS for all those situations where organizations emerge out of tentative interactions between human beings. Think, for instance, of the huge field of organizations emerging in emergency situations, such as fires or earthquakes. Science may well proceed "from funeral to funeral,"[1] but sooner or later the potentialities of ABMg will be certainly picked up by young scholars looking for distinctiveness.

This chapter offers a twofold contribution to the acceptance of ABMg within OS. First, it reviews a few applications that have been developed hitherto. Secondly, it points to concepts that might be useful for further applications.

Both in reviewing models and pointing to applications, ABMg is understood as encompassing any sort of model where relatively autonomous units interact with one another, including CA, ANNs, the NK model, the tangled nature (TN) model or other models of evolution, as well as models that are not cited in this chapter such as classifier systems. All of these models belong to the wider family of connectionist models (Farmer, 1990) and, from one particular but acceptable perspective, they can be viewed as ABMs whose agents are particularly simple.

2.2 A Few ABMs in Organization Science

In this section I shall review three models, or classes of models, where OS already met ABMg:

1. The Garbage Can Model (GCM) of organizational choice
2. Cellular automata and the NK as models of organizational interdependencies
3. ABMs of agile productive plants

These models will not be reviewed in any detail, nor their design and purpose will be discussed. Rather, I shall illustrate why specific organizational problems have been framed by means of ABMs.

[1]Max Planck is credited for the sentence "Science proceeds from funeral to funeral." It conveys the idea that novel theories are not accepted until the previous generation of scientists disappears.

Fig. 2.2 A snapshot of the GCM (Fioretti & Lomi, 2010): *Yellow* men represents organization members, *orange squares* represent choice opportunities, *red circles* represent solutions, and *violet triangles* represent problems

2.2.1 The GCM of Organizational Choice

The GCM of organizational choice by Cohen, March, and Olsen (1972) is among the most widely cited works in OS. Its amazing ability to generate unexpected and profound insights out of simple assumptions makes it a common reference to cite as well as a never-ending source of discussions.

The GCM can be thought as a sort of chemical reactor where "molecules" for organizational decision making have been dumped: organization members, choice opportunities, solutions, and problems jump around, meet, and interact according to rules specified by the model. Organization members make decisions depending on these encounters rather than according to individual utility functions, a circumstance that marks a difference between the GCM and many other models of decision making. Figure 2.2 illustrates a snapshot of the GCM.

The GCM is also a rare case of a piece of organizational theory that was constructed also *by means* of a computer simulation. While many models and theories may be supported and enhanced by computer simulation, the GCM was *defined* in terms of a computer simulation.

The GCM was designed in 1972. At that time, object-oriented programming did not exist. Thus, it is not surprising that the original code entailed a number of limitations as well as real mistakes (Bendor, Moe, & Shotts, 2001).

However, the very structure of the GCM calls for ABMg. The "chemical reactor" where organization members, choice opportunities, solutions and problems meet and interact reminds of a virtual space where agents operate. Somehow, it appears that the GCM was conceived ahead of its time. Indeed, a more recent agent-based version overcomes the main shortcomings of the GCM while its main results stay intact (Fioretti & Lomi, 2008a, 2008b, 2010).

2.2.2 Cellular Automata and the NK as Models of Organizational Interdependencies

Organizations are connected to one another, depending on one another for social legitimacy, strategy formulation, and implementation of decisions. On this issue, at least two streams of research can be identified that make use of specific ABMs.

On the one hand, Lomi and Larsen (1996, 1998) remarked that the local vs. global character of interactions between organizations is crucial in order to explain their diffusion over time. In their model, local competition couples with population-wide legitimation to explain the empirically observed pattern of organization diffusion—the number of novel organizations grows first slowly, and then rapidly, up to a peak. Previous theory had already pointed out that organization density increases legitimation at a decreasing rate while it increases competition at an increasing rate (Hannan, 1992; Hannan & Freeman, 1989), but building an ABM helped realizing that competition and legitimation work at different levels—competition mainly works at the local level, whereas legitimation mainly works at the population level.

On the other hand, Levinthal and others remarked that the fitness of an organization depends on component units that may be either tightly or loosely coupled to one another—for instance, an organization with lots of coordination roles is likely to be a tightly coupled one. Organizations whose units are tightly coupled to one another are subject to failure in rapidly changing environments unless they are capable of fundamental restructurings. By contrast, organizations whose component units are loosely coupled to one another can easily adapt to a changing environment by changing a few of their components (Levinthal, 1997; Levinthal & Warglien, 1999). This observation suggested several implications. One is that the strategies of tightly coupled organizations are difficult to imitate, precisely because imitation involves thorough reorganization (Rivkin, 2000). Another one is that organizations embedded in unpredictable environments cannot be managed by means of rational deduction, whereas analogical reasoning that allows to transfer useful wisdom from similar settings may work (Gavetti, Levinthal, & Rivkin, 2005). Still another one is that tightly coupled organization may not be selected in the short run, even if they would be perfectly fit at a later stage (Levinthal & Posen, 2007).

Lomi and Larsen employed cellular automata (CA), whereas Levinthal and his followers employed the NK model. None of their results could have been obtained without CA and NK reconstructing structures of relations between organizations. And both CA and the NK model can be seen as instances of ABMs.

The first of these tools, CA, originated with John Conway's *Game of Life* (Berlekamp, Conway, & Guy, 1982). In essence, CA can be seen as ABMs where agents are squares placed on a grid and whose state may change with time depending on the states taken by neighboring squares. In spite of their simplicity, CA are able to exhibit a huge variety of graphical patterns evolving and diffusing along the grid where they are placed. With proper mapping, they can constitute simple and yet powerful models of influence and diffusion.

In its turn, the NK model was conceived by Kauffman (1993) as a stylized model of interactions between living organisms and species in an ecosystem. It may be seen as an ABM where agents are strings of N characters which can either be zero or one: each zero/one has a fitness which depends on K neighboring characters as well as—in a more advanced version, called the NKC model—on some characters of other strings (the fitness value of each $(K+1)$-ple of characters is generated randomly before the actual simulation begins). The fitness of an agent, i.e., of a string, is the sum of the fitness values of its characters.

Suppose that an agent tries to improve its fitness and, therefore, mutates one of its characters. This mutation causes the fitness of the characters to change that are at a distance less or equal than K on the right. Thus, the greater the K—i.e., the greater the interdependencies between the units of an organization—the more difficult it is for an agent to improve its overall fitness unless several of its components are changed at a time. In spite of its simplicity, the NK model reproduces a crucial feature of ecologies, namely the fact that the fitness of organisms and species depends on their ability to change single features without impairing overall fitness and, in the more advanced NKC model, that the fitness of species depends on the relations they entertain with one another.

Figure 2.3 is designed to illustrate the similarities between cellular automata and the NK model. Left, CA A, B, and C are placed on a grid: each of them can be thought as an agent. Each agent contacts only neighboring agents. For instance, agent A contacts agent B because it lies within its neighboring positions (white pixels), but not agent C (which is on the brown pixels). Right, one of the strings of zeros and ones that make up an NK model: [0110]. The fitness of each character in the string depends on the two ensuing characters (black). For instance, the fitness of the first character on the left, i.e., 0, depends on the two 1 s in the middle.

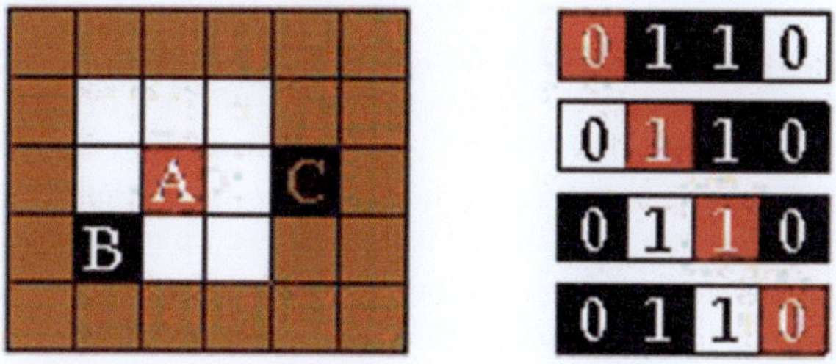

Fig. 2.3 Both CA and the NK model are ABMs that constrain the interactions between agents. *Left*, the agents are CA on a grid. *Right*, the agents are strings of zeros and ones in the NK model. In both models, elements on *red background* depend on elements on *black background* but not on elements on *white background*. CA can only see other automata that lie within their vision, delimited by the *brown area* for automaton A. On the *right*, an NK model with $N=4$ and $K=2$. The fitness of the element highlighted in *red* depends on the two elements on the right of it which, since the string is arranged in a *circle*, may find themselves at the other end of the string

Note that in both models each element (for instance, the one highlighted in red) depends on several but not all other elements (not on those highlighted in black, not included in the brown area). Indeed, both CA and the NK model can be seen as ABMs designed to constrain the interactions between agents along specific patterns.

2.2.3 ABMs of Agile Productive Plants

Since the 1980s, an increasing number of productive plants are being organized along *lean/agile manufacturing* principles rather than the more traditional Fordism focused on scale economies. One feature of the lean/agile manufacturing paradigm is that smaller, more flexible machines are typically employed. Workers and machines are eventually organized in "work teams" around "production islands" that can make independent decisions concerning work pace and routing of their semi-manufactured products (which can be processed by several flexible machines) while experimenting with workers' operations (with an incentive to keep production time as low as possible). Thus, many decisions are decentralized to production islands and their work teams, which eventually learn to interact along stable patterns and routines.

Several engineers have built ABMs of specific productive plants where agents are the "islands" where decisions are made (Nilsson & Darley, 2006; Pěchouček & Mařík, 2008). However, the problems of different lean manufacturing plants are similar to one another and, moreover, they are akin to those of many other organizations where decision making is decentralized, such as hospitals or public administrations.

These simulations are proving useful in at least two respects:

- *Identification and elimination of bottlenecks*. While no simulation may be necessary in order to observe bottlenecks in a real plant, ABMg can be very useful in order to evaluate the consequences of policies designed to eliminate bottlenecks. Eliminating bottlenecks is a tricky issue, because productive systems are typically characterized by nonlinearities such that, by increasing the productive capacity of a production island that has a long waiting queue, longer queues may arise at other points in the system. It is quite likely that productive capacity should be increased at different places; yet in practice it is very difficult to understand which are the relevant ones. Thus, a simulator may prove useful in order to experiment with organizational configurations searching for one where bottlenecks are actually eliminated.
- *Prediction and management of the organizational learning curve*. Production time decreases with cumulative production along a (negative) exponential curve whose slope is crucial in order to foresee production costs. Since learning curves are more pronounced in assembling rather than in machining operations, it is widely believed that they arise because workers learn to coordinate their efforts, developing routines that nearly optimize their interactions (Hirsch, 1952, 1956).

> The problem with learning curves is, however, that their slope is difficult to predict. In practice, engineers have collected empirical tables for the slope of learning curves in extremely narrowly defined industrial sectors, yet with no guarantee that a learning curve with the predicted slope will actually set in when new production starts. ABMs can prove useful in order to predict which routines may eventually emerge and how long it takes to approach minimum production time.

A simulation platform is under construction, which will be able to handle all sorts of organizations characterized by distributed decision making (AESOP, 2014). AESOP is based on the observation that albeit technologies may differ widely from one another, all agile production plants can be represented as bakery shops applying a set of recipes to a set of ingredients to yield a set of products. While the possible relations between work teams or production islands are in principle as many as their number and technical specifications allow, recipes constrain the set of feasible paths to a subset of meaningful ones. Just like cherries cannot be put on top of a cake before the cake is done, recipes set apart meaningful sequences from meaningless ones. However, recipes do much more. Recipes can specify batch processes—just like a bakery may wait that a tray is filled up with cakes before letting it enter the oven—as well as concurrent processes, bifurcations along different sequences that obtain the same result—inside a cake, it may make no difference whether cream or candies come first—and calls for shipments of ingredients. According to the AESOP framework, customers eventually place orders, which imply that some recipe must be applied—just like one may place an order for a chocolate cake, which requires the recipe for chocolate cakes to be applied.

Within AESOP, both orders and compounds of workers and machines (work teams, production islands, etc.) are agents. Agents representing compounds of workers and machines may be endowed with complex decision-making capabilities, ranging from heuristics to neural networks. Together, these agents generate possible stories of interactions within an organization—hence the name. AESOP can be applied to any organization where decision making is to some extent distributed, ranging from agile production plants to hospitals and administrative bodies.

Figure 2.4 illustrates a snapshot of a typical AESOP run. Nodes represent machines in a productive plant, whereas edges represent exchanges of semi-manufactured goods of various intensities. The simulator constructs possible developments of this graph, with stable patterns of interaction eventually emerging while organizational learning is taking place.

2.3 Concepts and Theories for New Applications

In the three above examples, ABMs were used in order to investigate the emergence of organizational arrangements out of interactions of some constitutive elements, or agents. In the GCM, interaction between the constitutive elements of decisions

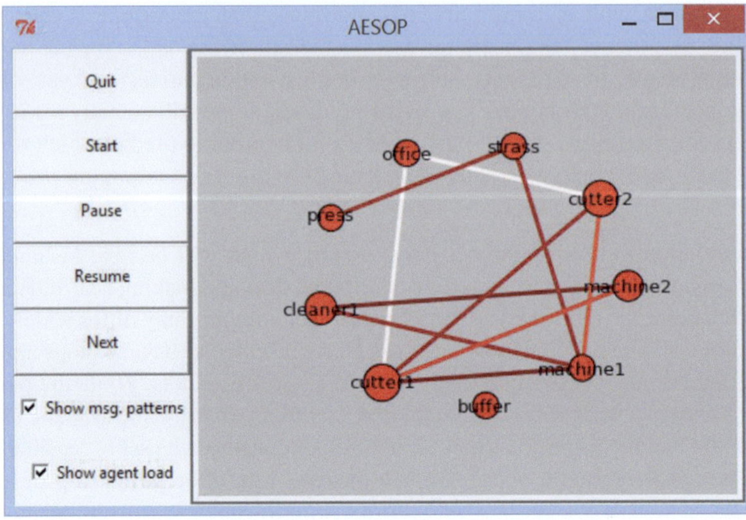

Fig. 2.4 The network of interactions between production islands as they are reconstructed by the AESOP simulator: edges of increasing thickness and darkness denote larger exchanges of semi-manufactured goods

would eventually yield organizational decision making. In CA- and NK-based models of organizational interdependencies, neighboring organizations would affect each organization's fitness and ability to survive. Finally, in ABMs of productive plants the production islands eventually settle down on stable patterns of shipments of semi-manufactured goods whose emergence corresponds to production time decreasing along the organizational learning curve.

Emergence of organizational arrangements is, indeed, a domain where ABMg and OS may meet. Potential unexploited applications may include the emergence of organizations in emergencies such as earthquakes, gaining insights into criminal and therefore fluid and unobservable organizations, exploring the possible outcomes of restructurings that require substantial horizontal communication—as it is currently happening in healthcare—or understanding network organizations in free software development and elsewhere. This list is certainly not exhaustive and, indeed, it could easily grow too long and too detailed to be useful. Rather, an indication of conceptual tools that may be relevant in several domains may be more appropriate to this stage of development.

Henceforth, I shall report on two pieces of knowledge that are quite well developed as ABMs and yet did not find corresponding applications in OS hitherto. It is neither obvious that they will, nor that these will be the leading ABMs in OS. Simply, I selected them because their current state of development is quite advanced, so applications to OS might be around the corner. These pieces of knowledge are relevant for the formation of organizational routines and for the evolutionary dynamics of organizational populations, respectively.

2.3.1 *Unsupervised Neural Networks and Organizational Routines*

Organizations are characterized by modes of behavior that are specific to each single organization, ways to react to contingencies, and ways to approach problems that exhibit some invariance with time and that are so intimately tied to organizational culture to persist in spite of organization members turning over with time. These modes of behavior are eventually known as *organizational routines*. One way to conceptualize organizational routines is that of conceiving them as sequences of actions that single organization members may undertake out of managerial directions, personal deliberation, or even unconscious responses (Becker, 2004; Pentland, Feldman, Becker, & Liu, 2012). Such sequences of actions can be activated by specific stimuli, but they can also repeat themselves indefinitely if they close in a loop (Hutchins, 1991). Either such loops may unfold within one single organization or they may involve several organizations if they include external actors such as long-standing customers and suppliers.

Closure in a loop is essential for a routine to be repeated over and over even without explicit directions while at the same time being open to change. The stability of routines is ensured by socialization of new organization members into groups where certain routines are practiced, which amounts for them to learn to perform a certain subset of actions along the loop. In its turn, the flexibility of routines arises both from top-down intervention and bottom-up fine-tuning. On the one hand, organizational routines can be influenced by leading personalities by means of personal example, involvement and socialization of other members in groups where different activity routines are used, or official regulations. On the other hand, the decision makers involved in a routine may change it by modifying their own actions, by adding new members to the loop, or by shortcutting it.

This view of organizational routines may suggest that there is some similarity between the behavior of human beings in an organization and the behavior of neurons in a brain. Just like individual behavior is the outcome of billions of neurons firing signals according to relatively simple principles, organizational behavior can be seen, to some extent, as the unintended outcome of the actions of many organization members pursuing a variety of goals. This understanding is actually at the core of the very concept of "organizational behavior" which—as an instance of the dictum that the whole is more than the sum of its parts—should capture the idea that organizations make decisions that cannot be fully explained by rational composition of the interests of their most powerful members.

All analogies are imperfect, and the analogy between human beings in an organization and neurons in a brain has limitations that organization scientists should not overlook. Its shortcomings are indeed evident to the extent a few members are able to steer the decisions and strategies of a whole organization. In more theoretical terms one may observe that this analogy is imperfect to the extent organization members optimize long-term strategies that they are able to put in practice, whereas it fits very well with an idea of organization members as boundedly rational, myopic, satisfycing decision makers (March & Simon, 1958). Since this last tradition is well established in OS, I deem that the analogy between neurons in a brain and human beings within an organization deserves careful attention. In particular, this analogy is likely to be fruitful with respect to:

- *Persistence of organizational routines independently of personnel turnover*
- *Organizational learning as formation of routines in response to environmental stimuli*
- *Enactment of routines when situations present themselves that remind of similar situations experienced in the past*

The connectionist revolution that swept across cognitive sciences in the 1980s provided a view of the brain which is absolutely relevant for the above aspects of organizational routines (McClelland, 2010; McClelland & Rumelhart, 1986; Smolensky, 1988). According to connectionism brain memory, just like organizational routines, consists of information circulating in loops. Cognitive scientists talk about *distributed memory*, as opposed to the *localized memory* of a computer (whose memory is localized on its hard disk) or a library (whose memory is localized on shelves). This explains the fact that patients who lost a substantial portion of their cortex as a consequence of accidents still retain their memories intact albeit their ability to learn new concepts is substantially reduced. Since memory does not reside in any particular place, circulating information may easily take on other paths if a subset of neurons is removed. However, a brain with less neurons may be too congested to allow the formation of new information loops, hence the difficulty of such patients to learn.

Compare the insight about information taking on other paths if a subset of neurons is removed with the observation that organizational routines persist in spite of personnel turnover (Stein, 1995): It is fair to recognize that opportunities for cross-fertilizations exist. Conversely, the insight about neuron removal causing inability to learn should be taken with some care. In organizations, inability to learn does not originate from removing employees but rather from stifling hierarchical relations into patterns where managers are happy to control whereas subordinates are happy to delegate responsibility (Argyris, 1994). In a sense, unempowered organization members are like "removed" from the organization. However, it would be much better that connectionist visions develop to the point of including control of low-level brain functions by high-level functions (including conscious activities) if a good matching with organizational problems is sought.

Organizational learning has a lot to do with connectionism, however. One important instance of organizational learning is the organizational learning curve, also known as progress ratio or learning by doing, which is the observation that throughput time decreases with cumulative production. At least a couple of models ascribe this fact to the formation of stable patterns of interaction (routines) among workers (Fioretti, 2007, 2010; Huberman, 2001; Schrager, Hogg, & Huberman, 1988). Connectionism, in its turn, understands the formation of stable connections among neurons as due to exposure to stable stimuli that deepen the "grooves" where information flows (Hebb, 1949). These statements may seem unrelated to one another, but consider that a few cases where the learning curve did not set in were due to continuous change of product specification (the Lockheed Tri-Star, cited in Huberman, 2001). Unless this happens, successful interactions among workers stabilize pretty much as connections between neurons do. Another hint on the conceptual linkage between organizational learning and connectionism is provided by the observation that the organizational learning curve is strongest in industries where assembling operations are paramount, such as the airframe industry or ship building (Hirsch, 1952, 1956). Similarly to the above issue, organizational learning is best understood by connectionist frameworks if all organization members are actively involved in creating novel routines, as it is the case of industries where assembling operations are paramount; by contrast, connectionism provides limited insight into organizational learning occurring under strong constraints on individual freedom.

Finally, connectionism is very relevant for the process of recalling and enacting organizational routines when proper situations appear (March, 1994). This is due to the fact that distributed memories are also *associative memories* (Clark, 1993; Kohonen, 1988), in the sense that their content is not retrieved by pointing to memory location (e.g., the position of a book on the shelves of a library) but rather by association with a neighboring concept (e.g., as students do when they make use of mnemonic rules). Likewise, we may understand an organization's reactions to environmental conditions as due to the fact that some features of those conditions trigger a routine that had been previously developed for other purposes. A trivial example may be the activation of bureaucratic rules in inappropriate contexts; a more complex one might be the construction of organizational narratives out of past experiences and occasional encounters (Lane & Maxfield, 2009).

However, the case for a cross-fertilization between connectionism and OS is not based on loose analogies only. Indeed the main issue at stake is that connectionism developed computational tools and mathematical formalizations that may be relevant for OS. The main tool is ANNs, particularly unsupervised neural networks.

Formally, ANNs are constituted by nodes, called neurons, connected to one another by edges according to a given architecture. Neurons produce an output y by summing inputs $x_1, x_2, \cdots x_N$ by means of coefficients $a_1, a_2, \cdots a_N$:

$$y = \sum_{i=1}^{N} a_i x_i \tag{2.1}$$

As previously hinted, ANNs can also be seen as ABMs whose agents simply weigh and sum up the inputs that they receive in order to yield an output that they pass on to other neurons.

The sort of neural networks I would suggest organization scientists to pay attention to are *unsupervised* neural networks. There exist substantial differences between unsupervised neural networks and the more common, more widely known supervised ones:

- In supervised neural networks, the weights of the neurons are settled during a training phase prior to the normal operation of the network. In unsupervised neural networks, no training phase takes place. Instead, each neuron adjusts its own weights by means of a positive feedback from its own inputs and output—it is more a sort of an agent. Expressions may take different forms, but the rationale is that the weights of a neuron grow when they receive inputs that already generated a high output, an effect that may be obtained by multiplying inputs x_i by output y (which amounts to deepening the groove of established paths between neurons), whereas they decrease if output grows too high. Here is an example, where **x** denotes the vector of neuron inputs, **a** denotes the vector of the coefficients of a neuron whereas μ and ν are constants:

$$\dot{\mathbf{a}} = \mu y \mathbf{x} - \nu \mathbf{y}\mathbf{a} \tag{2.2}$$

  The first term on the right makes each neuron specialize into reacting to stimuli to which its random initialization made it slightly more sensible than other neurons. This ensures the formation of stable linkages between neurons depending on the input patterns they have been exposed to. The second term on the right side of Eq. (2.2) is a forgetting term. It is simply there in order to ensure that the behavior of the network does not explode in the long run.
- While supervised ANNs are generally arranged in three layers, no a priori architecture exists for unsupervised ANNs. In general, each neuron of an unsupervised ANN is connected to all other neurons in the network. Eventually, special care is taken in order to ensure that loops can arise. Thus, only unsupervised neural networks are able to reproduce routine formation and routine retrieval.
- While most supervised ANNs are digital systems operating with zeroes and ones, unsupervised ANNs generally operate with continuous signals. Albeit biological neurons fire spikes, receiving neurons react to the frequency of spikes. Thus, employing continuous variables makes unsupervised ANNs somewhat closer to biological networks.

Suppose that an unsupervised ANN is endowed with linkages feeding the outputs of the neurons back into their inputs so that information loops are possible. Figure 2.5 illustrates one example taken from Kohonen (1988). Note that, for the sake of simplicity, neurons' coefficients weigh only the signals feeding back from neurons' outputs.

Let us focus on short-term dynamics, so the forgetting term (the second term on the right) of Eq. (2.2) can be neglected. Let us make the further simplification that coefficients μ and **A** can be subsumed by one single coefficient α when describing the variations of **A**. Then, the neural network of Fig. 2.5 can be described by

$$\mathbf{y} = \mathbf{x} + \mathbf{A}\mathbf{y} \tag{2.3}$$

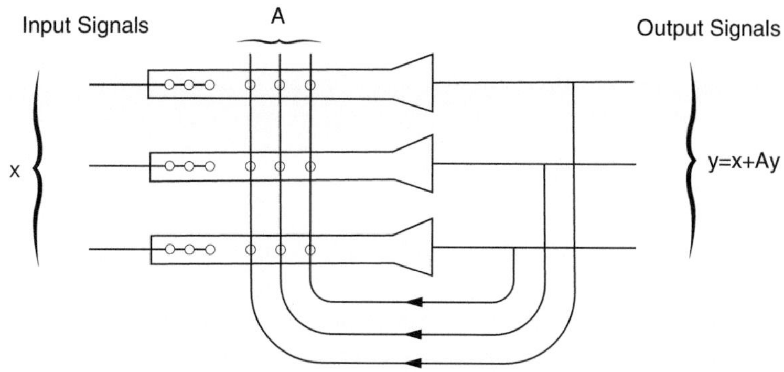

Fig. 2.5 An unsupervised ANN with feedbacks that enable the formation of information loops where, for simplicity, the coefficients entailed in matrix **A** weigh only the outputs that are fed back (from Kohonen, 1988)

$$\dot{\mathbf{A}} = \alpha \mathbf{y}\mathbf{y}^{\mathrm{T}} \tag{2.4}$$

From Eq. (2.3) we can write the transfer function $\mathbf{y} = \boldsymbol{\Omega}\mathbf{x}$ where $\boldsymbol{\Omega} = (\mathbf{I} - \mathbf{A})^{-1}$ provided that $(\mathbf{I} - \mathbf{A})$ exists, which is normally true. Kohonen (1988, Ch.IV) has the passages to obtain from Eq. (2.4):

$$\dot{\boldsymbol{\Omega}} = \alpha \boldsymbol{\Omega}^2 \mathbf{x}\mathbf{x}^{\mathrm{T}} \boldsymbol{\Omega}^{\mathrm{T}} \boldsymbol{\Omega} \tag{2.5}$$

Equation (2.5) has been obtained by neglecting the forgetting term. Thus, it makes sense to approximate it further in order to observe the short-term dynamics. By assuming $\boldsymbol{\Omega} \approx \mathbf{I}$ Eq. (2.5) becomes $\dot{\boldsymbol{\Omega}} \cong \alpha \mathbf{x}\mathbf{x}^{\mathrm{T}}$ which means that the first-order solution for the transfer operator is

$$\boldsymbol{\Omega}(t) \cong \mathbf{I} + \alpha \int_0^t \mathbf{x}(t')\,\mathbf{x}(t')^{\mathrm{T}} dt' \tag{2.6}$$

At this point, Kohonen (1988) asks to figure out that $\boldsymbol{\Omega}$ has been formed during some period $0 \leq t' \leq t$. Thus, $\boldsymbol{\Omega}$ represents what the network has learned up to time t as a consequence of stimuli $\mathbf{x}(t)$—it describes a configuration of neuron weights that make information circulate along certain loops. Assume that $\boldsymbol{\Omega}(0) = \mathbf{I}$. If at some later time $t_0 > t$ the network is excited by a stimulus $\mathbf{x}_0$, its response is

$$\mathbf{y} = \boldsymbol{\Omega}\mathbf{x}_0 = \mathbf{x}_0 + \alpha \int_0^t \left[\mathbf{x}^{\mathrm{T}}(t')\;\mathbf{x}_0\right] \mathbf{x}(t')\,dt' \tag{2.7}$$

The second term on the right side of Eq. (2.7) represents the recollection of information from the network's associative memory. That is, stimulus $\mathbf{x}_0$ generates a response that depends on its ability to reach the information that the network received in the $[0, t]$ interval, which is now circulating within the network. Its ability to recall the information stored in an associative memory depends on its similarity with stored information.

Kohonen's formulas could be usefully applied to organizations reacting to environmental stimuli by activating stored routines. It is true that quantitative data on organizational routines is hard to collect, but there are exceptions. Think, for instance, of Jazz ensembles learning "standards"[2] and activating them whenever a musician starts a phrase. Jazz ensembles are organizations; they are organizations whose members are encouraged to express themselves, so the analogy with neurons in a brain makes sense and, finally, for these organizations huge amounts of data could be obtained by analyzing recordings.

2.3.2 *Organizational Ecologies and Evolutionary Theory*

It is quite common for the popular management press to stress the qualities of prominent, successful CEOs with the aim to distill from their experiences some magical rule—often expressed in expressions like "the 5 A of management," "the 7 B of marketing," and the like—which would inevitably lead previously bankrupt organizations to success. Implicit in these statements is the view that organizations can easily change, and that they do so as a consequence of the involvement, passion, and power of their boss. The popular management press is echoed by substantial streams of scholarly research on "change management," i.e., what managers should do in order to change organizations.

The opposite view is that sunk investments, available competencies, established power structures, and organizational routines make it extremely difficult for organizations to change. Organizational populations do change, of course, but rather in the sense that new organizations are born which supersede the less efficient ones, pushing them to extinction. This view has a clear ecological flavor, with organizational competences and routines taking the role of a sort of DNA that cannot be changed by any single organism although random mutations may produce novel organisms with a different genome—i.e., new organizations with novel competences and routines (Hannan & Freeman, 1977, 1984).

Accepting the existence of this organizational ecology does not amount to claim that organizations are not capable of innovation. However, organizational ecologists would submit that organizations are only able to innovate within their established routines and competences. They would point to the fact that no producer of vacuum

[2]In Jazz jargon, "standards" are certain tunes that have been repeatedly used by Jazz musicians with infinite variations.

tubes was able to switch to transistors, no producer of chemical films was able to switch to digital cameras, and so on.[3] They would claim that organizations die rather than change.

Organizational ecology is absent from the popular management press, and it is relatively rare among academics. Casual search on Google Scholar yields 439,000 results for "organizational ecology" and 4,450,000 results for "change management." By restricting search to title words only, the figures were even more apart from one another: only 369 entries for "organizational ecology," but 27,200 entries for "change management" (Access: November 17th, 2014).

Whatever the merits of each point of view, as a matter of fact ABMg has little to say to a lonely enterprise as change management is. By contrast, ABMg actively concurred to our understanding of evolution (Gould, 2002), so it is a relevant tool for organizational ecology.

Organizational ecology is an approach that is still in its infancy. Arousal and diffusion of organizational populations is the only aspect that has been investigated hitherto. But many more issues are awaiting for proper research, for evolutionary theory is extremely insightful and complex.

A superficial understanding of evolution would equate it with the combination of mutation and selection in order to ensure "survival of the fittest." In particular, this expression is frequently misinterpreted as implying that whatever is empirically observed must have been "the fittest," or "the best" available option. This is particularly dangerous in the social sciences, where "social Darwinism" served as *ex post* justification of whatever organizations and institutions were eventually in place, including racist regimes. In reality, "survival of the fittest" can only be employed *ex ante*. It simply means that a specific organism is fittest with respect to the demands of other organisms in a particular niche at a specific point in time, for the fitness of an organism is constructed by all organisms that share its ecological niche. It is not, in any sense, an evaluation of how good an organism is with respect to "objectively" defined criteria (Lewontin, 1979).

Here are a few nontrivial aspects of evolutionary theory, which may convey how many interesting implications it has for organizational ecology:

- A substantial fraction of mutations are simply neutral with respect to fitness. Genetic drift makes organisms change quite independently of their fitness (Kimura, 1968).

  In organizational ecologies, neutral evolution has a counterpart in management fads. Some fads may be beneficial for some organizations or disruptive for

[3]Olivetti provides an apparently contrary example, since it used to be a producer of typing machines that did attempt to produce personal computers. However, this could only happen because its visionary leader, Adriano Olivetti, being aware of the opposition that computers would face by the typing machines people, set out a separate division. His early death marked the beginning of internal warfare against this division, which ultimately caused Olivetti to lose its leading position. Olivetti did switch to computers finally, but it was too late. It later stopped making computers altogether and, today, it no longer exists as a brand.

others, but for most organizations fads come and go with little or no effect on performance. Quite often management fads leave catchphrases and labels behind them, which persist insofar they are not terribly harmful. One simple example is organization charts where accounting, production, or marketing functions are called "divisions."

- Quite many features appear as necessary consequences of the features that are actually selected (Gould & Lewontin, 1979). These additional features do not arise because they are immediately useful, although they might be employed once they are available. By analogy with triangular spaces that arose out of the need to place a circular dome on a square basement of churches, which eventually provided unplanned opportunities for paintings, this sort of additional features is called *spandrels*.

  In organizational ecologies, new organizations are often created in order to put some invention into practice. And quite many of them originated from opportunities provided by other technical processes (Nooteboom, 2000). One example is the discovery of petrol as a by-product of the production of lubricants from crude oil. The whole automotive industry is a spandrel.
- Adaptation to current environmental requirements is not the only reason why certain mutations may be accepted. It happens quite often that mutations that had been selected for a specific purpose acquire a different function once they become available (e.g., small wings would have never been useful to fly, but devices that were originally selected for temperature regulation would be later used as wings). This is called *exaptation* in order to mark the difference with the more obvious "adaptation" (Gould & Vrba, 1982).

  Several examples of exaptation exist in organizational ecologies, mainly due to finding of a novel usage for a technology that had been developed for an entirely different purpose (Andriani & Cohen, 2013). One example is the microwave oven, which applies a radar technology into an entirely different domain. Just like exaptation of devices for temperature regulation into wings gave rise to qualitatively different organisms, the exaptation of technologies gives rise to different firms.
- Ecological niches may provide locally favorable environments to highly specialized organisms (Freeman & Hannan, 1983), who themselves concur to create the niche they exploit (Odling-Smee, Laland, & Feldman, 1996). Besides the curiosity of "living fossils" in remote places, niches may be important to allow organisms and species to grow before entering global competition.

  An example is provided by the pros and cons of closed vs. open economies. Closed economies shield domestic firms from international competition, allowing them to grow. However, protection from international competition may induce domestic firms not to innovate. Conversely, open economies prompt domestic firms to innovate in order to stand international competition but, if international competition is orders of magnitude stronger than domestic firms, domestic firms will not survive. Closed economies constitute niches for domestic firms.
- Dependencies between species are very intricate, with preys generally having many predators, predators chasing many preys, and symbiosis involving several

species at a time (e.g., insects favor pollination of very many vegetal species). This has the consequence that, while most mutations have no consequences, a few may trigger avalanches of extinctions and formation of new species. Evolution is said to proceed by *punctuated equilibria*, meaning that long intervals where little happens are interrupted by comparatively short times where dramatic events—such as dinosaurs' extinction—take place (Gould, 2002).

The consequences of the existence of firms producing smartphones on producers of simpler and smaller cellular phones, digital cameras, and music listening devices are one punctuation of an otherwise relatively stable equilibrium. And it is not an isolated instance, for punctuated equilibria are the rule in organizational ecologies. The empirical observation that innovations come in bursts (Silverberg & Verspagen, 2003, 2005) originates precisely from the tight linkages between firms in productive systems.

- Natural selection acts on different levels of aggregation at the same time: organisms, species, taxa, etc. (Gould, 2002; Lewontin, 1970). This may have the consequence, for instance, that single organisms are to be selected because their species is selected, independently of their individual performance.

  In the ecology of organizations, organizational forms such as the machine bureaucracy, the professional bureaucracy, and many others (Mintzberg, 1983) correspond to species whereas the single organizations correspond to the single organisms. Consider the neo-institutional stream in OS. It has emphasized that organizations may make substantial efforts to comply with expected behavior in order to gain social legitimacy (Meyer & Rowan, 1977; Powell & DiMaggio, 1991)—think, for instance, of a firm that restructures to comply with a fashionable organizational form in order to be positively valued by banks and rating agencies. This would be a case where selection, i.e., bank loans, accrues to the organizational form (the species) rather than the single organization.

Understanding the nuances and the implications of evolutionary theory is an ongoing enterprise that spans over biology, paleontology, philosophy, and, remarkably, ABMg. In particular, the NK model (Kauffman, 1993) has been useful in order to reproduce punctuated equilibria (Gould, 2002).

Today, the NK model may still make sense for very simple settings, but evolutionary modelers may want more realism and more detail. Consider, for instance, that the NK models handle the case of a multi-species ecology with one representative organism for each species. It is clear that punctuated equilibria are really the most that the NK model can do.

Other ABMs, such as the tangled nature model (Christensen, Di Collobiano, Hall, & Jensen, 2002), could be a better starting point to transfer evolutionary concepts to the world of organizational ecologies. This is a model where organisms reproduce themselves, species arise endogenously, and fitness depends on relations between organisms. Experimentations are at the very beginning, yet it seems safe to maintain that organizational ecologists have still a lot to learn from combinations of evolutionary dynamics and ABMg.

2.4 Conclusions

One interesting feature of ABMg is its ability to bridge the gap between the microscopic level of interactions between individuals and the macroscopic level of aggregate behavior of organizations. By including structures in quantitative analysis, it can give a precise meaning to the dictum "the whole is more than the sum of its parts." With these premises, one would expect ABMg to be a main tool in OS.

Reality is opposite, with ABMg still ignored or unknown to most organization scientists. My personal interpretation for this puzzling state of affairs is that, given the current mental frames and schemes among social scientists, ABMg deceives its true nature. Because it is computational, ABMg is perceived as one more quantitative technique. Thus, it is scrutinized by evaluating its ability to test given hypotheses. With this criterion, ABMg is rejected and finally ignored.

This sort of judgment is a misunderstanding, simply because ABMg is actually a tool to help researchers carry out sophisticated conceptual experiments. By allowing researchers to explore the implications of their hypotheses, it easily leads them to formulate new ones. It is a tool for creative researchers who do not content themselves with looking for databases by which the research hypotheses that are most popular in their discipline can be tested.

The contributors to this book constitute an exception. This book gathers organization scientists who know how relevant ABMg is to their discipline, and for what reasons. The question is how should this community proceed in order for ABMg to obtain the recognition that it deserves.

While several strategies can be conceived and should possibly be pursued at the same time, I would suggest that by enriching the cultural and conceptual content of ABMg, this tool may become more appealing to sophisticated scientists who are interested in formulating novel research questions. Connectionism has revolutionized cognitive sciences since the 1980s. Punctuated equilibria and other issues have deeply changed our understanding of evolution since the late 1970s. Hopefully, creative researchers will be attracted by the possibility to exploit these intellectual streams in order to gain a better understanding of organizing processes.

References

AESOP (2014). AESOP-ACP Enterprise Simulator. Available at http://aesop-acp.sourceforge.net.

Allen, P. M., & McGlade, J. M. (1987). Modelling complex human systems: A fisheries example. *European Journal of Operational Research, 30*, 147–167.

Andriani, P., & Cohen, J. (2013). From exaptation to radical niche construction in biological and technological complex systems. *Complexity, 18*, 7–14.

Argyris, C. (1994, July–August). Good communication that blocks learning. *Harvard Business Review*, pp. 77–85.

Becker, M. C. (2004). Organizational routines: A review of the literature. *Industrial and Corporate Change, 13*, 643–677.

Bendor, J., Moe, T. M., & Shotts, K. W. (2001). Recycling the garbage can: An assessment of the research program. *American Political Science Review, 95*, 169–190.

Berlekamp, E. R., Conway, J. H., & Guy, R. K. (1982). *Winning ways for your mathematical plays*. New York: Academic.

Christensen, K., Di Collobiano, S. A., Hall, M., & Jensen, H. J. (2002). Tangled nature: A model of evolutionary biology. *Journal of Theoretical Biology, 216*, 73–84.

Clark, A. (1993). *Associative engines*. Cambridge, MA: The MIT Press.

Cohen, M. D., March, J. G., & Olsen, J. P. (1972). A Garbage Can Model of organizational choice. *Administrative Science Quarterly, 17*, 1–25.

Drogoul, A., Vanbergue, D., & Meurisse, T. (2003). Multi-agent based simulation: Where are the agents? In J. S. Sichman, F. Bousquet, & P. Davidson (Eds.), *Multi agent based systems 2002, LNAI 2581* (pp. 1–15). Berlin/Heidelberg: Springer.

Epstein, J. M. (1999). Agent-based computational models and generative social science. *Complexity, 4*, 41–60.

Farmer, J. D. (1990). A Rosetta stone for connectionism. *Physica A, 42*, 153–187.

Fioretti, G. (2007). The organizational learning curve. *European Journal of Operational Research, 177*, 1375–1384.

Fioretti, G. (2010). A connectionist model of the organizational learning curve. *Computational and Mathematical Organization Theory, 13*, 1–16.

Fioretti, G., & Lomi, A. (2008a). An agent-based representation of the Garbage Can Model of organizational choice. *Journal of Artificial Societies and Social Simulation, 11*.http://jasss.soc.surrey.ac.uk/11/1/1.html.

Fioretti, G., & Lomi, A. (2008b). The Garbage Can Model of organizational choice: An agent-based reconstruction. *Simulation Modelling Practice and Theory, 16*, 192–217.

Fioretti, G., & Lomi, A. (2010). Passing the buck in the Garbage Can Model of organizational choice. *Computational and Mathematical Organization Theory, 16*, 113–143.

Freeman, J., & Hannan, M. T. (1983). Niche width and the dynamics of organizational populations. *The American Journal of Sociology, 88*, 1116–1145.

Gavetti, G., Levinthal, D. A., & Rivkin, J. W. (2005). Strategy making in novel and complex worlds: The power of analogy. *Strategic Management Journal, 26*, 691–712.

Gould, S. P. (2002). *The structure of evolutionary theory*. Cambridge, MA: The Bellknap Press of Harvard University Press.

Gould, S. P., & Lewontin, R. C. (1979). The Spandrels of San Marco and the Panglossian Paradigm: A critique of the adaptationist programme. *Proceedings of the Royal Society of London B, 205*, 581–598.

Gould, S. P., & Vrba, E. S. (1982). Exaptation – A missing term in the science of form. *Paleobiology, 8*, 4–15.

Gross, D., & Strand, R. (2000). Can agent-based models assist decisions on large-scale practical problems? A philosophical analysis. *Complexity, 5*, 26–33.

Hannan, M. T. (1992). Rationality and robustness in multilevel systems. In J. Coleman & T. Fararo (Eds.), *Rational choice theory: Advocacy and critique* (pp. 120–136). Newbury Park: Sage.

Hannan, M. T., & Freeman, J. (1977). The population ecology of organizations. *The American Journal of Sociology, 82*, 929–964.

Hannan, M. T., & Freeman, J. (1984). Structural inertia and organizational change. *American Sociological Review, 49*, 149–164.

Hannan, M. T., & Freeman, J. (1989). *Organizational ecology*. Cambridge, MA: Harvard University Press.

Hebb, D. O. (1949). *The organization of behavior*. New York: Wiley.

Hirsch, W. Z. (1952). Manufacturing progress function. *The Review of Economics and Statistics, 34*, 143–155.

Hirsch, W. Z. (1956). Firm progress ratios. *Econometrica, 24*, 136–143.

Huberman, B. A. (2001). The dynamics of organizational learning. *Computational and Mathematical Organization Theory, 7*, 145–153.

Hutchins, E. (1991). Organizing work by adaptation. *Organization Science, 2*, 14–39.

Kauffman, S. A. (1993). *The origin of order: Self-organization and selection in evolution*. Oxford: Oxford University Press.
Kimura, M. (1968). Evolutionary rate at molecular level. *Nature, 217*, 624–626.
Kohonen, T. (1988). *Self-organization and associative memory*. Berlin/Heidelberg: Springer.
Lane, D. A., & Maxfield, R. R. (2009). Building a new market system: Effective action, redirection and generative relationships. In D. A. Lane, S. Van der Leeuw, D. Pumain, & G. West (Eds.), *Complexity perspectives in innovation and social change* (pp. 263–288). Berlin/Heidelberg: Springer.
Levinthal, D. A. (1997). Adaptation on rugged landscapes. *Management Science, 43*, 934–950.
Levinthal, D. A., & Posen, H. E. (2007). Myopia of selection: Does organizational adaptation limit the efficacy of population selection? *Administrative Science Quarterly, 52*, 586–620.
Levinthal, D. A., & Warglien, M. (1999). Landscape design: Design for local action in complex worlds. *Organization Science, 10*, 342–357.
Lewontin, R. C. (1970). The units of selection. *The Annual Review of Ecology, Evolution, and Systematics, 1*, 1–18.
Lewontin, R. C. (1979). *Biology as ideology: The doctrine of DNA*. Concord: Anansi Press.
Lomi, A., & Larsen, E. R. (1996). Interacting locally and evolving globally: A computational approach to the dynamics of organizational populations. *The Academy of Management Journal, 39*, 1287–1321.
Lomi, A., & Larsen, E. R. (1998). Density delay and organizational survival: Computational models and empirical comparisons. *Computational and Mathematical Organization Theory, 3*, 219–247.
March, J. G. (1994). *A primer on decision making*. New York: The Free Press.
March, J. G., & Simon, H. A. (1958). *Organizations*. New York: Wiley.
McClelland, J. L. (2010). Emergence in cognitive science. *Topics in Cognitive Science, 2*, 751–770.
McClelland, J. L., & Rumelhart, D. E. (Eds.). (1986). *Parallel distributed processing: Exploration in the microstructure of cognition*. Cambridge, MA: The MIT Press.
Meyer, J. W., & Rowan, B. (1977). Institutionalized organizations: Formal structure as myth and ceremony. *The American Journal of Sociology, 83*, 340–363.
Mintzberg, H. (1983). *Structures in five: Designing effective organizations*. Englewood Cliffs: Prentice-Hall.
Nilsson, F., & Darley, V. (2006). On complex adaptive systems and agent-based modelling for improved decision-making in manufacturing and logistics settings: Experiences from a packaging company. *The International Journal of Operations and Production Management, 26*, 1351–1373.
Nooteboom, B. (2000). *Learning and innovation in organizations and economies*. Oxford: Oxford University Press.
Odling-Smee, F. J., Laland, K. N., & Feldman, M. W. (1996). Niche construction. *The American Naturalist, 147*, 641–648.
Pěchouček, M., & Mařík, V. (2008). Industrial deployment of multi-agent technologies: Review and selected case studies. *Autonomous Agents and Multi-Agent Systems, 17*, 397–431.
Pentland, B. T., Feldman, M. S., Becker, M. C., & Liu, P. (2012). Dynamics of organizational routines: A generative model. *Journal of Management Studies, 49*, 1484–1508.
Powell, W. W., & DiMaggio, P. J. (1991). *The new institutionalism in organizational analysis*. Chicago: The University of Chicago Press.
Rivkin, J. W. (2000). Imitation of complex strategies. *Management Science, 46*, 824–844.
Schrager, J., Hogg, T., & Huberman, B. A. (1988). A graph-dynamic model of the power law of practice and the problem-solving fan-effect. *Science, 242*, 414–416.
Silverberg, G., & Verspagen, B. (2003). Breaking the waves: A Poisson regression approach to Schumpeterian clustering of basic innovations. *Cambridge Journal of Economics, 27*, 671–693.
Silverberg, G., & Verspagen, B. (2005). A percolation model of innovation in complex technology spaces. *Journal of Economic Dynamics and Control, 29*, 225–244.
Smolensky, P. (1988). On the proper treatment of connectionism. *Behavioral and Brain Sciences, 11*, 1–74.

Stein, E. W. (1995). Organizational memory: Review of concepts and recommendations for management. *The International Journal of Information Management, 15*, 17–32.
Vidgen, R., & Padget, J. (2009). Sendero: An extended, agent-based implementation of Kauffman's NKCS model. *Journal of Artificial Societies and Social Simulation, 12*. http://jasss.soc.surrey.ac.uk/12/4/8.html.

Chapter 3
Cognition Beyond the Body: Using ABM to Explore Cultural Ecosystems

Stephen J. Cowley

Simulation is a thirdway of doing science.
Robert Axelrod, 1997

Abstract Cognitive science increasingly strives to avoid the gratuitous assumption that minds "represent" a world. For Anthony Chemero, a radical and embodied approach hypothesizes that agent–environment interactions ground all cognitive powers. Pursuing this bold view, the paper shows how agent-based modeling (ABM) can clarify how cultural resources (e.g., sound patterns) *enable* flexible adaptive behavior. They grant communities modes of action that arise as bodies sensitize to coordinated behavior (e.g. how /a/ is spoken). Using ABM, Stanford and Kenny (*Language Variation and Change, 25*(02), 119–153, 2013) examine pronunciation shifts. They show how future changes can be prefigured in simple child-agents: this pinpoints the premature theorization that all too often bedevils the human sciences. Given significant differences in how /a/ is pronounced, many mistakenly conclude that there must be an "underlying" (neural) mechanism. They ignore the diachronic nature of human cognition—much depends on history. Those who immediately posit inner mechanisms stumble into the *e-bar* (*∄*) *fallacy*: they assume that an intervening variable (or system) *must* explain any significant difference. ABM is thus a deflationary weapon to investigate cognition beyond the brain. Pursuing the positive agenda, I echo Robert Rosen in stressing that *biological* encoding is creative: models can show how social norms empower diachronic systems. While based in embrained bodies, humans depend on ascribing sense to events in cognitive cultural ecosystems. As living beings, persons use artifacts, institutions and the *said*—they exploit impersonal resources. A major advantage of ABM is that it can be used to model how such resources enrich body-based cognition.

Keywords Distributed cognition • Cultural ecosystem • Radical embodied cognitive science • Immergence • Vowel shift • The observer • Embodied cognition

---

S.J. Cowley (✉)
Department of Language and Communication, Centre for Human Interactivity (CHI), Research Cluster for Cognition, Management and Communication (COMAC), University of Southern Denmark, Slagelse Campus, Slagelse, Denmark
e-mail: cowley@sdu.dk

D. Secchi, M. Neumann (eds.), *Agent-Based Simulation of Organizational Behavior*, DOI 10.1007/978-3-319-18153-0_3

3.1 On the Outer Reaches of Science

The paper applies the logic of radical embodied cognitive science to agent-based modeling (ABM). Rather than invoke mental representations as the basis for cognition, Chemero (2011) proposes that all cognitive powers be traced to agent–environment interactions. As applied to humans, therefore, these constitute the process of culture.[1] As a "third way of doing science" ABM pursues how social context transforms human agency. While based in predictive models that allow inductive analysis, the method is also a heuristic for exploring multi-scalar systems. It opens up how biology uses temporality and humans develop special domains of activity (e.g., cockpits, means of navigation, the blogosphere). Rather than posit "levels"—or bottom-up processes—one can ask how these activity fields prompt agents to reconfigure as they interact. Accordingly, I turn to the question of embedded agency contributes to social organization in spatial and time scales that reach beyond the lived present. In other terms, I show that ABM can explore the cognitive importance of what Hutchins (2014) calls *cultural ecosystems*. Using Stanford and Kenny's (2013) model of phonetic change, I focus on an artificial environment where simulated speech influences how agents manage vowels in words like "cat."

The model shows that, given exemplar memory, agents link acts of articulation with ecosystemic factors. For Stanford and Kenny (2013), this shows the *reality* of the speech community or, strictly, that change can be modeled around the density of interactions. While formalisms capture what an agent knows in saying "cat" (i.e., /kæt/), they ignore a history of agent–environment dynamics. These, it is argued, enable an agent to self-configure. Events re-enact patterns in slow time-scales because, just as in living systems, exemplar memory allows agents to connect multiple records with later interactions. So what are the implications of cognitive diachrony? The question sets an agenda. Taking bodies and brains for granted, I present ABM as the basis for asking how embedded agents "use" interactions to appropriate a cultural ecosystem's normative resources. It suggests that an agent uses immergence to self-configure by linking what it does with ecosystemic norms.[2] On such a view new weight falls on observation. Echoing Robert Rosen (1991),

[1]Hutchins (1995) famously declares: "Culture is not any collection of things, whether tangible or abstract. Rather, it is a process. It is a human cognitive process that takes place inside and outside the minds of people. It is a process in which our everyday cultural practices are enacted." (1995: 354) Because culture adds value to human life, its adaptive products, cultural ecosystems, favor modes of action (e.g., flying planes, navigation, and blogging): designers and those who come before exert *direct* effects on those who follow.

[2]Conte, Andrighetto, and Campennì (2013) define immergence in terms of a recursive dimension of emergence where information flows from the social environment back into the individual. While they are interested in the internalization of cultural norms, I pursue the role of immergence in a cultural ecosystem where individuals from an earlier period exert a direct influence on those who follow them. Reading "God has no pleasure in the death of the wicked" brings forth echoes of the Biblical figure of Ezequiel (for discussion, see Markoš, Švorcová, & Lhotský 2013). This is

I suggest that models can be used to reach beyond objects and probabilities. One can understand the influence of Chicago pronunciation by considering how behavior draws on the nonlocal. Simulation science shows that *abstracta* can use diachronic cognition in action. Using this third way in science, it may therefore be possible to open up ecosystemic by-products—culture, consciousness, literal meaning—that elude inductive or deductive approaches. Given its considerable heuristic power, ABM can be applied where, in Søren Brier's (2008) disarming phrase, "information is not enough."

3.2 Observing and Diachrony: A Challenge for Science

The academy separates the natural sciences, the social sciences, and the humanities. Leaving aside the observer, it splits nature into objects whose investigation pertains to fields. Methods that throw light on phenomena like atomic particles, cells, or verbal patterns are also applied to, say, global warming or human well-being. This is odd: why should diachronic phenomena be approached through the privileged use of inductive and the deductive methods? After all, it is beyond doubt that multi-scalar processes do not reduce to observables. Rosen (1991) voiced similar concerns about the study of *life itself*. In addressing such concerns, I argue that ABM provides a valuable heuristic. Unlike other modeling, it can simulate the bidirectional dynamics that sustain human practice. Modeling opens up the bio-sociocognitive by exploring how natural processes might, in principle, influence interpretative powers. Like Peirce, Maturana, Polyani, von Foerster, and others, I emphasize the observer. However, far from offering a theory of observation or its origins, I ask how the bio-sociocognitive (or semiotic) can be clarified by agent-based models. First, however, I suggest that observing is based in using the results of noticing aspects. In the human species at least, this allows *the said* to ground much speaking and acting.[3]

Every situation can be seen in many aspects. Classically, the concept is introduced by considering when, in observing a face, one notices a likeness to another. Wittgenstein remarks, "I *see* that it has not changed; and yet I see it differently. I call this experience 'noticing an aspect'." (1957: 193c). He then pursues the nature of aspects in relation to a triangle.

---

taken to mesh the use of statistical evidence with how agents self-configure by using agent-internal processes (and, in living systems, sensorimotor activity).

[3]I use "observe" in roughly Maturana's (2002) sense (for discussion, see Raimondi 2014): extending second-order cybernetics, he traces the bio-logic of the *said* to the recursive structural coupling of human languaging of the "doings of the observer." In saying anything at all, the said thus takes on a subjective aspect. As an anonymous referee points out, this sets up a parallel between saying and using an ABM: in both cases an attentional technology (a model or a verbal pattern) brings about non-random events—a way of saying or a "chance" to see new aspects.

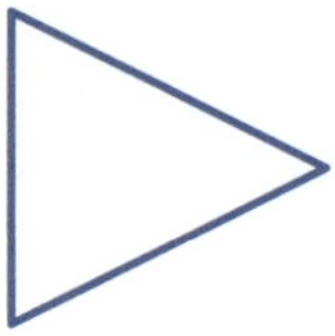

The connected lines can be seen as a mountain (on its side), a wedge (on an uneven surface), or even an arrow (which points in each of three ways). For Wittgenstein (1957), an observer draws on imagination thanks to his or her mastery of the *concepts* of mountain, wedge, and arrow.[4] As a result, people can shift perspectives or, perhaps, use experience to reconfigure the perceived. In this paper, it is claimed that a similar process applies during learning. Agents are taken to self-configure by using interactional experience to develop skills in taking stances to the perceived. Although many creatures can discriminate triangles, humans alone can choose how to look—their use of its many aspects is partly social, partly subjective, and partly linguistic. For Wittgenstein, using aspects grants shared "perceptions" and, thus, agreement in judgments. And that, he thinks, underpins all sophisticated thought. Further, similar concerns sustain Humberto Maturana's pursuit of how bio-logic produces observers (Maturana 1978, 2002). Not only must "everything that is said" draw on observing but only human practices (or a consensual domain) can shape the results—whether in cockpits, blogging, or medical diagnosis. In "cultural ecosystems" (Hutchins 2014), aspects of a shared world prompt human attunement. People make common use of instruments or aids to diagnosis: culture, for Hutchins, serves to reduce entropy and, thus, makes it easier to fly a plane or practice medicine. Concepts also simplify—and call up bundles of artifacts, practices, and *beliefs*. For example, if we do not "believe in minds" (whatever that means), this alters scientific practice. Yet, in everyday life, we act as if we had minds and treat others that way. For Ryle (1949) the *concept of mind* is indispensible or, in other terms, to predict behavior agents must take an intentional stance (Dennett 1989). Perceiving aspects shapes social skills that are appropriated by a history of stance taking. For Dennett, science uses a physical stance and engineers take a design stance: extending this logic, Cowley (2011a) argues that babies take a new stance when coming to hear utterance-activity in a verbal aspect. Since total language binds culture and metabolism with brains, this "language stance" opens up the shared world. People learn that trees, atoms, geometry, and words are certain: the stance permits literal meaning, deductive logic, and, of course, the development and use of artificial models. It also raises the question of how observing can be possible and, inseparably, if it can be simulated.

To reduce the argument's abstraction, I now exemplify by a blogger's observing. Enrico Torre's case study (2014) shows a diachronic process where events interlace

[4]While, for Wittgenstein's philosophical purposes, this is enough, a fuller view of how aspects are perceived would consider the "pre-conceptual" too. In modeling, this would be a necessary basis.

across (at least) three time scales. Initially, writing is dominated by experiential time; the blog is lived as action. The blogger brings cognitive resources to, not the experiential now, but making sense of her own writing. In this scale, working-memory meshes recall, perception, and writing. Even in the lived scale—the one at which this text becomes comprehensible observing links an individual past with current action. Blogging is a cultural ecosystem where writing is never wholly synchronic.[5] For Torre, blogging exploits two other crucial temporal dimensions. First, as people respond, the blogger increasingly uses *what other people write*. Observing and, thus, writing reorient to possible perspectives. Indeed, her sense making meshes with other views—immergent processes prompt engagement and, I suggest, help a blogger to self-configure. For Torre, this is in a dialogical scale: heightened emotion shapes a tendency to anticipate response. In his case study, the parties use the social context to consolidate what they regard as opposing political views. Slow scales of historical change thus bring a third temporal dimension into the blog. As the blogger self-configures in the role, she draws on anchor points from various sources. These stabilize her argument and, remarkably, shape future observation: perception alters as a result of blogging. As future attractors, blogs are able to sensitize a writer's perception and, thus, interpretations. The blog enacts political process. For Torre, future oriented writing-and-acting enacts a co-optative scale. The blogger writes, in part, to bring forth possible futures. Immergent processes thus enable bloggers to interlace events in, at least, enchronic, dialogical, and co-optative time-scales.

While blogging occurs in chronological time ("the blog lasted a month"), the results display the multi-scalar nature of human "thinking." People use a social domain to manage the quality of experience—feelings, ways of acting/reacting, and indeed what they say and observe. Bloggers pick up on aspects of situations, project what may be possible, and enact sociocultural processes. A blog thus constitutes a cultural ecosystem: events in historical scales are enmeshed with cultural products that influence acts of blogging. Since the activity of reading-and-writing is diachronic, a person self-configures as a blogger. In other words, while blogging is situated, it evokes events in other scales—to mention the Nazis is to evoke history.[6] For this reason, in becoming a blogger, what one writes changes future observing. This much is, I hope, uncontentious. In negative terms, its import is readily stated: blogging, writing, and observing elude the logic of input–output. More positively, I argue that social organizing depends on agents who manage the many scales of diachronic cognition. So how cognitive science pursue such issues?

[5]As a cultural ecosystem, blogging is cultural process where those who came before (and one's previous self) exert direct effects on later blogs (and one's later self). As in a cockpit, the blogger uses a designed environment where writing adds value to writing in ways that do not apply in, say, writing the same words on a scrap of paper.

[6]Uryu, Steffensen, and Kramsch (2014) describe a case where a Japanese visitor to America tries to help a German partner who is fishing for a delicate expression by saying that the then Pope had been a Nazi.

3.3 Towards a Sociocognitive View of Cognitive Science

Cognitive science began with modeling the already conceptualized (e.g., problem solving, vision) and, over time, shifted its focus to how conceptualizing arises. Machine models of "mind" were gradually replaced by enquiry into the conditions that *enable* human activity. In illustration, I sketch how symbol processing gave way to the connectionism, the rise of robotics, interest in life, its artificial counterpart, and a growing concern with the limits of embodiment. I invoke three waves in cognitive science—the first uses symbolic models and the second both how systems act and, at times, use first person experience. In the third wave, social resources become cognitive phenomena as, I suggest, events in rapid metabolic scales are transformed by the use of affordances that use the slow dynamics of cultural ecosystems.

In first wave cognitive science, computers modeled how tasks were conceptualized. Emphasis fell on how programs could use a search function to solve well-defined problems. Using functionalist insights, theorists sought, for example, to specify chess moves, generate sentences, and assemble a 3D model out of 2½ dimension visual sketch. Assuming that mind is in the head (or supervenes on the brain), strong claims were made. Chomsky (1972) claimed to have discovered a language "organ" and Fodor (1975) argued for the necessity of a language of thought. By analogy with von Neumann computers, brains and minds were assumed to function in a synchronic fashion. Language was reduced to grammar: the generative enterprise aimed to be an "explanatory" science where formalizations derived from Universal Grammar. Once found to be too ambitious, Chomsky's (1965) standard theory was revised—but not abandoned. Even today, minimalists posit operations that allegedly sustain a hypothetical neural "core" of I-language (Chomsky 1995). On such views, no theory independent observation of I-language is possible. Models can only be evaluated against the theory's own formal descriptions or, perhaps, against recurrent neural correlations. Such approaches elude empirically based development.

Second wave cognitive science looked towards the world. First, allowing that brains are, in part, self-organizing systems, connectionist models gave new weight to learning. Second, interest in the living brain roused interest in theoretical biology and the workings of living bodies. Third, robotics turned from classic representational architectures by making ingenious use of objects and physical invariants. Fourth, first person experience came to be seen as valid evidence and, as a result, action and perception were acknowledged to use artifacts, experience, and the world's scaffolding. Fifth, human cognition was seen as, at once, both individual and socially distributed. While leaving gaps—and allowing debate—today many accept that, while brains matter to cognition, human powers are also *e*mbodied, *e*mbedded, *e*nacted, and *e*xtended. Thus, what Menary (2010) calls 4E cognition emphasizes, not original intentionality, but how bodies accomplish cognitive tasks as they link artifacts, mental states, and action—experience exploits both memory and artifacts.

While stressing embodiment, Anthony Chemero (2011) rejects the representationalism that dominates first and second wave cognitive science. On methodological grounds, he traces cognitive processes to agent–environment interactions. Since these are multi-scalar, the not-here and not-now comes to the fore in this third-wave of cognitive science (Kravchenko 2008). Emphasis on the nonlocal (Steffensen 2012) can be traced to how process philosophy sustains Maturana's (1978) consensual domains and Edwin Hutchins' (1995, 2014) focus on distributed systems. While still underdeveloped, the approach grants the world beyond the body a major cognitive role. In blogging, a social realm links embodiment with agent-centered activity. Torre's bloggers manipulate alphabetic vehicles as they re-enact a multi-scalar world (in enchronic, dialogical, and pro-optative scales). While reliant on their central nervous system, blogging links writing to cultural history. Aspects of text perception contribute to both impersonal meaning and local construals. Blogging changes observing and observers: fast processes of the body mesh with slow historical ones. In pursuing how cultural ecosystems work, one must give due importance to how situated activity uses nonlocal or collective resources. For this reason ABM is a valuable tool for exploring how cultural ecosystems influence self-configuring agents-in-interaction.

3.4 Investigating Ecosystemically Embedded Agents

Before pursuing how ecosystems that work through embodied agents, it will be of value to consider parallels and contrasts with Axelrod's view of simulation. He says:

> "Simulation is a third way of doing science. Like deduction, it starts with a set of explicit assumptions. But unlike deduction, it does not prove theorems. Instead, a simulation generates data that can be analyzed inductively. Unlike typical induction, however, the simulated data comes from a rigorously specified set of rules rather than direct measurement of the real world. While induction can be used to find patterns in data, and deduction can be used to find consequences of assumptions, simulation modeling can be used as an aid in intuition". (1997: 5)

Whereas measurements ground inductive and deductive work, models use clearly specified rules. These appear more certain, more readily applicable, and thus aid intuition, if—and only if—they use correct assumptions.[7] They apply to aspects of the world that would otherwise remain unobserved. The approach appears, for example, in using Multi-agent models to explore the frog's behavioral ecology (Scheutz, Madey, & Boyd 2005). Using systems engineering, the model is designed to identify multi-level mechanisms. It mimics emergent behavioral patterns with

[7]In the frog's ecosystem, assumptions are "correct" where applicable to observations of frog populations in the wild or within the frame of ethology. Further, as an anonymous referee points out, many models assume, for example, that agents are rational actors: while the assumption appears zany as applied to living human beings, as economics shows, the results can characterize populations.

respect to, first, a habitat's specified affordances and, second, models of rapid neural processes that generate pattern recognition. By hypothesis, the levels draw on a mechanism—this is to be identified by using causal interdependence and distributed control. In focusing on "levels," the model allows swarm intelligence to contribute to behavior of frog-agents: it makes use of veridical assumptions that, by removing the modeler from the scene, have the capacity to identify mechanisms (whose real-world counterparts can be sought in nature).

Swarm intelligence is probably a factor in the self-maintenance of cultural ecosystems. For, as noted, humans also exploit aspects, perspectives, and, broadly, diachronic cognition. The question is thus one of its limits: do immergent processes enable agents to self-configure? Rather than presuppose distributed control and systemic interdependence, one can ask how the functionality of embedded systems can draw on the nonlocal. It matters that models can give rise to surprises (Axelrod 1997). Just as an observer–modeler can be prompted to change assumptions, people exploit diachronic integration—and discover new aspects in the familiar. Since no formal model captures all aspects of the world, rigorously specified rules bring out their necessarily *incomplete adequacy*. Observations of incompleteness can prompt an observer to new ways of looking. On this view ABM simulates agent–environment dynamics where the world is able to talk back to the modeler. Far from relying on the causal, like a blogger, he or she can self-configure. To use this insight in modeling human-simulacra, swarm intelligence needs agents with context sensitivity. While frogs are repetitive, a blogger's choices use cultural ecosystems that lack any parallel in the frog's world. Before turning to Robert Rosen's work, I briefly contrast natural and observer-based cultural ecosystems. Whereas systems engineering is bound to minimize the modeler, the study of cultural ecosystems depends on how results *fail to* mesh with expectations. One's concern is with ways of replacing past conceptualizations. By analogy, even if swarm intelligence is used, immergence can be used to grant agents a local signature.

3.5 The Northern Cities Shift

ABM is under-used in linguistics. This is because, in mainstream or code-views, language is traced to "utterances" and a mind and/or brain's production and processing. However, if reduced to the verbal, language is separated from society, individual skills, and local beliefs. In fact, in blogging, these are neither unsponsored nor independent of human subjects. As Linell (2004) argues, the code models of the mainstream fall foul of "written language bias." While code models are increasingly challenged (e.g., Cowley 2011b; Cummins 2014; Kravchenko 2007; Love 2004), few techniques have been developed to examine the ecological and distributed complexity of language. Indeed, this explains the striking nature of Torre's (2014) emphasis on the interplay of language and agency. While leaving aside subjectivity, sociolinguistics has long emphasized dynamics and multi-scalarity. Language variation correlates speech variables with most social factors and, of course, that

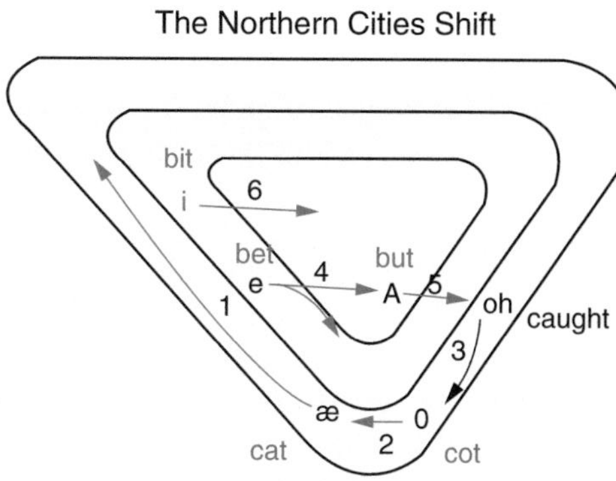

Fig. 3.1 The Northern cities shift

influences sociolinguistic change. Lacking space to describe this literature, I pursue how ABM connects issues of variability with agency. Specifically, I ask how interactions enable agents to self-configure by using sociolinguistic norms. Not only does this view of immergence challenge mainstream (or code) linguistics, but it shows that aspects of language also resemble a complex adaptive system. In part, at least, the multi-scalar structures of language co-evolve as people enact linguistic history.

All languages have vowel systems that change over time. In the United States, the so-called Northern cities shift (see, Labov 2007) contrasts with a shift found in the Southern States (Wolfram and Schilling-Estes 1998). Both cases involve a cascade or chain of interlocking changes where alterations in one vowel affect others. Thus, Chicago vowel pronunciation is slowly coming to influence the speech of people in a large area. The changes can be visualized by regarding Fig. 3.1 as showing vowels in an auditory space. Once the shift begins, the chain effect shown in the diagram affects individual pronunciation. While not a conscious phenomenon, the changes reflect (among other things) judgements of prestige. In the case of the Northern vowel shift, six stages can be identified—broadly, once a vowel such as that of "cat" comes to be spoken with a raised and tensed tongue position, this triggers a chain reaction in the other vowels. Leaving details aside, what matters is that the changes unite interactions, the neurophysiology of how a vowel is spoken and, crucially, how vowels are *heard*:

Stage 1 (trigger): Tensing and raising of /æ/ in words like cat.
Stage 2: Fronting of /ɑ/ in words like cot, and lowering of /ɛ/ in words like bet.
Stage 3: Lowering and fronting of /oh/ in words like caught.
Stage 4: Backing of /ɛ/ in words like bet toward /ʌ/ in but.
Stage 5: Backing of /ʌ/ in words like but.
Stage 6: Lowering and backing of /ɪ/ in words like bit.

When two vowels compete in an auditory space, pronunciation leads to the chain shift—vowels move in the auditory space shown.

Labov (2007) examined the chain shift across speakers. He found that, while diffusion between adults is erratic, child pronunciation is generally faithful to the norm. All things being equal, children speak as do their parents; however, once a vowel shift is underway, children exemplify a third category of change. In Chicago, but not the neighboring city of St Louis, children are able to anticipate future change. For Labov, this *incrementation* is surprising—though learning and imitation explain transmission and diffusion, they cannot account for anticipation of upcoming change. Accordingly, he attributed this to the child's superior linguistic ability and, perhaps, a learning device that favors language acquisition.

Stanford and Kenny explored this outcome with the help of ABM. Accordingly, they asked about the extent to which differences depend on adult/child agents, a learning mechanism or a history of interaction. Drawing on discoveries about exemplar based learning (e.g., Bybee 1994; Pierrehumbert 2001), agents are posited to develop exemplars of each vowel. In the model, they interact in an artificial environment that includes a Chicago and a St Louis setting. Agents interact randomly and, at times, move along a St Louis–Chicago highway. Inter-city contact is balanced by a homing mechanism that allows the population as a whole to remain relatively intact. Each agent has exemplars of three vowels which vary only with respect to the vowel [æ] as in "cat." Simply, [æ] was set differently in the $\pm$1,900 Chicago agents and the $\pm$250 strong St Louis population (agent births and deaths led to fluctuations in number). Since agents reset their vowels—by remembering and using exemplars—change was modeled around random interactions between agents. This was done by ensuring that, at any moment in the simulation, agents either stayed where they were or moved to an adjacent square. When agents encountered each other, they signaled: if their settings were sufficiently "similar" (i.e., based on simple calculations), they took on an exemplar of the other agent's signal (up to 140 exemplars). Further, in pursuing the adult/child dimension, when female and male agents met, age-based circumstances were used to calculate if they should produce a child-agent. In initial settings, while adult agents were given 50 exemplars, child agents came to the world without any.

The model replicated diffusion, transmission, and incrementation. Further, just as in the Northern cities, incrementation occurred only in Chicago child-agents. Density of interaction thus exerts variable influences on child- and adult-agents. Since they differ only in lacking initial exemplars, the results must draw on a history of remembering. For linguistic theory, this is a deflationary view: change is more parsimonious than in theories that posit a special learning device. For, given exemplar based memory, embedded agents self-configure by using population norms. In spite of statistical conformity, learning to say "cat" uses bundles of exemplars and not representations of a /kæt/ analogue. While this runs against a long history of linguistic theory and, specifically, the view that speech is "coded" with respect to sound patterns, the deflationary findings will not surprise all phoneticians. It confirms experimental work showing use of rich phonetic memory (see, Port

2007).[8] Equally, it is consistent with the observation that people change how they say “cat” as, for example, they accommodate or, perhaps, stress their own identity. In Stanford and Kenny’s terms, the model supports and explicates “the notion of speech community” (2013: 119). More forcefully, how “cat” is spoken reduces to neither synchronic mental processes nor knowledge of a form. Further the claim is consistent with radical embodied cognitive science in that, Chemero (2011) would argue, saying “cat” re-enacts a history of agent–environment dynamics. For our purposes, two lessons can be drawn. First, as basic an aspect of language as saying [kæt] is agent-specific—it uses a history of interactions. While it can be *described* by a form, “ways of speaking” depend on a history of immergence. Second, ABM illuminates such processes. Indeed, while Labov sought to explain his surprise at incrementation by positing a mechanism, there is a far simpler explanation. The implications reach across the social sciences in urging wariness about how to interpret statistically significant results. Often these use induction to establish a robust description or, simply, an observable aspect of the data. However, significant results do not necessarily involve underlying mechanisms. In parallel, seeing a triangle as a wedge is imaginative—there is no wedge-detecting mechanism. By hypothesis, in both cases, immergence leads to self-configuration. Observable effects (∋) do not always require a theoretical explanation. Conversely, by allowing agents to self-configure, one can play down black box explanations (a “learning device”) by allowing embedded agents to draw on diachronic processes.

3.6 Premature Theorization and Social Science

Many phenomena are pursued through inductive investigation of behavior. On finding a difference, theorists are tempted to offer explanations. Thus, in the case of the vowel shift, Labov sought to explain incrementation by appeal to a mechanism. The logic can seem infallible—where a significant effect is found, what is reliably measured (∋) is often mistakenly assumed to co-vary with a “lower level” entity. The effect seems to be—not an aspect of a phenomenon—but marker of a reality. Indeed much evidence-based enquiry leads to premature theorization that can be described in terms of what can be called the *e-bar (∌) fallacy*. It is not hard to see why. Once a scholar offers a theory to explain (∋), inductive work can be used to establish differences related to (∋). Losing sight of the phenomenon (e.g., how immergence contributes to vowel change), later scholars seek to refute the original claim or, perhaps, develop a theory around new evidence. At least in principle, ABM can deflate such moves: for, as Stanford and Kenny show, evidence of (∋) does not necessarily indicate an underlying mechanism.

---

[8] On a mainstream or code view, brains or minds are said to use inner words coded by a phonemic (or quasi alphabetic) system. Often this is called a “mental lexicon.”

The (∌) fallacy shows the power of the third way in science. A simple model can challenge a widely accepted view because, at times, no explanation is needed. In this case it is because, given agents with exemplar memory, all things being equal, learning leads to incrementation. As in much research based on psychological constructs or expert reports, any search for explanation may fall foul of (∌) fallacy. In this way, simulation exploits the observer and, thus, good old-fashioned skepticism. It offers much in areas where bogus constructs abound—such as attributing human behavior to "mechanisms" of the mind and/or brain. Of course, similar views motivated behaviorism and are used in sophisticated ways by those drawing on, for example, Ryle and Wittgenstein. However, folk psychology will inevitably nudge towards premature theorization. In challenging this, an embedded architecture offers alternatives. Just as immergence influences pronunciation, other social phenomena may use how agents self-configure in cultural ecosystems. Allowing agents exemplar memory not only challenges code linguistics (i.e., models where linguistic "forms" are said to be "used" by brains or individuals) but it shows the importance of diachrony to human cognition. While not the place to develop this view (but see Neumann & Cowley 2015; this volume), the example is indicative. First, saying "cat" is not determined by history (or a brain!) but, rather, connects neural factors with circumstances. This appears, for example, in whether "cat" is spoken automatically (e.g., in listing animals) or in specific cases ("The cat's eating the chicken"). Further, not only do people accommodate to show positive and negative attitudes (by negative accommodation) but saying "cat" can be emotional or indicative ("yes, you're a silly cat"). In mainstream or code linguistics, appeal to utterance (or sentence) production unjustifiably separates language from agency.[9] Further, it is manifestly true that saying "cat" derives from a history of social experience. Not only does this undermine unwarranted appeal to black boxes but it emphasizes how agents *detect* utterances of (what an observer hears as) "cat" and, over time, self-configure. In simple terms, just as in seeing cats, perceiving "cat," depends on, neither processing nor a naked brain, but a human observer.

The observer may have little relevance in certain areas of natural science. Applied to human life and, indeed, the ecology, this may be a dangerous view. Recognizing this, in ecological psychology, it is stressed that an individual's perspectives influence agency: the field is concerned with values. It is important to establish, for example, that people carry babies with more care than they do their shopping (Hodges 2007). This is likely to depend on immergence, sociocultural routines, and changes in neural bio-mechanisms—correlating, in part, with awareness. Thus while bound up with density of interactions and particular kinds of regularity, in themselves, such factors are sufficient to explain neither stance-taking nor human observation.

[9] Van Orden, Holden, and Turvey (2003) report on reaction times of ten subjects over 1,100 trials responded to a visual signal where they uttered /ta/ into a microphone. Similar patterns of variation arise in ten, a hundred and a thousand trials. The authors conclude that the fractal "signature of variation in the laboratory performance is the dynamical signature of intentional behavior" (p. 338).

3.7 Modeling: Life and Cognition

If cognitive science lives by modeling, its progress depends on what the models achieve. There is a parallel with living systems which, as is often argued, evolved increasingly complex modeling systems. If the artificial mimics the natural, it is worth reconsidering Robert Rosen's eloquent exposition of the view that *no* formal model excludes the observer. In so doing, he proposed a version of a diagram labeled as in Fig. 3.2.

On the surface, the model shows that a modeler uses a formal system to learn about what Rosen terms a natural system. Further, this is done by using inferences about causal processes. However, Rosen's labels bring out a contrast with Axelrod's work. This shows, above all, in his striking use of the code metaphor. Rather than draw parallels with an artificial system (e.g., Morse), encoding and decoding become acts (made possible by life). Further, this is necessary because the process "cannot be entailed by anything in the formalisms." Indeed, what formalisms show—even if they are models of an ecosystem—is bound to depend on "comparison of inferential structures." In other words, it depends on an observer's natural encoding or, for Rosen, it is "in effect a creative act, resulting in new formal objects." Creating modeling relations is, on this view, an art. Creative activity (shown on the upper and lower arrows) shapes modeling. How can this insight be used? On one hand, as Axelrod stressed, one can use simulated data that "comes from a rigorously specified set of rules" to benchmark "intuitions" about real world observations. On the other hand, as with the Northern vowel shift, one can use it in the spirit of Rosen to amplify intuitions and, thus, develop new conceptualizations. In comparing the formal structures of Labov's analysis with those used in running their ABM model, one finds that, given exemplar memory, a learning mechanism supported by interaction can produce incrementation.

General conclusions follow. While deflating the view that children have a special mechanism for language learning, it also shows the importance of the speech community. For Rosen, such intuitions are creative ways of decoding a model around what is known of sound change. The same applies to tracing acts of saying "cat" to local practices, bodies, and changing circumstances. Given exemplar based memory, immergent processes transform pronunciation. By implication, individuals

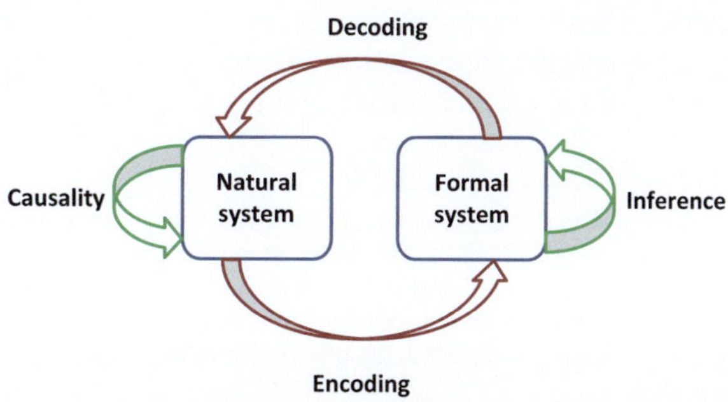

Fig. 3.2 Rosen's model of simulation

do not use phonetic types; rather, just as in seeing a triangle, there are *aspects* to hearing "cat." While we may attend to the "word," there are times when we focus on a cat, a speaker, or issues of status and attitude. We hear as observers: it is unwarranted to posit that an English speaking person perceives a "form" like /kæt/ when he or she hears "cat" (in English).[10] As Kenny and Stanford's model allows, agents rely on selections from a range of phonetic exemplars. This enables children-agents to pick up on how things are said, reconfigure the detail of speech, and "foresee" historical change. Remarkably, the agents act like simple observers.

The model features interactional asymmetry between the world for agents and how agents display "sames" to the world. This parallels, for example, what people hear and how they speak. Simple agents select constraints because their behavior draws on history. They mesh slow processes with fast ones. In Rosen's sense, they "encode" what they hear—the "natural system" of other agents—by developing an individual "formal system." Modeling now becomes a heuristic—a way of rethinking natural systems and (multi)causal processes. This provides grounds for being wary of the levels metaphor (results are decoded in terms of what might happen in the world). Plainly, ABM can be used in different ways. If, in Rosen's terms, one highlights the art of observing, the model can be seen as an ecosystem in which embedded agents self-configure—as they change modes of interaction. Eschewing mentalist assumptions, the rigor of ABM can pursue how use behavior shapes natural systems that reduce to neither structural types, regularities, nor sequential models. By focusing on embedded agents in cultural ecosystems, diachronic complexity can be examined in relation to recurrences, pivotal events, phases, and trajectories. On one hand, ABM complements other methods and, on the other hand, it opens up the issue of how social constraints enable cognitive activity. It offers heuristics for rethinking the bio-sociocultural as drawing on how social artifice contributes to and an observer's skills. By hypothesis, people take stances based on routines, know-how, roles, strategies, and collaborative projects. Seen thus, a stance taker's cognition is co-optative: the model serves to open up new ways of orienting to the future.

3.8 Cognition Beyond the Body

ABM allows cognitive science to examine how intelligent activity draws on agent–environment dynamics. Writing as an observer, I thus see it as part of the arsenal of radical embodied cognitive science. This is, above all, because it allows

[10]At the risk of being pedantic, a person who *reports* a phonetic pattern [kæt] is said to hear /kæt/ (i.e., what is spelled "cat"). Yet, where an outside observer hears an instance of "cat" as, say, [kɛt], an interlocutor may not notice the detail. He or she may, for example, be getting a cat off a table. In any case, there is no reason to suppose that she (or her brain) represents a form /kæt/; simply, like [kɛt], /kæt/ is a second-order description of how exemplars of "cat" can be spoken, heard, and reported.

bidirectional agent–environment coupling that exploits a range of time-scales. Agent behavior links (a) what is intrinsic to the agent; (b) how agents exploit interaction; and (c) how immergent products enable agents to self-configure. Focusing on the latter, I have emphasized how an agent appropriates ways of acting that draw on socio-cultural resources. Given exemplar memory, agents can use interaction to produce vowels in ways that are consistent with sociolinguistic findings. Crucially infant-agents show incrementation—their pronunciation anticipates future change.

ABM can be used in many ways. Classically, using Axelrod's logic, there are many cases when modelers rightly seek to minimize the observer's role. This applies, for example, to Scheutz et al.'s (2005) systems engineering approach to the frog ecology. In principle, at least, the approach can be used to develop hypotheses about possible mechanisms. This is because it uses, not measures of the world, but how these serve in constructing rules. Weight thus falls on swarm intelligence or interdependencies between levels that function under distributed control. On this view, agents are so deeply embedded in the world that their doings are integral parts of environments. In studying organism-environment systems, much can be gained from this view of possible outcomes—especially if parts and procedures depend on hidden mechanisms. In pursuing cultural ecosystems, however, I advocate a different approach. Humans rely on perceiving *aspects* because decision making draws on observations. Turning from swarm intelligence, I suggest that ABM can also be used to understand how sociocultural resources function—how agents use extra-bodily norms, procedures, artifacts, and, indeed, languages *qua* abstract pattern.

Pursuing how extra-bodily resources enable intelligent activity, I develop Rosen's view. Rather than minimize observing, I stress the necessary inadequacy of modeling—the world is irreducible to formal description. ABM is both a means of discovering possible mechanisms and a tool for extending an observer's powers. Indeed, because it is free of real-world measures, it can show unexpected effects. In illustration, I use agent-based simulation of the Northern Vowel shift. Given exemplar memory, density of interactions drives agents to mimic incrementation—where vowel shifts occur, they can prefigure future change. The model overthrows appeal to a special learning mechanism and issues a general warning about premature theorization. It presents what I term the (∌) fallacy, or the mistaken view that statistically significant effects always have some kind of underlying cause. In fact, inductively based results are often redescriptions: phonetic incrementation proves to be a correlate of exemplar-based memory. This, I claim, is nontrivial. At very least, it suggests that humans may use exemplar memory to sensitize to vocalizations and, thus, gain varying degrees of control over utterances of, say, "cat."

Viewing ABM as an observational tool opens up cognition beyond the body. Indeed, given community resources and exemplar memory, agents gain a repertoire that, in principle, allows for variable performance. Instead of idealizing speech and hearing as processes based on real-time coding, learning to say "cat" exemplifies diachronic cognition. A history of interactions links events in slow moving scales (e.g., Chicago speech) with agent-interaction. By extrapolation, human language is enmeshed with embodiment (see Cowley 2014). Immergence therefore prompts agents to self-configure and, as they do so, to appropriate cultural resources. Not only is this amenable to modeling but it fits Torre's (2014) view of how sophisticated human agents interlace experience across lived, dialogical, and pro-optative time-scales. In short, human individuals use the stamp of the past to lay down anchor points that, remarkably, affect who they become. Diachronic cognition thus brings a new directedness to human life.

No computational agent observes. However, ABM both serves as an observational tool and, remarkably, shows potential for simulation of observing. In principle, if agents use exemplar memory to self-configure, they too can sensitize to aspects of a world in ways that shape interaction. One human equivalent is, of course, coming hear speech in a verbal aspect, or gaining the ability to take a language stance. By so doing, it is possible to learn—not only through direct experience but also from monitoring what people do and say together. Indeed, intermeshing utterances with visible expression enables people to concert perception as the said exploits affective and attitudinal indices ("the cat's eating the chicken, again"). However, if language is traced to a synchronic system, such phenomena are repressed (utterances are said to be "produced" by brains). Radical embodied cognitive science thus has much to gain from ABM. Moving beyond reliance on a levels metaphor, the method can show how diachronic cognition prompts agents to use ecosystemic resources as they self-configure. Just as robots show how agency exploits embedding-in-the-world, ABM allows modeling of how the world beyond the body contributes to flexible, adaptive behavior. This arises, it seems, as agents self-configure by appropriating cultural resources. In taking this view, one raises new questions about how embedded agents interact in a multi-scalar cultural ecosystem. Such views can give rise to new types of modeling—and approaches based on designing environments for agents who are able to simulate simple observation.

Acknowledgements While, the paper's flaws draw on how humanity arises through the humanity of others, its merits owe much to two people. First, Martin Neumann both taught me about modeling and, in so doing, spurred me to extend a systemic view of cognition. Second, Sabine Thürmel, sought clarification about observers—why the human is no product of swarm intelligence. I still owe her a convincing answer. Sorry, Sabine. However, let the paper be a start; having constructed what stands here, I offer gratitude to both of them and my inspiring reviewers.

References

Axelrod, R. (1997). Advancing the art of simulation in the social sciences. In *Simulating social phenomena* (pp. 21–40). Berlin: Springer.

Brier, S. (2008). *Cybersemiotics: Why information is not enough!* Toronto: University of Toronto Press.

Bybee, J. (1994). A view of phonology from a cognitive and functional perspective. *Cognitive Linguistics, 5*, 285–305.

Chemero, A. (2011). *Radical embodied cognitive science*. Cambridge, MA: MIT Press.

Chomsky, N. (1965). *Aspects of the theory of syntax*. Cambridge, MA: MIT Press.
Chomsky, N. (1972). *Language and mind*. New York: Harcourt Brace Jovanovich.
Chomsky, N. (1995). *The minimalist program*. Cambridge, MA: MIT Press.
Conte, R., Andrighetto, G., & Campenni, M. (Eds.). (2013). *Minding norms: Mechanisms and dynamics of social order in agent societies*. Oxford: Oxford University Press.
Cowley, S. J. (2011a). Taking a language stance. *Ecological Psychology, 23*(3), 185–209.
Cowley, S. J. (2011b). *Distributed language*. Amsterdam: John Benjamins.
Cowley, S. J. (2014). Linguistic embodiment and verbal constraints: Human cognition and the scales of time. *Frontiers in Psychology, 5*, 1085. doi:10.3389/fpsyg.2014.01085.
Cummins, F. (2014). Voice, (inter-) subjectivity, and real time recurrent interaction. *Frontiers in Psychology, 5*, 760. doi:10.3389/fpsyg.2014.00760.
Dennett, D. (1989). *The intentional stance*. Cambridge, MA: MIT Press.
Fodor, J. A. (1975). *The language of thought*. Cambridge, MA: Harvard University Press.
Hodges, B. H. (2007). Values define fields: The intentional dynamics of driving, carrying, leading, negotiating, and conversing. *Ecological Psychology, 19*(2), 153–178.
Hutchins, E. (1995). *Cognition in the wild*. Cambridge, MA: MIT Press.
Hutchins, E. (2014). The cultural ecosystem of human cognition. *Philosophical Psychology, 27*(1), 34–49.
Kravchenko, A. (2008). *Biology of cognition and linguistic analysis: From non-realist linguistics to a realistic language science*. Frankfurt am Main, Berlin: Peter Lang.
Kravchenko, A. V. (2007). Essential properties of language, or, why language is not a code. *Language Sciences, 29*(5), 650–671.
Labov, W. (2007). Transmission and diffusion. *Language, 83*, 344–387.
Linell, P. (2004). *The written language bias in linguistics: Its nature, origins and transformations*. London: Routledge.
Love, N. (2004). Cognition and the language myth. *Language Sciences, 26*(6), 525–544.
Markoš, A., Švorcová, J., & Lhotský, J. (2013). Living as languaging: Distributed knowledge in living beings. In S. J. Cowley & F. Vallée-Tourangeau (Eds.), *Cognition beyond the brain* (pp. 71–92). London: Springer.
Maturana, H. R. (1978). *Biology of language: The epistemology of reality* (pp. 27–63).
Maturana, H. R. (2002). Autopoiesis, structural coupling and cognition: A history of these and other notions in the biology of cognition. *Cybernetics and Human Knowing, 9*, 5–34.
Menary, R. (2010). Introduction to the special issue on 4E cognition. *Phenomenology and the Cognitive Sciences, 9*(4), 459–463.
Maturana, H. R. (1978). Biology of language: The epistemology of reality. In G. A. Miller & E. Lenneberg (Eds.), *Psychology and biology of language and thought: Essays in honor of Eric Lenneberg* (pp. 27–63). New York: Academic Press.
Neumann, M., & Cowley, S. J. (2015). Criminal organisations and society: Learning from the Mafia. In D. Secchi & M. Neumann (Eds.), *Agent-based simulation of organizational behavior: New frontiers of social science research*. New York: Springer (this volume).
Pierrehumbert, J. (2001). Exemplar dynamics: Word frequency, lenition, and contrast. In J. Bybee & P. Hopper (Eds.), *Frequency effects and the emergence of lexical structure* (pp. 137–157). Amsterdam: Benjamins.
Port, R. (2007). How are words stored in memory? Beyond phones and phonemes. *New Ideas in Psychology, 25*(2), 143–170.
Raimondi, V. (2014). Social interaction, languaging and the operational conditions for the emergence of observing. *Frontiers in Psychology, 5*, 899. doi:10.3389/fpsyg.2014.00899.
Rosen, R. (1991). *Life itself: A comprehensive inquiry into the nature, origin, and fabrication of life*. New York: Columbia University Press.
Ryle, G. (1949). *The concept of mind*. London, UK: Hutchinson.
Scheutz, M., Madey, G., & Boyd, S. (2005). tMANS – The multi-scale agent-based networked simulation for the study of multi-scale, multi-level biological and social phenomena. In *Proceedings of Spring Simulation Multiconference (SMC 05), Agent-Directed Simulation Symposium*.

Stanford, J. N., & Kenny, L. A. (2013). Revisiting transmission and diffusion: An agent-based model of vowel chain shifts across large communities. *Language Variation and Change, 25*(02), 119–153.

Steffensen, S. V. (2012). Care and conversing in dialogical systems. *Language Sciences, 34*(5), 513–531.

Torre, E. (2014). Digital inscriptions as material anchors for future action: Multi-scalar integration and dynamic systems. *Cybernetics & Human Knowing, 21*(1–2), 128–142.

Uryu, M., Steffensen, S. V., & Kramsch, C. (2014). The ecology of intercultural interaction: Timescales, temporal ranges and identity dynamics. *Language Sciences, 41*, 41–59.

Van Orden, G. C., Holden, J. G., & Turvey, M. T. (2003). Self-organization of cognitive performance. *Journal of Experimental Psychology: General, 132*(3), 331–350.

Wittgenstein, L. W. (1957). *Philosophical investigations* (2nd ed.). Oxford: Blackwell.

Wolfram, W., & Schilling-Estes, N. (1998). *American English: Dialects and variation*. Malden, MA: Blackwell.

Part II
Modeling Organizational Behavior

Chapter 4
The Effects of Disorganization on Goals and Problem Solving

Dinuka Herath, Davide Secchi, and Fabian Homberg

Abstract This chapter presents an agent-based simulation of the ability of employees to solve problems. The primary aim of the chapter is to discern the difference in problem solving under two structural conditions. One has rigid structural constraints imposed on the agents while the other has very little structural constraints (called "disorganization" in this work). The simulation further utilizes organizational goals as a basis for motivation and studies the effects of disorganization on goals and motivation. Results from the simulation show that, under the condition of a more disorganized environment, the number of problems solved is relatively higher than under the condition of a less disorganized and more structured environment.

Keywords Agent-based modeling • Disorganization • Expectancy theory • Goals • Problem solving • Effectiveness

4.1 Introduction

This chapter presents a model of the occurrence of "disorganization" and its impact on goal setting and problem solving. In this work, we do not attempt to define disorganization per se, because that would be the scope of another article. Instead, we consider it as an umbrella concept to indicate the reduction of structural constraints and rules of interaction employees are subject to so that their work does not seem to follow any clear order or rule. Every organization sets countless goals (Brown, Jones, & Leigh, 2005) and each is perceived as having a given level

The Editors gratefully acknowledge the support of the Society for the Study of Artificial Intelligence and Simulation of Behavior (AISB) in developing this volume.

D. Herath (✉) • F. Homberg
Department of Human Resources and Organizational Behavior,
Bournemouth University, Poole, UK
e-mail: Dinuka.Herath@bournemouth.ac.uk; fhomberg@bournemouth.ac.uk

D. Secchi
Research Cluster for Cognition, Management and Communication (COMAC),
Centre for Human Interactivity (CHI), Department of Language and Communication,
University of Southern Denmark, Slagelse, Denmark
e-mail: secchi@sdu.dk

D. Secchi, M. Neumann (eds.), *Agent-Based Simulation of Organizational Behavior*, DOI 10.1007/978-3-319-18153-0_4

of difficulty, some are relatively trivial, others appear to be very hard (Locke & Latham, 2013). Goals ought to be well defined and measurable (Locke & Latham, 1990) and this, historically, led to the idea that a well-organized structure associated with goals makes them manageable (Shenhav, 2002). This principle goes deep down to the roots of management (e.g., Fayol, 1916; Taylor, 1911) since it reflects the belief that goals (as problems to solve) should be clearly associated with employees and managers such that they become easier to achieve. In other words, it is the clarity of instructions and effective organizational structures that facilitates goal attainment (Chandler, 1932; Simon, 1947). This is what classic or rational management theories claim (Scott, 2001). However, recent debates have questioned the effectiveness of organizational structure and highlighted the seemingly positive effects of disorganized work environments on work outcomes (Amabile, 1996; Deci & Ryan, 1991; Frost, Osterloh, & Antoinette, 2010).

This chapter is a first attempt to investigate the effects of disorganization and goal attainment (framed as problem solving; see below). Even though some argue that disorganization may bring some benefits (Abrahamson & Freedman, 2006), the effect of disorganization on specific organizational processes and procedures has received limited attention. There is some ambiguity in what is meant by "disorganization" (Abrahamson, 2002) and this is why, in this paper, it is used as an umbrella term to encompass multiple concepts (Abrahamson & Freedman, 2006). These can be, among many others, messiness (unwanted aggregation of things), reduction of organizational structure, and low levels of organizational control (Abrahamson & Freedman, 2006; Cohen, 1974; Warglien & Masuch, 1996). This chapter focuses on goal achievement under condition of more or less structure and of formal or informal rules of interaction for workers. Hence, it is apparent that the concept of "disorganization" dealt with in this chapter is built around studies on the effects of increasing control in organizations (Abrahamson & Freedman, 2006; Cohen, 1974; Crozier, 1969).

The research presented in this chapter has two primary objectives. First, the chapter explores the effects of disorganization on goal achievement. In order to do that, we use an agent-based computational simulation model (ABM) that unveils the effects of disorganization and organization on employee's access to problems and solutions in the light of available problem solving opportunities. The primary interest of the research is to compare the efficiency of both organization and disorganization in terms of achieving goals, namely problem solving, assuming that to "solve problems" a goal needs to be set beforehand. This is done considering how motivation fluctuates among employees when problems are solved. The second objective of the chapter is to contribute to building of a theory of disorganization (Abrahamson, 2002; Warglien & Masuch, 1996). Consequently the study aims to broaden the understanding of how disorganization affects organizations.

In the following sections, we first discuss the concept of disorganization, then introduce the components of the model, present some preliminary results, and discuss them in a concluding section.

4.2 Theoretical Framework

4.2.1 Disorganization

Disorganization is a concept which was first introduced and discussed in the 1970s (Cohen, 1972) and it can also be referred to as *organized anarchy*. This is how Cohen and March (1974) discuss it in relation to leadership under conditions of ambiguous power and its responsibilities, a situation that provides advantageous outcomes for leaders. In the 1960s, disorganization was defined as any deviation from the organizational protocol (Crozier, 1969). This definition soon revealed to be inadequate since it does not explain "what" disorganization is, nor does it define its characteristics, causes, and consequences (Abrahamson & Freedman, 2006; Shenhav, 2002; Warglien & Masuch, 1996). For clarification purposes, it should be noted that in the context of this study the word "disorganization" does not automatically imply the antithesis of "organization." This means that for disorganization to occur, it is not required that the organized allocation of a given environment, resources, thoughts ought to be known. To make a simple example, when we see what seems to be a dis-organized desk, it does not mean that we have clear in mind how the same desk would be if organized. Moreover, disorganization can be also seen as an occurrence which takes place within a more organized or structured context.

There is a semantic level in the discussion that needs to be clarified before we can move forward. We may refer to disorganization and organization as ways of distributing, assembling and connecting resources, thoughts, and elements. The word "organization" can also be referred to social structure as a way of pulling resources together in a limited and formal social environment (e.g., a company, the European Union). If the latter meaning is used, it is clear that dis-organization cannot be considered an antonym. The model discussed in this chapter focuses on the former set of meanings, where the mode of using or not using structure is the main focus. The way disorganization occurs in this model is within a given formal social structure. Hence, the two levels are nested.

The traditional view of how an organization should work vouched for isolating the organization and its functions from external disturbances, or for trying to focus on a limited set of external influences only (Thompson, 1967). Over the years this approach has fallen out of favor given that every organization is heavily influenced by external factors such as market fluctuations. Furthermore, due to geographical barriers and technological advancements traditional hierarchical control over employees seems to be ineffective and more flexibility is required (De Vulpain, 2005). The reasons for different forms of organizing are largely due to globalization (Featherstone, 1990). Additionally, the workforce has also undergone substantial change since the 1960s and, for example, employee turnover has increased over the years (Mobley & Fisk, 1982). This means that a constant inflow and outflow of employees is commonplace in most modern organizations. Another factor which heavily influences organizations is the technological development and the tendencies towards globalization (Jarvenpaa & Leidner, 1998). In adapting to the changes in the environment, new forms of organizing have emerged. These new forms of organizing are increasingly driven by advancements in technology that are sometimes managed via globally distributed virtual teams or via so-called network organizations (Nohria, 1994). Network organizations contain small and agile self-directed teams; these organizations usually utilize multiple forms of organizing where some teams can be highly organized while other teams can be self-governing and disorganized (De Vulpain, 2005). Network mediation ensures interoperability of these heterogeneously organized teams (De Vulpain, 2005; Nohria, 1994). These flexible forms of organizing with large elements of disorganization (lack of structure) are also known as hybrid enterprise sensible organization, and organizing through social technologies—constructive learning approaches and are driven by the exponential leaps in technological capabilities (Black & Edwards, 2000).

Disorganization has earlier been considered a detrimental factor for organizational performance (Shenhav, 1995, 2002). However starting in the 1970s (Cohen, 1972) this view has started to be challenged. Abrahamson (2002) points out that there are disadvantages to order such as inattentiveness towards emergence, decreased employee motivation, and deviation from primary goals and objectives. In light of new evidence (Abrahamson & Freedman, 2006; Warglien & Masuch, 1996), some scholars (Freeland, 2002; Warglien & Masuch, 1996) now agree that there are advantages of minimally structured organizational environments (disorganized environments). The primary benefits of disorganization can be traced in decision making, problem solving (Cohen, 1972), innovation (Freeland, 2002), and motivation (Warglien & Masuch, 1996). Some key benefits of disorganization highlighted by Abrahamson (2002) and Abrahamson and Freedman (2006) are efficiency advantages, enhancing creativity, political advantages—indispensability, less use of resources, allowance for nonstandard agents/processes.

Given the hypothesized benefits of disorganization, some scholars conceive of disorganization as something that can be managed (Abrahamson & Freedman, 2006; Freeland, 2002; Warglien & Masuch, 1996). In this context, management does not imply "structuring." Instead, it implies direction and optimization of disorganization (Abrahamson & Freedman, 2006). The utilization of an amount of disorganized components, relationships, and procedures when needed (in decision making, in innovating, etc.) can be seen as disorganization management. Given the hypothesized ability of disorganization to be managed to achieve better outcomes for an organization, understanding the levels of disorganization at which effective goals can be set is an important task.

Currently, research (e.g., Abrahamson, 2002; Muller, 2000; Stacey, 1993) aims to provide a theoretical clarification of the concept of disorganization. Disorganization itself has not received attention from mainstream management given that the field has been concerned with the organized, the rational, and the structured for quite a long time (e.g., the so-called rational systems theories; Scott, 2001). The current lack of consensus on what disorganization really is can also be seen as one such cause. Nevertheless, some authors (Muller, 2000; Nonaka, 1988; Stacey, 1993) directly or indirectly present the concept of disorganization from various vantage points (individual, group, and organizational level). Over the years the concept of disorganization has been addressed by researchers under different terminologies (Muller, 2000; Nonaka, 1988; Stacey, 1993). Nevertheless, currently there is no established definition of "disorganization" which has achieved consensus (Abrahamson, 2002; Eisenberg, 1984). Thus, "disorganization" is used interchangeably with other words such as "disorder" and "messiness."

In this study, we start from the basic working definition of disorganization as introduced by Abrahamson (2002). This can be seen as the only attempt to define disorganization as an independent concept. This particular definition was chosen because it provides significant detail and makes the concept easier to operationalize in a simulation. He posits that "[d]isorganization is the disorderly accumulation of varied entities in hierarchically ordered complex human structures" (p. 4).

According to the aforementioned definition, disorderly accumulation refers to unintended aggregation of both non-physical and physical components within an organization (varied entities in the definition). These entities are also hierarchically ordered, pointing at how an organization is conventionally structured. Even though this definition roughly encompasses the concept of disorganization it still does not provide much of an explanation of what "disorganization" is. Abrahamson (2002) further posits that disorganization as defined above is an unavoidable condition within an organization and should be embraced. The rate at which a disorderly accumulation of varied entities happens is dependent on the structure of an organization. The structure can be rigid (organized, hierarchy) or flexible (disorganized, anarchy). These features can be re-phrased to indicate a reduction of structural constraints (hierarchy) and rules of interaction that employees are subjected to (anarchy). The implication is that work does not seem to follow any clear pattern or rule.

4.2.2 Operationalizing the Concept

In developing the simulation discussed in this chapter, the so-called garbage can model by Cohen (1972) was taken as a starting point. The garbage can was the first attempt to model disorganization and organization and it defines a solution space in which participants, problems, solutions, and opportunities are put together in a minimally structured environment. However, the technology used in the garbage can model is obsolete by today's standards as shown in the modern agent-based simulation as updated by Fioretti and Lomi (2008) who defined a mechanism to implement disorganization (anarchy) within the simulation.

As already stated above, how disorganization impacts problem solving is the primary focus of the agent-based simulation presented in this chapter. This simulation attempts to compare disorganization and organization in terms of access to problems by employees under both hierarchy-based interactions and non-hierarchy-based interactions, matched with opportunities and solutions. These comparisons are needed in order to properly define the concept of disorganization. It further allows for an operationalization helping to understand what its imminent effects on the daily operations of a company are. In particular, this study focuses on the process of problem solving, involving individual abilities, motivations, available solutions, and problems.

Given that the primary aim of the model is to study the effects of disorganization on problem solving, it explores the impact of disorganization (interpreted as absence of hierarchical distribution of problem solving) on decision efficiency using several elements that characterize problem solving, including the decision maker's motivation, defined through goal setting theory. By modeling the effects of disorganization (as defined) on goal setting and task performance, an understanding of why disorganization occurs, and how it materializes can be gained. Ultimately, the ABM approach allows for an investigation of what emerges once disorganization happens.

4.2.3 Goal Setting

One of the ways to better understand and study disorganization is that of associating it with a tangible and pervasive element of organizing (Warglien & Masuch, 1996). In this study, we claim that one such element is "goal setting" (Locke & Latham, 1990, 2013). In order for a goal to be achieved, workers need to make decisions and solve problems. In this paper, we are not interested in how goals are actually "set" or in the individual or social decision making process leading to a shared understanding of prioritizing goals and identifying what they should look like. It is worth noting that some of these goals are ambiguous (Cohen & March, 1974), thus making it difficult to deal with them. Not all goals are straightforward and easily measurable, as the theory seems to recommend (Locke & Latham, 1990). If we consider elements of goal ambiguity, we may realize the more individuals dealing with the same goal may help defining the shared meaning it has for the organization, employees, and management (Cannon-Bowers & Salas, 2001). Moreover, the dynamic of advice giving and taking between members of a team and/or hierarchical levels (Bonaccio & Dalal, 2006) affects how people think and act on particular goals and tasks. These broader processes can also be described cognitively, providing an externally and socially distributed version of the goal setting process (Cowley & Vallee-Tourangeau, 2013; Hutchins, 1995). This is why it is useful to approach solving problems related to goals using a less-organized (or disorganized) perspective.

Additionally, disorganization and goal setting share some common attributes. Both disorganization and goal setting occur at every hierarchical level of an organization (be it the mailroom or the boardroom). Furthermore, both disorganization and goal setting can be observed regardless of the reference point from which the observation is conducted (individual perspective, group perspective, organizational perspective). Additionally, goal setting and disorganization are inevitable attributes of any organization (Seijts & Latham, 2001). Moreover, setting goals acts as a platform for increasing employee motivation. Finally, the effects of disorganization on goal setting have not been studied before and this provides an added incentive to explore how the two variables interact together (Abrahamson & Freedman, 2006).

Goal setting theory (Locke & Latham, 1990) was developed over a 25-year period based on 400 laboratory and field studies (Locke & Latham, 2013). More recent studies have looked at components of goal setting theory as learning goals and individual efficacy (Donovan & Williams, 2003; Drach-zahavy & Erez, 2002; Seijts & Latham, 2001; Wiese & Freund, 2005). The basic premises of the theory state that hard and clearly defined goals lead to better task performance than vague (less defined) or easy goals if the individual has the efficacy, commitment, and does not have other conflicting goals (Locke & Latham, 1990).

The aforementioned relationship between goal difficulty and task performance has been well established both conceptually (Locke & Latham, 1990, 2013) and empirically (Donovan & Williams, 2003; Seijts & Latham, 2001). Furthermore, Bandura (1997) and Brown et al. (2005) found that self-efficacy, past performance, and various external influences affect the way goals are set. Even though the relationship between goal difficulty and performance is well understood, the external environmental or social effects of disorganized work environments on goal setting have not garnered the same attention (Locke & Latham, 2013). In the simulation model discussed in this chapter a goal is considered a prerequisite for a problem to be solved. This means that when a problem is solved a goal has been achieved.

Nevertheless, as already stated above, one of the impacts of disorganization on goals is that they can become ambiguous (Cohen & March, 1974). Of course, there are many ways goals can be perceived that way. For example, a goal can be perceived differently from employee to employee, be defined independent of the hierarchical level(s) in which it is first defined, and its achievement may be judged differently due to the goal being ill-defined (i.e., ambiguous) in the first place.

4.3 The Model

We explore the effects of disorganization on goal setting and task performance using agent-based modeling. ABMs can be seen as a direct solution for understanding complexities involved in an organizational environment (Miller & Lin, 2010). ABM can be used to simulate various organizational dynamics in a simple yet detailed manner (Lomi & Harrison, 2012; Secchi, 2013). The primary advantage ABM has over its alternatives is the ability to be more flexible and adaptable (Gilbert & Terna, 2000), characteristics that have increased its use among contemporary scholars (Gilbert, 2008).

Complementing the flexibility of ABM to study disorganization is the fact that this tool has already been used to model effects of disorganization in decision making. Fioretti and Lomi (2008) used an ABM to simulate the garbage can model (Cohen, 1972) of decision making. In developing the model for studying effects of disorganization on goal setting and task performance, a similar approach to that of Lomi and Harrison (2012) is adopted. In fact, a set of rules is derived from the underlying theory which can then be modeled into parameters. Thus the work of Fioretti and Lomi (2008) and Lomi and Harrison (2012) can be used as a foundation for the research proposed here. These rules were modeled using conditional statements.

The two main scenarios are modeled as "organization" and "disorganization." Hierarchy (organization) represents the structured working environment with rigid rules, regulations, and operational procedures where agents can only move based on sufficient conditions. Anarchy (disorganization) represents the loosely structured work environment where agents are fully autonomous and free to move.

The intention of this exploratory work is to assess whether some theoretical assumptions hold and to assess under what circumstances they do hold. ABM allows conducting more accurate theoretical refinements before getting to the testing phase. Moreover, this class of models is particularly well suited to represent complex adaptive systems, such as organizational problem solving dynamics.

4.3.1 Space and Agents

The world in which the agents reside is three dimensional. The dimensionality of the simulation space allows each agent to move along the x, y, and z axes. A three dimensional simulation space is used instead of a two dimensional simulation space in order to give more variability to agent movements.

The model consists of four agents which have a set of variables defined under them. Table 4.1 shows agent types and their attributes (parameters in the simulation) while Table 4.2 shows parameters, values, and a short description of what they represent.

Independent of its type, each agent is associated with a level that is used to specify where each agent is situated within the organizational hierarchy. These levels are defined by numbers from 0 to 4. The number '0' represents the lowest tier of the hierarchy (e.g., mailroom) while the number '4' represents the highest level (i.e. boardroom).

The agent employee represents the typical worker within a given organization. Efficacy, ability, and motivation are characteristics of each employee and are attributed through a random normal distribution with a mean of 0 and standard deviation of 1.

Table 4.1 Agent and attributes

Agent	Attributes
Employee (E)	Efficacy (e), ability (a), motivation (m), level (l)
Problem (P)	Difficulty (d), level (l)
Solution (S)	Efficiency, level (l)
Opportunity (O)	Level (l)

Table 4.2 Model parameters

Parameters	Values	Description
Levels	0, 1, 2, 3, 4	Each agent is assigned a hierarchical level randomly. This parameter allows the creation of a hierarchy with the model.
Efficacy	$N \approx (0, 1)$	Unique to an employee. Represents an employee's capability in solving problems.
Ability	$N \approx (0, 1)$	Unique to an employee. Represents an employee's level of skill and competency in solving problems.
Motivation	$N \approx (0, 1)$	Represents an employee's intrinsic and extrinsic motivation.
Problem difficulty	$N \approx (0, 1)$	Represents the inherent level of complexity or simplicity of the problem.
Solution efficiency	$N \approx (0, 1)$	Represents the suitability of available resources to be used for problem solving.
Range	1–10	The range determines the amount of patches an agent will scan. i.e., if the range is set at 5 an agent will scan 5 patches around itself at every step.
Similar wanted	0.00–1.00	Under the organization condition, the similar wanted parameter determines the percentage of agents of the same hierarchical level that a given agent is satisfied with. I.e., when similar wanted is set to 70 % an agent will be satisfied if agents in range were of similar level 70 % of the time.

The problem agent represents both physical and non-physical problems which arise within an organization (e.g., unruly employees, broken computers, delayed projects, low sales, and angry customers). This agent in the context of the model is used as a placeholder to represent all the multitude of problems an organization faces. Each problem has a difficulty assigned to it through a random normal distribution with a mean of 0 and standard deviation of 1. The difficulty of a problem represents the inherent complexity (or simplicity) or any given problem and is used in the decision making process. A problem is perceived more or less difficult depending on how this inherent complexity matches with an employee's abilities, efficacy, motivation, solutions, and opportunities. Such matching reflects problem difficulty relative to each agent-employee.

The solution agent represents both physical and non-physical options available (e.g., repairman, various tools, will power, collective action, political capital) which can be used to solve problems. The solution agent acts as a placeholder to represent all the various solutions available within a given organization. Each solution has an efficiency assigned to it through a random normal distribution with a mean of 0 and standard deviation of 1.

The opportunity agent is used to represent the occasion when a problem can be solved and when solutions are available. This variable takes into account the fact that in any given organization the opportunity to solve problems arise and cease to exists, thus the opportunities need to be grabbed once presented. A given opportunity does not have any attribute which is unique to it but shares the level attribute with all the other agent types.

4.3.2 Movement

Movement in the model represents the real world movement of agents within an organization. The orientation of a given agent (the direction which they are moving towards) depends on its type. Once an agent turns to a random direction it scans its surroundings and moves toward other agents within its range or randomly, depending on the following rules:

1. Problems move freely (i.e., randomly) within the solution space. Upon every step a given problem turns to a random angle and moves a patch before repeating the procedure ad infinitum until the simulation is stopped or the problem is solved in which case it exits the solution space.
2. Solutions tend to move around problems. In this context a solution represents resources available for solving a problem. The solution agent parallels the resources available in the real world, both physical and non-physical. A given solution scans its surroundings and moves towards the maximum valued problem in range.
3. Opportunities represent the window of time and circumstance where a given problem can be solved. In the real world some problems can only be solved at an opportune time or place thus this agent represents the reality of the window of opportunity. A given opportunity scans its surroundings and moves towards the maximum valued problem in range.
4. Employees within the model are fully mobile and move randomly in the simulation space. This represents an organization where employees tend to move around and are not stationary. Even if an employee is stationed to a physical location they have the opportunity to handle multiple problems and move around their designated physical location. Employees move towards problems at any given time. A given employee scans its surroundings and moves towards the maximum valued problem in range.

In order to impose the conditions of both "organization" and "disorganization" within the solution space, various movements based on a set of rules have been developed. First, once "disorganization" is switched-on all the agents within the solution space move with complete autonomy and each agent turns to a random direction and moves forward freely. Under this condition agents are free to interact with one another without any restrictions. This form of movement represents a "disorganized organization" where employees, solutions, opportunities, and problems move freely within the organization and interact without any restrictions. All the single agent movement conditions are applied under this setting. The distance a given agent travels under the disorganization setting is determined by the "range" parameter which is an initial condition.

In contrast, when the "organization" is switched on the agents are only allowed to move to a certain set of other agents within the solution space. The condition of "organization" is designed to represent the hierarchical nature of a real world organization where, for example, a problem in the mail room tends to be handled by an employee from the mailroom rather than an executive from the boardroom. This hierarchical restriction is implemented through the use of the "level" variable of each agent. The algorithm for hierarchical movement is as follows:

$$E_l \neq P_l \text{ OR } E_l \neq S_l \text{ OR } E_l \neq O_l$$

In the above algorithm let "E" be employee, "P" be problem, "S" be solution, and "O" be opportunity that are available at a given "level," "l." The employee's hierarchical level is checked against the hierarchical level of the solution, problem, and the opportunity so that the agents are dispersed without any interaction if the levels are not equal. In order to implement the aforementioned algorithm fitting a real world scenario some inter-level interactions were allowed. The extent to which the inter-level employees interact is dependent on the randomly defined position they find themselves in. In a real world scenario employees on a higher level might solve problems appearing in lower levels, eventually.

Therefore, in order to implement a more practical hierarchical rule, the so-called segregation algorithm is used (Wilensky, 1997), based on Schelling's racial segregation model (Schelling, 1969, 1971). The purpose of the segregation algorithm is to separate agents in a way that agents with similar levels cluster together. This clustering allows agents with different hierarchical levels to interact to a small extent. For example, if the segregation is set to 70 %, this implies that 70 % of the times agents will only interact with other agents who have the same level and they tend to interact with agents from other levels 30 % of the times.

4.3.3 Decision Rules

The same decision making logic is used both when movement is disorganized and organized. A problem is solved when a participant has sufficient ability (a), efficacy (e), motivation (m), and a sufficiently efficient (Sme) solution such that their product is greater or equal to the difficulty of the problem. This is called a "completed solution" in the model. Completed solutions take place when at least one participant, one opportunity, one solution, one problem are on the same simulated place (the so-called patch). The sum of the abilities (including motivation) of the participants on the patch, multiplied by the efficiency of the most efficient solution on the patch, is greater or equal to the sum of the difficulties of the problems on the patch (Eq. 4.1).

$$E\left(a^{*}m^{*}e\right) + \text{Sme}\,(\text{ef}) \geq P\,(d) \tag{4.1}$$

Most often, completed solutions occur when just one participant, one goal opportunity, one solution, and one problem happen to be on the same patch and the ability of the participant, multiplied by the efficiency of the solution, is greater or equal to the difficulty of the problem as shown succinctly in Eq. (4.1).

When the difficulty of a given problem is greater than the product of the employee efficacy, ability, motivation and the efficiency of the solution in range no decision is made (Eq. 4.2). If that is the case then, all agents immediately disperse.

$$\mathrm{E}\left(\mathrm{a}^{*}\mathrm{m}^{*}\mathrm{e}\right) + \mathrm{Sme}\,(\mathrm{ef}) < \mathrm{P}\,(\mathrm{d}) \tag{4.2}$$

4.3.4 *Motivation*

For the purpose of the simulation it is assumed that in order for a problem to be solved a goal has to be set by an employee. It is assumed that setting a goal is only possible if an employee is sufficiently motivated. It is assumed as a precondition that the external rewards and incentives are present within the model which provides the necessary extrinsic motivation. It is also assumed that employees are intrinsically motivated by the interest and the enjoyment of the tasks at hand to some extent. The levels of motivation among employees are randomly assigned among the employee population within the simulation.

In line with motivation theories (e.g., self-determination theory) we assume that the experience of successfully solving a problem has a positive effect on motivation (Deci & Ryan, 1991; Steel & Konig, 2006). An employee can set themselves either a "hard" or an "easy" goal. A hard goal is set if the following condition is satisfied:

$$2^{*}\left(\mathrm{E}\left(\mathrm{a}^{*}\mathrm{m}^{*}\mathrm{e}\right)\right) \leq \mathrm{P}\,(\mathrm{d}) \tag{4.3}$$

where "E" is employee, "a" ability, "m" motivation, and "e" efficacy. "P" denotes problem while "d" denotes the difficulty of the problem. As Eq. (4.3) depicts, if a problem's difficulty is greater than or equal to two times the product of an employee's ability, motivation and efficacy then the problem can be seen as a difficult problem to be solved. Thus an employee in such a predicament has to complete a hard goal. The term "hard" here implies that the problem a given employee is trying to solve is a very difficult one (i.e., 2 times one's own capabilities). Even though the problem might be hard it can still be solved using a highly efficient solution, where the combined value of both the employee's attributes and the solution's efficiency will be adequate to solve the problem at hand. In such a case where a "hard" problem is solved, the employee's motivation increases by a predefined value (i.e., 2).

On the other hand, if the product of the employee's attributes is greater than the problem's difficulty, then the problem can be easily solved once a solution is utilized.

$$2\left(E\left(a^{*}m^{*}e\right)\right) > P\left(d\right) \tag{4.4}$$

Therefore in a situation where the above condition (Eq. 4.4) is satisfied, where two times the product of an employee's attributes are greater than a given problems difficulty a problem is classified as an "easy" problem. This implies that the employee does not have to set a "hard" goal. In this case the employee's motivation does not increase as much compared to a "hard problem" but does increase slightly (i.e., 1).

4.3.5 Testing

Upon completion, the model was subjected to tests in order to determine whether the simulation was working as expected and if the results produced were consistent over multiple runs. The tests were divided into two categories. The organized movement test and the disorganized movement test.

In order to test the organized movement within the model both the segregation algorithm which enforces the hierarchical dynamics to the simulation and the decision making of the overall model had to be considered. A time limit of 5,000 steps was imposed on each test and 10 runs were carried out to check the consistency of the results obtained. The runs of the simulation were used to check if the simulation did not halt, segregation among agents happened according to specified percentages, if the problems were solved and were terminated and if the overall motivation increased.

In the disorganized movement test only the decision making capability of the model had to be considered. In order to compare results between disorganized movement and organized movement these tests were also given a time limit of 5,000 steps. A total of 10 runs were carried out. The runs under the "disorganization" condition was used to check if the simulation did not halt, if the random movement conditions worked, if the problems were solved and were terminated and if the overall motivation increased.

4.4 Findings

At any given instance the employees are divided into five employee types (levels) with a default distribution which is: low level workers (50 %), supervisors (25 %), managers (10 %), middle management (10 %), and top management (5 %). The default percentages tend to reflect the most common composition of employees within a standard organization.

Table 4.3 "Disorganization" results

Test number	Number completed	Completed percentage	MMAS	MMAE	Range
1	34/100	34	0.730702	14.04572	5
2	42/100	42	0.804362	20.79112	5
3	51/100	51	0.792403	58.61872	5
4	47/100	47	0.643094	42.64631	5
5	48/100	48	0.729849	33.67737	5
6	53/100	53	0.757948	89.20042	5
7	42/100	42	0.74192	36.94125	5
8	42/100	42	0.74043	25.70379	5
9	45/100	45	0.898174	59.5295	5
10	55/100	55	0.752668	107.3486	5
Total			7.59155	488.5028	5
Average	45.9 %		0.759155	48.85028	5

MMAS mean motivation at start, *MMAE* mean motivation at end

The range parameter determines the number of patches a given agent will scan during a single step. The scanning allows an agent to acquire some knowledge about its soundings namely if any other agent is present in the vicinity. Using this knowledge the agent can either move towards an agent or move away from an agent accordingly. It was initially set to 5.

Upon conducting 20 runs (10 runs per condition) we can draw some tentative and preliminary results. The following table presents the findings obtained through running the simulation in the "disorganized" movement condition under a specific set of initial conditions. The initial number of problems, employees, solutions, and opportunities were set to 100 at the start of the simulation.

Through the results obtained (Table 4.3) it can be observed that under the "disorganization" movement condition i.e., where all agents interact freely—46 % of problems are solved when the model is run for 5,000 steps. On average, it takes around 10,000 steps for 95 % of the problems to be solved under this condition. However, the number of problems solved decreases significantly when running the simulation under "organization" movement condition (Table 4.4).

Under the "organization" condition, the percent of similarity is set to 70 % which means that a given agent will only interact with other agents from the same level as itself 70 % percent of the time while engaging with agents with other hierarchical levels 30 % of the time.

Table 4.4 shows that, on average, under the "organization" condition 17 % of problems are solved when the simulation model runs for 5,000 steps. This is a 29 %-points drop in efficiency compared to the disorganized movement condition. This drop in efficiency is anticipated given the fact that under the "organization" condition agents are mostly expected to only interact with other agents on the same level. Furthermore the range and SW (similar wanted) parameters also affect the overall efficiency of the model. The tests conducted above were used to check the

Table 4.4 "Organization" results

Test number	Number completed	Completed percentage	MMAS	MMAE	SW (%)	Range
1	7/100	7	0.8126	1.4396	70	5
2	11/100	11	0.9057	2.3621	70	5
3	12/100	12	2.0156	0.7709	70	5
4	12/100	12	0.7044	2.0109	70	5
5	2/100	2	0.8099	0.8166	70	5
6	17/100	17	0.6664	2.3183	70	5
7	29/100	29	0.8166	7.3511	70	5
8	38/100	38	0.8229	15.9551	70	5
9	8/100	8	0.7945	1.7031	70	5
10	36/100	36	0.7320	12.7969	70	5
Total			9.0805	47.5246	70	5
Average	17.2 %		0.9081	4.7525	70	5

MMAS mean motivation at start, *MMAE* mean motivation at end

accuracy of the simulation. Given the vast number permutations and combinations which can be set through the simulation further testing will be conducted in order to gauge an understanding of the models behavior under a range of initial conditions.

4.5 Discussion and Conclusions

Results show that the "disorganization" condition provides a better structural environment for employees to solve problems rather than under the "organization" condition. Disorganization provides faster access to problems, opportunities, and solutions. This result must be further substantiated with more testing, with wider parameter ranges and additional conditions. Nevertheless, these findings seem to indicate that disorganization is not completely detrimental for an organization, contrary to what posited by rational management theorists (Scott, 2001). Although these are only tentative findings, they can be discussed as follows.

First, results from the model indicate that there seems to be a good chance that some disorganization is helpful to an organization. This confirms the findings of Cohen (1972) and Fioretti and Lomi (2008) who, under different circumstances, established that disorganization is a more efficient condition than organization in decision making. Results further provide support to the claims by Abrahamson and Freedman (2006) that disorganization is beneficial to problem solving. However, this is a starting point and further analysis is needed to circumstantiate these claims on a more robust and consistent basis.

Second, current findings indicate that a rigid organizational structure may be detrimental to problem solving due to constraints on how agents interact and solve problems. The model shows that sometimes solutions are available to people that are not directly related to a particular problem, thus disorganizing the rigid organizational structure to allow such indirect associations is advisable for organizations.

Third, making agents freely move on the organizational ground with minimal constraints means that abilities are more likely to be matched with the "right" problem or solution. The employee that is "stuck" to one hierarchical level may see his/her own abilities go to waste because they do not match any problem to be solved.

Fourth, there is an issue with scope in employees allocating themselves to problems. Through the reduction of structural constraints and rules of interaction, the disorganization condition increases the personal discretion available to employees. Personal discretion is defined as the degree to which a task provides substantial freedom, independence, and choice to individuals in determining the procedures to be used in carrying the task out (Hackman & Oldham, 1980). These preliminary results show that under the condition of disorganization the employees have increased individual discretion in the problem solving process. This also means that different agents/employees "see" and apply different solutions to problems, enhancing the probability that it gets solved. This also adds to the level of motivation among employees. A given employees will be able to self-determine the best problem to solve.

Fifth, modern organizations consist of teams; some teams often compete to accomplish same or similar tasks. An out-group looking at another team might underestimate or overestimate the capabilities of its rival team which leads to false perceptions and expectations (Cohen & March, 1974). In order to avoid unnecessary and unfair judgment based on subjective reasoning, a disorganized decision making process which involves actors from various groups can be used. The preliminary results of the simulation show that decreasing rules of interaction does contribute to a larger number of problems being solved. This decreasing of the rules of interaction ensures that the employee who previously was unable to interact with others due to rigid structures can now do so with relative ease. Agents in the model can be interpreted as teams of individuals, if one gives that interpretation to it. From our findings, we are not able to define whether individual and team problem solving is affected by organization or disorganization. However, this is clearly an interesting area to move this research further.

Sixth, organizational issues are always linked to other issues (Cohen & March, 1974). Once one issue is about to be tackled other linked issues come into the decision making process (e.g., construction of a new building brings in environmental issues). Trying to isolate and deal with a single issue is not always a sustainable approach. In instances where issues are isolated only stakeholders on that issues will play a part in the decision making process. In only focusing on one issue without any consideration for the linked issues can have drastic consequences for organizations (i.e., constructing a building without considering any linked environmental issues can have severe legal ramifications). Therefore integration of stakeholders representing the major issues and its sub-issues is essential. The findings of the simulation show that providing a low structured environment actors addressing multiple problems can come together in order to solve problem.

Seventh, the preliminary results show that when employees are given more freedom in interacting with problems, solutions, and opportunities there is a greater level of productivity (Table 4.3). These results feed in as a solution for a more general problem which is stakeholder involvement in decision making. In order to make the organizational mission work top management and everyone else down the hierarchy has to believe in its promise. Such a decision cannot be made in isolation as it will not consider the viewpoints of other key stakeholders. Therefore as the results show decreasing hierarchical structures will provide a faster channel for information to trickle down the hierarchy unhindered. Such an issue is an ideal locus for a disorganized decision making process (garbage can Cohen 1972).

Eighth, the advent and the increase of network organizations is a clear indicator that totally rigid management approaches do not provide viable results any more (De Vulpain, 2005; Nohria, 1994). The results obtained suggest that rigid hierarchical structure does not perform well compared to disorganized structure in terms of problem solving. Results show that the ideas which propose rigid hierarchical structure and tight control are not necessarily effective in relation to problem solving. Instead, the results are more in line with research (Hackman & Oldham, 1980) which claims that increasing productivity through rigid structure are outdated and which propose that teams should be autonomous and fluid in structure. Through the introduction of disorganization into management the organizations will be able to take a flexible approach to external influences using fluid structures which allow better cooperation among employees and adaptable rules of interaction.

Ninth, the preliminary findings of the simulation show that increasing disorganization increases productivity. Increasing disorganization in the context of the simulation involves giving employees more autonomy in engaging with problems. There is a link between increased autonomy and creativity (Hackman & Oldham, 1980). Shalley (1995) posits increased individual discretion leads to higher creativity. Creativity is the key ingredient in innovation (Amabile, 1983; Blumenthal, Inouye, & William, 2003; Terhurne, 2010). For an organization, adaptation is a necessity; adaption requires innovation and creativity. There is no guarantee that all efforts to innovate will yield positive results. However it is a necessary task in order to survive (Amabile, 1983). A key ingredient in innovation is creative autonomy and flexibility in planning and thinking. This flexibility can be facilitated by disorganizing certain structures within the organization. The results of the simulation show that the process of disorganizing can be started and stopped as and when required. It should be mentioned that in a real world scenario this change from organization to disorganization or vice versa can take substantial amount of time and is dependent on the scale and the contexts of the organization. In an organization currently innovating, disorganizing certain processes within the organization can incubate creativity. Once the necessary level of innovation is achieved the disorganized components can be re-organized as needed. Therefore, disorganizing the control structures within an organization will provide more chances of innovation.

Finally, the results indicate that the average motivation among employees is higher under disorganization compared to motivation levels under organization.

This difference in motivations levels can be attributed to the higher number of problems solved under disorganization compared to organization. Under a rigid organizational structure with multiple constraints employees are limited and lack flexibility to solve problems that suit their abilities. This limitation was observed while running the simulation and the results confirm that lack of "elbow room" decreases an employee's efficiency as posited by Crozier (1969). However, under disorganization employees are more autonomous and have more freedom of choice both in the problems and the solutions available to solve those problems.

This chapter presents the first version of this model to study disorganization. Increasing the granularity of details within the model will enable the model to be more and more accurate with each addition. Some of these additions are the implementation of multi-type agents. In a multi-type environment each agent type will be further divided into smaller sub-agents. For example, the agent "problem" can be divided into stationary problems (i.e., broken air conditioner on 3rd floor) and mobile problems (i.e., unruly employee). This division can also be done to solutions and opportunities. Splitting the agents into sub-types makes the simulation to closer to the real world environment. Furthermore, another addition can be the constant arrival and departure of employees, problems, opportunities, and solutions. Another dynamic which can be added is "training" where when an employee fails to solve a given number of problems (i.e., 5) they will be either fired or sent for training depending on the importance of the employee to the organization. This importance can be derived from the hierarchical position a given employee resides in. At training an employee will get its variables incremented thus enhancing its survivability.

In further developing the simulation, more variables can be added. These variables can either be other essential components in an organization. Ideally in further developing the model, the ability to select the organization type, the management type, and other parameters would provide an even more accurate representation of the real world.

4.5.1 Limitations and Prospects for Further Research

The main limitation of the simulation as it stands now is the granularity of the simulation itself. Granularity refers to the fineness of details considered. Even though the simulation does mimic real world conditions at a crude rather abstract level, in order for the accuracy of the results to be more applicable to a real world setting the level of details need to be upgraded. This can be accomplished by increasing its functionality by introducing team problem solving, prioritization of goals, clear preferences, skills, and multiple attempts to solve the same problem by the same individual or team of individuals, for example. Furthermore, conducting empirical studies will also enable the simulation to be more directly validated using real world data.

Another limitation of the simulation is the assumptions underlying the decision making of the simulation. The primary assumption of the simulation is "for a problem to be solved, an employee has to set goals; for goals to be set an employee has to have some motivation." This assumption is used in order to imply that when a problem is solved a goal was set prior to solving it. This assumption is directly derived from goal setting theory. This implication can be more explicitly modeled in the simulation in the future. Doing so will also increase the autonomy and granularity of the simulation.

Finally, considering employees' "ability × efficacy" may lead to distortions in the model, given that the agent is left with a low impact of the two parameters and that it makes it impossible to distinguish between the impact of either ability or efficacy. Tests conducted on the model so far did not raise any particular concern although further checks may be carried on in the future.

Building on the limitations discussed above, it is apparent that the simulation developed can be improved in multiple areas. A first area of improvement is that of collective forms of goal setting. Currently the model only deals with individual problem solving and goal setting. However, some of its processes may be thought of as sequential team work, where one employee engages on a problem, cannot solve it, and another employee starts being on the problem at a second time. A logical next step would be to simulate collective goal setting and team-based problem solving. Adding collective aspects to the simulation will provide a greater range of data which is even more closely related to the real world.

Another interesting direction can be that of considering multiple types of goals. The model presented in this chapter does not distinguish between types of goals and considers only basic view of goal setting. A future expansion would be to take into account the various types of goals such as productivity goal, compliance goals, stretch goals, and creativity goals. Each of these types of goals has nuances that need to be modeled separately to accurately mirror the real world.

Moreover, the introduction of concepts such as training, promotion/demotion, and other employee-related concepts may also increase the appealing of the model.

Developing the simulation further to encapsulate the points discussed above will increase the fineness of detail within the simulation, thus mirroring the real world in a greater manner. Furthermore the improvements will also generate valuable new data which upon analysis might provide some interesting insights into disorganization.

4.5.2 Conclusions

The purpose of the simulation was to utilize the unique functional capabilities offered by agent-based modeling to represent a real world organizational environment. The simulation is used to develop an understanding on how disorganization affects organizational problem solving (goal achievement) and motivation. The model is designed to simulate two contrasting environments one in which a clear hierarchy is present while in the other rules of interaction are minimal. Upon developing and running the simulation it was found that neither complete disorganization nor complete organization was conducive for efficient problem solving within an organization. It was further uncovered that in an environment where 70 % of organization and 30 % disorganization were present provided the most efficient performance in tests conducted. These results were consistent in all the tests conducted. Furthermore, we were able to unveil that, in some instances, shifting from a highly organized operation to a slightly more disorganized environment mid-simulation provides an increase in the number of problems solved 60 % of the time. It should be noted that the results currently uncovered cannot be considered conclusive yet clearly provides preliminary evidence for disorganization as a conducive condition for increasing problem solving efficiency.

References

Abrahamson, E. (2002). Disorganization theory and disorganizational behavior: Towards an etiology of messes. *Research in Organizational Behavior, 24*, 139–180.

Abrahamson, E., & Freedman, D. H. (2006). *A perfect mess: The hidden benefits of disorder*. London: Weidenfeld & Nicolson.

Amabile, T. M. (1983). *The social psychology of creativity*. New York: Springer.

Amabile, T. M. (1996). *Creativity and innovation in organizations*. Boston, MA: Harvard Business School.

Bandura, A. (1997). *Self-efficacy: The exercise of control*. New York: Freeman.

Black, J., & Edwards, S. (2000). Emergence of virtual or network organizations: Fad or feature. *Journal of Organizational Change Management, 13*(6), 267–276.

Blumenthal, M. S., Inouye, A. S., & William, J. (2003). *Beyond productivity: Information, technology, innovation, and creativity*. Washington, DC: National Academies Press.

Bonaccio, S., & Dalal, R. S. (2006). Advice taking and decision-making: An integrative literature review, and implications far the organizational sciences. *Organizational Behavior & Human Decision Processes, 101*(2), 127–151.

Brown, S. P., Jones, E., & Leigh, T. W. (2005). The attenuating effect of role overload on relationships linking self-efficacy and goal level to work performance. *Journal of Applied Psychology, 90*(3), 972–986.

Cannon-Bowers, J. A., & Salas, E. (2001). Reactions on shared cognition. *Journal of Organizational Behavior, 22*, 195–202.

Chandler, A. D. (1932). *Strategy and structure*. Cambridge, MA: Harvard University Press.

Cohen, M. D. (1972). A garbage can model of organizational choice. *Administrative Science Quarterly, 12*(2), 1–25.

Cohen, M. D., & March, J. G. (1974). *Leadership and ambiguity, the American college president*. New York: McGraw-Hill.

Cowley, S. J., & Vallee-Tourangeau, F. (Eds.). (2013). *Cognition beyond the brain. Computation, interactivity and human artifice*. London: Springer.

Crozier, M. (1969). *The bureaucratic phenomenon*. Piscataway, NJ: Transaction Publishers.

De Vulpain, A. (2005). Listening to ordinary people: The process of civilization on the way to a new society. *Society for Organizational Learning, 6*(7), 6–7.

Deci, E., & Ryan, R. (1991). A motivational approach to self: Integration in personality. In R. Dienstbier (Ed.), *Nebraska symposium on motivation: Perspectives on motivation* (Vol. 38, pp. 237–288). Lincoln: University of Nebraska Press.

Donovan, J. J., & Williams, K. J. (2003). Missing the mark: Effects of time and causal attributions on goal revision in response to goal-performance discrepancies. *Journal of Applied Psychology, 88*, 379–402.

Drach-zahavy, A., & Erez, M. (2002). Challenge versus threat effects on the goal-performance relationship. *Organizational Behavior and Human Decision Processes, 88*, 667–682.

Eisenberg, E. M. (1984). Ambiguity as strategy in organizational communication. *Communication Monographs, 51*(3), 227–242.

Fayol, H. (1916). Administration industrielle et generelle. Comptes Rendus Mensuels des Reunions de la, Societe de l'Industrie Minerale [Translated by: Garzon del Camino, 1985].

Featherstone, M. (1990). *Global culture: Nationalism, globalization and modernity*. Thousand Oaks, CA: Sage.

Fioretti, G., & Lomi, A. (2008). An agent-based representation of the garbage can model of organizational choice. *Journal of Artificial Societies and Social Simulation, 11*(1), 1.

Freeland, R. F. (2002). When organizational messiness works. *Harvard Business Review, 80*, 24–25.

Frost, J., Osterloh, M., & Antoinette, W. (2010). Governing knowledge work: Transactional and transformational solutions. *Organizational Dynamics, 39*(2), 126–136.

Gilbert, N. (2008). *Agent-based models*. Thousand Oaks, CA: Sage.

Gilbert, N., & Terna, P. (2000). How to build and use agent-based models in social science. *Mind & Society, 1*, 57–72.

Hackman, J. R., & Oldham, G. R. (1980). *Work redesign*. Boston, MA: Addison-Wesley.

Hutchins, E. (1995). *Cognition in the wild*. Cambridge, MA: MIT Press.

Jarvenpaa, S. L., & Leidner, D. E. (1998). Communication and trust in global virtual teams. *Journal of Computer-Mediated Communication, 3*(4).

Locke, E. A., & Latham, G. P. (1990). *A theory of goal setting & task performance*. Englewood Cliffs, NJ: Prentice Hall.

Locke, E. A., & Latham, G. P. (2013). *New developments in goal setting and task performance*. London, UK: Routledge.

Lomi, A., & Harrison, J. R. (2012). *The garbage can model of organizational choice: Looking forward at forty*. Bingley, UK: Emerald.

Miller, K. D., & Lin, S. J. (2010). Different truths in different worlds. *Organization Science, 21*, 97–114.

Mobley, W. H., & Fisk, M. J. (1982). *Employee turnover, causes, consequences, and control*. Reading, MA: Addison-Wesley.

Muller, F. (2000). *Handbook of ecosystem theories and management*. New York: CRC Press.

Nohria, N. (1994). *Networks and organizations: Structure, form and action*. Boston, MA: Harvard Business School Press Books.

Nonaka, I. (1988). Creating organizational order out of chaos: Self-renewal in Japanese firms. *California Management Review, 30*(3), 57–73.

Schelling, T. (1969). Models of segregation. *American Economic Review, 59*, 488–493.

Schelling, T. (1971). Dynamic models of segregation. *Journal of Mathematical Sociology, 1*, 143–186.

Scott, W. R. (2001). *Institutions and organizations*. Thousand Oaks, CA: Sage.

Secchi, D. (2013). Agent-based models for management: An overview of advantages with one example. In *European Academy of Management Annual Conference*.

Seijts, G. H., & Latham, G. P. (2001). The effect of distal learning, outcome, and proximal goals on a moderately complex task. *Journal of Organizational Behavior, 22*, 291–307.

Shalley, C. E. (1995). Effects of coaction, expected evaluation, and goal setting on creativity and productivity. *Academy of Management Journal, 38*(2), 483–503.

Shenhav, Y. (1995). From chaos to systems: The engineering foundations of organization theory, 1879–1932. *Administrative Science Quarterly, 21*, 557–585.

Shenhav, Y. (2002). *Manufacturing rationality: The engineering foundations of the managerial revolution*. Oxford: Oxford University Press.

Simon, H. A. (1947). *Administrative behaviour*. New York: Free Press.

Stacey, R. (1993). Strategy as order emerging from chaos. *Long Range Planning, 26*(1), 10–17.
Steel, P., & Konig, C. J. (2006). Integrating theories of motivation. *Academy of Management Review, 31*(4), 889–913.
Taylor, F. W. (1911). *Principles of scientific management*. New York: Harper and Row.
Terhurne, H. (2010). *Innovation by creativity*. Herts, UK: Ecademy Press Limited.
Thompson, J. (1967). *Organizations in action: Social science bases of administrative theory*. Classics in Organization and Management Series. London, UK: Transworld Publishers.
Warglien, M., & Masuch, M. (1996). *The logic of organizational disorder*. Berlin: Walter de Gruyter.
Wiese, B., & Freund, A. (2005). Goal progress makes one happy, or does it? Longitudinal findings from the work domain. *Journal of Occupational and Organizational Psychology, 78*, 287–304.
Wilensky, U. (1997). *NetLogo segregation model*. Evanston, IL: Center for Connected Learning and Computer-Based Modeling, Northwestern University. URL: http://ccl.northwestern.edu/netlogo/models/Segregation.

Chapter 5
Constructing Agent-Based Models of Organizational Routines

Cara H. Kahl and Matthias Meyer

Abstract Organizational routines represent a form of organizational behavior currently studied in multifarious scientific domains, such as economics, organization science, sociology, and psychology. The diverse perspectives on this phenomenon produce a plethora of models reflecting, for instance, what a routine is and how it emerges from and changes within a socio-technical system. Newcomers to the topic of organizational routines may be easily confused by this substantial scientific diversity, discovering many maps for seemingly the same territory. This chapter presents descriptors to facilitate the comparison of work on organizational routines, and applies them to a contemporary method employed to investigate the phenomenon: agent-based modeling. This insight is related to technical issues relevant to simulating organizational routines, such as model design, implementation, and validation.

Keywords Routines • Organizational behavior • Agent-based modeling • Complexity • Context • Personification • Map-territory relation • Target • Simulation • Model • Micro-foundations • Operationalization • Sense-making • Construct • Validation

5.1 Introduction

Organizational routines are currently an object of study in a multitude of scientific disciplines. In the domains of economics, organization science, sociology, and psychology alone, three special issues on routines were recently published (Felin, Foss, Heimeriks, & Madsen, 2012; Jack & Mundy, 2013; Lazaric, 2011), and three

C.H. Kahl (✉)
Institute of Technology, Work Processes and Vocational Education, Hamburg University of Technology, Hamburg, Germany
e-mail: cara.kahl@tuhh.de

M. Meyer
Institute of Management Control and Accounting, Hamburg University of Technology, Hamburg, Germany
e-mail: matthias.meyer@tuhh.de

D. Secchi, M. Neumann (eds.), *Agent-Based Simulation of Organizational Behavior*, DOI 10.1007/978-3-319-18153-0_5

others are forthcoming (D'Adderio, Feldman, Lazaric, & Pentland, 2012; Gevers, Passos, & Uitdewilligen, 2014; Murji & Neal, 2014). There is a plethora of empirical work on organizational routines (Cohen & Bacdayan, 1994; Narduzzo & Warglien, 2008; Parmigiani & Howard-Grenville, 2011; Pentland & Feldman, 2008; van der Steen, 2009), as well as an increasing number of computer models simulating them or similar phenomena (Breslin, 2014; Cohen, Levinthal, & Warglien, 2014; Gao, Deng, & Bai, 2014; Holtz, 2014; Kunz, 2011; Meyer & Carley, 2007; Miller, Choi, & Pentland, 2014; Miller, Pentland, & Choi, 2012; Pentland, Feldman, Becker, & Liu, 2012).

Admittedly, scientific work on organizational routines is not lacking. The issue, rather, is how to integrate the abundance of accumulating work, especially when findings appear incongruent, scholars use different expressions for seemingly the same phenomenon (e.g., habit, practice, collective action), or investigate particular parts subsequently generalized to the whole (Becker, 2004; Becker, Lazaric, Nelson, & Winter, 2005; Cohen et al., 1996). Contemporary debates cover questions such as the following: Does the concept of a routine encompass behavior *and* cognition of the respective entity performing it (Hutchins, 1995)? Who has more influence on an organizational routine, the individual contributing to it or the organization managing it (Geiger & Schröder, 2014)? Do the steps within a routine need to occur in the same or a similar order every time to be considered a "routine" (Pentland et al., 2012)?

One way to view the plethora of work on organizational routines is to identify the general question or problem a scholar is addressing with the concept. In the seminal contribution by Nelson and Winter (1982), routines form a central element in their "evolutionary theory of the firm." They represent a unit of selection, required as a building block for an evolutionary model, and can be interpreted as the "genes" of a firm. In this vein, the strategic management literature uses the concept as a way to specify the idea of "capabilities," a source of value creation and competitive advantage for firms (Amit & Schoemaker, 1993). The organizational learning literature, focusing on another scientific question, addresses how these competences can be acquired and maintained by a firm (Marengo, 1992). The literature in accounting, as a further example, takes quite a different stance on organizational routines (Burns & Scapens, 2000; Quinn, 2014). In early contributions, the main scientific issue addressed there regarding routines was the apparent stability of many accounting activities (e.g., annual budgeting). In more recent literature, this focus has widened to include the circumstances under which changes in accounting take place (Burns & Scapens, 2000).

Nevertheless, the abundance of accumulating work on organizational routines may be overwhelming to newcomers to the topic, scholars stepping over the boundaries of their discipline to gain a more integral understanding, or scientists using more than one method to study the phenomenon. This chapter is intended for the latter group, in particular those employing agent-based modeling to explore conceptualizations and formalizations of organizational routines. The aim is to address issues considered key to describing what an organizational routine is, and highlight how they are implemented in contemporary models. This chapter proceeds with a description of how routines are defined in the literature (Sect. 5.2), followed by a comparison of models constructed to simulate conceptualizations of organizational routines (Sect. 5.3). The chapter closes by highlighting issues considered crucial for advancing research organizational routines (Sect. 5.4).

5.2 Conceptualizing Organizational Routines

Although scientists agree on the existence and relevance of routines as constituents of organizational behavior, they remain difficult to be unambiguously defined (Becker, 2004; Cohen et al., 1996; Parmigiani & Howard-Grenville, 2011). For instance, Vromen (2011) related "a widely agreed upon definition and understanding are still lacking" (p. 175). Becker et al. (2005) referred to routines as "indeed a complex and wide-ranging subject" (p. 780), while Felin and Foss (2009) described the definitions, concepts, and levels of analysis of routines a matter of ongoing debate. Admittedly, the matter is not a lack of definitions, but rather their seeming incongruity. In this section, exemplary definitions of organizational routines are presented and several characteristics frequently attributed to this phenomenon are derived in order to attain a common denominator for work discussed in later sections.

Nelson and Winter (1982) defined routines as "regular and predictable behavior patterns of firms" (p. 14). Another seminal definition was provided later by Cohen et al. (1996). According to them, a routine is "an executable *capability* for repeated performance in some *context* that has been *learned* by an organization in response to *selective pressures*" (p. 638). Vromen (2011) viewed routines as "multi-level mechanisms" (p. 175) as well as "recurrent *intra*organizational, *multi*-person *inter*action patterns displayed in specific artificially created physical environments" (p. 180). Similarly, Parmigiani and Howard-Grenville (2011) defined routines as "repetitive patterns of interdependent organizational actions" (p. 419). In Pavlov and Bourne (2011), routines are described as "a set of organizational processes . . . which perform specific functions, respond to performance feedback . . . and carry out organizational change in a number of distinct ways" (p. 102). Ter Bogt and Scapens (2014) stated routines are "not actions per se, but they have the potential to shape actions" (p. 5). Breslin (2014) emphasized that routines are "collective phenomena" (p. 64), and Pentland, Hærem, and Hillison (2010) conceived routines as "generative systems" (p. 934).

By no means exhaustive, the above definitions nevertheless relay the diversity of fundamental ideas routines scholars build their research upon. One approximation to consolidating definitions of organizational routines is to contemplate which specifics characterize them (Cohen et al., 1996). Such an approach generates labels, or descriptors, for the target of observation. Moreover, it creates an abstraction from particular conceptualizations and therewith a common denominator among them, perhaps even facilitating a "truce" among scholars representing dissimilar stances.

In the remainder of this section, aspects described in the literature as crucial to defining what an organizational routine is are elaborated.

Routines occur in an **organization** and are carried out to **accomplish work** (Becker, 2004, 2005; Breuker & Matzner, 2014; Cohen et al., 1996; Geiger & Schröder, 2014). **Multiple actors** are involved in the generation of routines (Cohen et al., 1996). Routines therefore reflect the behavior of groups instead of individuals (Lazaric, 2011). The actors are usually represented by individuals (Becker, 2004), but they can also be represented by organizational subunits (Nelson & Winter, 1982), multiple organizations (Zollo, Reuer, & Singh, 2002), technologies (D'Adderio, 2008), more generally physical or non-physical artifacts (Parmigiani & Howard-Grenville, 2011; Pentland & Feldman, 2005), or combinations of these entities. Actors contributing to a routine may possess distributed (identical) to dispersed (disparate) cognitive phenomena such as knowledge, skills, goals, preferences, or decision-making strategies (Becker, 2004; Felin & Foss, 2009; Howard-Grenville, 2005; Nelson & Winter, 1982). Furthermore, the actors may be **vertically or horizontally** located within the organization in question (Becker, 2004).

Routines are described as **patterns**, implying a recurring and regular form (Becker, 2004; Nelson & Winter, 1982). The regularity of a routine implies the **interdependence**, **order**, or **sequence of actions** (Feldman & Pentland, 2003; Felin & Foss, 2009) **belonging to**, **or *within***, **the routine**. The strength of actions' interdependence varies depending on the task at hand (Becker et al., 2005). The recurrence of a routine implies **path-dependence *between* routines** (Becker, 2004). Additionally, routines are triggered by internal (intraindividual) or external (extraindividual) cues, that is, they occur based on some form of prior stimulation (Becker, 2004; Felin & Foss, 2009). A routine as a pattern, therefore, refers to a **process** and is fluid as well as organic. It is in this sense that a routine is distributed in terms of when and where it occurs (Becker, 2004).

Substantial differences exist in terms of what routines as patterns consist of (Becker, 2004). Two aspects, **behavior** and **cognition**, are generally denoted as their contents. Parmigiani and Howard-Grenville (2011) speak of them as the "dual character" (p. 422), Becker et al. (2005) as the "dual ontology" (p. 782) of routines. Behavior refers to human activity which is observable, in particular intentional motor activity such as moving or speaking (Becker, 2004; Cohen et al., 1996; Winter, 2012). Other expressions denoting the behavioral aspect of routines are routine enactment (Miner, Ciuchta, & Gong, 2008), routine in practice (Parmigiani & Howard-Grenville, 2011), routine actualization (Hodgson, 2008), performative part (Pentland & Feldman, 2005), routine instantiation (Miller et al., 2014), phenotype (Becker et al., 2005), and interactor (Hodgson & Knudsen, 2006; Vromen, 2007).

Which human activity cognition specifically refers to regarding organizational routines remains a matter of ongoing debate (Cohen et al., 1996; Lazaric, 2011; Pentland et al., 2012). Becker et al. (2005) noted that the abstract, cognitive aspect of routines is "much less obvious" and "causes the main trouble" in conceptualizing and operationalizing routines (pp. 782–783). Nelson and Winter (1982) described the cognitive part of individuals carrying out a routine in the following way: "the ability to receive and interpret a stream of incoming messages from other members and from the environment . . . the member uses the information contained therein in the selection and performance of an appropriate routine from his own repertoire" (p. 100). Other expressions denoting the cognitive aspect of routines are routine representation (Miner et al., 2008), routine in principle (Parmigiani & Howard-Grenville, 2011), routine potentiality (Hodgson, 2008), ostensive part (Pentland & Feldman, 2005), typification of the routine (Miller et al., 2014), genotype (Becker et al., 2005), and replicator (Hodgson & Knudsen, 2006; Vromen, 2007).

Irrespective of the particular definition, both human activities—behavior and cognition—are associated with and considered to contribute to the generation of routines. Their distinction from one another is perhaps more pragmatic than valid, as it is difficult to conceive one without the other (Becker et al., 2005). As Becker (2004) noted, the "... nature of the linkages between cognitive and behavioral levels is still unclear..." (p. 652). One approach to combining behavioral and cognitive aspects is described by Hodgson (2008) and Hodgson and Knudsen (2006), who refer to routines as organizational propensities or dispositions. More specifically, Hodgson (2008) defined routines as "organizational dispositions to energize conditional patterns of behavior within an organized group of individuals, involving sequential responses to cues" (p. 21). In this chapter, behavior and cognition are conceived as separate constructs and used as general labels for the human activities underlying organizational routines.

Apart from distinguishing behavior and cognition as "contents" of routines, it is crucial to reemphasize the collective nature of routines and consequently the collective nature of behavioral and cognitive activities contributing to their emergence. Behavior, therefore, does not only refer to individual behavior, but also to social interaction. Cognition, likewise, does not only imply individual cognitive activities, but also some form of socially dispersed or distributed cognition (Hutchins, 1995). Behavioral and cognitive aspects of routines are occasionally subsumed under the expression *micro-foundations* (Bapuji, Hora, & Saeed, 2012; Cohen, 2012; Felin et al., 2012; Felin & Foss, 2009; Lazaric, 2011). This term refers to any theoretical constructs and/or operationalizations chosen to represent the individual and interactional (i.e., social, socio-technical) levels of a macro-level phenomenon.

Another aspect essential to conceptualizing organizational routines is their relation to concepts such as norms, institutions, and rules. While this connection is not commonly addressed in the majority of the literature cited above, the domain of accounting provides a solid example for its explicit conceptualization: The influential framework by Burns and Scapens (2000) describes external and internal institutions as presumptuous ways of thinking in an organization, rules as "the formalised statement of procedures" and routines as "the procedures actually in use" (p. 7). The latter two can be interpreted as the "accounting version" of cognitive and behavioral aspects of organizational routines. More recent literature emphasizes that rules and routines are separate concepts. For example, Quinn (2014) reports a case study at the Guinness company to support his claim that routines and rules should be unbundled and "that the concepts are at best considered ontologically and empirically separate" (p. 14).

Finally it is noted that organizational routines are related to organizational capabilities in the literature (Becker, 2004; Becker et al., 2005; Cohen et al., 1996; Cyert & March, 1963; Feldman, 2003; Feldman & Pentland, 2003; Felin & Foss, 2009; March, 1991; Nelson & Winter, 1982; Zollo et al., 2002). The relation between routines and capabilities has, however, been disputed, especially regarding what exactly a capability is, how it differs (or not) from a routine, and how both are interrelated (Felin & Foss, 2009; Parmigiani & Howard-Grenville, 2011). Cohen et al. (1996), for instance, defined capability as the "capacity to produce action" (p. 683), while a decade earlier Nelson and Winter (1982) defined it as "the range of things a firm can do anytime" (p. 52). Moreover, distinctions between operational and dynamic capabilities are made in the literature (Eisenhardt & Martin, 2000; Felin et al., 2012; Felin & Foss, 2009; Parmigiani & Howard-Grenville, 2011; Winter, 2012). On a general level, organizational processes, such as routines, are assumed to have the potential to become capabilities in the respective organization (Amit & Schoemaker, 1993; Nelson & Winter, 1982). It has, for instance, been argued that routines are a repository for organizational capabilities (Becker et al., 2005; Nelson & Winter, 1982; Winter, 2012).

Figure 5.1 summarizes the aspects characterizing routines as discussed in this section. The compilation is not intended to be exhaustive; rather, it developed to

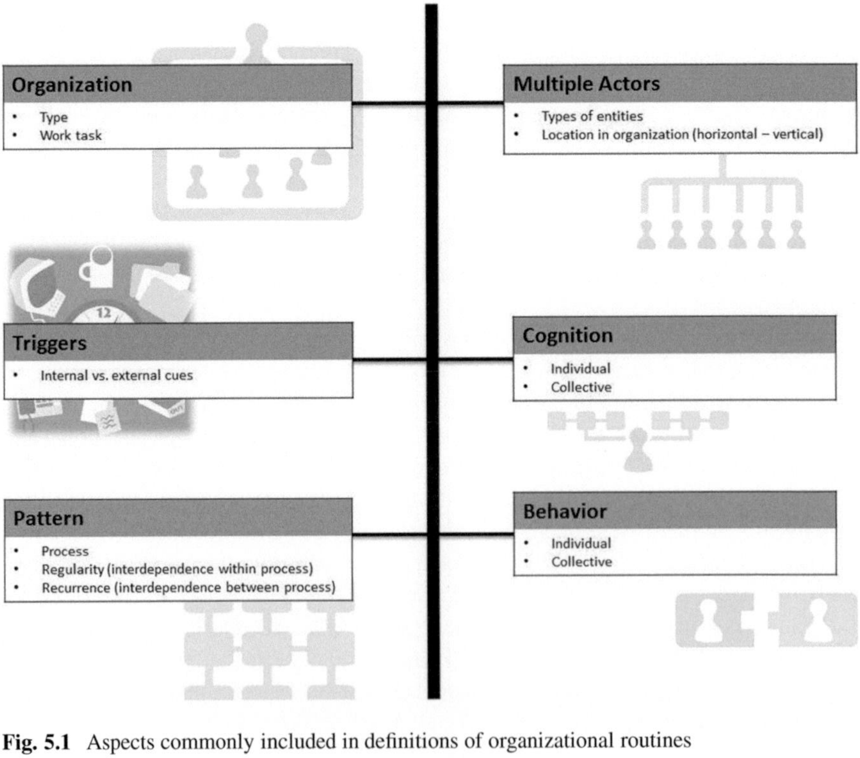

Fig. 5.1 Aspects commonly included in definitions of organizational routines

relay a common denominator for comparing simulation models of organizational routines. In the next section, recently published models are presented and compared based on this compilation.

5.3 Contemporary Agent-Based Models of Organizational Routines

Agent-based modeling has been proposed as a method for advancing the understanding of routines, and in particular, the micro-dynamics leading to their emergence within an organization (Felin & Foss, 2009; Wall, 2014). Several agent-based models specifically formalizing behavioral and cognitive representations of routines, as well as the interdependence within and between routines, were recently published (Breslin, 2014; Cohen et al., 2014; Gao et al., 2014; Miller et al., 2012, 2014). Such aspects are among those explicitly debated in reviews regarding how exactly a routine can be conceptualized (Becker, 2004; Becker et al., 2005; Cohen et al., 1996; Geiger & Schröder, 2014; Parmigiani & Howard-Grenville, 2011). In this section, a selection of models are described and compared based on the way they incorporate common conceptualizations (Fig. 5.1). The aim is to examine how they address and operationalize these characteristics.

The models selected for comparison were retrieved with an extensive literature search. Articles containing the word pairs "routine" and "agent-based" or "routine" and "multi-agent" in their titles, abstracts or keywords were searched in the following databases: *Ebsco*, *Web of Science*, *Jstor*, *Science Direct*, *EconBiz,* and *SSRN*. Afterwards, and in a similar manner as reported by Parmigiani and Howard-Grenville (2011), the same word pairs were searched in the following journals: *Academy of Management Journal*, *Administrative Science Quarterly*, *Management Science*, *Organization Science*, *Strategic Management Journal*, *Industrial and Corporate Change*, *Journal of Management Studies*, *Organization Studies and Strategic Organization*. Databases as well as journals were searched from 1996 to 2014; 1996 was chosen as a limit due to the seminal paper by Cohen et al. (1996) summarizing their Santa Fe Institute conference to establish a common conceptualization of organizational routines. The search resulted in 22 contributions, whereas some do not incorporate conceptualizations of organizational routines as discussed in Sect. 5.2, and others do not portray agent-based models.

The four models discussed in this section were chosen based on the following process. Firstly, their authors model an organizational routine specifically based on accounts derived from literature discussing how the phenomenon can be conceptualized in the first place (see Sect. 5.2). Secondly, an organizational routine is the intended emergent outcome of the simulation. Thirdly, they were chosen based on the differential way they incorporate theoretical work on organizational routines, therewith creating diversity in the sample: The first model focuses on actions as basic entities, while the second models an empirical socio-technical system. The third model incorporates a form of distributed cognition, and the fourth sophisticated assumptions about individual cognition in context.

Among the models not chosen for comparison were those depicting business design processes, workflow management systems, or process systems engineering (Siirola, Hauan, & Westerberg, 2003; Sikora & Shaw, 1998; Yang, Sung, Wu, & Chen, 2010). Others focus primarily on the exploration and exploitation of knowledge (Aggarwal, Siggelkow, & Singh, 2011; Geisendorf, 2009; Kim & Rhee, 2009; Siggelkow & Levinthal, 2005), capabilities (Maritan & Coen, 2004), norms (Criado, 2013), or other aspects of organizational design (Bruderer & Singh, 1996; Levitt, 2012; Siggelkow, 2011). Some contributions explicitly model routines without reference to the conceptualizations elaborated in Sect. 5.2 (Groff, 2007; Rouchier, Bousquet, Requier-Desjardins, & Antona, 2001; Silva, Gonçalves, Dimuro, Dimuro, & Jerez, 2013); nonetheless, they describe targets which, in a face valid way, constitute organizational routines, such as meeting scheduling (Chun, Wai, & Wong, 2003) or the process of entrepreneurship (McMullen & Dimov, 2013). A final paper worth noting is authored by Gaskin, Berente, Lyytinen, and Yoo (2014), who report a computational model of sociomaterial routines. These models were briefly mentioned here to inform the interested reader of similar developments beyond the ones compared later in this section.

In Sect. 5.3.1, all four models selected for comparison are summarized. The information presented for each one is based on the ODD+D protocol (Müller et al., 2013), a tool used to describe human decisions in agent-based models. Thereafter in Sect. 5.3.2, the models are compared based on the descriptors inferred in Sect. 5.2.

5.3.1 Overview of Models

Pentland et al. (2012) reported an abstract, generative model of organizational routines. Its purpose is to explore the dynamics of organizational routines as actions *and* as dispositions. The authors based it on their previous work describing routines as having performative and ostensive parts (Feldman & Pentland, 2003; Pentland & Feldman, 2005, 2008), as well as on work conceiving routines as dispositions (Hodgson, 2008; Hodgson & Knudsen, 2004a, 2004b). Apart from those concepts, two others underlie the model: evolutionary theory (variation and selected retention) and sociomateriality (indifference about who or what carried out an action). The routine which can emerge in the model refers to a sequence of disparate actions (routine enactment) as well as a disposition for executing a particular sequence of actions (routine representation). As the model depicts an abstract, generative system, it does not possess specific, real-world temporal or spatial resolutions. Moreover, the actions constitute the basic entities. It is in this manner the authors account for sociomateriality: No distinction is made between entities carrying out the actions; they could be humans or artifacts. The model was built with Matlab and is intended for scientists, managers, and organizational designers. Strictly, one cannot speak of heterogeneous agents in this model, as actions represent its basic entities. It was nevertheless selected for comparison as it specifically simulates the emergence organizational routines as interacting performative and ostensive parts.

Gao et al. (2014; see also Gao, 2012) reported an agent-based model depicting an empirical scenario from the domain of higher education (college). Specifically, the target refers to the management and usage of classroom audio and video (AV) equipment by administrators and teachers. Two routines are possible: Administrators lock and unlock the equipment themselves, or teachers borrow the keys from administrators and return them after class. If teachers often complain about defect equipment, administrators lock and unlock it themselves. Otherwise, teachers commonly manage that subtask. The simulation model is based on field data collected by interviewing administrators, randomly observing teachers and studying activity logs. Conceptually, the routine the authors described is based on work by Pentland and Feldman (2008); it includes ostensive and performative parts, as well as artifacts. In addition, individual agent behavior is based on the concept of habit as developed by Hodgson and Knudsen (2004a). The authors also incorporated the concept of a "narrative network." This is similar to the transition or history matrix in the simulation reported by Pentland et al. (2012), but it is based on the authors' field data. Created with the Swarm package, this model is the only one among the ones compared in this section simulating a genuine situation in practice.

Miller et al. (2014) reported an abstract agent-based model of organizational routines. The organizational task is represented by a recurring problem consisting of k subtasks which must be fulfilled in an exact, stable order in order to solve it. The agents, representing individuals, do not possess an established response (i.e., correct order of subtasks) to the problem in the beginning of the simulation. They know what needs to be done, but they do not know who can accomplish which part. By exchanging information about who possesses which skill to solve a particular subtask, agents build a knowledge base about the actor sequence necessary to solve the problem. Miller et al. (2014) based their model on concepts such as decentralized coordination, collective-centric organizational cognition (Michel, 2007), and transactive memory ("who knows what"). Transactive memory is viewed as a bridge between individual and collective cognition. Programed with Matlab, this model was chosen for comparison as it specifically addresses distributed cognition, formalizes it, and presents a unique stance on routines by emphasizing the actors'—and not the actions'—ties.

Cohen et al. (2014) presented a comprehensive framework to model "collective performance," a term they introduced to substitute as well as encompass concepts such as "organizational routine," "practice," and "standard operating procedure." Although they based their framework on previous work, the authors introduced a completely new terminology along with the substantial concepts they deem essential in modeling collective performance. The scientific issue Cohen et al. (2014) address pertains to the lack of formal theory regarding collective performance, in particular the formalization of micro-foundations. They aim to provide a general architecture for modeling any kind of collective performance based on individual habit systems or skills. In doing so, they developed 12 properties (A to L) to denote aspects such models could include. Four supplementary models implementing different properties of their framework are available online. Due to the volume of their theoretical framework, however, it will be the sole focus of this comparison.

5.3.2 Comparison of Models

The four models outlined in Sect. 5.3.1 are compared in Tables 5.1 and 5.2 based on the descriptors derived in Sect. 5.2 and depicted in Fig. 5.1. Each model, therefore, is described regarding how its authors implemented the aspects *organization type*, *triggers*, *patterns*, *multiple actors*, *cognition* and *behavior*. In this section, the results from this comparison are highlighted.

The way an organization is represented in all four examples reveals a prominent difference in how conceptions of organizational routines are translated into models. While Gao et al. (2014) modeled a concrete case in practice, Cohen et al. (2014), Miller et al. (2014), and Pentland et al. (2012) each depicted an abstract setting with no direct connection to a theoretical or real-world organization. Cohen et al. (2014) intentionally conceive their framework as overarching and therewith suitable for all models of organizational routines.

All models compared incorporate triggers. Gao et al. (2014) view their empirical routine's trigger to be the start of class, an environmental cue. Similarly, Miller et al. (2014) and Pentland et al. (2012) set certain actions or subtasks as triggers for following ones. Cohen et al. (2014) view triggers as something internal, that is, located in an individual's perception of the situation and to which behavior is an appropriate response. Not all models encompass fixed end points or "stopping actions" in the routines. This indicates a conceptual difference regarding the form of routine: Does it possess an action which defines its termination a priori, or is the routine terminated when a certain goal is achieved regardless of the last action leading to goal attainment?

The patterns depicted in the four models differ in several ways. Gao et al. (2014), Miller et al. (2014), and Pentland et al. (2012) refer to a concrete number of actions constituting a routine as a process. Cohen et al. (2014), on the other hand, describe their process in a more qualitative manner. The processes also differ according to whether their constituting actions must occur in a predefined sequence or not in order to be understood as "the routine." In other words, is there one correct routine (Miller et al., 2014) or does the routine refer to an emerging regularity in the model (Cohen et al., 2014; Gao et al., 2014; Pentland et al., 2012)? The interdependence within a routine as a process is implemented by most authors as a relation between two disparate actions (Gao et al., 2014; Miller et al., 2014). Cohen et al. (2014), however, refer to a previous situational outcome and the subsequent perception it triggers in the next individual in the process as the connection between parts of the routine. The four models differ substantially in the way they implement interdependence between routines as processes. Gao et al. (2014) and Pentland et al. (2012) explicitly incorporated some kind of weighting to enforce interdependence (e.g., preferences, retention parameters). Miller et al. (2014) did not focus on this kind of interdependence; rather, they investigated how long it takes for agents to establish a predefined routine. Cohen et al. (2014) did not explicitly address interdependence between routines in their framework. However, it is implicitly accounted for in their concepts of stably perceived situations, goals, and behavioral options, all of which reinforce a particular collective performance (e.g., routine).

Table 5.1 Comparison of models based on their implementation of organization type, triggers, and patterns

	Organization		Triggers	Pattern		
Model	Type	Work task	Cues	Process	Interdependence within process	Interdependence between processes
Gao et al. (2014)	College	Management of audio & video (AV) equipment	Start of class	Process of 11 disparate, interdependent actions	Frequency of ties between 11 actions	Preference for particular process (strategy) based on feedback
Pentland et al. (2012)	Unspecified	Unspecified	Particular first ("1") and last ("10") actions	Sequence of 10 disparate, interdependent actions	Conditional probabilities of one action occurring after another	Selective retention
Miller et al. (2014)	Unspecified	Unspecified	Particular first ("1") and last ("*k*") subtasks of work task	Accomplishing all subtasks in order (1 to *k*)	Predefined subtask order	Not focus of model; indicated by number of cycles (efficiency) needed to solve problem (*k* subtasks)
Cohen et al. (2014)	Generic	Generic	Individually perceived situation	Combining perceived situations and behavioral options into new situation to reach goal	"Mutual compatibility" (situational outcome triggers goal in next individual)	Stable perceived situations, goals and behavioral options reinforce process

Table 5.2 Comparison of models based on actor types, cognition, and behavior

	Multiple actors		Cognition		Behavior	
Model	Entities	Location	Individual	Collective	Individual	Collective
Gao et al. (2014)	Administrators, teachers, AV equipment	Unspecified	**Perception** (Admins can observe their nearest neighbor admins) **Adaptation/ learning**: (Admins change behavior strategy based on number of teacher complaints. Admins can imitate nearest neighbor with lowest teacher complaints.) **Uncertainty** (accuracy of info transmission from teachers to admins)	**Administrators & teachers**: Frequency table of all action-pair ties at time *t*	**Administrators**: locking, unlocking, repairing, recording info, checking info **Teachers**: getting key, unlocking equipment, using equipment, complaining, locking equipment, returning key	**Administrators & teachers**: Frequency table of all action-pair ties at time *t*
Pentland et al. (2012)	Intentionally unspecified	Unspecified	**Perception** (knowledge of prior action) **Disposition** (conditional probability of action occurring after prior action) **Variation** (probability of random variation of action; uncertainty) **Action cost** (random normal distribution)	**Retention** (memory; number of action sequences retained; 1–100) **Forgetting**: (Oldest sequence(s) dropped) **Disposition history** (first-order Markov transition matrix $A \times A$; conditional probabilities of all actions occurring after each other) **Sequence cost** (total of action costs) **Selection** (decision-making; sequences selected based on retention value OR average costs of current retained sequences)	Single action	Sequence of actions

Miller et al. (2014)	Individuals	Intentionally unspecified	**Skill/ capability** for a subtask **Transactive memory** Own "linked" infos (who can do which subtask; workflow relationships)	**Transactive memory** Others' "linked" infos (who can do which subtask; workflow relationships)	Perform subtask, search for actor with subtask skill	Pattern (frequencies) of workflow relationships between actors
Cohen et al. (2014)	Individuals	Unspecified	"**Situation-set**" ***A***: Perceived world (observed & expected actions of others) ***B***: Perceived similarity among situations ***C***: Dynamic change in dimensions/properties attributed to situations ***D***: Reflection of categorization of possible worlds " **Desirable ends**" ***E***: Encode "activated-ends" (classes of desirable situations)" **Relation between perception & action**" ***J***: Feedback from "acts" (alters situation structures and action spaces) ***K***: mutual development of situation perception, action to be taken, ends to be pursued	"**Relation between perception & action**" ***L***: Model of processes aligning actions (e.g., joint categorization of contexts, inputs, outputs)	"**Action representation**" ***F***: Model of an individual "act"	"**Action representation**" ***G***: Model of collective "action" (mathematical function) " **Relation between actions**" ***H***: Model of composition of "acts" or "actions" ***I***: Model of compilation of "actions"

The multiple actors implemented in all four models reflect substantially different concepts of routine "carriers." While Cohen et al. (2014) and Miller et al. (2014) model human individuals as actors, Pentland et al. (2012) intentionally omit actors to emphasize the significance of actions in forming routines. Gao et al. (2014), in comparison, incorporate human individuals as well as technical artifacts in their simulated, practice-based case. No model represents actors (or actions) in terms of their vertical or hierarchical distance from each other within the organization. Miller et al. (2014) purposely omit this aspect, as they argue it is more about who can fulfill a task rather than what position or title that person possesses.

In all models, individual behavior refers to single actions. In other words, no entity can carry out all possible actions. Most of these models represent actions as contingent upon the respective actor's role, skills or perception (Cohen et al., 2014; Gao et al., 2014; Miller et al., 2014). Collective behavior in all four models refers to some collection of actions related to each other in a way that quantitatively or qualitatively distinguishes them from other potential collections of actions (i.e., due to frequencies of their co-occurrence).

Individual cognition is implemented in all four models, albeit with differing emphasis. Firstly, individual perception of some sort is incorporated in all of them. It refers either to the sensing of other prior actions or of other agents' capabilities (Gao et al., 2014; Miller et al., 2014; Pentland et al., 2012). The framework presented by Cohen et al. (2014) is an exception. Perception in their case refers to a conglomerate of situations, goals, and relations between actions and situations as sensed by an individual. Moreover, all models incorporate some kind of learning. This concept is implemented in simple forms, that is, as retained and updated contingencies between actions, actors, etc. Distributed cognition is part of all four models, but it is implemented in substantially different ways depending on the model. Gao et al. (2014) appear to equate distributed cognition ("narrative network") with collective behavior, that is, frequencies of action-pair occurrences. Pentland et al. (2012) elaborate it as a "history matrix" containing the conditional probabilities of actions. Miller et al. (2014) conceive distributed cognition as "transactive memory," specifically what an individual agent can know about others' skills by communicating with other agents. Cohen et al. (2014) describe it in their framework as processes of joint categorization.

This section highlighted prominent similarities and differences based on the comparison of models summarized in Tables 5.1 and 5.2. It also demonstrated that the descriptors inferred in Sect. 5.2 can be used to structure and compare contrasting simulation models of organizational routines. In Sect. 5.3.3, the use of agent-based modeling to simulate organizational routines is reflected.

5.3.3 Reflections on Constructing Simulations of Organizational Routines

The subtle differences between the models compared as well as the potential complexity of an agent-based model per se pose challenges to constructing and using a simulation model of organizational routines. The challenges particularly refer to decisions a modeler needs to make when dealing with model design, implementation, and validation. They are reflected in the following with specific reference to organizational routines as well as to the models compared above.

General Scientific Approach The general scientific approach pertains to whether a routine is modeled as given, its structure or its dynamics (Pentland & Feldman, 2005). Modeling a routine as given means conceiving it at some aggregate level, for instance, as a single numerical value or outcome. The agent-based model of organizational co-evolution reported by Breslin (2014) is an example of this type of approach. Modeling a routine as its structure refers to its behavioral (expressed) or cognitive (represented) part. In the model reported by Gao et al. (2014), for example, the emerging routine ultimately reflects a routine as behavior (i.e., who did what in which order). Modeling a routine based on its dynamics means studying the interaction between the behavioral and cognitive aspects of its multiple actors. This is reflected in the models reported by Cohen et al. (2014), Miller et al. (2014), and Pentland et al. (2012).

Analogy A particular analogy may be implicitly or explicitly employed to describe a routine. Common analogies used in the past are computer programs, genes, or individual habits (Feldman & Pentland, 2003; Hodgson, 2008). Three models compared above, for instance, refer to routines as an emergent property of individual habit systems (Cohen et al., 2014; Gao et al., 2014; Pentland et al., 2012).

Entities and Levels Included organizational levels and entities characterize the target's decomposition into a system to be simulated. The models compared in Tables 5.1 and 5.2 exhibit notable differences regarding these design aspects, as indicated by the diverging selection of types of multiple actors. Psychological and sociological constructs are concepts selected to describe human entities and social structures. These design aspects specifically relate to the way behavior and cognition are conceptualized in the four models compared in Sect. 5.3. For example, while Miller et al. (2012, 2014) construct their agents psychologically as having skills and transactive memories, Cohen et al. (2014) emphasize the necessity of human perception and categorization in the formation of organizational routines. Moreover, Schulz (2008) compiled numerous psychological and sociological constructs scientists have adopted to describe and explain the stability of routines, for example, habitualization, priming, institutionalization, competency traps, and escalation of commitment.

Process Theory Process theories refer to any kind of scientific assumptions or practical simplifications used to represent what happens in a simulation. They are present in, for instance, how a routine is designed as a pattern, and how multiple agents' cognitive and behavioral parts interact. The models reported by Gao et al. (2014) and Pentland et al. (2012) depict the emergence of a routine as the development of conditional probabilities among pairs of actions. Miller et al. (2014), as another example, represented the development of agents' transactive memories as a process of asking one another about who can do what. This implies some process of verbal communication, whereas, hypothetically, such a process could also be represented by observation alone (Posada & Lopez, 2008).

Initiation, Termination and Boundaries Routine initiation and termination refer to initializing and terminating cues for a routine, while routine boundaries refer to a routine's first and last actions, given a routine is conceived as a sequence of actions. The models compared in Sect. 5.3.2 incorporate these implementation aspects via triggers (Table 5.1). Gao et al. (2014) interpreted the start and end of class as initializing and terminating cues for their routine. Miller et al. (2014) and Pentland et al. (2012), on the other hand, did not implement specific initializing and terminating cues. Instead, the boundaries set for their routine, that is, numbers marking its start and end, function without them.

Routine Indicators Routine indicators refer to concrete entities or variables chosen to technically characterize the routine in terms of its representation and enactment. In empirical research as well as in practice, narratives, ISO standards, SOPs, and rules are exemplary indicators for a routine's representation, while protocols, log files, historical accounts, testimonials, and observations serve as exemplary indicators for its enactment (Geiger & Schröder, 2014; Pentland & Feldman, 2005). In the model reported by Miller et al. (2014), the routine's representation is indicated by agents' transactive memories, while its enactment is indicated by the concrete subtasks solved by agents.

Routine Measurement Apart from implementing a routine based on the way its representation and enactment are conceptualized, further implementation is necessary to measure how the routine emerges or performs. For instance, routines are recurrently described as exhibiting certain qualities such as recognizability, repetitiveness, adaptability, or generativity (Becker, 2005). While these qualities imply a routine's measurement, they are not tied to explicit, generally accepted functions or measures to assess a routine: When exactly may a routine be considered *recognizable* or *repetitive*? When can the *survival* of a routine be spoken of? What does *noisiness* in routine recurrences indicate? While initially depending on the purpose of the simulation model at hand, the implementation of measures indicating routine quality or performance varies substantially in the models compared in Sect. 5.3.2.

Modeled Perspectives The number and types of perspectives incorporated in a simulation model of an organizational routine may differ from those accounted for in its empirical assessment. The model reported by Gao et al. (2014) draws on administrators' and teachers' specifications, indicating a topological fit between both worlds—simulated and empirical. The model described by Miller et al. (2014) assumes an agent not able to fulfill a task randomly asks another agent for support. While no doubt conceivable, an alternative empirical scenario could be that individuals do not ask just anyone for help, but perhaps most likely those they like, trust, respect, etc. (Dignum, Prada, & Hofstede, 2014). An empirical target with sufficient similarity to their abstract model could, hypothetically, produce quite diverging results based on routine enactors' contribution to the emergence of the empirical routine. Moreover, a routine may be quite differentially perceived in terms of its triggers (i.e., initiation, termination, boundaries) depending on whether it is being observed or enacted (Pentland & Feldman, 2008). Furthermore, there is potential for deviance between what routine enactors say they do and what they actually do (Clancey, Sachs, Sierhuis, & van Hoof, 1998). This discrepancy is not necessarily intentional, as routine enactors may not be completely aware of or capable of fully verbalizing what they do or how they do it (Cohen, 2012).

Simulation-Empiricism Fit Scholars assessing organizational routines empirically have noted the high variability these collective phenomena exhibit depending on the domain and particular instance investigated (Howard-Grenville, 2005; Pentland & Feldman, 2008). Organizational routines differ in their exogenous and endogenous stability depending on the domain they occur in (Bapuji et al., 2012; Kozica, Kaiser, & Friesl, 2014). Even within one particular domain, instances of a routine are subject to high variability as Pentland and Feldman (2008) showed for help-desk routines in the IT branch and van der Steen (2009, 2011) for management accounting rules in the banking industry. Empirical validation of agent-based models simulating organizational routines, in conclusion, requires the accommodation of a versatile empirical context and the distinction between meaningful and irrelevant variability.

5.4 Conclusion

The aim of this chapter was to address aspects considered key to describing what an organizational routine is, and how they are incorporated in contemporary agent-based models intended to formalize them. The key descriptors derived from extensive literature discussing definitions and facets of this phenomenon refer to the organization type, routine triggers, routines as patterns, multiple actors carrying out a routine, as well as cognition and behavior on individual and collective levels (Fig. 5.1). Four recently published models were compared based on how these descriptors are implemented in them (Tables 5.1 and 5.2). A number of technical aspects regarding the usage of agent-based modeling to gain insight on organizational routines arose from the comparison and were subsequently reflected.

5.4.1 Limitations

Several issues limit the generalizability of the ideas and conclusions presented in this chapter. Firstly, the descriptors derived in Sect. 5.2 are to a certain extent debatable. Although they were extracted from a comprehensive survey of influential scientific literature on organizational routines, this does not imply another routines scholar would have arrived at exactly the same compilation. Secondly, the search procedure and criteria chosen to select models for comparison were predefined, but subjectively set. Conceivably, other procedures and criteria may have retrieved different returns. Thirdly, only four models were selected for comparison. While all build upon the content in Sect. 5.2, they nevertheless represent a small sample. Fourthly, the contents provided in Tables 5.1 and 5.2 reflect our interpretations of the models. Given the potential difficulty of describing as well as comprehending described models, other readers may have understood the models' contents differently. Lastly, models simulating similar phenomena yet not referring to the literature reviewed in Sect. 5.2 were not selected for comparison. While the purpose of this chapter was to highlight how scientific conceptualizations of organizational routines are formalized in simulation models, similar models based on other theoretical foundations may have provided comparable insight.

5.4.2 Future Research

Admittedly, the current work could be refined and extended in several ways. One avenue could be to assess other routines scholars' essentials for characterizing organizational routines, and appraise whether they coincide with the ones derived in this chapter. This would provide an expert validation of our inferences. Another avenue could be to enlarge the sample discussed here to include more and in particular other kinds of models, that is, ones not directly grounded in the literature discussed here. This would provide more insight on how to formally conceptualize organizational routines or similar phenomena, perhaps illuminating parts of the whole still obscure to routines scholars, such as the relation between behavior and cognition or the interplay between organizational and individual levels. In making a final suggestion, taking other models simulating similar empirical phenomena into consideration could provide valuable ideas on how to validate a computer model of organizational routines, and more generally, which practical purposes it could be used for.

Conceptually, an organizational routine is a multifarious phenomenon. Routines scholars contend manifold aspects are necessary for its emergence, yet how to scientifically construct as well as interconnect them remain a matter of ongoing debate (Becker, 2004; Cohen et al., 1996; Parmigiani & Howard-Grenville, 2011). In particular, the individual and interactional (i.e., social, socio-technical) levels continue to intrigue scholars investigating organizational routines (Cohen, 2012; Felin et al., 2012; Felin & Foss, 2009; Lazaric, 2011). Regarding the individual level, future conceptual work could focus on disentangling what is called "behavior" and what "cognition," as well as which manifestations indicate them. Moreover, the relation between individual and distributed cognition embedded in concepts of organizational routines remains obscure and could benefit from further distinction, especially when routines are considered moments of organizational learning.

The lack of formal concepts and the porous understanding of routine dynamics on the micro-level, consequently, render agent-based modeling a fitting as well as promising method for disentangling these scientific knots. Translating conceptual ideas and their interconnectedness into code forces explicitness and reflection of theory, while the micro-level focus challenges lofty assumptions about what might be happening "down there" (Squazzoni, 2012). Elements such as a (common) task, heterogeneous actors, emerging organization, as well as distinct cognitive and behavioral parts of a complex whole are features of agent-based modeling (Meyer, Lorscheid, & Troitzsch, 2009). Nevertheless, future agent-based modeling of organizational routines could be advanced by taking the context in which an organizational routine emerges into stronger focus. This means explicitly characterizing the social or socio-technical system under investigation and incorporating the distinct perspectives participating in the construction, that is, the enactment and the observation, of the phenomenon.

Acknowledgements The authors greatly appreciate the feedback provided by two anonymous reviewers, Jonas Hauke and Bruce Edmonds on an early draft of this chapter. Your remarks have considerably helped us to communicate our ideas.

References

Aggarwal, V. A., Siggelkow, N., & Singh, H. (2011). Governing collaborative activity: Interdependence and the impact of coordination and exploration. *Strategic Management Journal, 32*(7), 705–730. doi:10.1002/smj.900.

Amit, R., & Schoemaker, P. J. H. (1993). Strategic assets and organizational rent. *Strategic Management Journal, 14*(1), 33–46.

Bapuji, H., Hora, M., & Saeed, A. M. (2012). Intentions, intermediaries, and interaction: Examining the emergence of routines. *Journal of Management Studies, 49*(8), 1586–1607. doi:10.1111/j.1467-6486.2012.01063.x.

Becker, M. C. (2004). Organizational routines: A review of the literature. *Industrial and Corporate Change, 13*(4), 643–678. doi:10.1093/icc/dth026.

Becker, M. C. (2005). A framework for applying organizational routines in empirical research: Linking antecedents, characteristics and performance outcomes of recurrent interaction patterns. *Industrial and Corporate Change, 14*(5), 817–846. doi:10.1093/icc/dth072.

Becker, M. C., Lazaric, N., Nelson, R. R., & Winter, S. G. (2005). Applying organizational routines in understanding organizational change. *Industrial and Corporate Change, 14*(5), 775–791. doi:10.1093/icc/dth071.

Breslin, D. (2014). Calm in the storm: Simulating the management of organizational co-evolution. *Futures, 57*, 62–77. doi:10.1016/j.futures.2014.02.003.

Breuker, D., & Matzner, M. (2014). Performances of business processes and organizational routines: Similar research problems, different research methods – A literature review. In *Proceedings of the European Conference on Information Systems (ECIS 2014)*. Tel Aviv, Israel. Retrieved from http://aisel.aisnet.org/cgi/viewcontent.cgi?article=1242&context=ecis2014.

Bruderer, E., & Singh, J. V. (1996). Organizational evolution, learning, and selection: A genetic-algorithm-based model. *Academy of Management Journal, 39*(5), 1322–1349.

Burns, J., & Scapens, R. W. (2000). Conceptualizing management accounting change: An institutional framework. *Management Accounting Research, 11*(1), 3–25. doi:10.1006/mare.1999.0119.

Chun, A., Wai, H., & Wong, R. Y. (2003). Optimizing agent-based meeting scheduling through preference estimation. *Engineering Applications of Artificial Intelligence, 16*(7), 727–743. doi:10.1016/j.engappai.2003.09.009.

Clancey, W. J., Sachs, P., Sierhuis, M., & van Hoof, R. (1998). Brahms: Simulating practice for work systems design. *International Journal of Human-Computer Studies, 49*(6), 831–865.

Cohen, M. D. (2012). Perceiving and remembering routine action: Fundamental micro-level origins. *Journal of Management Studies, 49*(8), 1383–1388. doi: 10.1111/j.1467-6486.2012.01078.x.

Cohen, M. D., & Bacdayan, P. (1994). Organizational routines are stored as procedural memory: Evidence from a laboratory study. *Organization Science, 5*(4), 554–568.

Cohen, M. D., Burkhart, R., Dosi, G., Egidi, M., Marengo, L., Warglien, M., et al. (1996). Routines and other recurring action patterns of organizations: Contemporary research issues. *Industrial and Corporate Change, 5*(3), 653–698.

Cohen, M. D., Levinthal, D. A., & Warglien, M. (2014). Collective performance: Modeling the interaction of habit-based actions. *Industrial and Corporate Change, 23*(2), 329–360. doi:10.1093/icc/dtu005.

Criado, N. (2013). Using norms to control open multi-agent systems. *AI Communications, 26*(3), 317–318. doi:10.3233/AIC-130560.

Cyert, R. M., & March, J. G. (1963). *Behavioral theory of the firm.* New Jersey: Prentice Hall.

D'Adderio, L. (2008). The performativity of routines: Theorising the influence of artefacts and distributed agencies on routines dynamics. *Research Policy, 37*(5), 769–789. doi:10.1016/j.respol.2007.12.012.

D'Adderio, L., Feldman, M., Lazaric, N., & Pentland, B. (2012). Call for papers – Special issue on routine dynamics: Exploring sources of stability and change in organizations. *Organization Science, 23*(6), 1782–1783. doi:10.1287/orsc.1120.0800.

Dignum, F., Prada, R., & Hofstede, G. J. (2014). From autistic to social agents. In *Proceedings of AAMAS '14 International Conference on Autonomous Agents and Multi-Agent Systems* (pp. 1161–1164). Richland, SC: International Foundation for Autonomous Agents and Multiagent Systems.

Eisenhardt, K. M., & Martin, J. A. (2000). Dynamic capabilities: What are they? *Strategic Management Journal, 21*(10–11), 1105–1121.

Feldman, M. S. (2003). A performative perspective on stability and change in organizational routines. *Industrial and Corporate Change, 12*(4), 727–752.

Feldman, M. S., & Pentland, B. T. (2003). Reconceptualizing organizational routines as a source of flexibility and change. *Administrative Science Quarterly, 48*(1), 94–118.

Felin, T., & Foss, N. J. (2009). Organizational routines and capabilities: Historical drift and a course-correction toward microfoundations. *Scandinavian Journal of Management, 25*(2), 157–167. doi:10.1016/j.scaman.2009.02.003.

Felin, T., Foss, N. J., Heimeriks, K. H., & Madsen, T. L. (2012). Microfoundations of routines and capabilities: Individuals, processes, and structure. *Journal of Management Studies, 49*(8), 1351–1374. doi:10.1111/j.1467-6486.2012.01052.x.

Gao, D. (2012). Multi-agent based simulation of organizational routines from an actor-based view. In *2012 3rd International Conference on System Science, Engineering Design and Manufacturing Informatization (ICSEM)* (Vol. 1, pp. 311–314). doi:10.1109/ICSSEM.2012.6340736.

Gao, D., Deng, X., & Bai, B. (2014). The emergence of organizational routines from habitual behaviours of multiple actors: An agent-based simulation study. *Journal of Simulation, 8*(3), 215–230. doi:10.1057/jos.2014.1.

Gaskin, J., Berente, N., Lyytinen, K., & Yoo, Y. (2014). Toward generalizable sociomaterial inquiry: A computational approach for zooming in and out of sociomaterial routines. *MIS Quarterly, 38*(3), 849–871.

Geiger, D., & Schröder, A. (2014). Ever-changing routines? Toward a revised understanding of organizational routines between rule-following and rule-breaking. *Schmalenbach Business Review, 66*, 170–190.

Geisendorf, S. (2009). The influence of innovation and imitation on economic performance. *Economic Issues, 14*(1), 65–94.

Gevers, J. M. P., Passos, A. M., & Uitdewilligen, S. (2014). Call for papers: Special issue on "Team adaptation and the dynamics of team cognition." *European Journal of Work and Organizational Psychology*. Retrieved from http://www.tandf.co.uk/journals/cfp/pewocfp.pdf.

Groff, E. R. (2007). Simulation for theory testing and experimentation: An example using routine activity theory and street robbery. *Journal of Quantitative Criminology, 23*(2), 75–103. doi:10.1007/s10940-006-9021-z.

Hodgson, G. M. (2008). The concept of a routine. In M. C. Becker (Ed.), *Handbook of organizational routines* (pp. 15–28). Cheltenham, UK: Edward Elgar Publishing Limited.

Hodgson, G. M., & Knudsen, T. (2004a). The complex evolution of a simple traffic convention: The functions and implications of habit. *Journal of Economic Behavior & Organization, 54*(1), 19–47. doi:10.1016/j.jebo.2003.04.001.

Hodgson, G. M., & Knudsen, T. (2004b). The firm as an interactor: Firms as vehicles for habits and routines. *Journal of Evolutionary Economics, 14*(3), 281–307. doi:10.1007/s00191-004-0192-1.

Hodgson, G. M., & Knudsen, T. (2006). Why we need a generalized Darwinism, and why generalized Darwinism is not enough. *Journal of Economic Behavior & Organization, 61*, 1–19. doi:10.1016/j.jebo.2005.01.004.

Holtz, G. (2014). Generating social practices. *Journal of Artificial Societies and Social Simulation, 17*(1), 17. Retrieved from http://jasss.soc.surrey.ac.uk/17/1/17.html.

Howard-Grenville, J. A. (2005). The persistence of flexible organizational routines: The role of agency and organizational context. *Organization Science, 16*(6), 618–636. doi:10.1287/orsc.1050.0150.

Hutchins, E. (1995). *Cognition in the wild*. Cambridge, MA: MIT Press.

Jack, L., & Mundy, J. (2013). Routine and change: The role of management accounting and control. *Journal of Accounting & Organizational Change, 9*(2), 112–118.

Kim, T., & Rhee, M. (2009). Exploration and exploitation: Internal variety and environmental dynamism. *Strategic Organization, 7*(1), 11–41. doi:10.1177/1476127008100125.

Kozica, A., Kaiser, S., & Friesl, M. (2014). Organizational routines: Conventions as a source of change and stability. *Schmalenbach Business Review, 66*, 334–356.

Kunz, J. (2011). Group-level exploration and exploitation: A computer simulation-based analysis. *Journal of Artificial Societies and Social Simulation, 14*(4), 18. Retrieved from http://jasss.soc.surrey.ac.uk/14/4/18.html.

Lazaric, N. (2011). Organizational routines and cognition: An introduction to empirical and analytical contributions. *Journal of Institutional Economics, 7*(02), 147–156. doi:10.1017/S1744137411000130.

Levitt, R. E. (2012). The virtual design team. Designing project organizations as engineers design bridges. *Journal of Organization Design, 1*(2), 14–41. doi:10.7146/jod.1.2.6345.

March, J. G. (1991). Exploration and exploitation in organizational learning. *Organization Science, 2*(1), 71–87.

Marengo, L. (1992). Coordination and organizational learning in the firm. *Journal of Evolutionary Economics, 2*(4), 313–326.

Maritan, C. A., & Coen, C. A. (2004). An agent-based model of investing in capabilities: Processes, decisions and performance. In *Academy of Management Proceedings* (Meeting Abstract Supplement, Vol. 2004, pp. N1–N6). Briarcliff Manor, NY: Academy of Management. doi:10.5465/AMBPP.2004.13863777.

McMullen, J. S., & Dimov, D. (2013). Time and the entrepreneurial journey: The problems and promise of studying entrepreneurship as a process. *Journal of Management Studies, 50*(8), 1481–1512. doi:10.1111/joms.12049.

Meyer, M., & Carley, K. (2007). Costs and benefits of budgeting in dynamic environments – An information processing model. In *European Accounting Association Annual Conference*. Lisbon, Portugal, April 2007.

Meyer, M., Lorscheid, I., & Troitzsch, K. G. (2009). The development of social simulation as reflected in the first ten years of JASSS: A citation and co-citation analysis. *Journal of Artificial Societies and Social Simulation, 12*(4), 12. Retrieved from http://jasss.soc.surrey.ac.uk/12/4/12.html.

Michel, A. A. (2007). A distributed cognition perspective on newcomers' change processes: The management of cognitive uncertainty in two investment banks. *Administrative Science Quarterly, 52*(4), 507–557.

Miller, K. D., Choi, S., & Pentland, B. T. (2014). The role of transactive memory in the formation of organizational routines. *Strategic Organization, 12*(2), 109–133. doi:10.1177/1476127014521609.

Miller, K. D., Pentland, B. T., & Choi, S. (2012). Dynamics of performing and remembering organizational routines. *Journal of Management Studies, 49*(8), 1536–1558. doi:10.1111/j.1467-6486.2012.01062.x.

Miner, A. S., Ciuchta, M. P., & Gong, Y. (2008). Organizational routines and organizational learning. In M. C. Becker (Ed.), *Handbook of organizational routines* (pp. 152–186). Cheltenham, UK: Edward Elgar.

Müller, B., Bohn, F., Dreßler, G., Groeneveld, J., Klassert, C., Martin, R., et al. (2013). Describing human decisions in agent-based models – ODD+D, an extension of the ODD protocol. *Environmental Modelling & Software, 48*, 37–48.

Murji, K., & Neal, S. (2014). Call for papers – Sociology special issue on the sociologies of everyday life. *Sociology*. Retrieved from http://www.britsoc.co.uk/media/61136/sociologies_of_the_everyday_CFP.pdf.

Narduzzo, A., & Warglien, M. (2008). Conducting experimental research on organizational routines. In M. C. Becker (Ed.), *Handbook of organizational routines* (pp. 301–324). Cheltenham, UK: Edward Elgar Publishing Limited.

Nelson, R. R., & Winter, S. G. (1982). *An evolutionary theory of economic change*. Cambridge, MA: Harvard University Press.

Parmigiani, A., & Howard-Grenville, J. (2011). Routines revisited: Exploring the capabilities and practice perspectives. *The Academy of Management Annals, 5*(1), 413–453. doi:10.1080/19416520.2011.589143.

Pavlov, A., & Bourne, M. (2011). Explaining the effects of performance measurement on performance: An organizational routines perspective. *International Journal of Operations & Production Management, 31*(1), 101–122. doi:10.1108/01443571111098762.

Pentland, B. T., & Feldman, M. S. (2005). Organizational routines as a unit of analysis. *Industrial and Corporate Change, 14*(5), 793–815. doi:10.1093/icc/dth070.

Pentland, B. T., & Feldman, M. S. (2008). Issues in empirical studies of organizational routines. In M. C. Becker (Ed.), *Handbook of organizational routines* (pp. 281–300). Cheltenham, UK: Edward Elgar Publishing Limited.

Pentland, B. T., Feldman, M. S., Becker, M. C., & Liu, P. (2012). Dynamics of organizational routines: A generative model. *Journal of Management Studies, 49*(8), 1484–1508. doi:10.1111/j.1467-6486.2012.01064.x.

Pentland, B. T., Hærem, T., & Hillison, D. (2010). Comparing organizational routines as recurrent patterns of action. *Organization Studies, 31*(7), 917–940. doi:10.1177/0170840610373200.

Posada, M., & Lopez, A. (2008). How to choose the bidding strategy in continuous double auctions: Imitation versus take-the-best heuristics. *Journal of Artificial Societies and Social Simulation, 11*(1), 6. Retrieved from http://jasss.soc.surrey.ac.uk/11/1/6.html.

Quinn, M. (2014). Stability and change in management accounting over time—A century or so of evidence from Guinness. *Management Accounting Research, 25*(1), 76–92. doi:10.1016/j.mar.2013.06.001.

Rouchier, J., Bousquet, F., Requier-Desjardins, M., & Antona, M. (2001). A multi-agent model for describing transhumance in North Cameroon: Comparison of different rationality to develop a routine. *Journal of Economic Dynamics and Control, 25*(3), 527–559.

Schulz, M. (2008). Staying on track: A voyage to the internal mechanisms of routine reproduction. In M. C. Becker (Ed.), *Handbook of organizational routines* (pp. 228–255). Cheltenham, UK: Edward Elgar Publishing Limited.

Siggelkow, N. (2011). Firms as systems of interdependent choices. *Journal of Management Studies, 48*(5), 1126–1140. doi:10.1111/j.1467-6486.2011.01010.x.

Siggelkow, N., & Levinthal, D. A. (2005). Escaping real (non-benign) competency traps: Linking the dynamics of organizational structure to the dynamics of search. *Strategic Organization, 3*(1), 85–115. doi:10.1177/1476127005050521.

Siirola, J. D., Hauan, S., & Westerberg, A. W. (2003). Toward agent-based process systems engineering: Proposed framework and application to non-convex optimization. *Computers & Chemical Engineering, 27*(12), 1801–1811. doi:10.1016/S0098-1354(03)00152-2.

Sikora, R., & Shaw, M. J. (1998). A multi-agent framework for the coordination and integration of information systems. *Management Science, 44*(11-part-2), 65–78.

Silva, C., Gonçalves, E., Dimuro, G., Dimuro, G., & de Manuel Jerez, E. (2013). Modeling agent periodic routines in agent-based social simulation using colored petri nets. In *2013 BRICS Congress on Computational Intelligence and 11th Brazilian Congress on Computational Intelligence (BRICS-CCI & CBIC)* (pp. 644–650). doi:10.1109/BRICS-CCI-CBIC.2013.112.

Squazzoni, F. (2012). *Agent-based computational sociology*. Hoboken, NJ: John Wiley & Sons.

Ter Bogt, H. J., & Scapens, R. W. (2014). *Institutions, rationality and agency in management accounting: Rethinking and extending the Burns and Scapens Framework*. Available at SSRN: http://dx.doi.org/10.2139/ssrn.2464980.

van der Steen, M. (2009). Inertia and management accounting change: The role of ambiguity and contradiction between formal rules and routines. *Accounting, Auditing & Accountability Journal, 22*(5), 736–761. doi:10.1108/09513570910966351.

van der Steen, M. (2011). The emergence and change of management accounting routines. *Accounting, Auditing & Accountability Journal, 24*(4), 502–547. doi:10.1108/09513571111133072.

Vromen, J. (2007). Generalized Darwinism in evolutionary economics: The devil is in the details. *Papers on Economics and Evolution*. Evolutionary Economics Group, Max Planck Institute of Economics, Jena, Germany (0711), pp. 1–26.

Vromen, J. (2011). Routines as multi-level mechanisms. *Journal of Institutional Economics, 7*(2), 175–196.

Wall, F. (2014). Agent-based modeling in managerial science: An illustrative survey and study. *Review of Managerial Science*, 1–59. doi:10.1007/s11846-014-0139-3.

Winter, S. G. (2012). Capabilities: Their origins and ancestry. *Journal of Management Studies, 49*(8), 1402–1406. doi:10.1111/j.1467-6486.2012.01081.x.

Yang, Y. J., Sung, T.-W., Wu, C., & Chen, H.-Y. (2010). An agent-based workflow system for enterprise based on FIPA-OS framework. *Expert Systems with Applications, 37*(1), 393–400.

Zollo, M., Reuer, J. J., & Singh, H. (2002). Interorganizational routines and performance in strategic alliances. *Organization Science, 13*(6), 701–713.

Chapter 6
CoopNet: A Social, P2P-Like Simulation Model to Explore Knowledge-Based Production Processes

Gian Paolo Jesi and Edoardo Mollona

Abstract A prevalent claim is that we are in a knowledge economy, where firms can be viewed as intra-organizational networks of knowledge nodes. Accordingly, firms' competitive advantage relies on their ability to support intellectual production processes that bridge talents and (possibly) foster durable work relations among employees in the organization. In this work, we propose a social, P2P-like simulation model, CoopNet, to investigate how intra-organizational networking and organizational mechanisms interact to affect intra-organizational cooperation. More specifically, we examine how (a) different reward mechanisms and (b) alternative assumptions on workers' mobility within an intra-organizational network combine to influence cooperation. As a result, we highlight the role of (a) co-workers' selection and (b) continuity of working relationships as alternative mechanisms to foster cooperation within intra-organizational networks.

Keywords Knowledge economy • Agent-based • Self-emergent • Cooperation • Peer-to-peer

6.1 Introduction

A recent survey conducted by McKinsey & Company (2007) reports that, to facilitate knowledge sharing among co-workers (for example in product design), firms are investing in collaborative technology (Guo, 2009), peer-to-peer networks, and social networks (Chunhui, Xufang, & Harris, 2010). In addition, MacDuffie (2007), quoting the Wall Street Journal (de Lisser, 1999) and data from the

G.P. Jesi (✉)
Fondazione Bruno Kessler (FBK), via S.Croce, 77, 38122 Trento, Italy
e-mail: gpjesi@fbk.eu

E. Mollona
Department of Computer Science, University of Bologna, via Mura Anteo Zamboni, 7, 40126 Bologna, Italy
e-mail: edoardo.mollona@unibo.it

D. Secchi, M. Neumann (eds.), *Agent-Based Simulation of Organizational Behavior*, DOI 10.1007/978-3-319-18153-0_6

Gartner Group (Jones, 2004), reports that more than half of U.S. companies with more than 5,000 employees use virtual teams and that more than 60 % of the professional employees surveyed reported working in a virtual team. Ultimately, management scholars describe the twenty-first-century firm as an intricately woven web of dispersed operations that are managed via collaborative technologies and are organized around networks rather than by rigid hierarchies (Cascio & Aguinis, 2008). Despite firms' increasing investments in collaborative technologies such as peer-to-peer communities and social networks, the managerial problems that follow from the adoption of such technologies have been fairly neglected by the literature in management and organization theory.

The evidence that knowledge-intensive production processes require, at least partially, self-organized and voluntary organization of work relationships is a well-accepted tenet in organization theory (Ouchi, 1979, 1980; Saxberg & Slocum, 1968; Smith, Carroll, & Ashford, 1995). Yet, despite the well-recognized role that clans (Ouchi, 1980) or relational teams (Williamson, 1981) might play in organizing hard to monitor intellectual production, the literature is fairly vague on the micro-processes that enhance reciprocation in intra-organizational exchanges. The relaxation of authority-based control mechanisms shifts focus on the dynamics of individual exchange behavior. Knowledge-based productive processes resemble peer-to-peer networks in which task execution implies exchanges among workers (of information or effort) that are likely to be governed by unspecified personal obligations, intrinsic rewards, and trust.

The aim of this paper is at analyzing the circumstances under which cooperative behavior emerges in knowledge-based organizations. More specifically, we are interested in contexts in which traditional hierarchical control mechanisms are weak in preventing free-riding. We present a model, CoopNet, that describes production processes as an intra-organizational network in which workers interact within local structures of exchange. We then explore the unfolding aggregate behavior of the network. This behavior stems from the local interaction among workers who respond to the incentives that are crystallized in specific reward mechanisms. We adopted computer simulation in order to investigate the non-obvious emergent consequences of changing reward mechanisms and of adopting different individual policies of social interaction. CoopNet has fundamental commonalities with large-scale P2P models, where each node has a limited, local knowledge about the network and the communication is message-driven.

The remainder of this paper is organized as follows: we briefly discuss relevant literature in the theory of economic organization and we present our methodology; in the following three sections, we describe our model and its algorithms in detail. Then we describe our experimental setup and our achieved results. Finally, we conclude with a discussion about related work and our specific contribution.

6.2 Hierarchy and Reciprocity

A prevalent claim is that we are in a knowledge economy (Foss, 2005; Hodgsson, 1999; Xu, Wang, Luo, & Zhongzhi, 2006). What characterizes a knowledge economy is a growing importance of human capital in productive processes (Foss, 2005) and the mounting knowledge intensity of jobs (Hodgsson, 1999). In addition, an increasingly influential argument is that the division of labor is becoming complex and firms can be viewed as networks of knowledge nodes (Benkler, 2006; Foss, 2005; Grandori, 2001; Hilton, 2008; Zenger & Hesterly, 1997), that is, sets of interacting individuals with key skills and competencies. Such networks crystallize firm-specific knowledge and provide ground upon which firms build their heterogeneity. In this context, production processes require the joint effort of a number of individuals with very specific know-how so that firms play a role of integrators of such a variety of individual talents (Xu et al., 2006).

For example, biotechnology firms require a complex mix of social networks, interpersonal skills, and technical skills. This implies that these firms need to build collaborative interdisciplinary environments attracting top scientists (Hilton, 2008). In this vein, Grandori (2001) reports the employment by large firms of knowledge translators, or knowledge brokers, that are professionals that facilitate communication and information exchange among specialists of different disciplines.

As knowledge specialization increases, however, the integration becomes a difficult endeavor and reliance on creativity of individual specialists may weaken the effectiveness of authority-based hierarchical mechanisms.

The reason is twofold; first, specialization often implies a supervisor dilemma when supervisors have less knowledge than employees within specific domains (Hodgsson, 1999). In this respect, He and Wang (2009) suggest that information asymmetry between holders of highly innovative knowledge assets and other stakeholders makes monitoring less effective and, in some cases, even counterproductive. Second, human creativity may be very difficult to standardize into contracts enforceable through hierarchical control (Benkler, 2006). In such circumstances, evaluating the potential outcome of a productive process, allocating rewards and detecting free-riding all become cumbersome attempts. This is the well-known problem of *metering* (Alchian & Demsetz, 1972) that makes contracts incomplete and hardly enforceable.

As imposing a top-down structure may be inefficient for this kind of intellectual and over-socialized production processes, a rising attitude is for allowing the self-organization of knowledge workers. To this aim, collaborative technology spread within large organizations that increasingly let the aspects of workers' interaction to emerge bottom-up (McAfee, 2006).

In addition, as production processes are intertwined with social processes (Ouchi, 1980), exchange behavior among agents that are embedded in joint production processes is likely to be informal and reciprocal rather than formal and negotiated. If knowledge-based productive processes are likely to take place in intra-organizational P2P networks, rather than in hierarchical structures, a question emerges regarding the real effectiveness of traditional organizational mechanisms and the role played by firms in organizing economic activity.

Intrigued by this perspective, in this article, we focus on reciprocal exchange to explore collaboration within organizations. From this angle, we define *pro-social* and *free-riding* behavior referring to social exchange theory. According to social exchange theory, a dyadic exchange relationship is maintained if it is mutually rewarding (Blau, 1964; Homans, 1958, 1961; Thibaut & Kelley, 1959). For the relationship to be established, a *starting mechanism* is necessary (Blau, 1964, p. 92), that is, an individual offer of help from one agent to another; for example, the first agent offers a valuable information to the second agent. This act of altruism may be moved by an entrenched norm of reciprocity that suggests that people should help those that help them and, therefore, those whom you have helped have an obligation to help you in the future (Gouldner, 1960, p. 173). In laboratory experiments with sequential prisoner's dilemma, in which a first-mover chooses to cooperate or defect, and a second-mover responds with either cooperation or defection, Clark and Sefton have demonstrated that second-movers are likely to reciprocate an initial act of cooperation (Clark & Sefton, 2001). Had the individual that received help to reciprocate this help, the original giving behavior would be reinforced (Homans, 1958) and, eventually, a reciprocal flow of valued behavior (Emerson, 1976, p. 347), for example information exchange, would be established. As suggested by Emerson, the concept of reinforcement implies that, for an exchange relationship to emerge and to be maintained, a longitudinal series of mutually rewarding transactions is required. The concept of reciprocal exchange, which is at the core of social exchange theory, is also used in the framework of game theory as well. As Molm suggests, reciprocal exchange, which is a non-negotiated exchange (Molm, 2003, p. 3; Molm, Takahashi, & Peterson, 2000), fits in non-cooperative game theory in which actors make choice independently, without knowledge of others' choice (Molm, 2003, p. 4). Along these lines, in non-cooperative game theory, cooperation based on reciprocation has been modeled within the framework of the Prisoner's Dilemma (PD). The emergence of cooperation in a game theoretic setting is equivalent to the emergence of a reciprocal exchange behavior between to exchange partners. In the PD setting, cooperation emerges as the result of a repeated interaction among two rational players who are bound to interact and have the possibility to punish each others' defection (Kreps, Milgrom, Roberts, & Wilson, 1982; Rapoport & Chammah, 1965). Moving our analysis from the general into the specific context of organizations, the focus on the continuity of a longitudinal exchange relationship remains central in both social exchange theory and game-theoretic cooperation theory. Akerlof (1982) and Fehr, Kirchler, Weichbold, and Gachter (1998), for example, suggest that norms of reciprocity may give rise to wages that are persistently above market-clearing level. This phenomenon is interpreted as the result of repeated interaction between workers and their employer, where workers develop a feeling of obligation and, thus, they reward with cooperative behavior an employer who has signaled its good intentions by paying high salaries. On similar lines, in the work of Korsgaard, Schweiger, and Sapienza (1995), perceived procedural fairness is an antecedent to the creation of trust and commitment of employees to leaders' decisions. Grounding on the concept of reciprocation as built in both social exchange theory and game theoretic approaches to cooperation theory, we describe the collaboration among co-workers as a social exchange and we define pro-social and free-riding behaviors accordingly. More specifically, we define as pro-social an agent that reciprocates a co-worker's contribution of effort to a specific joint task. In the wording of PD, pro-social actors do not defect given a cooperative act from a co-worker. On the other hand, we define as free-rider an actor that does not entirely reciprocate the co-worker's effort contribution. The aim of our experiments is at capturing the ambiguous, and frequently contradictory, effects that traditional organizational mechanisms, such as reward systems, have on the emerging cooperation among co-workers.

6.3 Computer Simulation Models as *Theoretical Laboratories*

Modeling and simulation (Barjis, 2007) constitute a fundamental element of our research design. Computer simulation helps rigorously to deduce consequences from modeled assumptions when complexity of modeling makes it difficult obtaining closed-form solutions. We employ a computer simulation model as a theoretical laboratory to explore the circumstances in which different patterns of cooperation among workers emerge. In particular, we analyze how different hiring, firing, and reward strategies produce aggregate organizational performances. In our work, computer simulation is used to investigate (a) how variations in the parameters that describe hiring, firing, and reward strategies affect individual decision-making and (b) how individual decision-making interacts to generate emergent aggregate behavior. The system that we describe behaves as a *complex, adaptive system* (CAS) (Chunhui et al., 2010) and the dynamics of intra-organizational interaction can be extremely complex and almost impossible to predict *a priori*. Yet, the simulation of the system allows exploring the rich repertoire of behaviors (Gilbert & Doran, 1994; Gilbert & Troitzch, 2005) that can potentially arise.

This approach has the advantage of creating an appropriate testing field for conducting controlled experiments. We adopted this method to perform computational "thought experiment" in which we ask "what if" questions in an artificial world. In our intentions, this speculation facilitates the process of generating and testing candidate ideas in a rigorous reproducible and deductive way.

Thus, in our inquiry, the CoopNet model describes an intra-organizational network that embeds knowledge workers. Using computational experiments, we highlight the conflict between hierarchically imposed and emergent structures of exchange. In addition, we are able to analyze how workers respond to the incentives that are crystallized in the reward mechanisms and to the information that is available to them concerning co-workers' productivity.

6.4 Model

We designed and implemented an agent-based model (Zhang & Bhattacharyya, 2007)—the CoopNet model—to simulate the interaction among employees. Using computer simulation models in this way (see Axelrod, 1997) is a well-established paradigm within the social sciences (artificial social systems: Hales, Edmonds, Norling, & Rouchier, 2003). Increasingly, social scientists use multi-agent based simulation (Li & Wang, 2007) to explore complex dynamics in artificial social systems (Axelrod, 1997; Hales et al., 2003).

Among similar lines, the CoopNet model should be viewed as an "artificial society" type model [i.e., similar to the SugarScape model (Epstein & Axtell, 1996)] that allows representing in a stylized manner the processes that may occur in a real organization.

More specifically, in the CoopNet model, collaboration relationships among workers are represented by an undirected network where the employees are the nodes and each relation is a link between a couple of nodes. The communication between nodes is managed in a P2P-like fashion, using message passing and local knowledge about the network.

Each node in the system holds a list of links to other nodes, which we call CACHE. Therefore, a network defined by the relation "who knows whom" is induced by the cache's information. We can define more formally the CoopNet network as an undirected graph $G_{\text{coop}}(V, E_{\text{coop}})$, where V is the set of vertices (nodes) and E_{coop} is the corresponding set of links or edges. In our model, the notion of time is not strict because our P2P-like approach needs not be synchronized (Jelasity, Voulgaris, Guerraoui, Kermarrec, & van Steen, 2007). We measure time in generic *cycles* during which each node has the possibility to run the protocol once.

Each node i holds a variable e_i representing its current *productivity effort* and a variable w_i representing its *wage*. With $e_i(j)$ we indicate the portion of the effort spent by node i in reciprocating with node j.

Each node i can behave *pro-socially* or *free-riding*; the node's behavior is assigned at bootstrap and may change during time (see Sect. 6.5.2). Pro-social nodes will try to invest more effort in their relations, while free-riding nodes prefer maximizing the ratio between reward and effort spent. The system wide parameter MAX_{eff} represents the maximum allowed value for e_i $\forall$ node i.

The system rewards each node for its spent effort at regular time intervals. The wage w_i assigned to node i is calculated according to specific *reward policies* (see Sect. 6.6.1). In addition, we consider the *utility* of a node i, which is defined as the difference between its wage and its actual effort: $u_i = w_i - e_i$.

Finally, we consider that each node has the capability to contact a limited number of random nodes in the whole network independently of the CoopNet overlay.

The content of this set is dynamic as it changes over time. This limitation mimics the real world, as a person can hardly contact all the other persons in the company especially when the company is multi-business and geographically dispersed. In P2P terms, this feature can be achieved by a sampling service (Jelasity et al., 2007).

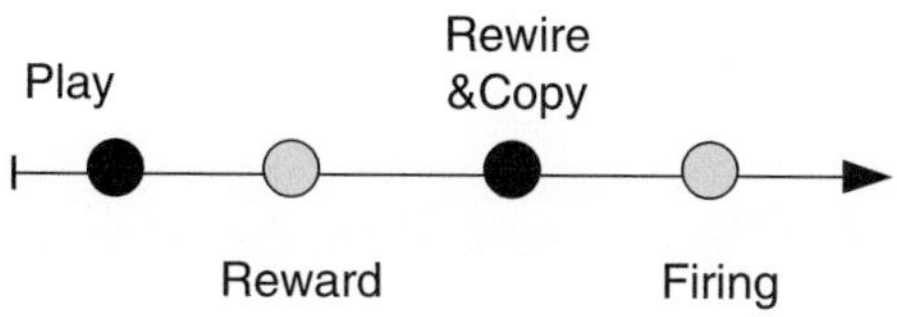

Fig. 6.1 The CoopNet model schema. The *dark circles* represent the *Individual Decision Making* phases, while the *light ones* represent the *Human Resource Management* phases

The simulation of the CoopNet model unfolds in four sequential phases (shown in Fig. 6.1): (a) Play, (b) Reward, (c) Rewire&Copy, and (d) Firing phase.

In phase (a) nodes interact with their neighbors according to their behavior, in (b) each node receives a reward according to a specific *reward policy* (see Sect. 6.6.1), in (c) each node tries to find a new neighbor having "interesting" characteristics (e.g., such as having a high wage or utility) with which to join; in addition, a node may imitate (copy) the behavior of the new acquired neighbor. Finally, in phase (d) a node can be fired (i.e., removed from the system) if it does not achieve a minimum productivity threshold. The productivity threshold mimics an institutional context in which firing is very rare and it is applied only for extremely low performing employees. The four simulation phases portray the two core features of our model: the structure *of individual decision making* (i.e., phases (a), (c)) and the *human resource management* mechanisms (i.e., phases (b), (d)).

6.5 Individual Decision Making Algorithm

In the following, we discuss in detail how the individual decision making algorithm is designed by the Play and Rewire&Copy phases.

6.5.1 *Play Phase*

In this phase, each node tries to obtain the highest possible wage by interacting with its neighbors. If the interaction with one or more neighbors is not satisfactory, then those neighbors are blacklisted and dropped from the current node's cache.

Each node i starts the simulation by committing a specific effort $e_i(j) = \frac{e_i}{\text{degree}_i}$ in the interaction with each neighbor j. In the next cycles, each node has to adjust its effort according to the other party's efforts. The basic idea is that when two nodes i and j play distinct values, say x_i and x_j, they tend to close the difference gap between x_i and x_j.

```
1 e ← Array[] # effort commited ∀ neighbor
2 wait ← Array[] # time waiting ∀ neighbor
3 black_list ← Array[]
4 t ← max time to wait for lower performing neighbors
5 repeat periodically every time units
6     foreach neighbor ∈ neighborhood do
7         if behavior == PROSOCIAL then
8             if e[neighbor] < neighbor.e[this] and e[neighbor] < MAX_eff then
                  # the prosocial tries to glose the gap with its better performing
                    neighbor
9                 black_list.add(neighbor)
10                close_gap(neighbor)
11                redistribute_effort()
12            else
13                if wait[neighbor] < t then
14                    wait[neighbor] ++
15                else if neighbor.e.total_effort > e.total_effort then
16                    wait[neighbor] ← 0
17                else
18                    disconnect(neighbor)
19        if behavior == FREERIDER then
20            if e[neighbor] > neighbor.e[this] then
21                close_gap(neighbor)
```

Fig. 6.2 Play phase algorithm in pseudo code format. It is run by each node

The actual algorithm run by each node is summarized in Fig. 6.2 by using a pseudo code language which adopts object oriented syntax and imperative statements. The algorithm code works as follows.

The management of the gap between efforts depends on each node's individual behavior (i.e., lines 10 and 21, function *close_gap()*). A pro-social node i, for instance, will try to play the same amount of a neighbor j, but if j has played less than i, it will not modify its effort waiting and hoping that neighbor j is willing to play more in the next future. Node i will wait node j for a limited amount of t consecutive interactions (i.e., $t = 4$); if node j is cooperative (pro-social), it will likely fill—at least partially—the effort gap.

Conversely, a free rider node i will not modify its effort when its neighbor j is playing more, **but** it will play less if its neighbor's effort is less than its own effort. The PLAY phase is iterated t consecutive times to allow multiple opportunities to achieve a reciprocally satisfactory relation in terms of effort spent.

In a relationship, a *reciprocal satisfaction* is achieved when both parties contribute the same amount of effort. Such an ideal situation is fairly difficult to achieve; for this reason, we included in the model a relaxed notion of satisfactory relation. More specifically, we assume that for pro-social nodes to maintain a relationship it is sufficient that they perceive that the weaker party in the relationship (i.e., the party spending less effort) shows its *willingness to cooperate*. We represent the *willingness to cooperate* of the weaker party as an increase in the effort spent by this latter that produces a *partial* closure of the effort gap.

Also, it is realistic considering that a neighbor might be unable to reciprocate just because it is already busy in many, and possibly valuable, activities.

This condition is managed in lines 15–16, where it is considered the total effort that each node deploys in the interaction with its entire neighborhood, that is e_i and e_j. When evaluating whether to drop or to maintain a relationship, in addition to effort reciprocation, a node i weighs the total effort that its neighbor j contributes to the organization. When the total effort contributed by j to the neighborhood is larger than the total effort contributed to the neighborhood by the worker i itself, i keeps the link with j independently of the reciprocating behavior of j in the dyadic relationship between i and j.

This mechanism allows nodes to maintain links with nodes that are pro-social but, being linked to many other nodes, cannot commit much effort to each node. When these mechanisms fail to detect any willingness to cooperate or value in the relation, the link is dropped.

Our modeling here is strongly grounded on social exchange theory and we assume a relationship between reciprocity and perceived justice (Eckhoff, 1974; Molm, Quist, & Wiseley, 1993); workers interrupt dyadic relationships when they perceive that partners show an unfair behavior.

As links are undirected, when a worker drops a relationship with a neighbor, also the neighbor loses a link as well. After having terminated a relation, pro-social nodes redistribute effort uniformly among the neighbors left. This effort is dissipated when the node that has terminated the relation is a free rider.

6.5.2 Rewire and Copy Phase

As in the Play phase, the rewiring process is related with a node's behavior. Two general behavioral assumptions are crystallized in our modeling. First assumption is that nodes try to find a (possibly) good new neighbor to join with. Having a new good neighbor will eventually improve the average effort of the cluster and hence will improve the agents' wage from a local point of view and the system's performance from a global one.

The second assumption is that nodes tend to imitate the behavior of those newly joined neighbor that show higher performances in the hope to achieve similar performance results.

```
e ← Array[] # effort commited ∀ neighbor
black_list ← Array[]
candidates ← Set{}
candidate ← None
repeat periodically every k time units
    with search_policy=NSR or GSR do
        candidates ← search()
    with select_policy=WAGE or UTILITY do
        candidate ← select(candidates)
    if candidate ∉ black_list and candidate.accept(this) then
        this.neighborhood.add(candidate)
        if behavior == PROSOCIAL then
            e[candidate] ← rnd(0, MAX_eff - e.total_effort)
        if behavior == FREERIDER then
            e[candidate] ← rnd(0, e(t0))
        with P(p_bcopy) do
            this.behavior ← candidate.behavior
```

Fig. 6.3 Rewire&Copy phase algorithm in pseudo code format. It is run by each node

When a node executes the rewire phase, it has to grant some effort to the neighbor with which he joins. If the node i is a pro-social, he will grant a random effort in the range [0, $\text{MAX}_{\text{eff}} - e_i$]; otherwise, he will grant a random effort in the range [0, $e_i(t_0) - e_i$], where $e_i(t_0)$ is the node's initial effort.

To simulate the evolution of the network topology, we adopted two mechanisms: *unilateral tie severance* and *consensual tie creation*, that have been formerly presented in Hanaki, Peterhansl, Dodds, and Watts (2007). The idea is to allow for the emergence of social plasticity, that is, the ability of an individual agent to select partners thereby changing their neighborhood as time goes by Eguiluz, Zimmermann, Cela-Conde, and San Miguel (2005). In the following, we describe the phases in detail.

The algorithmic steps required to manage this phase are summarized in Fig. 6.3.

Search: a node always searches for new neighbors if it has effort to spend. In case of a free rider node i, the effort can never exceed its initial effort $e_i(t_0)$. We designed two different policies to search for candidates; the search can be performed over the CoopNet network or over random links.

- **Neighborhood Search Rewire** (NSR): the candidate set is composed of a random CoopNet neighbor s and all the neighbors of s
- **Global Search Rewire** (GSR): the set is composed by k distinct nodes taken at random from the whole intra-organizational network, where k is a system wide constant

Select: the aim of the selection policy is to find the "best" candidate for a node i among the elements of S. We designed two alternative mechanisms to select partners. Nodes select partners either on the basis of the wage that potential partners receive or on the basis of the utility that accrues to potential partners. A node i checks if there is at least a candidate having a higher wage (or a higher utility). Then, it selects the candidate j that maximizes the difference $w_j - w_i > 0$ (or the difference $u_j - u_i > 0$) where $j \in \{1 \ldots \|S\|\}$.

Accept: this step is performed when a request for linking is received from a neighbor node. If a node i has some effort to spend, whether it is a pro-social or a free rider, it accepts the newcomer.

Copy: when selecting another node j for rewiring, nodes chose potential partners on the basis of performances. We assume that a node i, when rewiring with a node j, may decide to imitate individual behavioral policy of the newly connected node in the attempt to replicating the performance of the latter. The actual adoption of the possibly new behavior is a stochastic process with probability p_{bcopy}.

6.6 Human Resource Management Processes Algorithm

In the following, we discuss in detail the algorithms that capture the focal organization's human resource management processes. We adopt a stylized representation that focuses on two processes: REWARD and FIRING which activate two further phases of our model.

6.6.1 Reward Phase

At the end of the PLAY phase, an organizational hierarchy (i.e., an oracle) measures the average productivity (AP) level: $AP = \sum_{i=1}^{N} \frac{e_i}{N}$, where e_i is the *effort* played by each node and N is the size of the network. However, when the COOPNET overlay eventually splits in distinct connected components, due to the node's behavior or due to the rewiring process, the AP is computed on per-component. In other words, it is computed on the set of efforts of each component: $\sum_{i=1}^{N_k} \frac{e_i}{N_k}$, where N_k is the size of the k-th connected component. For simplicity, we consider AP_i as the AP of component-i. We considered two different ways of calculating the node wage: WAGEBONUS and WAGENEIGHBOR. Both policies are based on the AP value.

The actual algorithm run by the hierarchy oracle is depicted in Fig. 6.4.

WAGEBONUS (lines 5–11): the wage of node i is calculated as follows: $w_i = \frac{\sum_{j=1}^{N} e_j}{N} \cdot (1 + \alpha)$, where α is an *added value* constant and N is

```
1  AP ← Array[NETWORK.#of_components]
2  repeat periodically every k time units
3      for i = [0 : NETWORK.#of_components] do
4          AP[i] ← ∑(node.effort ∀node ∈ NETWORK[i])
5      if WAGEBONUS then
6          foreach node ∈ NETWORK.nodes do
7              my_cluster ← NETWORK.cluster_of(node)
8              wage ← AP[my_cluster] / NETWORK[my_cluster].size (1 + α)
9              if AP[my_cluster] ≥ BONUS_T then
10                 wage ← wage(1 + RND([0 : 1]))
11             node.wage ← wage
12     if WAGENEIGHBOR then
13         foreach node ∈ NETWORK.nodes do
14             node.wage ←
                   (node.effort + ∑(neighbor.effort ∀neighbor ∈ node.neighborhood)) / (sizeof(node.neighborhood) + 1) (1 + α)
```

Fig. 6.4 Reward phase algorithm in pseudo code format. It is run by an oracle

the size of the cluster in which node i is embedded or the size of the whole network if the CoopNet overlay is not split. When the overlay splits into clusters, if the wage assigned to a cluster is $\geq$ Bonus_T, where Bonus_T is a specific threshold, then each node i of the cluster will receive $w_i = w_i * (1 + x)$, where $x \in [0 : 1]$ and has a stochastic nature; when node i's has an effort $\geq$ Bonus_T, x takes a uniformly distributed value. On the contrary, when the effort is $<$ Bonus_T, $x = 0$ node i does not receive any bonus. The idea is that the system is able to measure the effective effort that each node is contributing and, consequently, it encourages individual performances by assigning bonus rewards to single nodes.

WageNeighbor (lines 12–14): the idea underpinning this reward mechanism is to associate each node's wage with the performance of a small group of nodes that are embedded in a neighborhood of close relationships. This *small group* is described by a node's *n*eighborhood; at the beginning of the simulation, the size d_{cnet} of the neighborhood is initialized with a constant value (see Sect. 6.7) and can grow or shrink over time according to the node's behavior and the evolution of the system. The value of *AP* for node i is calculated over the effort of each neighbor and i's effort itself in the following manner: $w_i = \frac{e_i + \sum_{j=1}^{c} e_j}{d_{\text{cnet}}+1} \cdot (1 + \alpha)$, where α is an *added value* constant.

The idea here is testing different designs of group rewards. As suggested in Zenger and Hesterly (1997), by facilitating selective intervention, technological innovation may increase the easiness with which firms are able to disaggregate large firms into small autonomous sub-units to which high-powered incentives may be applied. In this respect, our alternative types of rewarding mechanisms reflect two logics applied to the definition of the unit to which the monitoring of productivity is applied and rewards accrue.

In WageBonus, the unit of reward accrual is the larger set of workers that collaborate directly and indirectly; on the other hand, in WageNeighbor, the definition of the unit of accrual is more fine-grained and considers only direct collaboration relationships. On the other hand, however, in WageBonus mechanism, a finer analysis of individual effort is possible while in WageNeighbor the evaluation applies to groups' performance only.

6.6.2 Firing Phase

In the model we included a component that, when activated, allows focal organization to fire employees that underperform. The algorithm is shown in Fig. 6.5.

In general, the system can fire any node i that is committing an effort e_i lower than a certain threshold value. However, in our model, the firing mechanism can be calibrated in order to mimic different degrees of freedom in firing employees by real-world organizations. In the real world, knowing the actual productivity of an employee is not a trivial task and it is not fail-proof.

Thus, when the firing mechanism is activated, any node spending an effort in the interval $[0, \delta_{\mathrm{LOW}}]$ is purged from the system with perfect accuracy (lines 3–5), while any node spending effort in the interval $[\delta_{\mathrm{LOW}}, \delta_{\mathrm{HIGH}}]$ is purged according to a p_{fire} probability (lines 6–9).

The idea is that when a node's performance is at the lowest extreme (e.g., in the range of $[0, \delta_{\mathrm{LOW}}]$), it is easy to detect shirking but when the performance of the node is closer to the average performance, then the system is unable to

```
1 repeat periodically every k time units
2     foreach node ∈ NETWORK.nodes do
3         if node.effort ∈ [0 : δLOW] then
4             purge(node)
5             injectNewNode()
6         if node.effort ∈ [δLOW : δHIGH[ then
7             with P(pfire) do
8                 purge(node)
9                 injectNewNode()
```

Fig. 6.5 Firing phase algorithm in pseudo code format. It is run by an oracle

discriminate the difference with perfect accuracy. The nodes that are eventually purged are substituted by an equal amount of "fresh" nodes whose initialization is identical to the bootstrap initialization (i.e., line 9, function *injectNewNode()*).

6.7 Experiments

We adopted PeerSim[1] (i.e., an open source, P2P simulator) as a simulation platform and we wrote a Java implementation of our model.

The goal of our experiments is to generate hypotheses on the role that the context in which employees interact plays in facilitating or hindering cooperation. We explore four elements that characterize such a context.

A first element is the rewarding strategy at work in the focal organization. We experimented with different simulated mechanisms to evaluate individual productivity and reward employees. Moving towards ill-defined intellectual production processes, in which tasks are interconnected, precision in defining individual productivity may decrease dramatically.

Strictly connected with the first element, the second element that we consider is the capability of a firm to detect and fire free-riders.

Flexibility that employees are assigned in modifying the set of co-workers, for example by moving from one team to another, is the third element that we consider. This element is particularly important because it has not been previously considered when investigating how to counter free riding within organizations.

Lastly, we analyze the role of available information concerning co-workers' performances.

6.7.1 Experimental Setup

In our experimental protocol, we simulated (a) the presence/absence of the firing mechanism, (b) different search policies (i.e., NSR, GSR), (c) different rewiring and peer selection policies (i.e., wage or utility-based), and (d) different rewarding mechanisms.

As the parameters involved in configuring the simulations are many, in order to simplify the reading and to provide a faster lookup, we summarized them in Table 6.1. The lines marked with symbol "$*$" correspond to the variable parameters (e.g., (a), (b), (c) and (d)), while the others are kept constant for all the simulation experiments.

We run two sets of experiments in which individual contribution to a collaborative production process is ambiguous. In the first set, we assumed that the focal

[1] http://peersim.sf.net/.

Table 6.1 Simulation features and parameters with their respective values or states and a short description

Feature or parameter	Value	Description
*search policy	NSR, GSR	How to look for possible candidates
*select policy	WAGE, UTILITY	How to choose among candidates
*firing mechanism	true, false	Whether to purge poor performing nodes or not
*reward mechanism	WAGEBONUS, WAGENEIGHBOR	How nodes are rewarded for their performance
d_{cnet}	5	Degree of the bootstrap network
MAX_{eff}	50	Max effort a node can spend for time unit
μ	27.5	Effort mean
σ	5.5	Effort variance
α	0.2	Reward added value constant
p_{bcopy}	0.9	Probability to copy the behavior of a newly joined neighbor
p_{fire}	0.6	Probability to fire a poor performing node
BONUS_T	40	Threshold to get the productivity bonus
δ_{LOW}	10	Threshold under which the firing is deterministic
δ_{HIGH}	15	Threshold under which a node is considered "poor performing"

company can only assess the average productivity of a network of connected co-workers. Yet, the firm is able to assess individual productivity and to consequently assign a bonus to specific workers that show above-average productivity (this is the WAGEBONUS rewarding scheme).

In the second set, we assumed that the focal company is able to more accurately recognizing smaller isles of productivity and applying a fine-grained analysis of teams' productivity (each neighborhood). On the other hand, the company is less efficient in assessing individual productivity (this is the WAGENEIGHBOR rewarding scheme). Consequently, the focal firm assigns wages to workers on the basis of the average productivity of the neighborhood they belong to.

In both sets of experiments, we run our simulations with two different individual decision-making routines to select co-workers.

The GSR rewire policy gives the employees the freedom to look for new suitable neighbors over a wider horizon, increasing the chance to find a good match while the NSR policy allows employees to search only over own neighborhood.

In addition, in both sets of experiments, we included a third selection routine, labeled UNSR that considers the node's utility, rather than wage, when selecting co-workers. More specifically, when the UNSR policy is applied, an employee selects a co-worker i by maximizing $u_i = w_i - e_i$.

If not stated otherwise, we focus on a scenario involving 500 agents. The data presented have been collected from 10 distinct simulation runs with randomly generated seeds.

We calibrated model's parameters by following two steps. First, we used sensitivity analysis to select parameters that have strong influence on model's behavior. Second, we calibrated these parameters by (a) replicating of similar setups found relevant literature and (b) adopting a general criteria of plausibility. For example, the network (i.e., work relations) is randomly wired at bootstrap using $d_{\text{cnet}} = 5$ degree. This value has been selected by looking at degree values used in previous work. In Riolo, Cohen, and Axelrod (2001), degree ranges from 1 to 10, being 3 the more frequently used value. In the simulation experiments reported by Eguiluz et al. (2005), average degree is 8. Thus, we set $d_{\text{cnet}} = 5$ degree.[2] The links in the CoopNet overlay represents the actual work relations. The maximum effort a node can spend in a *time unit* is fixed to the constant $\text{MAX}_{\text{eff}} = 50$ and it is considered a system wide parameter. The unit of measure of effort is hours per week of labor. The choice of 50 as the maximum effort that a node can spend is defined with reference to a standard of 8 h work week plus a plausible supplementary effort that a worker can devote to a company by, for example, working beyond the daily required time or on Saturdays and Sundays. The logic underpinning the calibration of this parameter is grounded on the literature on corporate citizenship according to which pro-social behavior in organization is defined as employee behavior that is above or beyond the call of duty and is therefore discretionary (Konosky & Pugh, 1994; Moorman, Blakely, & Niehoff, 1998; Niehoff & Moorman, 1993; Organ, 1988; Smith, Organ, & Near, 1983; Van Dyne, Graham, & Dienesch, 1994).

The effort with which each node starts to work is assigned by a normal distribution having parameters: $\mu = 27.5$, $\sigma = 5.5$. These values are motivated by the fact that we want to start the system having the most of the population close to an average value and few nodes at the extremes. This setting was chosen to explore how the aggregate behavior of the system can be attracted either to an extreme of widespread collaboration and high global performances of to another extreme characterized by high level of individual opportunism and diffused free-riding behavior. For the same reason, the initial node's behavior (i.e., pro-social or free-rider) is assigned randomly to a 50–50 % proportion.

The added value constant is $\alpha = 0.2$; it is a multiplier that represents the willingness of the focal firm to reward effort spent by workers. The parameter is useful to reproduce situation in which labor is rewarded more or less generously. Within the range [0.1 , 0.3] changes in α do not affect emerging global behavior.

The initial node's behavior (i.e., pro-social or free-rider) is assigned randomly according to a 50–50 % proportion.

The probability to copy the behavior of a newly joined neighbor is $p_{\text{bcopy}} = 0.9$. The newcomer behavior is copied with high probability because it is supposed that its behavior is the cause of observed superior performances. However, a door is left open for a deviation (i.e., "mutation") in the copying behavior as in genetic, epidemic, dilemma-game algorithms (Hales et al., 2003; Marcozzi, Hales, Jesi,

[2] Having a (constant) degree of 5, it is safe to assume that the network is connected at the beginning of the simulation, regardless its size.

Arteconi, & Babaoglu, 2005). Multiple simulation experiments proved that values for p_{bcopy} in the range [0.6,0.9] produce similar aggregate behavior of the system.

The threshold over which the system assigns a node's wage bonus is BONUS_T $= 40$ because the company's rewarding system tends to prize effort superior to standard call of duty. Indeed, 40 h are the standard work week of eight daily hours per five work days

When the firing mechanism is enabled, we adopt $\delta_{strict} = 10$ and $\delta_{rnd} = 15$ and the firm fires nodes having an effort in the $[\delta_{strict}, \delta_{rnd}]$ with probability $p_{fire} = 0.6$. These settings reflect the idea that the system can just detect the actual performance of its employees with barely sufficient accuracy. When the performance of an employee is extremely low (i.e., ≤ 10), it can be detected and isolated easily, but when the performance is in the $[\delta_{strict}, \delta_{rnd}]$, the system detection ability becomes fuzzy and its results are no better than average.

When the organizational structure requires the presence of the firing feature (see Sect. 6.6.2), any new node introduced in the system is initialized with the same network, effort and behavior distribution as described above.

Each data represents an average value collected from 10 distinct simulation runs.

6.7.2 *Experimental Results*

Figure 6.6a, b shows the performance of the system when the WAGEBONUS reward policy is adopted. We performed experiments both activating and deactivating the firing mechanism.

As we measure the performance in terms of effort spent, the performance of each policy setup can be compared with a *benchmark* in which each node achieves to spend the maximum allowed effort: $e_i = 50\ \forall i$ (e.g., overall effort $E = 25{,}000$).

This benchmark is highlighted by a horizontal line in the upper part of each effort plot.

Figure 6.7 instead reports percentage of free riders in each experiment.

This first set of experiments presents two findings worth of being discussed. In Fig. 6.6, we notice that, when it is possible to detecting and firing individuals that perform very low, performances of GSR and NSR are very similar. On the other hand, when detecting free-riding and, consequently, firing becomes difficult, the two selection routines yield very different performances.

In particular, the selection routine in which workers are allowed to search beyond the cluster of neighbors (GSR) yields much higher performances.

This finding suggests that, when organizational hierarchy is weakened by the ambiguity of individual contribution to a shared endeavor, a firm ought to assign to individual workers larger autonomy in selecting co-workers all over the entire network of organizational employees.

In this way, people willing to collaborate are given the opportunity to both punish free-riders, by severing specific working relationships, and to find and select co-workers willing to cooperate. As clusters of cooperators emerge, the information

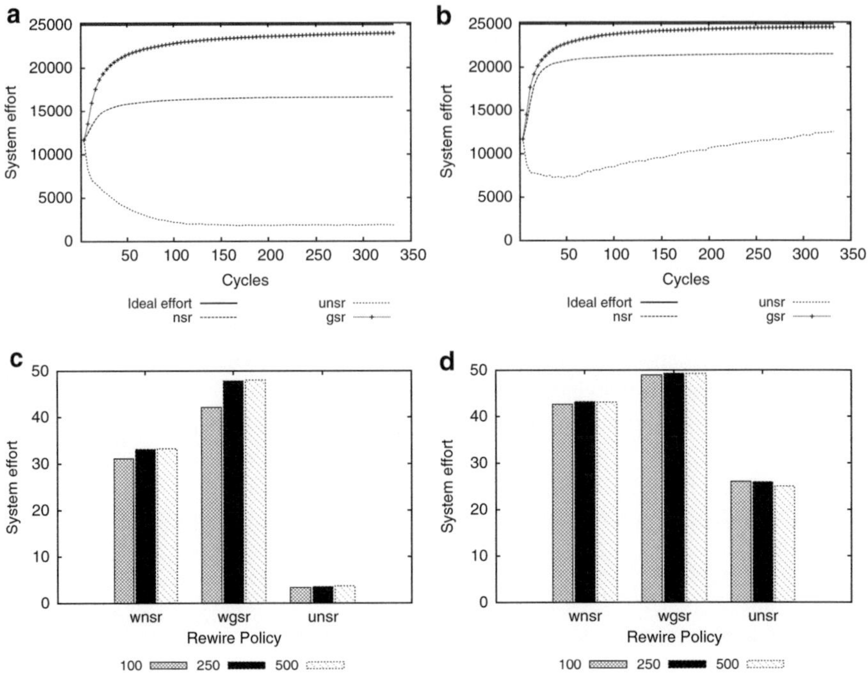

Fig. 6.6 System effort and scalability effort achieved by each policy using WAGEBONUS reward. Both no-fire and fire scenarios are considered. Network size is 500. (**a**) System effort, no-fire scenario. (**b**) System effort, fire scenario, (**c**) Effort scalability, no-fire scenario. (**d**) Effort scalability, fire scenario

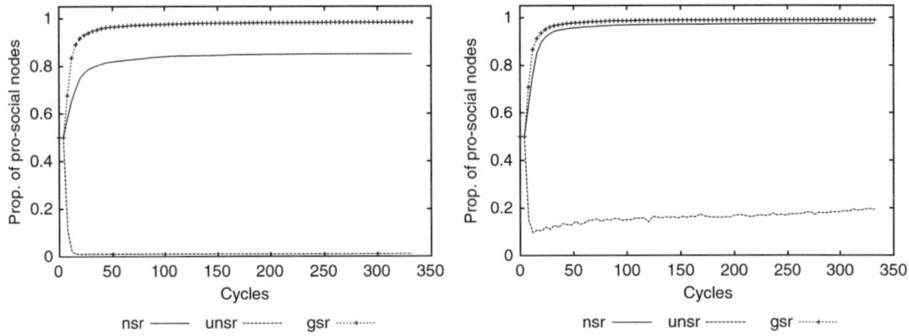

Fig. 6.7 Proportion of pro-socials and free-riders over time. Both no-fire (on the *left*) and fire (on the *right*) scenarios are considered. WAGEBONUS reward policy is adopted. Network size is 500

that is conveyed by the high performances of such clusters spread within the organizational network inducing imitation of cooperative behaviors (see Fig. 6.7).

A second insight that surfaces from this first set of experiments regards the role of available information to individual decision-makers. As reported in Fig. 6.6, when the UNSR selection protocol is activated, the performance of the system is extremely low. By using UNSR, the utility drives the selection of new neighbors. By definition (see Sect. 6.4) this makes nodes to minimize their effort and to profit by the work of others. Quickly, almost the entire population converges towards free-riding behavior and the firm's productivity collapses (see Fig. 6.7, left plot).

Having the possibility to compare the wage received by co-workers with real effort produced, easy reveals free-riding behavior. The problem is that, when wage is assigned to a connected cluster or to a neighborhood of co-workers, free-riders employees have, at least in the beginning of the simulation, higher utility (with similar wage they dedicate less effort).

Thus, they will be more frequently selected by other workers, and their behavior will be imitated. The idea here is that, at least at the beginning of the simulation, it is important to conceal the fact the free-riders have higher utility due to their behavior. In general, as the process of interaction evolves, the emerging of clusters of cooperators allows pro-social workers to yield higher reward, this process, however, requires that at the beginning a firm covers up the gains produced by free-riders, in order to inhibit imitation of dysfunctional behaviors.

When designing a system based on incentives, it is important to understand which information is necessary to make it public or to hide. A free access to all the information available does not necessarily represent an advantage, rather it may lead to unexpected and undesired results.

A last remark concerns scalability of results. Although poor performing, the UNSR policy is perfectly scalable. NSR is scalable as well, but GSR seems to favor larger networks since as the size of intra-organizational networks reduces, search capabilities of GSR wear off. When firing is involved (Fig. 6.6d) and the action of free riders is minimized, all the policies are scalable.

In the second set of experiments we applied the WAGENEIGHBOR policy. In this case, the reward is locally evaluated and assigned to small groups of co-workers. Figure 6.8a, b show that while the absolute performance is not as high as with the previous policy, the difference gap among GSR and NSR is much lower. Both reach their results almost at the same time. This set of experiments elicits another important insight.

In general, Fig. 6.8 reports that, when a WAGENEIGHBOR policy is assumed, GSR protocol loses strength in comparison with NSR. The message conveyed by these experiments is that, when reward is assigned by evaluating productivity of small groups, it is important that co-workers within each group learn how to collaborate by both increasing their efforts, in case they are pro-social workers, and isolating free-riders. Such learning process requires stability of groups of co-workers.

In this light, the NSR selection protocol, by constraining individual search for partners in the neighborhood, facilitates groups stability and intra-groups learning. On the other hand, the GSR protocol, which increases workers' mobility, by allowing partners' selection over the entire employees network, delays intra-group learning. Concluding, GSR and NSR illustrate virtues of two different mechanisms that facilitate emerging of cooperation.

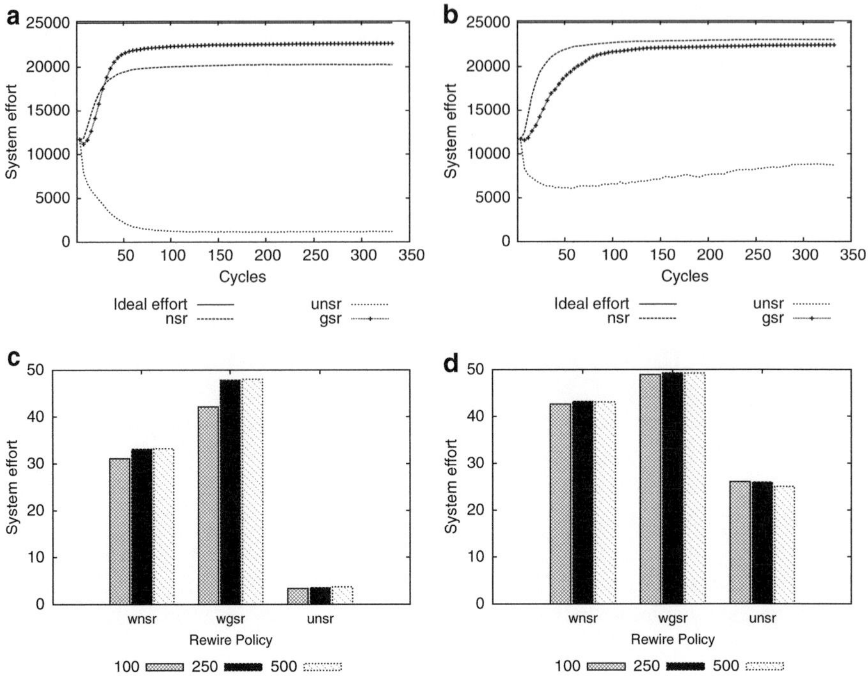

Fig. 6.8 System and scalability effort achieved by each policy using WAGENEIGHBOR reward. Both no-fire and fire scenarios are considered. Network size is 500. (**a**) System effort, no-fire scenario. (**b**) System effort, fire scenario. (**c**) Effort scalability, no-fire scenario. (**d**) Effort scalability, fire scenario

The GSR speaks in favor of the mobility of workers in selecting co-workers. Mobility allows pro-social workers to select appropriate co-workers punishing free riders by unilaterally terminating work relationships. On the other hand, NSR brings forth advantages of limiting mobility of co-workers forcing intra-group learning. In this case, the continuity of the relationships among co-workers leads pro-social employees to increase their efforts. In addition, free-riders, being limited in their mobility, are forced to remain in a group where they will be soon or later isolated by co-workers. Furthermore, groups that eliminate free-riders will not easily replace links severed. Consequently, groups are formed by neighborhoods of nodes in which each node is connected to a limited number of other nodes. In this way, each node will more easily be able to respond to neighbors' requests of effort reciprocation.

6.8 Discussion on Related Work and Contribution

Firms use hierarchical authority to punish opportunism and for rewarding workers' cooperative behavior. In this vein, traditionally, literature in management and organizational theory has investigated the effectiveness of different rewarding mechanisms (Gibbons, 1998; McAdams & Hawk, 1994).

As monitoring of individual productivity becomes cumbersome, along with the use of hierarchical authority, a typical response is to shift attention to such social mechanisms as clans, relational teams (Ouchi, 1980; Williamson, 1981) or intra-organizational (Lida, Huimin, Song, & Kanliang, 2009) social networks (Cross & Cummings, 2004).

Both approaches, in our perspective, emphasize the relationship between an individual and the corporate, this latter interpreted as a reified entity.

In this light, for example, studies on corporate citizenship focus on the employee's behavior that is above and beyond the call of duty and is therefore discretionary and not necessarily rewarded but follows from the attitude to show attachment to the firm in which he/she works (Konosky & Pugh, 1994; Moorman et al., 1998; Niehoff & Moorman, 1993; Organ, 1988; Smith et al., 1983; Van Dyne et al., 1994).

Interestingly, even in the case in which the pro-social behavior takes the form of a cooperative act towards an individual co-worker, the inner force that explains such behavior is the attachment to the corporate, not to the particular co-worker. Thus, the reciprocal behavior that is apparently directed toward particular others is inherently a manifestation of indirect reciprocity.

We suggest that such a point of view, which is often oblivious to the role of dyadic relationships that emerge within joint productive process, is inadequate to address the interaction dynamics that characterize intellectual production processes in which co-workers collaborate in flexible virtual (Wenan, Bosheng, Weiming, Lida, & Ling, 2008; Wenan et al., 2010) teams and workplaces, in social networks and in company intra-nets.

Our approach encompasses a two-folded shift in the analysis of cooperative behavior in organization.

First, our approach focuses on dyadic relationships in intellectual productive processes within organizations. Second, and consequently, we propose that a company ought to shift from controlling the content of behaviors to controlling the networking behavior of employees and the mobility with which employees move within intra-organizational networks deciding to initiate or terminate working relationships with co-workers.

Though articulated into an artificially built organizational context, we suggest that our work contributes to the analysis of what features virtual intra-organizational collaboration ought to have, what the consequences might be of employees' collaboration through social networks and what issues and problems collaboration in virtual teams and workplaces bring about.

In this vein, our experiments provide a number of managerial implications. Indeed, we suggest that a company willing to design, promote, and control employees' cooperation in virtual teams and workplaces needs to look at three interconnected aspects.

First, the firm needs to regulate the degree of mobility allowed to employees within intra-organizational collaborative networks. Mobility means the possibility to easily and frequently starting and interrupting collaborative relationships with potential co-workers. High mobility fosters collaboration by allowing workers to select appropriate co-workers and to interrupt relationships with allegedly opportunistic co-workers. These findings advocate that the regulation of mobility of workers, and the connected plasticity of intra-organizational collaboration networks, represents a possible avenue to build competitive advantages. The experience of firms such as software producer Valve confirms how, in specific organizational contexts and given specific tasks to be completed, the issue of flexible collaboration receives paramount attention. In the Handbook for New Employees, the company advises newcomers that working desks have wheels to be moved and encourages employees to move their desks around in order to flexibly create and reshape teamwork. At Valve, "desk wheels" is a metaphor to remind that "There is no organizational structure keeping you from being in close proximity to the people who you'd help or be helped by most" (Valve, 2012, p. 6). Thus, managers ought to carefully consider whether organizational structure represents an obstacle to organization productivity. As our work explained, however, limiting workers' mobility and forcing employees to maintain stable relationships, may lead to cooperation via another avenue. Precisely, once forced to work in stable teams, workers learn to reciprocate others' effort and to expel opportunistic colleagues. In a nutshell, reported simulation experiments suggest to managers that the issue of co-workers intra-organizational mobility has to be taken seriously.

Second, our simulation experiments contribute to articulating previous work on human resource management. Zenger and Hesterly (1997), for example, suggest that, by facilitating selective intervention, technological innovation may increase the easiness with which firms are able to disaggregate large firms into small autonomous sub-units to which high-powered market-like incentives may be applied. They invite managers to consider the decomposition of organizations into small and definable sub-units. In our work, we show that sub-units need to spontaneously emerge. More precisely, rather than designing size and shapes of sub-groups, managers ought to invest their effort in associating mobility and reward mechanisms to guide the self-organization of intra-organization collaboration networks. More specifically, managers need to pair reward mechanisms that do not discriminate among workers effort to high intra-organizational mobility and local, neighborhood-based, rewards to low mobility.

Finally, our work highlights the role of information made available to individual workers when they decide to starting or interrupting collaborative relationships with potential co-workers. Interestingly, the reported experiments unveil the negative consequences that accurate information may have on the aggregate dynamics of intra-organizational collaboration. While researches on electronic markets have addressed the role of electronic reputation or feedback mechanisms that, by providing the type of information available in more traditional close-knit, mitigate the moral hazard problems that are associated with exchange among strangers (Bolton, Katok, & Ockenfels, 2004), our findings suggest that too much information, for example regarding asymmetry in rewards, may reveal opportunism of colleagues. This disclosure may lead to an early unilateral termination of collaborative relationships that prematurely interrupts learning and the emerging of cooperation.

Beside the insights for managers, our work contributes a useful point of view to the literature on emerging cooperation.

Previous conventional game-theoretic analysis of cooperation in dyadic relationships typically suggests that the possibility to punish a defeating partner in a stable relationship is a factor that facilitates cooperation (Axelrod, 1984; Rapoport & Chammah, 1965). In this perspective, continuity of association between partners, and the unfeasibility to terminate the relationship, encourage partners to learn how to cooperate. More recently, however, an alternative hypothesis proposes that the possibility to walk away from an exchange relationship to select specific exchange partners is a mechanism to build cooperation (Boone & Macy, 1999; Eguiluz et al., 2005; Hanaki et al., 2007).

In our work, we compare these two mechanisms and we find that their effectiveness depends on the structure of a firm's rewarding mechanisms and, ultimately, on the ability of monitoring employers' productivity.

When monitoring of productivity focuses on large networks of interconnected co-workers, the more employees are allowed to navigate within intra-organizational networks, flexibly activating or interrupting working collaboration, the greater are performances in terms of emerging collaboration.

On the other hand, when monitoring is applied locally, at the level of closed neighborhoods of co-workers, advantages of intra-networks mobility weakens and gains from learning increase. In this scenario, limiting workers' mobility leads to cooperation by forcing workers to learn how to reciprocate others' efforts and to detect and to select away free riders.

Interestingly, the scenario of low mobility and learning offers its best results when firing mechanism is deactivated and, thus, it does not interrupt the learning processes at work by expelling nodes from the network of relationships. In addition, being intra-organizational network fragmented in a large number of small neighborhoods that are rewarded differently, such differences produce a tension towards imitating successful behaviors. Furthermore, our findings further support research on the possibly dysfunctional effects of individually assigned reward mechanisms. Individual rewards create more wage dispersion than group-based bonuses (Barth, Bratsberg, & Haegeland Raaum, 2009). Wage dispersion creates inequality perceptions and dysfunctional consequences such as reduced effort and turnover (Zenger & Marshall, 2000; Zenger & Hesterly, 1997), which, we suspect, are not germane for the emergence of cooperation among workers. In this respect, rewards based on individual performances become more costly as the size of a firm increases (Zenger & Marshall, 2000; Zenger & Hesterly, 1997) because it creates reward differentials that increase as the boundary of a firm increases. Along these lines, Zenger (1994) found that small scale firms more efficiently attract talented engineers by offering contracts that reward individual performances. Our work points at a future research that deals with how visible the variance in individual rewards is. In this respect, we illuminate a direction for further investigation by suggesting that workers may react to free-riding rather than just variance in rewards. In other words, workers may match higher rewards with colleague's higher effort thereby accepting rewards differences as procedurally fair. What upset workers is the association of high rewards and low effort. This association, in our experiments, produced a self-reinforcing wave of free-riding behavior. When workers are able to capture the difference between paid salaries and effective effort spent, free-riding strategies would immediately manifest their higher payoffs and maintaining cooperation within the firm would result impossible. A final remark on the validity of our findings. As Cohen and Cyert (1961) suggest, computer models can be divided into two types: synthetic and analytic. In synthetic models, the modeler knows the behavior of the component units of the phenomenon under scrutiny. On the other hand, in analytic models, the behavior of the phenomenon is known and the problem is capturing the mechanisms that produce the behavior.

Referring to this categorization, we suggest that our computer model is synthetic since it moves off from the description of plausible individual decision-making rules, as grounded in relevant literature, and typical organizational rewarding processes to deduce unfolding aggregate consequences.

Thus, our simulations are theoretical experiments that elicit dynamic hypotheses to analyze the consequences of plausible assumptions regarding individual exchange behavior and organizational rewarding mechanisms.

As Hughes suggests, experiments conducted by the means of computer simulations may bring about information on actual worlds, about possible worlds, or about impossible worlds (Hughes, 1999), they are at par with all other kinds of theoretical speculation. In this light, findings obtained with computer experiments are to be judged in their ability to deduce interesting inferences starting from plausible assumptions.

When devising possibly relevant but unrealized states of the world, simulation experiments may hardly be compared with available empirical data. Yet, in their anticipating possible scenarios, they produce their value by building stimulating preliminary conceptualizations that guide further empirical research.

6.9 Conclusions and Future Work

The aim of our work was at investigating the role of modern firms at the verge of a fast and dramatic metamorphosis of the nature of production processes and of employment relationships themselves.

To appropriately addressing the consequences that such a transformation will bring about, we suspect that different disciplines need to be integrated. More specifically, we suggest that organizational theory may gain a great deal from borrowing the concepts and techniques that computer scientists developed to explore behavior of P2P systems.

In this article, we reported results from a research project in which we looked at organizations as hybrids that combine mechanisms that are typical of firms, such as rewarding mechanisms, and processes that characterize interaction within P2P systems.

Under a methodological point of view, we developed our insights by simulating the behavior of a large organization with an agent-based model that worked as a virtual laboratory for our analysis.

We believe that our work discloses two avenues of future research.

First, since organizations increasingly let people interact in virtual teams through a repertoire of collaborative tools, we suggest that an important issue to investigate is the coherence between the specific features of these tools and the attributes of the specific organization's structure and processes, and of the specific content of production processes. For example, is it possible to associate specific features of collaborative tools to specific types of organizations, or to specific types of products or services produced by an organization?

A second avenue of research is connected to the role that the information available to individual decision-makers has in inducing or hindering cooperative behaviors in intra-organizational networks. Our simulations conveyed a counterintuitive finding by suggesting that, in specific circumstances, less information is better than more, and that being aware of the level of efforts that our peers contribute may tempt nodes to imitate free riding behaviors. This outcome invites researchers to empirically test whether a correlation exists between information made available to co-workers by different collaborative tools, cooperative behavior, and virtual teams' productivity. Concluding, we hope that our work was able to highlight the gains that may potentially arise from an interdisciplinary approach to the study of the role of information technology in firms' organization.

Acknowledgements The authors acknowledge financial support from the research project FIRB 2003 no. RBNE03HJZZ named "The evolution of clusters of firms: emerging technological and organizational architectures".

References

Akerlof, G. A. (1982). Labor contracts as partial gift exchange. *Quarterly Journal of Economics, 97*(4), 543–569.

Alchian, A., & Demsetz, H. (1972). Production, information costs, and economic organization. *American Economic Review, 62*(5), 777–795.

Axelrod, R. (1984). *The evolution of cooperation*. New York: Basic Books.

Axelrod, R. (1997). Advancing the art of simulation in the social sciences. *Complex, 3*(2), 16–22.

Barjis, J. (2007). Automatic business process analysis and simulation based on DEMO. *Enterprise Information Systems, 1*(4), 365–381.

Barth, E., Bratsberg, B., & Haegeland Raaum, O. (2009). Performance pay and within-firm wage inequality. Technical Report 4137. IZA - Institute for the Study of Labor.
Benkler, Y. (2006). *The wealth of networks. How social production transforms markets and fredom*. New Haven: Yale University Press.
Blau, P. M. (1964). *Exchange and power in social life*. New York: Wiley.
Bolton, G. E., Katok, E., & Ockenfels, A. (2004). How effective are electronic reputation mechanisms? An experimental investigation. *Management Science, 50*(11), 1587–1602.
Boone, R. T., & Macy, M. W. (1999). Unlocking the doors of the prisoner's dilemma: Dependence, selectivity, and cooperation. *Social Psychology Quarterly, 62*(1), 32–52.
Cascio, W. F., & Aguinis, H. (2008). Chapter 3: Staffing twenty-first-century organizations. *The Academy of Management Annals, 2*(1), 133–165.
Chunhui, P., Xufang, H., & Harris, W. (2010). Research on e-commerce transaction networks using multi-agent modeling and open application programming interface. *Enterprise Information Systems, 4*(3), 329–353.
Clark, K., & Sefton, M. (2001). The sequential prisoner dilemma: Evidence on reciprocation. *The Economic Journal, 111*(468), 51–68.
Cohen, K., & Cyert, R. (1961). Computer models in dynamic economics. *The Quarterly Journal of Economics, 75*(1), 112–127.
Cross, R., & Cummings, J. R. (2004). Tie and network correlates of individual performance in knowledge-intensive work. *Academy of Management Journal, 47*(6), 928–937.
de Lisser, E. (1999). Update on small business: Firms with virtual environments appeal to workers. Wall Street Journal, October 5.
Eckhoff, T. (1974). *Justice: Its determinants in social interaction*. Rotterdam: Rotterdam University Press.
Eguiluz, V. M., Zimmermann, M., Cela-Conde, C. J., & San Miguel, M. (2005). Cooperation and the emergence of role differentiation in the dynamics of social networks. *America Journal of Sociology, 110*(4), 977–1008.
Emerson, R. M. (1976). Social exchange theory. *Annual Review of Sociology, 2*, 335–362.
Epstein, J., & Axtell, R. (1996). *Growing artificial societies: Social science from the bottom up*. Washington, DC: Brookings Institute Press.
Fehr, E., Kirchler, E., Weichbold, A., & Gachter, S. (1998). When social norms overpower competition: Gift exchange in experimental labor markets. *Journal of Labor Economics, 16*(2), 324–351.
Foss, N. J. (2005). *Strategy, economic organization, and the knowledge economy*. Oxford: Oxford University Press.
Gibbons, R. A. (1998). Incentives in organizations. *Journal of Economic Perspective, 12*(4), 115–132.
Gilbert, G., & Doran, J. (1994). *Simulating societies: The computer simulation of social phenomena*. London: UCL Press.
Gilbert, N., & Troitzch, K. (2005). Simulation for the social scientist. *Journal of Management and Governance, 12*(2), 225–231.
Gouldner, A. W. (1960). The norm of reciprocity: A preliminary statement. *American Sociological Review, 2*(2), 161–178.
Grandori, A. (2001). Neither hierarchy nor identity: Knowledge-governance mechanisms and the theory of the firm. *Journal of Management and Governance, 5*, 381–399.
Guo, J. (2009). Collaborative conceptualization: Towards a conceptual foundation of interoperable electronic product catalogue system design. *Enterprise Information Systems, 3*(1), 59–94.
Hales, D., Edmonds, B., Norling, E., & Rouchier, J. (2003). Multi-agent-based simulation III, MABS 2003. In *MABS*. Lecture Notes in Computer Science (Vol. 2927). New York: Springer.
Hanaki, N., Peterhansl, A., Dodds, P. S., & Watts, D. J. (2007). Cooperation in evolving social networks. *Management Science, 53*(7), 1036–1050.
He, J., & Wang, H. (2009). Innovative knowledge assets and economic performance. *Academy of Management Journal, 52*(5), 919–938.

Hilton, M. (2008). Skills for work in the 21st century: What does the research tell us? *Academy of Management Perspectives, 22*(4), 63–78.
Hodgsson, G. M. (1999). *Economics and Utopia*. New York: Routledge.
Homans, G. C. (1958). Social behavior as exchange. *American Journal of Sociology, 63*(6, Émile Durkheim-Georg Simmel 1858-1958), 597–606.
Homans, G. C. (1961). *Social behaviour: Its elementary form*. New York: Brace & World.
Hughes, R. I. (1999). *The Ising model, computer simulation, and universal physics*. New York, NY: Cambridge University Press.
Jelasity, M., Voulgaris, S., Guerraoui, R., Kermarrec, A.-M., & van Steen, M. (2007). Gossip-based peer sampling. *ACM Transactions on Computer Systems, 25*(3), 8.
Jones, C. (2004). Teleworking: The quiet revolution. Technical report, The Gartner Group.
Konosky, M. A., & Pugh, S. D. (1994). Citizenship behaviour and social exchange. *Academy of Management Journal, 37*(3), 656–669.
Korsgaard, M. A., Schweiger, D. M., & Sapienza, H. J. (1995). The role of procedural justice in building commitment, attachment, and trust in strategic decision-making teams. *Academy of Management Journal, 38*(1), 60–84.
Kreps, D. M., Milgrom, P., Roberts, J., & Wilson, R. (1982). Rational cooperation in the finitely repeated prisoners' dilemma. *Journal of Economic Theory, 27*(2), 245–252.
Li, H., & Wang, H. (2007). A multi-agent-based model for a negotiation support system in electronic commerce. *Enterprise Information Systems, 1*(4), 457–472.
Lida, X., Huimin, L., Song, W., & Kanliang, W. (2009). Modeling and analysis techniques for cross-organizational workflow systems. *Systems Research and Behavioral Science, 26*(3), 367–389.
MacDuffie, J. P. (2007). Chapter 12: HRM and distributed work. *The Academy of Management Annals, 1*(1), 549–615.
Marcozzi, A., Hales, D., Jesi, G. P., Arteconi, S., & Babaoglu, O. (2005). Tag-based cooperation in peer-to-peer networks with newscast. *Frontiers in Artificial Intelligence and Applications, 135*, 396.
McAdams, J. L., & Hawk, E. J. (1994). *Organizational performance and rewards: 663 experiences in making the link*. Phoenix: American Compensation Association.
McAfee, A. P. (2006). Enterprise 2.0: The dawn of emergent collaboration. *MIT Sloan Management Review, 47*(3), 21–28.
McKinsey & Company (2007). How businesses are using Web 2.0: A McKinsey's Global Survey. Technical Report, McKinsey & Company.
Molm, L. D. (2003). Theoretical comparison of forms of exchange. *Sociological Theory, 21*(1), 1–17.
Molm, L. D., Quist, T. M., & Wiseley, P. A. (1993). Reciprocal justice and strategies of exchange. *Social Forces, 72*(1), 19–44.
Molm, L. D., Takahashi, N., & Peterson, G. (2000). Risk and trust in social exchange: An experimental text of a classical proposition. *American Journal of Sociology, 105*(5), 1396–1427.
Moorman, R. H., Blakely, G. L., & Niehoff, B. P. (1998). Does perceived organizational support mediate the relationship between procedural justice and organizational citizenship behaviour. *The Academy of Management Journal, 41*(3), 351–357.
Niehoff, B. P., & Moorman, R. H. (1993). Justice as a mediator of the relationship between methods of monitoring and organizational citizenship behaviour. *The Academy of Management Journal, 36*(3), 527–556.
Organ, D. (1988). *Organizational citizenship behavior: The good soldier syndrome*. Lexington: Basic Books.
Ouchi, W. (1979). A conceptual framework for the design of organization control mechanisms. *Management Science, 25*(9), 833–848.
Ouchi, W. G. (1980). Markets, bureaucracies, and clans. *Administrative Science Quarterly, 25*(1), 129–141.

Rapoport, A., & Chammah, A. (1965). *Prisoner's dilemma*. Ann Arbor: University of Michigan Press.

Riolo, R. L., Cohen, M. D., & Axelrod, R. (2001). The evolution of cooperation without reciprocity. *Nature, 414*(22), 441–443.

Saxberg, B. O., & Slocum, J. W. (1968). The management of scientific manpower. *Management Science, 14*(8), B473–B489.

Smith, C. A., Organ, D. W., & Near, J. P. (1983). Organizational citizenship behavior: Its nature and antecedents. *Journal of Applied Psychology, 68*, 653–663.

Smith, K. G., Carroll, S. J., & Ashford, S. J. (1995). Intra and interorganizational cooperation: Towards a research agenda. *Academy of Management Journal, 38*(1), 7–23.

Thibaut, J., & Kelley, H. H. (1959). *The social psychology of groups*. New York: Wiley.

Valve. (2012). *Handbook or new employees*. Bellevue: Valve Press/Valve Corporation.

Van Dyne, L., Graham, J. W., & Dienesch, R. M. (1994). Organizational citizenship behavior: Construct redefinition, measurement and validation. *The Academy of Management Journal, 37*(3), 765–802.

Wenan, T., Bosheng, Z., Weiming, S., Lida, X., & Ling, L. (2008). A business process intelligence system for enterprise process performance management. *IEEE Transactions on SMC Part C, 38*(6), 745–756.

Wenan, T., Yichen, X., Wei, X., Lida, X., Xianhua, Z., Li, W., et al. (2010). A methodology toward manufacturing grid-based virtual enterprise operation platform. *Enterprise Information Systems, 4*(3), 283–309.

Williamson, O. (1981). The economics of organization: The transaction cost approach. *American Journal of Sociology, 87*, 548–577.

Xu, L., Wang, C., Luo, X., & Zhongzhi, S. (2006). Integrating knowledge management and ERP in enterprise information systems. *Systems Research and Behavioral Science, 23*(2), 147–156.

Zenger, T. D. (1994). Explaining organizational diseconomies of scale in R&D: Agency problems and the allocation of engineering talent, ideas, and effort by firm size. *Management Science, 40*(6), 708–729.

Zenger, T. D., & Marshall, C. R. (2000). Determinants of incentive intensity in group-based rewards. *Academy of Management Journal, 43*(2), 149–163.

Zenger, T. R., & Hesterly, W. S. (1997). The disaggregation of corporations: Selective intervention, high-powered incentives, and molecular units. *Organization Science, 8*(3), 209–222.

Zhang, Y., & Bhattacharyya, S. (2007). Effectiveness of Q-learning as a tool for calibrating agent-based supply network models. *Enterprise Information Systems, 1*(2), 217–233.

Chapter 7
Conceptualizing and Modeling Multi-Level Organizational Co-evolution

Dermot Breslin, Daniela Romano, and James Percival

Abstract This chapter stresses the need for research in organizations to reflect the co-evolutionary and complex nature of the changing world we live in today. We argue that key concepts can be abstracted from biological evolution, and used as a starting point for the conceptual development of such approaches. In addition, computational modeling techniques can be used not only as a tool for shaping this conceptual development, but simulating changing behaviors at multiple levels in real organizations. While a number of researchers have developed co-evolutionary accounts of organizational change, these efforts have been constrained by an entity interpretation of the unit of co-evolution. In this latter view, it is assumed that organizations act as vehicles for bundles of routines, being subject to external selection forces only. As a result change occurs largely through the actions of customers or senior executives. We argue that practice-based interpretations offer an alternative approach in the modeling of co-evolution, unpacking the complexity and interconnected agency within and beyond organizations. Building on these conceptual foundations, we outline key conceptual, empirical, and ethical challenges in developing related computational models. We argue that such simulation models can be used by managers to help them navigate complex future worlds.

Keywords Organizational co-evolution • Multi-level studies • Agent-based modeling • Routines • Variation-selection-retention

D. Breslin (✉)
Sheffield University Management School, Conduit Road, Sheffield, UK
e-mail: d.breslin@Sheffield.ac.uk

D. Romano
Department of Computer Science, University of Sheffield, Regents Court, Sheffield, UK
e-mail: d.romano@sheffield.ac.uk

J. Percival
Sheffield University Management School, Conduit Road, Sheffield, UK

Department of Computer Science, University of Sheffield, Regents Court, Sheffield, UK
e-mail: aca08jsp@sheffield.ac.uk

D. Secchi, M. Neumann (eds.), *Agent-Based Simulation of Organizational Behavior*, DOI 10.1007/978-3-319-18153-0_7

7.1 Introduction

As we move into the twenty-first century, organizations find themselves increasingly interconnected with other firms, customers, and stakeholders in fast moving business environments. Faced with these turbulent and competitive changes, firms need not only to adapt, but also to co-evolve in order to survive (Murmann, 2013). In addition to the pace of environmental change, business environments are increasingly complex and interconnected (McCarthy, Lawrence, Wixted, & Gordon, 2010), and a co-evolutionary approach is well suited to study such regimes of change, with some calling for research to adopt a "more encompassing, co-evolutionary perspective" (Lewin & Volberda 2011, p. 242). In the co-evolutionary view practices, competences and strategic initiatives are seen to co-evolve through the interaction of individuals, groups, and managers (Lewin & Volberda, 1999; Rosenkopf & Nerkar, 1999; Volberda & Lewin, 2003), as organizations adapt to meet the changing needs of the external environment. In this sense, co-evolution can be defined as the joint evolution of entities at multiple levels (Campbell, 1990; Lewin & Volberda, 1999; Murmann, 2003) where changes of one entity/level influence changes at other entity/levels (Kauffman, 1993; McKelvey, 1999). In this narrative, the focus of the story shifts from that of the visionary, directional entrepreneur or senior executive (that one still finds in the financial and business press), to a complexity of voices, interrelationships and co-evolving parts, reflective of what most practicing managers experience in their daily lives.

The notion of co-evolution offers scholars the potential to draw from similar approaches taken in other areas of research beyond organization studies, "integrating micro- and macro-level evolution within a unifying framework, incorporating multiple levels of analyses and contingent effects, and leading to new insights, new theories, new empirical methods, and new understandings" (Lewin & Volberda, 1999, p. 520). A number of researchers have explored the notion of co-evolution (Rodrigues & Child, 2003; Volberda & Lewin, 2003), with studies examining (co)evolutionary processes in internationalization strategies (Koza, Tallman, & Ataay, 2011), off-shoring of business services (Lewin & Volberda, 2011), networks (Dantas & Bell, 2011), organizational adaptation (O'Reilly & Tushman, 2008), organizational learning (Crossan, Maurer, & White, 2013), and organizational practices (Pentland, Feldman, Becker, & Liu, 2012; Pentland, Hærem, & Hillison, 2010). Despite these recent calls for a co-evolutionary narrative, few studies have drawn from the theoretical approaches used to study co-evolutionary processes in other scientific domains such as biology, psychology, or cultural evolution (Abatecola, 2012, 2014; Breslin, 2014; Murmann, 2013). A number of these latter researchers have used the variation, selection, and retention framework from evolutionary theory to put forward conceptual descriptions of multi-level evolution within organizations (Aldrich, 1999; Baum & Singh, 1994; Breslin, 2011a; Murmann, 2003; Rosenkopf & Nerkar, 1999). We argue that this variation-selection-retention framework provides a solid foundation for the conceptual development of organizational co-evolution.

Given the complexity of organizational co-evolution, some researchers have developed computational models as a means of advancing theory, building on the evolutionary concepts of variation-selection-retention (Breslin, 2014; Bruderer & Singh, 1996; Lant & Mezias, 1990, 1992; Mezias & Glynn, 1993). However many of these accounts assume that the organization behaves as one, with an all powerful top management team making choices on behalf of the wider firm (Bruderer & Singh, 1996; Lant & Mezias, 1992; Mezias & Glynn, 1993). As argued above, this latter perspective seems to be at odds with the view that most organizations are characterized by a complexity of interacting parts. Therefore in this chapter, we seek to make a contribution towards this project, exploring the potential of a co-evolutionary approach to study multi-level change in organizations. Given the complex longitudinal nature of changing behavior in organizations, we argue that the development of theory can be further enhanced through the use of simulation models, which allow the researcher to explore these complex processes over time (Carley & Hill, 2001; Lant & Mezias, 1990; Lomi, Larsen, & Wezel, 2010). Such computational models can capture the contextual and historical complexity of changing organizational behavior (March, 2001), as the path-dependent co-evolution of interacting parts is modeled over time. However unlike previous studies of this nature, this study focuses on the co-evolution of behavior at multiple-levels between interacting individuals, based on the evolutionary mechanisms of variation, selection, and retention. In addition, we examine key empirical challenges relating to the development of such modeling techniques in the simulation of change in real organizations.

7.2 Conceptualizing Organizational Co-evolution

In developing theory-led co-evolutionary accounts, Baum and Singh (1994) stress the importance of defining and identifying units of analysis at each level within an organizational hierarchy. This need to explicitly define units of co-evolution becomes even more paramount when developing simulation models. These co-evolving units need to be discrete classes of "entities" with their own evolutionary path, yet at the same time interact with "entities" at other levels. As noted above, while a number of scholars have adopted the word co-evolution to describe the multi-level interactions within organizations (see Huygens, Van Den Bosch, Volberda, & Baden-Fuller, 2001; Jones, 2001; Rodrigues & Child, 2003; Volberda & Lewin, 2003), few have drawn from other domains of study to further develop the theoretical foundations of such a co-evolutionary approach. Over the past 40 years an emerging group of researchers have explored the possibility of developing a theory-led evolutionary approach to studying organizational adaptation (Aldrich, 1999; Breslin, 2011b; Burgelman, 1991; Campbell, 1965; Hannan & Freeman, 1977; Hodgson & Knudsen, 2004; McKelvey, 1982; Nelson & Winter, 1982; Weick, 1979). As noted above, a number of these have developed the mechanisms of variation, selection, and retention to give a conceptual account of evolution in organizations, and populations of organizations. More recently a consensus amongst a group of these scholars has emerged around the use of these three mechanisms and the additional concepts of the replicator and interactor. The replicator-interactors are abstracted concepts from biological evolution, where the replicators are defined as anything in the universe of which copies are made such as genes in the biological world. Interactors have been defined as entities that interact as a cohesive whole with their environment in a way that causes differential replication of these elements (Hull, 1988). The use of the replicator-interactor concept, alongside variation-selection-retention, has been labeled the Generalized Darwinist approach, which argues that at a sufficiently general level of abstraction a core set of general "Darwinian" principles can be used to describe evolution within a variety of domains (Aldrich et al., 2008; Breslin, 2011b; Campbell, 1965; Hodgson, 2003; Hodgson & Knudsen, 2004), including biology, psychology, culture, and economics. In this manner, whilst the details of socio-economic evolution may be different from biological evolution, the concept of Generalized Darwinism can nonetheless be used as the starting point for the development of theory in both.

Scholars who have studied organizational co-evolution through this evolutionary lens have focused on the routine as the unit that co-evolves. In many respects the adoption of the routine dates back to the notion of the "routine as gene" introduced in Nelson and Winter's (1982) seminal work "An evolutionary theory of economic change." While the concept is generally defined as a collective phenomenon, whose enactment results in recurrent patterns of action (Becker, 2005; Nelson & Winter, 1982), different conceptualizations have resulted in quite distinct evolutionary narratives emerging. Some have tended to conceptualize the routine as a capability or entity (Breslin, 2015; Rerup & Feldman, 2011), with a focus on how these phenomena influence wider organizational performance (Parmigiani & Howard-Grenville, 2011). For instance, Nelson and Winter (1982) conceptualized the routine as a reflex-like, automatic process in which individuals within a group respond to certain stimuli with a particular set of repeated actions. Through reinforcement or conditioning certain behavioral responses become associated with certain stimuli over time, resulting in repeated patterns of actions. Interlocking, conditional, and sequential behaviors between individuals (Hodgson, 2008), and associated socio-political truces and coalitions (Cyert & March, 1963; Nelson & Winter, 1982) act to maintain the status quo. As a result, it is assumed that routines are enacted in an automatic sense, varying little over time, and so their evolution largely depends on external selection forces acting on the organization, as opposed to endogenous change by the individuals enacting them (Feldman & Pentland, 2003). This dualism of the routine and organization is carried over in the conceptualization of the replicator-interactor (Breslin, 2015). It is thus argued that the fate of these routines is inextricably linked to that of the organization (Hodgson, 2008; Hodgson & Knudsen, 2010). Over time organizations coalesce as entities, as founding entrepreneurs gain control of resources, with externals treating it "as an ecological entity, a social unit with a life of its own" (Aldrich & Ruef, 2006, p. 94). The greater the pressures for coherence within the organization, the more change will occur at the "level of the entire entity" (Aldrich & Ruef, 2006, p. 129). Organizational evolution is thus viewed as the study of self-replicating entities (i.e., routines), where replication is affected by external selective pressure (Warglien, 2002), overlooking the internal dynamics of change *within* routines themselves. However this routine-organization dualism (and associated evolutionary accounts) has been criticized, as the voice of the individual and agency is lost, excluding the possibility of intentionality, learning (Witt, 2004), motivation, creativity, imagination, and deliberate adaptations (Cordes, 2006).

This routine-as-entity view has been heavily criticized not only from an evolutionary perspective (Breslin, 2011b; Witt, 2004) but from within the routines literature itself (Parmigiani & Howard-Grenville, 2011; Rerup & Feldman, 2011). Some have put forward a "practice" view of routines (Parmigiani & Howard-Grenville, 2011), in which the focus shifts to parts of routines (Rerup & Feldman, 2011), how they are enacted day-to-day and their internal dynamics. Parmigiani and Howard-Grenville (2011) argue that the practice perspective opens the black box of routines and their internal workings in specific organizational contexts. While the definition of the routine as a repetitive pattern of actions is similar to the entity approach, the emphasis here is on how these patterns are produced and reproduced, and to what extent the patterns remain stable versus change over time (Parmigiani & Howard-Grenville, 2011). Pentland and Feldman (2005) introduced the ostensive-performative duality to conceptualize this adaptive, improvisational nature of routines. They define the performative aspect of the routine as the "actual performances by specific people, at specific times, in specific places," as opposed to the ostensive aspect of routines which are "abstract or generalized patterns that participants use to guide, account for and refer to specific performances of a routine" (Pentland & Feldman, 2005, p. 795). Feldman and Pentland (2003) argue that making a distinction between these two levels, captures the interaction between them as they adapt over time to suit changing contexts. Evolutionary accounts have likewise been developed in which the replicator-interactor is defined through the ostensive-performative duality (Breslin, 2008, 2011b; Feldman & Pentland, 2003; Pentland et al., 2010, 2012). In this manner, behaviors (as represented by the performative aspect) are varied and selectively retained through the ostensive aspect over time, or in other words variations in performance are selectively retained through the guiding story or ostensive aspect (Feldman & Pentland, 2003).

This "practice" move marks a conceptual shift in emphasis in the story of organizational change and co-evolution. In the entity approach, change is seen to occur through the selection "of" organizations which act as vehicles "for" the underlying routines (Hodgson & Knudsen, 2010). In this sense, the routine represents the replicator and the organization the interactor (Baum & Singh, 1994; Hodgson & Knudsen, 2010; Murmann, 2003; Nelson & Winter, 1982). In the practice view, change is seen to occur within the routine, with variation-selection-retention acting on the mutually constitutive duality of the ostensive-performative aspect. In this "evolution-as-practice" account, the performances are thus the phenotypic expression of an underlying genotypic logic as represented by the ostensive aspect (Breslin, 2015).

7.2.1 From Entity to Practice: Implications for the Conceptualization of Co-evolution

In this move from entity to practice, a replicator-interactor duality is proposed with the former interpreted as the "stored information," and the latter it's behavioral "expression" or enacted "manifestation" (Breslin, 2015; Breslin & Jones, 2012; Plotkin, 1994; Warglien, 2002). In this view knowledge cannot be seen to be accumulated or indeed separated from the specific activity or practice involved (Orlikowski, 2002). As Miner (1994) notes, many evolutionary accounts treat knowledge as entities independent of the individuals enacting them, thus ignoring social interaction. Therefore to link the replicator (as a repository of knowledge) with the socially constructed concept of the organization becomes problematic. For example, accumulated knowledge can pass between organizations and through spin-outs (Aldrich & Ruef, 2006; Breslin, 2011b; Szulanski, 2000; Szulanski & Winter, 2002). "So organizational boundaries are not sealed, because cultural norms and practices, institutional requirements, and flows of people permeate them" (Aldrich & Ruef, 2006, p. 130). Moreover, knowledge can be discontinued within organizations, as groups innovate, change, and improvise behaviors (Argyris & Schon, 1978). Given differences in personal dispositions and life histories, pockets of knowledge can also form within subgroups, despite the pressure for coherence at an organizational level (Aldrich & Ruef, 2006). As a result organizations are rarely truly monolithic (Aldrich & Ruef, 2006). As a consequence the "life" of the knowledge is not always tied to the "life" of one particular group or organization. Knowledge-in-practice, on the other hand, is tied to the fate of the practice and not the organization. It cannot be assumed that this continually evolving knowledge-in-practice is a static entity, subject to forces acting beyond the boundaries of the group or even organization. Its maintenance or variation occurs through the continual interrelationship between local performances and abstracted structure (Feldman & Orlikowski, 2011). Therefore, it is through the individuals enacting and participating in the activity, that this knowledge is played out, and not through the actions of some distant managers pulling strings like puppeteers. The "replication" of knowledge can only occur through involvement and participation of others in the activity (Brown & Duguid, 1991; Lave & Wenger, 1990), as opposed to being "transferred" in some entity-like fashion. In sum, in this view the evolution of knowledge is subsumed within the practice, as individuals "learn to evolve" (Breslin & Jones, 2012).

As noted above the entity view of the replicator-interactor concept assumes the organization acts as a vehicle for bundles of replicators (Hodgson & Knudsen, 2010). So with increasing levels of organizational coherence, selective forces shift from evolving routines and schemata to the organization itself as an entity (Aldrich & Ruef, 2006). The focus of attention thus remains largely at the level of the organization, with at best managers making choices on behalf of the firm (Levitt & March, 1988), and as a result above the level of individual learning (Schulz, 2002). This becomes somewhat problematic when examining the co-evolution of routines within the organization itself. Addressing this problem, some have expanded the entity view by identifying units of evolution at different levels of analysis (Baum & Singh, 1994; Hodgson & Knudsen, 2010). For example, Baum and Singh (1994) make a distinction between genealogical entities (replicators) that "pass on their information largely intact in successive replications," and ecological entities (interactors) that are the "structural and behavioral expressions of the genealogical entities, interact with the environment and this interaction causes replication to be differential" (Baum & Singh, 1994, p. 4) at each level in the organizational hierarchy. So the "routine-job" represents the micro-level, moving to the "organization-organization" and "species-population" at higher levels 2. Nascent and growing organizations can use abstractly defined idiosyncratic jobs to build organizational knowledge and so develop routines which are better fit to the emerging market (Aldrich & Ruef, 2006). More recently Hodgson and Knudsen (2010) argue that the "habit-individual" represent the micro-level, with the "routine-group" and "routine-organization" representing higher levels.

Despite the multi-level nature of these proposed solutions, there is still an inherent assumption that evolving routines are terminally tied to the individuals, groups, and organizations concerned (Breslin, 2015). As noted above in many cases, this link has been focused on the organization as an entity, with the assumption being that integrative forces within the organization result in change largely occurring at the level of the firm (Aldrich & Ruef, 2006). If one assumes, however, that organizational cultures are fragmented or differentiated, then clearly the unit of selection shifts within the firm itself. So, selection "of" these individuals and groups results in the selection "for" associated ideas, routines, and knowledge (Hodgson & Knudsen, 2010). However, such an interpretation of selection downplays choices made by the individuals concerned (Witt, 2005). Selection "for" routines gives primacy to the selective powers "of" the world external to the phenomena (e.g., managers, customers, etc). In this way, poorly performing routines eventually become extinct as managers select different groups and individuals, or customers select different organizations. On the other hand, if individuals are viewed as "selecting" habits or routines for enactment through the choices they make, then clearly foresight, anticipation of futures, and the interpretation of feedback from the external world come to the fore.

With practice-based evolutionary accounts, the replicator-interactor concept is represented as a mutually constituted duality of cognitive representations and manifest behaviors. However most of these accounts again tend to focus exclusively on only one level of analysis. For example, Pentland et al. (2012) focus on the group as a level of analysis, with routines evolving and adapting in a mutually constitutive relationship between the ostensive guide and performative aspect. However, as noted above some have identified units of analysis at different levels in the development of co-evolutionary accounts (Mesoudi, 2010; Plotkin, 1994). So individuals and collective cognitive structures represent the replicators at the level of the individual, group, and organization, respectively (Breslin, 2008). The corresponding interactor depends on the "micro-environment within which selection occurs, namely the set of actions performed by individuals, groups or firms" (Breslin, 2008, p. 412). A simple example of a product design group can help illustrate Breslin's (2008) account of the co-evolutionary processes acting at each level.

Individual Level When completing a task such as an engineering calculation, individuals within the product development group can chose to select either a collective routine associated with that task, such as a "standard calculation" routine, which they share with other members of the group, or they may chose to carry out a calculation habit which only they use. The individual can also attempt to vary replicators at both levels by changing their individual calculation habit or by persuading others to alter the more collective "standard calculation" routine. Once selected by the individual, the routine or habit is then enacted through the individual's actions, which in turn receive feedback from external parties, such as other members of the group, managers, and customers (Breslin, 2008). Based on the particular strength of these feedback signals, these variants of replicators are retained over time. So, for instance, if the individual interpreted the use of the calculation habit as resulting in better quality designs, the individual might choose to retain this habit over time. This individual-level evolutionary process is in turn nested within the evolution of collective routines within the group.

Group Level At the level of the group, each individual might choose to enact both individual habits, as outlined above, and collective routines. Again individuals are capable of attempting to vary and select these replicators. However, now the enactment and feedback from other group members is played out within the selection mechanism of the group. Through communication, dialogue, and negotiation (Brown & Duguid, 1991; Lave & Wenger, 1990), the individual selection mechanisms are reconciled within the collective selection mechanism, resulting in a set of group actions which then receive feedback from the world external to the group. Each individual will interpret feedback both from other individuals and the world outside the group, including managers and customers (Daft & Weick, 1984; March & Olsen, 1975). In this way whilst one individual might interpret feedback based on the use of the collective standard calculation routine as positive, another individual might interpret this differently and call for a modification in the calculation routine. Over time different interpretations are resolved within the group through dialogue, negotiation, and socialization (Lave & Wenger, 1990) as routines are retained.

Organizational Level At a higher level, the evolutionary processes of each group are played out within the context of the organization. The organization will thus be a polythetic collection of individual habits, collective routines, and now organizational routines. This collection of replicators is polythetic in the sense that the existence of routines does not exclude the coexistence of individual habits and after the formation of the routine individuals can continue to adopt both group routines and individual habits. In this way, whilst individuals may be the agents enacting both group routines and individual habits, the replicators at each level are discrete in the sense that selection occurs at both levels, depending on the differential degree of fitness. Therefore whilst different groups within the organization develop routines in the completion of activities such as *idea generation, idea screening,* and *product development*, they also "share" broader organizational routines associated, for instance, with the management of project documentation and information through the company's information system. Individuals and groups can attempt to persuade others within the company to vary these organizational routines, perhaps by presenting alternative approaches to, for instance, project documentation. Individuals and groups can also choose to select this organizational routine, or may even choose to select alternative group-level routines or even individual-level habits associated with data management. Again these decisions to retain individual habits, group or organizational routines will depend upon the feedback from other groups, managers, and agents external to the organization, such as customers.

In summary, the co-evolutionary narrative one develops differs depending on whether one uses an entity- or practice-based interpretation of the replicator-interactor. In the former account, routines are viewed as repositories tied to the life of individuals and groups. The evolution of these entities is experiential and as a result path dependent. In practice-based narratives, knowledge is viewed as being enacted in practice, and having an existence through those actions. As a result they are not necessarily tied to the fate of the individuals and groups concerned. Individuals can change and learn, with capabilities and knowledge struggling for survival in the collective "mind space" (Dobson, Breslin, Suckley, Barton, & Rodriguez, 2013). Examining these differences in approach taken, the choice to use a practice- or entity-perspective depends on the relationship between organizational and environmental change. In the entity view, one largely assumes that the external environment (or that external to the entity in question) changes more rapidly than the associated individual or group. As a result, routines are selected "for," by the selection "of" carrying individuals. On the other hand, if one adopts a practice view, then one assumes that individuals and groups can adapt dynamically (and indeed prospectively) to external change. So while multi-level narratives can be developed using both approaches, the different positions taken reflect the long-standing dichotomy between deterministic and voluntaristic perspectives (Abatecola, 2012). In the former it is assumed that structural inertia and environmental change have primacy, whereas in the latter adaptation and strategic choice hold sway (Abatecola, 2012; Breslin, 2008).

7.3 Modeling Organizational Co-evolution

Conceptualizations of organizational co-evolution can be further developed through computational modeling techniques. A variety of computational techniques have been used to simulate evolving behavior in organizations, including nonlinear differential equation modeling (Rahmandad & Sterman, 2008), system dynamics (Larsen & Lomi, 2002), and agent-based approaches. System dynamics models are designed to depict dynamic causal theories in which interacting variables influence each other over time (Sastry, 2001). This approach thus highlights feedback processes, or circular causal relationships in which variables influence and, in turn, respond to each other. Agent-based approaches, on the other hand, view the organization as a complex social system, and recognize that much of this complexity is due to the interactions between multiple heterogeneous agents. These agent–agent interactions thus shape the emergence and development of wider system-level patterns of behavior. A key advantage in using computational techniques in general is that they can capture the contextual and historical complexity of changing organizational behavior (March, 2001), and as a result help develop formal theories (Lomi et al., 2010; Sastry, 1997). Agent-based approaches can simulate the path-dependent co-evolution of interacting parts is modeled over time, allowing the researcher to carry out experiments that would be impossible in live organizations. In this manner, one can test for counterfactual conditionals, where the experimenter seeks to identify what would have been the case if the antecedent in a causal relationship were true (although it is not true). In addition to the conceptual advantages of developing computational models, they can also be used to simulate and validate real-life case studies. Models can therefore allow researchers and practitioners to unpack the complexity of organizational life, and uncover "hidden" generative mechanisms driving or resisting change over time.

A number of scholars have thus used simulation techniques to model change within organizations, both using the variation-selection-retention framework (Bruderer & Singh, 1996; Lant & Mezias, 1990, 1992; Mezias & Glynn, 1993; Pentland et al., 2012) and focusing on the tension between stability and change (Lant & Mezias, 1992), or incremental and radical change (Mezias & Glynn, 1993), in which routines are the focus on analysis. In many of these previous simulation studies, an entity approach has been taken as outlined above. In many respects, conceptualizing organizational change through the mechanisms of variation-selection-retention has many similarities with models of learning (Bruderer & Singh, 1996; Lant & Mezias, 1990, 1992; Mezias & Glynn, 1993). Agency is introduced with managers varying, selecting and retaining routines in response to performance and organizational aspiration levels. So managers search for variations in routines in response to shortfalls between actual and aspired levels of performance. These variants are selected if managers perceive the performance to be favorable (Levitt & March, 1988)—though uncertainty and ambiguity surround this interpretation (March & Olsen, 1975). And finally "successful" routines are retained which in the process can lead to organizational inertia. Given the entity approach taken in these models, the link between the routine and the organization as a level of analysis is still retained. In this sense, the routine-organization might be seen as the replicator-interactor. As in most entity approaches, external selection forces are viewed as the key driving force behind the evolution of the organization over time. It is therefore assumed that the firm behaves as one, with an all powerful top management team making choices on behalf of the wider organization (Bruderer & Singh, 1996; Lant & Mezias, 1992; Mezias & Glynn, 1993). For example, Bruderer and Singh (1996) accommodate both choice and learning by a top management team, and subsequent selection of the organization based on its performance. Thus we have an external "selected of" organizations and groups, "for" the underlying routines (Hodgson & Knudsen, 2010; Lant & Mezias, 1992; Larsen & Lomi, 2002; Mezias & Glynn, 1993). More recently researchers have modeled organizational change, shifting the focus of attention onto groups and individuals within the organizations (Breslin, 2014; Holtz, 2014; Kahl, this edition; Miller et al., 2014; Thomsen, this edition). Given the focus of agent-based modeling on multi-agent interaction, the approach is thus clearly well suited to simulating changing patterns of behavior within organizations. Taking a co-evolutionary approach, the mechanisms of variation-selection-retention are now played out in the choices, interactions and behaviors of agents, as represented by the individuals and groups in the organization (Breslin, 2014). In addition, selection is now represented through the choices made by agents based on feedback received from all others (not just external selection) following enacted behaviors. In this way, a practice-based interpretation of the replicator-interactor is assumed.

Assuming such a practice-based interpretation of organizational change, and following the multi-level conceptualization given above, computational representations can be developed. In such models the co-evolution of routines at different hierarchical levels in the organization is simulated including the individual-, group- and organizational-levels. Given the practice-based assumptions, all individuals and groups can influence the evolution of organizational routines over time, through the mechanisms of variation-selection-retention as shown in Fig. 7.1. Selection therefore is not assumed to occur at the level of the organization or group only, but through the choices made by individuals at all levels. It should be noted that the account presented below is one of the many possible practice-based accounts, and is used here to highlight key empirical issues associated with the development of

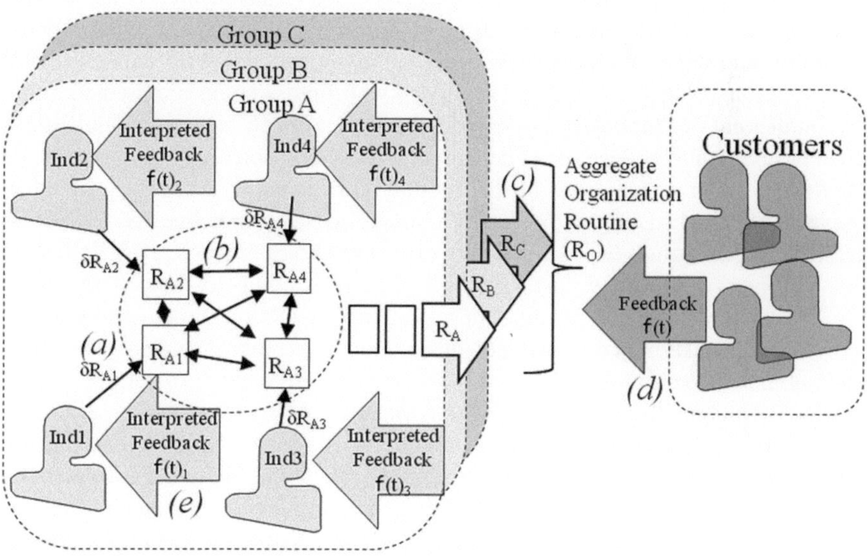

Fig. 7.1 Outline of co-evolutionary model using variation-selection-retention

such approaches. Finally a variety of approaches have been used to represent the routines in these models, ranging from abstract numerical representations (Breslin, 2014), to action sequences (Pentland et al., 2012). For a more complete review of these approaches, please see Kahl's contribution to this volume.

Variation Each individual in the organization makes a unique contribution to the wider organizational routine. In the first instance however, an individual can only directly influence their immediate group of colleagues. At each iteration of the model, each individual (Ind_i) can potentially change the routine, and he/she differs in their capacity to do so. So a more innovative employee will be more able to alter the routine than a less innovative colleague. During each iteration of the model, individual 1 (Ind_1) can change the routine by an amount δR_{A1}, as shown in Fig. 7.1a. Clearly, these values will be different for each individual, and a group consensus is reached through a process of negotiation (see Fig. 7.1b). The more influential the individual, the more they influence this group-level choice (Mezias & Glynn, 1993). So if all individuals have equal influence and power within the group, the consensus value is represented by the "mean" of the individual values. In this way, a negotiated routine R_A emerges (with values R_B and R_C representing groups B and C, respectively). Given that these group routines may also differ, a consensus is similarly reached between the groups through a process of negotiation (see Fig. 7.1c) to arrive at an organizational level routine R_O. Again the degree to which group level routines (R_A, R_B, R_C) influence the aggregate organizational level routine R_O will depend on the influence and power of each group. In this way, individual choices are reconciled within those of the group, whose choices are in turn reconciled within that of the organization as a whole.

Selection The organization routine is then presented to the customer for feedback (see Fig. 7.1d). Past attempts at modeling organizational evolution have used fitness curves or landscapes to represent feedback on organizational performances (Bruderer & Singh, 1996; Lant & Mezias, 1992), with fitness being represented either as a numerical fit (Mezias & Glynn, 1993), or as a match between combinations of gene-like routines (Bruderer & Singh, 1996). As noted above, selection is interpreted in an active sense in this model, with individuals choosing to select routines. So for instance, individual 1 chooses to select practice R_{A1}, which is presented to the group (as outlined above). These choices involve each individual first interpreting customer feedback, and then responding to this, as shown in Fig. 7.1e. The "accuracy" of this interpretation depends on the closeness of the individual in question to the customer, or customer proximity. The greater the value of customer proximity, then the more accurate the individual's interpretation of feedback (Bruderer & Singh, 1996; Lant & Mezias, 1990). Indeed Abatecola (2012) stresses the importance of management (mis)perception on wider organizational adaptation. So it is assumed that frontline employees are closer to the customer and have a more accurate view of what customer wants. Individuals therefore "select" practice R_{A1}, if they perceive the associated "performance" to be favorable—though uncertainty and ambiguity surround this interpretation (March & Olsen, 1975; Levitt & March, 1988). In common with other models of organizational change (Bruderer

& Singh, 1996; Lant & Mezias, 1990, 1992; Mezias & Glynn, 1993), individuals are seen to search for variations in response to shortfalls between actual and aspired levels of performance. The greater the shortfall, then the more the individual will act to change the routine (Bruderer & Singh, 1996; Levitt & March, 1988). So if individual 1 interprets customer feedback to be poor, he will act to change the routine by δR_{A1} (as outlined above). Crucially in this multi-level model, the individual can only propose a change at the level of the individual, based on their interpretation of feedback given at the aggregate level of the organization.

Retention "Successful" routines are retained over time, when an individual interprets feedback as positive. However the exploitation of knowledge in this manner can lead to a build up of behavioral and socio-political inertia within the organization, which can in turn act to suppress subsequent variations (Miller, 1999), thus impairing the firm's ability to respond creatively to changing external conditions (Aldrich, 1999). In this way, success through positive feedback can lead to over-exploitation of existing knowledge, and an inability to adapt to changing customer expectations. So the longer individual 1 continues to enact the same routine R_{A1}, then the more difficult it becomes for that same individual to initiate change (via δR_{A1}) in subsequent iterations. As with other models, and using the metaphor of the inertial clock, it is assumed that this inertial effect of experiential learning is "reset" after each innovative change above a given threshold (Mezias & Glynn, 1993). Given the advantages of increasing learning through competence enhancing (Tushman & Anderson, 1986), individuals will only attempt change when the perceived performance is below a certain aspiration level or threshold.

7.4 Implications for Empirical Investigations

While such multi-level models can be used as a conceptual tool in the development of organizational co-evolutionary theory, they can also be developed to model changing practices in real organizations, provided appropriate representations of those routines are chosen. A number of empirical challenges need to be considered when developing such simulation models. First key characteristics of the organization need to be represented through the model inputs. Second empirical studies need to be designed to capture co-evolving outputs over time.

7.4.1 Model Inputs

Referring to the model description given above, the following key organizational characteristics at a minimum need to be represented.

Organizational Structure As outlined above, the interaction between individuals and groups is determined by key characteristics of the organizational structure

(Breslin, 2014). Therefore, a key input for any model of organizational co-evolution is the structure of the organization, including the identity of individuals and groups, and how they are interconnected. Actual interactions between individual may differ from formal divisional structures, and through techniques such as social network analysis, clearer representations of these interconnections can be made (Dobson et al., 2013; Hanneman, 2001).

Relative Power The negotiation of consensus between individuals and groups, as seen in Fig. 7.1b, c, is determined by the relative power of individuals within groups (Fig. 7.1b), and groups within the organization (Fig. 7.1c). A number of approaches might be taken to capture this. For instance, group leaders and managers can be asked to rate the influence of each individual (or group) relative to others within the group (or organization), using a Likert scale. Such data can be gathered via interviews with managers and based on a range of projects worked on, or a typical project worked on over a period of time. Other approaches might be used to capture the actual interactions between individuals over time. For instance, sociograms can be developed from social network analysis (Cross & Borgatti, 2004), further supported through qualitative research methods, such as periods of observation and interviews. These maps can capture key dimensions of interconnectedness, including how individuals are influenced by others across a range of activities.

Creativity As noted above, each individual i can alter the routine by an amount δR_{Ai}, as shown in Fig. 7.1a. As a result, a measure of creativity is needed for each individual within the organization. A number of measures might be used to capture this. For example, drawing on Holman et al. (2012) a measure for employee creativity is given using self-completion questionnaires (see Table 7.1).

Customer Proximity Finally as noted above each individual interprets customer feedback, and then responds to this, as shown in Fig. 7.1e. The "accuracy" of this interpretation depends on the closeness of the individual in question to the customer, or customer proximity. Drawing on marketing literature, Sin, Tse, Yau, Chow, and Lee's (2005) customer proximity measures can be used again using self-completion questionnaires (see Table 7.2).

Ethical Issues There are clear ethical issues associated with such modeling exercises, and related attempts to represent individuals and groups in simulation studies. Therefore it is imperative that full ethical approval is obtained before

Table 7.1 Measure of individual creativity

In the last year, and in a work context, how often have you done the following (1 = not a lot to 5 = a great deal)?
1. Thought of new ideas
2. Had ideas about how things might be improved
3. Found new ways of doing things
4. Attempted to get support from others for your ideas
5. Tried to get approval for improvements you suggested
6. Got involved in persuading others to adopt your proposals for doing things differently

Table 7.2 Measure of customer proximity

When dealing with the customer to what extent to you agree with the following statements (1 = not a lot to 5 = a great deal)?
1. We both try very hard to establish a long-term relationship
2. We work in close cooperation
3. We keep in touch constantly
4. We communicate and express our opinions to each other frequently
5. We can show our discontent toward each other through communication
6. We can communicate honestly
7. We share the same worldview
8. We share the same opinion about most things
9. We share the same feelings toward things around us
10. We share the same values
11. We always see things from each other's view
12. We know how each other feels
13. We understand each other's values and goals
14. We care about each other's feelings
15. My company regards "never forget a good turn" as our business motto
16. We keep our promises to each other in any situation
17. If our customers gave assistance when my company had difficulties, then I would repay their kindness
18. They are trustworthy on important things
19. My company trusts them

embarking on interviews and questionnaires. Crucially the anonymity of individuals must be assured, to ensure that participants complete the questionnaires as honestly as possible. In this respect, it is important that the gathering of data is administered by researchers, independent to the operational activities and management of the organization. Nonetheless, the representation of individuals and groups, and the process through which these individuals interact is key to developing such simulation studies.

7.4.2 *Model Outputs and Validation*

While a number of scholars have developed conceptual models of organizational evolution (Bruderer & Singh, 1996; Lant & Mezias, 1990, 1992; Mezias & Glynn, 1993; Pentland et al., 2012), few of these have attempted to validate their results using actual data from organizations. Key to validating the model is the choice of output variable which is used to represent changing behaviors within the organization. While change can be captured through the routine, the practice-view clearly presents some challenges for research design. Considering key elements of the preceded narrative above, a number of core issues come to the fore. First co-evolution is by definition a process which occurs over time (Winter, 2012), and as such this temporal dimension must be captured in proposed research methods and design. As a result, longitudinal studies must be seen as key research method. Indeed Parmigiani and Howard-Grenville (2011) note that in general, scholars exploring a practice-view of routines tend to use single case studies, derived from ethnographies and direct observation (Feldman, 2000; Howard-Grenville, 2005; Lazaric & Denis, 2005; Szulanski, 2000). This longitudinal nature gives researchers the opportunity to explore key aspects of the evolutionary dynamic including the emergence, development, and extinction of routines over time (Parmigiani & Howard-Grenville, 2011). In this manner, empirical studies can explore how routines are varied, selected, and replicated within the multi-level complexity of the organization.

Second the replicator-interactor concept is a multi-faceted concept, incorporating interpretive frameworks and enacted behaviors. When studying these routines, some give primacy to the study of performative side (i.e., actions) of the replicator-interactor duality (Pentland et al., 2010; Pentland et al., 2012). For instance, Pentland et al. (2010) argue that expressed behaviors and not potentialities are the best foundation for empirical research on routines. In the absence of observable patterns of behavior it is impossible to tell if a routine exists, and difficult to "observe" the underlying generative mechanisms (Pentland et al., 2010). Instead they argue that the underlying generative mechanisms (ostensive aspect) can be inferred from these patterns of action (Pentland et al., 2012). A number of means of inquiry might be used to capture these performances. First detailed observations can record the "what" and "how" of enacted performances over time. Such methods require a strict adherence to a set recording system, followed by all researchers involved. Ultimately this method is limited to the exposure of the researcher to expressed behaviors.

Alternatively, the actors themselves can record their actions and behaviors. This can be done either by prompting participants to record behaviors at random or regular intervals. In many cases, actors already record their activities through on-line or off-line daily logs of records. The clear advantage in recording such action sequences is that it allows the modeler to capture details of the changing routine, at multiple levels within the organization. A number of techniques might be used to process this longitudinal data into a form useful for validation purposes. For instance, sequential analysis methods (Abbott, 1990) can be used to identify similarities in recorded sequences of activities over time (Salvato, 2009; Turner & Fern, 2012). In this way, each specific activity recorded in daily logs is coded, with similar actions being coded together. Following this coding exercise, each enacted activity is translated into a sequence of coded actions. A distance matrix is generated in which the distances between all pairs of sequences in the data set are computed. Clusters are subsequently generated from this distance matrix to aggregate the sequences into a smaller number of groups, which represent emerging routines (Turner & Fern, 2012). In this manner a detailed log of emerging routines as represented by clusters of action sequences within the organization is captured, which can be compared with outputs from the simulation model via statistical methods.

7.5 Conclusions

This chapter stresses the need for research which reflects the co-evolutionary and complex nature of changing organizations in the world today. We argue that key concepts can be abstracted from biological evolution, and used as a starting point for such approaches. While a number of researchers have taken this latter approach, these efforts have been constrained by an entity interpretation of the unit of co-evolution. Assuming that organizations are vehicles for bundles of routines, and subject to external selection forces only, seems to draw too close a parallel to related biological analogies (Dawkins, 1976). We argue that the practice-based interpretation of the routine, and related co-evolutionary accounts unpacks the complexity and interconnected agency within organizations. Building on these conceptual foundations computational models can be developed to model and simulate behaviors in real organizations. While there are clear ethical considerations in doing so, such simulation models can be used by managers to help them navigate the complex worlds they face on a daily basis.

References

Abatecola, G. (2012). Interpreting corporate crises: Towards a co-evolutionary approach. *Futures, 44*(10), 860–869.

Abatecola, G. (2014). Research in organizational evolution. What comes next? *European Management Journal, 32*(3), 434–443.

Abbott, A. (1990). A primer on sequence methods. *Organization Science, 1*(4), 375–392.

Aldrich, H. (1999). *Organizations evolving*. London: Sage.

Aldrich, H., Hodgson, G., Hull, D., Knudsen, T., Mokyr, J., & Vanberg, V. (2008). In defence of generalized Darwinism. *Journal of Evolutionary Economics, 18*, 577–596.

Aldrich, H., & Ruef, M. (2006). *Organizations evolving*. London: Sage.

Argyris, C., & Schon, D. (1978). *Organizational learning: A theory of action perspective*. Reading, MA: Addison-Wesley Publishing Co.

Baum, J., & Singh, J. (1994). Organizational hierarchies and evolutionary processes: Some reflections on a theory of organizational evolution. In J. Baum & J. Singh (Eds.), *Evolutionary dynamics of organizations* (pp. 3–20). New York: Oxford University Press.

Becker, M. (2005). A framework for applying organizational routines in empirical research: Linking antecedents, characteristics and performance outcomes of recurrent interaction patterns. *Industrial and Corporate Change, 14*(5), 817–846.

Breslin, D. (2008). A review of the evolutionary approach to the study of entrepreneurship. *International Journal of Management Reviews, 10*(4), 399–423.

Breslin, D. (2011a). Interpreting futures through the multi-level co-evolution of organizational practices. *Futures, 43*(9), 1020–1028.

Breslin, D. (2011b). Reviewing a generalized Darwinist approach to studying socio-economic change. *International Journal of Management Reviews, 13*(2), 218–235.

Breslin, D. (2014). Calm in the storm: Simulating the management of organizational evolution. *Futures, 52*, 62–77.

Breslin, D. (2015). What evolves in organizational co-evolution? *Journal of Management & Governance*, DOI 10.1007/s10997-014-9302-0.

Breslin, D., & Jones, C. (2012). The evolution of entrepreneurial learning. *International Journal of Organizational Analysis, 20*(3), 294–308.
Brown, J., & Duguid, P. (1991). Organizational learning and communities-of-practice: Toward a unified view of working, learning, and innovation. *Organization Science, 2*, 40–57.
Bruderer, E., & Singh, J. (1996). Organizational evolution, learning, and selection: A genetic-algorithm-based model. *Academy of Management Journal, 39*(5), 1322–1349.
Burgelman, R. (1991). Intra-organizational ecology of strategy making and organizational adaptation: Theory and field research. *Organization Science, 2*, 239–262.
Campbell, D. (1965). Variation, selection and retention in socio-cultural evolution. In H. Barringer, G. Blanksten, & R. Mack (Eds.), *Social change in developing areas: A reinterpretation of evolutionary theory* (pp. 19–49). Cambridge, MA: Schenkman.
Campbell, D. (1990). Levels of organization, downward causation, and selection-theory approach to evolutionary epistemology. In G. Greeberg & E. Tobach (Eds.), *Theories of the evolution of knowing* (pp. 1–17). Hillsdale, NJ: Lawrence Erlbaum.
Carley, K., & Hill, V. (2001). Structural change and learning within organizations. In A. Lomi & E. Larsen (Eds.), *Dynamics of organizations* (pp. 63–92). Cambridge, MA: The MIT Press.
Cordes, C. (2006). Darwinism in economics: From analogy to continuity. *Journal of Evolutionary Economics, 16*, 529–541.
Cross, R., & Borgatti, S. P. (2004). The ties that share: Relational characteristics that facilitate information seeking. In M. Huysman & V. Wulf (Eds.), *Social capital and information technology* (pp. 137–159). Cambridge, MA: MIT Press.
Crossan, M., Maurer, C., & White, P. (2013). Multilevel mechanisms of organizational learning. Paper presented at the International Conference on Organizational Learning, Knowledge and Capabilities, April, Washington, USA.
Cyert, R., & March, J. (1963). *A behavioral view of the firm* (2nd ed.). Oxford: Blackwell.
Daft, R. L., & Weick, K. E. (1984). Toward a model of organizations as interpretation systems. *Academy of Management Review, 9*(2), 284–295.
Dantas, E., & Bell, M. (2011). The co-evolution of firm-centered knowledge networks and capabilities in late industrializing countries: The case of Petrobras in the offshore oil innovation system in Brazil. *World Development, 39*, 1570–1591.
Dawkins, R. (1976). *The selfish gene*. New York: Oxford University Press.
Dobson, S., Breslin, D., Suckley, L., Barton, R., & Rodriguez, L. (2013). Small firm growth and innovation: An evolutionary approach. *The International Journal of Social Entrepreneurship and Innovation, 14*(2), 69–80.
Feldman, M. (2000). Organizational routines as a source of continuous change. *Organization Science, 11*(6), 611–629.
Feldman, M., & Orlikowski, W. (2011). Theorizing practice and practicing theory. *Organization Science, 22*, 1240–1253.
Feldman, M., & Pentland, B. (2003). Reconceptualizing organizational routines as a source of flexibility and change. *Administrative Science Quarterly, 48*(1), 94–118.
Hannan, M., & Freeman, J. (1977). The population of ecology of organization. *American Journal of Sociology, 82*, 929–964.
Hanneman, R. A. (2001). *Introduction to social network methods*. Riverside: University of California.
Hodgson, G. (2003). The mystery of the routine: The Darwinian destiny of an evolutionary theory of economic change. *Revue économique, 54*, 335–384.
Hodgson, G. (2008). The concept of a routine. In M. Becker (Ed.), *Handbook of organizational routines* (pp. 15–28). Cheltenham, UK: Edward Elgar.
Hodgson, G., & Knudsen, T. (2004). The firm as an interactor: Firms as vehicles for habits and routines. *Journal of Evolutionary Economics, 14*, 281–307.
Hodgson, G., & Knudsen, T. (2010). *Darwin's conjecture: The search for general principles of social and economic evolution*. Chicago: University of Chicago Press.

Holman, D., Totterdell, P., Axtell, C., Stride, C., Port, R., Svensson, R., et al. (2012). Job design and the employee innovation process: The mediating role of learning strategies. *Journal of Business & Psychology, 27*, 177–191.

Holtz, G. (2014). Generating social practices. *Journal of Artificial Societies and Social Simulation, 17*(1).

Howard-Grenville, J. (2005). The persistence of flexible organizational routines: The role of agency and organizational context. *Organization Science, 16*, 618–636.

Hull, D. (1988). *Science as a process*. Chicago: The University of Chicago Press.

Huygens, M., Van Den Bosch, F., Volberda, H., & Baden-Fuller, C. (2001). Co-evolution of firm capabilities and industry competition: Investigating the music industry, 1877–1997. *Organization Studies, 22*, 971–1011.

Jones, C. (2001). Co-evolution of entrepreneurial careers, institutional rules and competitive dynamics in American film, 1895–1920. *Organization Studies, 22*, 911–944.

Kauffman, S. (1993). *The origins of order: Self-organization and selection in evolution*. Oxford: Oxford University Press.

Koza, M., Tallman, S., & Ataay, A. (2011). The strategic assembly of global firms: A micro-structural analysis of local learning and global adaptation. *Global Strategy Journal, 1*, 27–46.

Lant, T., & Mezias, S. (1990). Managing discontinuous change: A simulation study of organizational learning and entrepreneurship. *Strategic Management Journal, 11*, 147–179.

Lant, T., & Mezias, S. (1992). An organizational learning model of convergence and reorientation. *Organization Science, 3*(1), 47–71.

Larsen, E., & Lomi, A. (2002). Representing change: A system model of organizational inertia and capabilities as dynamic accumulation processes. *Simulation Modelling Practice and Theory, 10*, 271–296.

Lave, J., & Wenger, E. (1990). *Situated learning: Legitimate peripheral participation*. Cambridge, UK: Cambridge University Press.

Lazaric, N., & Denis, B. (2005). Routinization and memorization of tasks in a workshop: The case of the introduction of ISO norms. *Industrial and Corporate Change, 14*, 873–896.

Levitt, B., & March, J. (1988). Organizational learning. *The Annual Review of Sociology, 14*, 319–340.

Lewin, A., & Volberda, H. (1999). Prolegomena on co-evolution: A framework for research on strategy and new organizational forms. *Organization Science, 10*(5), 519–534.

Lewin, A., & Volberda, H. (2011). Co-evolution of global sourcing: The need to understand the underlying mechanisms of firm-decisions to offshore. *International Business Review, 20*, 241–251.

Lomi, A., Larsen, E., & Wezel, F. (2010). Getting there: Exploring the role of expectations and preproduction delays in processes of organizational founding. *Organization Science, 21*(1), 132–149.

March, J. (2001). Forward. In A. Lomi & E. Larsen (Eds.), *Dynamics of organizations* (pp. i–xviii). Cambridge, MA: The MIT Press.

March, J., & Olsen, J. (1975). The uncertainty of the past: Organizational learning under ambiguity. *European Journal of Political Research, 3*, 147–171.

McCarthy, I., Lawrence, T., Wixted, B., & Gordon, B. (2010). A multidimensional conceptualization of environmental velocity. *Academy of Management Review, 35*(4), 604–626.

McKelvey, B. (1982). *Organizational systematics: Taxonomy, evolution, classification*. Berkeley, CA: University of California Press.

McKelvey, B. (1999). Avoiding complexity catastrophe in co-evolutionary pockets: Strategies for rugged landscapes. *Organization Science, 10*(3), 294–321.

Mesoudi, A. (2010). *Cultural evolution: How Darwinian theory can explain human culture & synthesize the social sciences*. London: University of Chicago Press.

Mezias, S., & Glynn, M. (1993). The three faces of corporate renewal: Institution, revolution, and evolution. *Strategic Management Journal, 14*(2), 77–101.

Miller, D. (1999). Selection processes inside organizations: The self-reinforcing consequences of success. In J. Baum & B. McKelvey (Eds.), *Variations in organization science. In honor of Donald T. Campbell* (pp. 93–109). New York: Sage.
Miller, K.D., Choi, S., & Pentland, B.T. (2014). The role of transactive memory in the formation of organizational routines. *Strategic Organization, 12*, 109–133
Miner, A. (1994). Seeking adaptive advantage: Evolutionary theory and managerial action. In J. Baum & B. McKelvey (Eds.), *Evolutionary dynamics of organizations* (pp. 76–89). New York: Oxford University Press.
Murmann, J. (2003). *Knowledge and competitive advantage: The co-evolution of firms, technology and national institutions*. New York: Cambridge University Press.
Murmann, J. (2013). The co-evolution of industries and important features of their environments. *Organization Science, 24*, 58–78.
Nelson, R., & Winter, S. (1982). *Evolutionary theory of economic change*. Cambridge, MA: Bellknap.
O'Reilly, C., & Tushman, M. (2008). Ambidexterity as a dynamic capability: Resolving the innovator's dilemma. *Research in Organizational Behavior, 28*, 185–206.
Orlikowski, W. (2002). Knowing in practice: Enacting a collective capability in distributed organizing. *Organization Science, 13*(3), 249–273.
Parmigiani, A., & Howard-Grenville, J. (2011). Routines revisited: Exploring the capabilities and practice perspectives. *The Academy of Management Annals, 5*, 413–453.
Pentland, B., & Feldman, M. (2005). Organizational routines as a unit of analysis. *Industrial and Corporate Change, 14*(5), 793–815.
Pentland, B., Feldman, M., Becker, M., & Liu, P. (2012). Dynamics of organizational routines: A generative model. *Journal of Management Studies, 49*(8), 1484–1508.
Pentland, B., Hærem, T., & Hillison, D. (2010). Comparing organizational routines as recurrent patterns of action. *Organization Studies, 31*, 917–940.
Plotkin, H. (1994). *Darwin machines and the nature of knowledge*. Cambridge, MA: Harvard University Press.
Rahmandad, H., & Sterman, J. (2008). Heterogeneity and network structure in the dynamics of diffusion: Comparing agent-based and differential equation models. *Management Science, 54*(5), 998–1014.
Rerup, C., & Feldman, M. (2011). Routines as a source of change in organizational schemata: The role of trial-and-error learning. *Academy of Management Journal, 54*, 577–610.
Rodrigues, S., & Child, J. (2003). Co-evolution in an institutionalized environment. *Journal of Management Studies, 40*(8), 2137–2162.
Rosenkopf, L., & Nerkar, A. (1999). On the complexity of technological evolution. In J. Baum & B. McKelvey (Eds.), *Variations in organization science. In honor of Donald T. Campbell* (pp. 169–183). New York: Sage.
Salvato, C. (2009). Capabilities unveiled: The role of ordinary activities in the evolution of product development processes. *Organization Science, 20*(2), 384–409.
Sastry, M.A. (1997). Problems and paradoxes in a model of punctuated organizational change. *Administrative Science Quarterly, 42*, 237–275.
Sastry, M. A. (2001). Understanding dynamic complexity in organizational evolution: A system dynamics approach. In A. Lomi & E. R. Larsen (Eds.), *Dynamics of organizations* (pp. 377–404). Cambridge: The MIT Press.
Schulz, M. (2002). Organizational learning. In J. Baum (Ed.), *The Blackwell companion to organizations* (pp. 415–441). Oxford: Blackwell.
Sin, L., Tse, A., Yau, O., Chow, R., & Lee, J. (2005). Market orientation, relationship marketing orientation, and business performance: The moderating effects of economic ideology and industry type. *Journal of International Marketing, 13*(1), 36–57.
Szulanski, G. (2000). Appropriability and the challenge of scope: Banc One routinizes replication. In G. Dosi, R. Nelson, & S. Winter (Eds.), *The nature and dynamics of organizational capabilities* (pp. 69–97). Oxford: Oxford University Press.

Szulanski, G., & Winter, S. (2002). Getting it right the second time. *Harvard Business Review, 80*, 62–69.

Turner, S., & Fern, M. (2012). Examining the stability and variability of routine performances: The effects of experience and context change. *Journal of Management Studies, 49*(8), 1407–1434.

Tushman, M. L., & Anderson, P. (1986). Technological discontinuities and organizational environments. *Administrative Science Quarterly, 31*, 439–465.

Volberda, H., & Lewin, A. (2003). Guest editors' introduction co-evolutionary dynamics within and between firms: From evolution to co-evolution. *Journal of Management Studies, 40*(8), 2111–2136.

Warglien, M. (2002). Intraorganizational evolution. In J. Baum (Ed.), *The Blackwell companion to organizations* (pp. 98–118). Oxford: Blackwell.

Weick, K. (1979). *The social psychology of organizing*. Reading, MA: Addison-Wesley Publishing.

Winter, S. (2012). Capabilities: Their origins and ancestry. *Journal of Management Studies, 49*, 1402–1406.

Witt, U. (2004). On the proper interpretation of 'evolution' in economics and its implications for production theory. *Journal of Economic Methodology, 11*(2), 125–146.

Witt, U. (2005). The evolutionary perspective on organizational change and the theory of the firm. In K. Dopfer (Ed.), *The Evolutionary Foundations of Economics* (pp. 339–364). Cambridge: Cambridge University Press.

Chapter 8
Exploring Aspects of Coordination by Mutual Adjustment in Fluid Teams: An Agent-Based Modeling Approach

Svend E. Thomsen

Abstract This chapter applies an agent-based modeling approach to explore some aspects of team coordination by mutual adjustments. The teams considered here are cross functional teams, either co-located or distributed where individuals with specialized knowledge and skills work simultaneously together to accomplish an interdependent team task. Coordination by mutual adjustment is the joint activity whereby each team member aims to align his actions so that they fit those actions contributed by the other team members. Simon's construct, docility is used as a theoretical lever to cast light on how the composition of teams with respect to individual level differences play out during team members' interaction and the resulting consequences of these differences for team coordination. An agent-based simulation model with agents that worked together on an interdependent team task was created and coded in Java-based NetLogo language. The results from a series of experiments with the model suggest that homogenous teams with team members with moderate rates of docility outperform teams where individuals have either high levels or low levels of docility. The results further suggest that intra-team heterogeneity with respect to team members' docility in most cases makes coordination by mutual adjustment harder to achieve. Discussions of the findings, the contribution to theory, the managerial implications, the limitations, and suggestions for future research finalize the chapter.

Keywords Docility • Agent-based model • Coordination • Mutual adjustment • Fluid teams

S.E. Thomsen (✉)
Department of Leadership and Corporate Strategy, University of Southern Denmark, Slagelse, Denmark
e-mail: set@sdu.dk

D. Secchi, M. Neumann (eds.), *Agent-Based Simulation of Organizational Behavior*, DOI 10.1007/978-3-319-18153-0_8

8.1 Introduction

For a long time teams have proliferated in organizations as a preferred way of organizing work that requires joint effort and diversity with respect to knowledge and skills. According to Hollenbeck, Beersma, and Schouten (2012) firms have shown a steady increase in the use of team based structures since 1980. Interest from researchers has also grown as a response to the increased use of teams in organizations (Davison, Hollenbeck, Barnes, Sleesman, & Ilgen, 2012). In addition to the increased use of team based structures, researchers have reported recent changes in the way today's organizations apply teams. Tannenbaum, Mathieu, Salas, and Cohen (2012) noted that teams in organizations have changed from being fairly stable to today's much more fluid teams, e.g. in professional service firms tasked with jobs in accounting, marketing, engineering, law, information technology, and consulting. Within these organizations teams are often temporary with rapid changes in team membership. Other examples of temporary teams that are formed to complete a particular team task are medical trauma teams (Klein, Ziegert, Knight, & Yan, 2006), product development teams (Edmondson & Nembhard, 2009), and computer software teams (Huckman, Staats, & Upton, 2009). In such settings individuals are often part of a resource pool in possession of specialized knowledge to high level. The organization can draw team members from this pool and compose teams that are able to work together with others in order to meet the needs of a pressing task that requires complementary expertise and high levels of specialization. Edmondson (2012) reports on the phenomenon of temporary teams by the verb, "teaming" as the gathering of experts in temporary teams to solve problems they encounter and then move on to address other cases. According to Edmondson today's organizations face a faster speed of change, more intensity of market competition, and unpredictability of customers' needs. As a consequence there is often not enough time to build stable teams and organizations must increasingly compose teams as and when needed.

Team literature fully recognizes that coordination and integration of team members' contributions is an important process that is related to team effectiveness and performance (e.g., Brannick, Roach, & Salas, 1993; Ilgen, Hollenbeck, Johnson, & Jundt, 2005; Kozwlowski & Bell, 2003). Some scholars have proposed that team coordination becomes more difficult when teams are cross functional with different specialized knowledge that they must combine to solve the team task (Majchrzak, More, & Faraj, 2012). It has also been suggested that the challenge of team coordination is greater in temporary teams because their members lack common experiences in learning from each other (Tucker, Nembhard, & Edmondson, 2007), and may lack team psychological safety (Edmondson, 1999) and have not developed transactive memory that could facilitate coordination (Reagans, Argote, & Brooks, 2005).

Given that the need for teams is increasing, coordination is an important process for achieving effectiveness in teamwork, team members often bring deep and specialized knowledge to the teams task, and teams are becoming more fluid lacking a shared history of working together, it follows that today's organizations increasingly face the challenge of composing teams that are capable of coordination from the very first time they are gathered as a team.

As will become evident in the literature review in the subsequent sections research has so far neglected this important and topical challenge. This is remarkable, as the importance of team coordination is well recognized in much of the literature. The literature on team coordination has so far paid scant attention to the possible impact of team composition on team coordination. This means that we currently lack answers to questions such as this: Will teams coordinate better if they are composed of similar—or dis-similar members?

This study aims to contribute to the team literature by exploring some aspects related to this research gap. This is undertaken by pursuing the following research question, which seems to be both important and topical in today's organizations:

How does team composition impact coordination?

The remaining part of the chapter is structured as follows: The following section reviews prior research from two so far unrelated streams of literature, i.e. (1) literature on team coordination and (2) literature on team composition. In the third section some methodological issues are discussed and it is argued why the chosen approach: agent-based modeling is an appropriate method for exploring the research question. The fourth section provides a description of the developed model and its underlying theoretical assumptions. In the fifth section the experiments conducted are described followed by a presentation of the obtained results. The penultimate section concludes by discussing the study's contribution to theory and the managerial implications, before a section on the limitations and suggestions for future research finalizes the chapter.

8.2 Literature Review

8.2.1 Team Coordination Defined

Prior research has established that task work and teamwork are distinct and both important for team effectiveness (e.g., Marks, Mathieu, & Zaccaro, 2001). According to these authors task work represents interaction with tasks, tools, machines, and systems, i.e. what the teams are doing. In order to accomplish task work the team must possess knowledge and skills about all aspects of the team task. When a team of specialists divide the collective task each team member can hold a part of the necessary task work knowledge and skills as long as the sum of knowledge and skills held by the entire team covers all aspects of the team's task. Teamwork, on the other hand, refers to team processes that enable team members to orchestrate task work activities for goal accomplishment, i.e. how they integrate their contributions to the team task (Marks et al., 2001). The process of integrating team members' contribution has been referred to as team coordination by Brannick et al. (1993). They defined team coordination as team members' contribution to the team task and orchestrating the sequence and timing of interdependent actions. Similarly (Gopal, Espinosa, Gosain, & Darcy, 2011) defined team coordination as the activity of managing dependencies among task activities carried out by various actors to integrate the work. Other authors have defined team coordination as the activity whereby multiple agents synchronize, integrate, and apply order to the working situation (Salas, Burke, & Cannon-Bowers, 2000). As demonstrated there is across a range of studies a high degree of consensus on the meaning of team coordination. Team coordination has also been described as an outcome resulting from the successful integration, sequencing, and timing of team members' interdependent actions. There is also a high degree of consensus across a range of studies that team coordination is a critical enabler of team effectiveness and team performance (e.g., Kozlowski & Ilgen, 2006).

8.2.2 How Teams Achieve Coordination

While there is consensus on the meaning of team coordination either as a process or as the resulting outcome and the importance of coordination for performance there is a wide variety of descriptions of how teams achieve coordination. Within the field of organization science coordination has been studied extensively. According to this literature, organizations achieve coordination by two generic strategies, (1) reliance on planned standardized procedures to achieve coordination and (2) creation of opportunities for the interdependent actors to make mutual adjustments in order to align their actions. These generic strategies have been described as coordination by plan versus coordination by feedback (March & Simon, 1958; Thompson, 1967). Mintzberg (1979) has referred to these two coordination mechanisms as coordination by standardization and coordination by mutual adjustment. In addition he has also referred to coordination by direct supervision where a leader coordinates the work on lower levels. Within the team literature there are numerous studies that consider these broad types of coordination mechanisms on the team level and also some studies conducted in settings with temporary teams. Faraj and Xiao (2006) described how coordination was achieved by medical trauma teams where the work was coordinated both by means of standardization of work prescribed in medical protocols and mutual adjustments in the process of treating patients. The authors described how team members used dialogic practices such as continuous interactions, joint sensemaking, common responsibility, and cross-boundary interventions to coordinate their work. Klein et al. (2006) focused, in their study from a similar setting, on the important role of team leaders for coordinating the work of the team. They reported that the team leader was critical for providing strategic direction for the team, directing the team's focus and procedures during moments of choice or uncertainty. Bechky (2006) conducted an ethnographic study of temporary teams working in film projects and focused on how coordination was achieved by means of work roles. Team members in the studied film settings were found to rely on role expectations to guide relationships and tasks. These field studies provide rich descriptions of how coordination takes place in the temporary teams in the studied settings. However, the studies reviewed seem to emphasize the role of structural coordination mechanisms, e.g. the importance of team members' adherence to work roles, standardized work practices, and team leader's directions. However, the studies do not provide any clear answers to the question of what will cause coordination success in situations when no structural mechanisms are available and teams must rely on mutual adjustments.

8.2.3 Antecedents to Team Coordination

There are some studies that have found important antecedents of team coordination. Gittell, Weinberg, Bennett, and Miller (2008) found in a field study from a hospital setting that job designs that offered opportunities for individuals to work together and strengthen their relations were conductive of team coordination. A large and growing stream of work on transactive memory systems (Wegner, 1986; Wegner, Giuliano, & Hertel, 1985) has considered how teams that have developed a shared knowledge of how knowledge and expertise is distributed among the team members have an advantage in coordinating their work compared to teams lacking such knowledge (Reagans et al., 2005). Many studies have shown that teams where team members have a shared experience of working together are better able to coordinate their work (Huckman et al., 2009). Scholars have argued that this shared experience helps in different ways, e.g. by providing teams with psychological safety (Edmondson, 1999) and provide a shared collective mind that fosters heedful interrelation among team members in stressed situations (Weick & Roberts, 1993). The antecedents of coordination considered in the reviewed studies all seem to require that teams work together for substantial periods of time whereby team members learn to coordinate their work. As a consequence the considered antecedents cannot be expected to play a role in fluid teams where team members must coordinate with others that they are not familiar with.

8.2.4 Team Composition

Team composition has been defined as the question of how people are matched to teams and roles within the teams (Hollenbeck, DeRue, & Guzzo, 2004). There is a long line of research that has studied how team composition affects performance, cohesion, and social interaction, and team members' commitment, satisfaction, and other indicators of subjective well-being (van Knippenberg & Schippers, 2007). An important question in this stream of research is whether teams should be composed of similar—or dis-similar team members. This question has largely been guided by two research traditions: the social categorization perspective and the information/decision-making perspective. Where the former perspective emphasizes the value of working with similar others the latter emphasizes the value of bringing together team members with diverse information, knowledge, and perspectives. Social categorization processes may result in teams that function more smoothly when they are composed of homogeneous team members rather than diverse team members and as a result team members are more satisfied with and attracted to the team when it is homogeneous and they are similar to the other team members. In contrast to the social categorization perspective, the information/decision-making perspective emphasizes the positive effects of team member diversity. The starting point for this perspective is the notion that diverse teams are likely to possess a broader range of task-relevant knowledge, skills, and abilities. The team members with different opinions and perspectives give a larger pool of resources that may be helpful in dealing with non-routine problems (van Knippenberg & Schippers, 2007). From other lines of research we know that diverse teams need to coordinate and integrate the contributions of the members (Hinsz & Vollrath, 1997), but it seems from this review of the literature that we lack research that considers how team composition impacts coordination. Few studies have focused on team composition in organizations that apply fluid teams. Huckman and Staats (2011) studied fluid software development teams and considered how diversity in team members' experience impacted different aspects of performance. However, the study did not consider coordination as an explanation of performance.

8.2.5 *Summarizing the Reviewed Literature*

As demonstrated in the condensed literature review there is a long line of research on both team coordination and team composition. There are a number of studies on coordination in temporary and fluid teams. These studies have mainly provided rich descriptions of how coordination is achieved, mainly by means of structural coordination mechanism. The reviewed studies have not aimed at explaining why some teams are better able to coordinate by mutual adjustment than others. From the stream of research on team composition very little was found on how team composition impacts team coordination. Based on this review it is suggested that there is an important gap in the literature that is worthy of research attention. It is shown that we lack studies that consider how team composition impacts fluid teams' ability to coordinate by mutual adjustment.

8.3 Methodological Issues

An agent-based model is a computer program in which the actors are represented by segments of program code. By running the program it is possible to observe actions over the course of simulated time. Large scale studies of team composition and team coordination are neither possible in rigorous laboratory experiments nor in field studies. This may explain why scant research has focused on this problem despite its importance in many applied settings. It is proposed that agent-based modeling is a useful approach for exploring some aspects of this problem. The agent-based approach allows the researcher to run controlled quasi-experiments in an isolated system and observe what happens. Agent-based modeling is particularly suitable to topics where understanding processes and their consequences is important. The agent-based model can include agents that are heterogeneous in their features and abilities, and can deal directly with the consequences of interaction between agents (Gilbert, 2008). Dependencies among the agents are of crucial importance when studying team coordination by mutual adjustment. It is possible with an agent-based model to examine how interactions between multiple heterogeneous agents cause structures at a higher level of aggregation to emerge as a result of their interaction over time (Siggelkow & Rivkin, 2006).

Of course the computer simulation does not claim to precisely portray the real social world. Rather, deriving the behavior of a model analytically is useful because it provides information about how the model will behave given a range of inputs, and by experimenting with different inputs it is possible to learn how the model behaves. By using the model in this way we may be able to learn more about team coordination in the real world as it might be in a variety of circumstances (Gilbert, 2008).

8.4 The Agent-Based Model of Team Coordination

With inspiration from the literature on behavioral game theory (Camerer, 2003; Lave & March, 1975) we can think of coordination by mutual adjustment as the familiar situation where two pedestrians must avoid a collision when they pass each other on a narrow lane. If one of them makes a change of direction and the other does not, they have coordinated their actions successfully by mutual adjustment and avoided the collision. In contrast, if neither of them change direction they will end up in a collision, which may also be the result if they both change their direction and end up on a new collision path. As can be seen from this simple coordination problem the outcome depends on how the two agents mutually adjust to the situation. Drawing on the intuition from this familiar situation it is suggested that the way the team members mutually adapt their behavior to the situation matters for coordination. To keep matters relatively simple it is assumed that the agents have perfectly aligned interest. This assumption precludes situations where team members end up in "prisoner-dilemma situations." Even under these restricting assumptions the agents' behavioral adaptation matters for team coordination in a non-trivial way because of the interdependence between the agents. The behavior of one agent can be either successful for coordination or the opposite depending on the behavior of the other agents.

To study the impact of team composition on teams' ability to coordinate a simple simulation model coded in Java-based NetLogo language was created. NetLogo is a multi-agent programmable modeling environment developed by The Center for Connected Learning and Computer-Based Modeling at Northwestern University in Evanston, IL (Wilensky, 1999). The simulation model contained only the features essential to this problem as intentional simplification is strongly endorsed in modeling approaches (e.g., Axelrod, 1997; Gilbert, 2008). It means that the model focused on team members' characteristics that play a role for coordination while it is agnostic about all other characteristics of the team members.

The model simulates nine agents that work together simultaneously on an interdependent team task with nine subtasks. Each agent must undertake exactly one subtask in the team task, which means that all nine agents must contribute to the solution of the team task. In each time step agents move with the goal of taking care of one of the subtasks. Interdependence among agents is modeled by letting the success of agents' moves be dependent on whether other agents move to the same subtask. If more than one agent moves to the same subtask, i.e. a coordination failure takes place, each of them must decide whether they will stay with the subtask or move to another subtask in the next time step. The team task is solved when each of the agents is matched with exactly one subtask. This corresponds to a situation where none of the agents overlap on the same subtask and none of the subtasks are omitted. In other words: the team members have coordinated their work and integrated their individual contributions to the collective team task by means of mutual adjustment.

The model measures performance of the teams by counting how many time steps are needed before the team task is solved. This measure assumes that the shortest possible time for coordination is always preferable. While this may be a true representation of the situation in some teams, e.g. medical trauma teams that must coordinate the treatment of a seriously wounded patient in a limited time frame (window of opportunity), it may not be the case in all teams, that time is a critical factor that should unanimously be minimized. It is possible to think of teams, where a prolonged period of interaction may benefit the solution that the team decides on. If teams are tasked with finding creative solutions fast coordination may be detrimental if the team decides on premature solutions.

The agents in the model are assumed to be adaptively rational meaning that each of them take an action, the world responds to the action, and the agent adapts his behavior so as to secure desirable responses in the subsequent time step. The agents are similar in all respects except for their level of docility. Docility refers to the individuals' capacity to accept instructions and the tendency to accept and believe instructions received through social channels (Simon, 1997). In this study docility is modeled as an individual level attribute that explains how agents behave based on the "instructions" they receive when they interact with other team members. The agents can find themselves in a situation where they are in conflict with another agent trying to do the same subtask or they can find themselves in a conflict-free situation. Depending on their level of docility, they react differently when they receive the instruction that they are in conflict with others. Agents' level of docility is implemented in the model as a probability that the agents will move to a new subtask in the next time step after a coordination failure in the current time step. The probability that the agent will move to a new subtask following a coordination failure can take on values from $p = 0.1$ to $p = 0.9$ with increments of 0.10. Agents' levels of docility are assumed to be exogenous variables set by the modeler before the simulation starts. E.g., he can make a homogeneous team where all nine agents have the same level of docility. As opposed to this he can compose a heterogeneous team where the nine agents have different levels of docility. Once the teams are composed the simulation runs the team task and repeats it 1,000 times to obtain consistent and reliable results. The resulting numbers of time steps for completing these 1,000 tasks are reported along with the arithmetic mean, i.e. number of time steps per completed task.

8.5 Experiments and Results

The aim of the experiments was to explore the model's behavioral space with respect to how team homogeneity, team heterogeneity, and different levels of docility among team members impacted teams' ability to coordinate by mutual adjustment. The strategy for doing that was to focus first on eight possible compositions of teams with completely homogeneous team members. The results from these experiments were used as base-line results in a subsequent series of experiments that aimed to explore the impact of team heterogeneity by considering how intra-team distribution of docility levels impacted teams' ability to coordinate.

8.5.1 Homogenous Teams

The first experiment considered a team composed of nine team members all with the same level of docility (0.1). The next experiment considered a team composed of nine team members all with a level of docility = 0.2 and so on. All eight experiments and the obtained results are listed in Table 8.1 and illustrated in Fig. 8.1.

The results of the experiments suggest that among the teams with homogeneous agents, those with a moderate level of docility (0.5) are more capable of coordinating, as these teams achieved coordination while minimizing simulated time. However, as can be seen from the plot in Fig. 8.1 the differences are small for experiment 3–7 which suggests that coordination is tolerant to some variations in the teams' level of docility as long as they stay within the mid-range territory, whereas coordination seems to suffer when teams have docility levels in either the high— or the low end. An interpretation of these results suggests that team coordination by mutual adjustment deteriorates when homogeneous teams are composed of team members that are overly reluctant to be instructed by others as well as team members that are overly willing to lean on instructions received from others.

Table 8.1 Experiments with eight homogeneous teams

		Mean of 1,000 simulations
Experiment number	Level of docility	Number of time steps
1	0.1	11.79
2	0.2	7.15
3	0.3	5.52
4	0.4	5.04
5	0.5	4.70
6	0.6	4.86
7	0.7	5.36
8	0.8	7.91

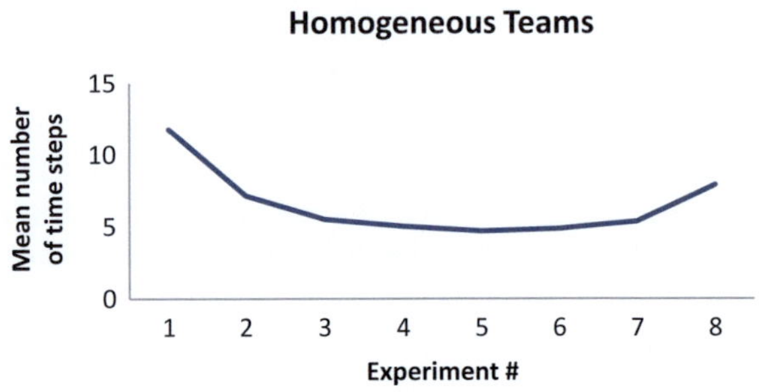

Fig. 8.1 Plot of mean number of time steps on 1,000 experiments with homogeneous teams

8.5.2 Heterogeneous Teams

In order to explore the impact of team compositions with different levels of intra-team heterogeneity 14 teams were composed with the same average rate of docility as considered in the experiments with homogenous teams. This time the teams had intra-team distributions of docility equal to standard deviation, SD = 1.0; SD = 2.0; and SD = 3.0. The obtained results from the experiments with heterogeneous teams are shown in Table 8.2 with results obtained from the experiments with homogeneous teams included for comparison.

The results from the experiments with heterogeneous teams suggest that there is little to be gained from composing heterogeneous teams rather than homogenous teams. Compared to the base-line results with homogenous teams only team compositions in the mid-range of docility (from 0.4 to 0.7) with a moderate intra-team distribution (SD = 1) yielded slightly better results. All other experiments revealed that intra-team heterogeneity was detrimental to team coordination.

Table 8.2 Results from experiments with heterogeneous teams

Level of docility	Homogenous teams	Heterogeneous teams		
Team average		SD=1	SD=2	SD=3
0.1	11.79			
0.2	7.15	8.00	9.73	
0.3	5.52	6.14	6.44	
0.4	5.04	4.88	5.13	6.03
0.5	4.70	4.68	4.76	5.11
0.6	4.86	4.74	4.92	
0.7	5.36	5.45	6.06	
0.8	7.91			

8.5.3 Summing Up the Results

Together the results suggest that both the teams' average level of docility and the intra-team distribution of team members' levels of docility matters for teams' ability to coordinate by mutual adjustment. Teams with average levels of docility in the mid-range territory are better coordinators and too low—and too high levels of docility should be avoided. In addition it seems that teams with homogeneous team members with respect to docility in most cases are better coordinators than teams with heterogeneous team members. However homogeneous teams seem to be preferable for coordination, the results also suggest that teams can tolerate some heterogeneity before coordination is severely deteriorated as the results obtained for SD = 1.0 and SD = 2.0 are close to the results obtained for the homogeneous teams.

8.6 Discussion and Conclusion

This chapter has demonstrated how an agent-based model can be applied in order to explore aspects of team coordination by mutual adjustment. The model was designed to explore how composition of teams with respect to team members' level of docility impacted teams' ability to coordinate by mutual adjustment. A series of experiments were tried with the model in order to learn how various team compositions impacted on team coordination. It was found that homogeneous teams with team members' level of docility in the mid-range were most capable of coordination. This result confirms the intuitive notion that team members should neither rely too much nor too little towards instructions obtained from others. The second result, that homogeneous teams in general are better coordinators than heterogeneous teams is more surprising and counterintuitive. Intuition based on the familiar situation where two pedestrians must coordinate their actions to avoid a collision would prompt us to foresee that an ideal team composition would be one where some team members have high levels of docility and some have low levels of docility. This was not what was found by letting the model run the experiments.

Although the study is explorative in nature it makes some contributions and signals a direction that seems promising for future research. The study is to this author's best knowledge the first to focus on the relation between team composition and team coordination by mutual adjustment. By doing that the study relates two well-established streams of research, and this intersection may well be a fruitful ground for future research. It is suggested that research into the relation between team composition and team coordination in particular seems promising with respect to contributing to the growing research interest in fluid teams in the team literature (Edmondson & Nembhard, 2009; Huckman & Staats, 2011) as these teams cannot rely on building coordination capabilities based on team member familiarity, as they do not acquire experience of working together in stable relations.

The study also contributes to the team composition literature by suggesting that team composition research should focus on team coordination as an outcome. There is the reason to believe that future research will be able to resolve some of the conflicting evidence that plagues the team composition literature (van Knippenberg & Schippers, 2007) by focusing research attention on variables that impact team coordination.

8.6.1 Managerial Implications

The findings of the study have important implications for the managers tasked with leading team-based organizations. First, managers should aim to compose teams with team members with levels of docility in the mid-range. Managers should encourage newcomers in their team-based organizations to rely on their own judgment to avoid that they demonstrate too high levels of docility. On the other hand managers should also emphasize that the most experienced team members should remember also to rely on instructions received from others, to avoid demonstrating too low levels of docility. Second, managers should try to compose teams that are homogeneous or moderately heterogeneous, as too much intra-team heterogeneity with respect to docility seems unwarranted. In addition, it may be possible for managers to promote practices in their team-based organizations that allow team members to discuss and evaluate their team work experience after they have completed their team tasks. Thereby they can develop a shared understanding of what it means to have an "appropriate level of docility" which in turn will improve teams' ability to coordinate and enhance their performance. Finally, the findings may prompt new ideas as to how managers should design and apply team training interventions in their organizations.

8.7 Limitations and Suggestions for Future Research

As this study has applied an agent-based modeling approach and is explorative in nature there are several limitations that should be noted. The first concern is the chosen methodological approach where the experiments were made with simulated agents rather than real teams. It is recommended that additional research with alternative research designs should be undertaken to strengthen and corroborate the results. Field studies seem warranted at the current stage of knowledge. While team composition arguably plays an important role for team coordination, it is certainly not the only factor that matters. Prior research has established that organizations can support their teams in coordination, e.g. by standardizing the work and providing teams with protocols and guidelines that prescribe appropriate ways of solving the team task (Faraj & Xiao, 2006), appointing team leaders to take care of coordination (Klein et al., 2006), assigning people to fixed work roles (Bechky, 2006), and providing training that emphasizes coordination (Salas & Cannon-Bowers, 2001). Future research is needed to explore how team composition interacts with these other coordination mechanisms to impact team coordination and performance.

The model has considered nine team members as a given team size. It is very likely that team size matters for the reported results. Future research should be undertaken to clarify through experiments how smaller—and larger team sizes impact the relation between team composition and team coordination. The study has highlighted some aspects of how organizations should compose teams with respect to team members' level of docility. The answer to this question raises new questions, e.g. how can we in real organizations identify team members' with different levels of docility? Are newcomers more likely to exhibit high levels of docility and are employees with extensive experience more likely to be non-docile? How do individuals' levels of docility change over time as they acquire experience as team members in various teams? These are questions for future empirical research to consider. Related to these questions, it is also a task for future research to explore to what extent it is possible to change individuals' level of docility in team work settings, e.g. by applying different sorts of team training interventions. Finally, the model in this study has assumed that team coordination emerges from the individual level to the team level. Future research should also consider how individuals' level of docility emerges one level further up to the organizational level. In doing so this study relates to recent calls for research that aims at furthering our understanding of the birth of organizational routines and their role in supporting individuals' coordination in team based work (Dionysiou & Tsoukas, 2013).

References

Axelrod, R. (1997). *The complexity of cooperation: Agent-based models of competition and collaboration*. Princeton, NJ: Princeton University Press.

Bechky, B. A. (2006). Gaffers, gofers, and grips: Role-based coordination in temporary organizations. *Organization Science, 17*(1), 3–21.

Brannick, M. T., Roach, R. M., & Salas, E. (1993). Understanding team performance: A multimethod study. *Human Performance, 6*(4), 287.

Camerer, C. F. (2003). *Behavioral game theory: Experiments in strategic interaction*. New Jersey: Princeton University Press.

Davison, R. B., Hollenbeck, J. R., Barnes, C. M., Sleesman, D. J., & Ilgen, D. R. (2012). Coordinated action in multiteam systems. *Journal of Applied Psychology, 97*(4), 808–824.

Dionysiou, D. D., & Tsoukas, H. (2013). Understanding the (re)creation of routines from within: A symbolic interactions perspective. *Academy of Management Review, 38*(2), 181–205.

Edmondson, A. (1999). Psychological safety and learning behavior in work teams. *Administrative Science Quarterly, 44*(2), 350–383.

Edmondson, A. C. (2012). Teamwork on the fly. *Harvard Business Review, 90*(4), 72–80.

Edmondson, A. C., & Nembhard, I. M. (2009). Product development and learning in project teams: The challenges are the benefits. *Journal of Product Innovation Management, 26*(2), 123–138.

Faraj, S., & Xiao, Y. (2006). Coordination in fast-response organizations. *Management Science, 52*(8), 1155–1169.

Gilbert, N. (2008). *Agent-based models*. Thousand Oaks, CA: Sage.

Gittell, J. H., Weinberg, D. B., Bennett, A. L., & Miller, J. A. (2008). Is the doctor in? A relational approach to job design and the coordination of work. *Human Resource Management, 47*(4), 729–755.

Gopal, A., Espinosa, J. A., Gosain, S., & Darcy, D. P. (2011). Coordination and performance in global software service delivery: The vendor's perspective. *IEEE Transactions on Engineering Management, 58*(4), 772–785.

Hinsz, V. B., & Vollrath, D. A. (1997). The emerging conceptualization of groups as information processors. *Psychological Bulletin, 121*(1), 43.

Hollenbeck, J. R., Beersma, B., & Schouten, M. E. (2012). Beyond team types and taxonomies: A dimensional scaling conceptualization for team description. *Academy of Management Review, 37*(1), 82–106.

Hollenbeck, J. R., DeRue, D. S., & Guzzo, R. (2004). Bridging the gap between I/O research and Hr practice: Improving team composition, team training, and team task design. *Human Resource Management, 43*(4), 353–366.

Huckman, R. S., & Staats, B. R. (2011). Fluid tasks and fluid teams: The impact of diversity in experience and team familiarity on team performance. *Manufacturing & Service Operations Management, 13*(3), 310–328.

Huckman, R. S., Staats, B. R., & Upton, D. M. (2009). Team familiarity, role experience, and performance: Evidence from Indian software services. *Management Science, 55*(1), 85–100.

Ilgen, D. R., Hollenbeck, J. R., Johnson, M., & Jundt, D. (2005). Teams in organizations: From input-process-output models to IMOI models. *Annual Review of Psychology, 56*(1), 517–543.

Klein, K. J., Ziegert, J. C., Knight, A. P., & Yan, X. (2006). Dynamic delegation: Shared, hierarchical, and deindividualized leadership in extreme action teams. *Administrative Science Quarterly, 51*(4), 590–621.

Kozlowski, S. W. J., & Ilgen, D. R. (2006). Enhancing the effectiveness of work groups and teams. *Psychological Science in the Public Interest (Wiley-Blackwell), 7*(3), 77–124.

Kozwlowski, S., & Bell, B. S. (2003). Work groups and teams in organizations. In W. C. Borman, D. R. Ilgen, & E. J. Klimoski (Eds.), *Handbook of psychology: Industrial and organizational psychology* (Vol. 12). London: Wiley.

Lave, C. A., & March, J. G. (1975). *An introduction to models in the social sciences*. Lanham, MD: University Press of America, Inc.

Majchrzak, A., More, P. H. B., & Faraj, S. (2012). Transcending knowledge differences in cross-functional teams. *Organization Science, 23*(4), 951–970.

March, J. G., & Simon, H. A. (1958). *Organizations*. New York: Wiley.

Marks, M. A., Mathieu, J. E., & Zaccaro, S. J. (2001). A temporally based framework and taxonomy of team processes. *Academy of Management Review, 26*(3), 356–376.

Mintzberg, H. (1979). *The structuring of organizations*. Englewood Cliffs, NJ: Prentice-Hall.

Reagans, R., Argote, L., & Brooks, D. (2005). Individual experience and experience working together: Predicting learning rates from knowing who knows what and knowing how to work together. *Management Science, 51*(6), 869–881.

Salas, E., Burke, C. S., & Cannon-Bowers, J. A. (2000). Teamwork: Emerging principles. *International Journal of Management Reviews, 2*(4), 339.

Salas, E., & Cannon-Bowers, J. A. (2001). The science of training: A decade of progress. *Annual Review of Psychology, 52*(1), 471.

Siggelkow, N., & Rivkin, J. W. (2006). When exploration backfires: Unintended consequences of multilevel organizational search. *Academy of Management Journal, 49*(4), 779–795.

Simon, H. A. (1997). *Models of bounded rationality, Vol. 3. Empirically grounded economic reason*. Cambridge, MA: The MIT Press.

Tannenbaum, S. I., Mathieu, J. E., Salas, E., & Cohen, D. (2012). Teams are changing: Are research and practice evolving fast enough? *Industrial & Organizational Psychology, 5*(1), 2–24.

Thompson, J. D. (1967). *Organizations in action*. New York: McGraw-Hill.

Tucker, A. L., Nembhard, I. M., & Edmondson, A. C. (2007). Implementing new practices: An empirical study of organizational learning in hospital intensive care units. *Management Science, 53*(6), 894–907.

van Knippenberg, D., & Schippers, M. C. (2007). Work group diversity. *Annual Review of Psychology, 58*(1), 515–541.

Wegner, D. (1986). Transactive memory: A contemporary analysis of the group mind. In B. Mullen & G. Goethals (Eds.), *Theories of group behavior* (pp. 185–208). New York: Springer.

Wegner, D., Giuliano, T., & Hertel, P. (1985). Cognitive interdependence in close relationships. In W. J. Ickes (Ed.), *Compatible and incompatible relationships* (pp. 253–276). New York: Springer.

Weick, K. E., & Roberts, K. H. (1993). Collective mind in organizations: Heedful interrelating on flight decks. *Administrative Science Quarterly, 38*(3), 357–381.

Wilensky, U. (1999). *NetLogo*. Evanston, IL: Northwestern University, Center for Connected Learning and Computer-Based Modeling. http://ccl.northwestern.edu/netlogo/.

Chapter 9
Boundary Conditions for the Emergence of "Docility" in Organizations: Agent-Based Model and Simulation

Davide Secchi

Abstract The idea that individuals do not make decisions in isolation is not new in the behavioral sciences. In fact, it was one of the founding fathers of the discipline, Herbert A. Simon, who suggested individuals depend on opinions, recommendations, information, and advice coming from other human beings and labeled it "docility." Limited attention has been devoted to the study of this key characteristic of decision makers. This chapter takes the original model of docility, expands it, and applies it to individuals in structured or formal social systems (e.g., organizations). This exercise is performed using agent-based modeling and it explores under what circumstances organizational "docility" is supported or not.

Keywords Docility • Organizations • Prosocial behavior • Distributed cognition

9.1 Introduction and Problem Statement

In recent years there has been an increase in referencing, if not in the use of the concept of "docility" (Bardone, 2011; Miller & Lin, 2010; Ossola, 2013; Secchi, 2011; Secchi & Bardone, 2013; York, Sarasvathy, & Wicks, 2013). This is the human tendency to lean on information coming from (Simon, 1990, 1993) and provide information to social channels (Secchi & Bardone, 2009) when making decisions. According to these studies, docility relates to prosocial behavior and for this reason has been associated to altruism (Knudsen, 2003; Simon, 1993). As a behavioral rule based on mutual exchange of information, docility requires some level of institutionalization (Secchi, 2011). This means that organizations (or communities) should allow, value, and support docile individuals. It remains unclear under what conditions docility would emerge, stabilize, or disappear from a given population.

D. Secchi (✉)
Research Cluster for Cognition, Management and Communication (COMAC), Centre for Human Interactivity (CHI), Department of Language and Communication, University of Southern Denmark, Slagelse, Denmark
e-mail: secchi@sdu.dk

D. Secchi, M. Neumann (eds.), *Agent-Based Simulation of Organizational Behavior*, DOI 10.1007/978-3-319-18153-0_9

Another way of describing docility is that of thinking of organizations that create the conditions for distributed cognitive mechanisms—*à la* Hutchins (1995)—to be practiced. This clearly sets the grounds for docile behaviors to emerge (Secchi & Bardone, 2009, 2013). All in all, this is one of the elements that makes the organization a cohesive unity of individuals despite being also a complex (hence unpredictable) and adaptive social system (Miller & Page, 2007). Docility may balance this inherent complexity, being one of the elements that makes human behavior adaptation and evolution lean more towards a more organized or disorganized system (cfr. in this book Herath, Secchi, & Homberg, 2016).

This paper uses an agent-based model (ABM) to study what are the conditions under which a community facilitates the emergence of docility. The model explores what happens to it when some of the conditions that define its appearance vary significantly.

This study offers two significant novelties. First, it studies boundary conditions for this concept to emerge. Existing studies agree that "docility" is a behavioral and cognitive disposition and, as such, it is something that either explains (Knudsen, 2003; York et al., 2013) or helps (Secchi, 2011; Secchi & Bardone, 2009) decision makers make better choices in organizational environments (e.g., Miller & Lin, 2010). However, there is limited knowledge on what are the conditions for these behaviors to emerge and stabilize at the organizational level. Second, the use of ABMs is increasing in social sciences but it is still not so popular in organizational and management studies. In his seminal article, Simon used an equation-based simulation. In bringing the agent-based paradigm in, the present work offers advancements in continuity with the traditional origins of the concept.

Before a short description of the model is provided, the following pages offer four arguments that support the study and provide a theoretical background.

9.1.1 Rationale for the Study

There are many reasons why the study of human "docility" appears to be particularly relevant today as opposed to 25 years ago, when it was first introduced (Simon, 1990, 1993). I have selected four that are particularly relevant to the study presented in this chapter. I do not claim that these are *the* most important elements when it comes at the study of docility however, they are significant aspects of any decision making process. Still, they point out why the study of docility (a) is *timely*, (b) can be considered a *distributed* phenomenon, (c) may happen to bear cognitive and/or behavioral *costs*, and (d) there is a need to update the original model.

9.1.1.1 Timeliness and Fitness

One of the first important aspects that indicates the relevance of docility for the understanding of organizational interactions is that it is *timely*. Most of the technological advancements in the recent past have been "social" or labelled as such. This means that they bring people "closer," to some extent, in that they offer easier ways to exchange information. This happens when real world socially based practices for decision making are replicated on a virtual tech-based platforms, such as that of the chat line associated with the largest online shopping business in China (Ou, Pavlou, & Davison, 2014). Exchange of information also happens taking new forms, opening up human social interactions to unexplored territories, such as the use of social networking websites for recruitment (e.g., Ross & Bohnert, 2010) or, more simply, to establish friendship (e.g., Ellison, Steinfield, & Lampe, 2007). This implies that what Simon referred to as "social channels" (Simon, 1993), having in mind just live human-to-human interaction, has today reached scope and range that was unthinkable just about one decade ago. As an implication of this, studies on advice giving and taking (e.g., Bonaccio & Dalal, 2006; Dalal & Bonaccio, 2010; Gino, Brooks, & Schweitzer, 2012; Gino & Moore, 2007) appear today more and more relevant to the way social interactions happen within organizations. Put differently, not only we have the social interaction that Simon had in mind but employees and managers are today exposed to the Internet, social networking websites (e.g., LinkedIn, Facebook), chat platforms (e.g., QQ, WeChat, Whatsapp), multi-media platforms (e.g., Skype), other information stored in the computer. This puts an emphasis on cognitive stimuli and emphasizes the fact that decision making is mostly a socially based process.

The phenomenon of socially distributed and socially based decision making cannot be considered a secondary and minor aspect of the way individual gather and process information any more. One of the elements that may be offered as a complement to what was proposed in the original model of docility is that of redefining the concept of "fitness." This was introduced as a way through which the adoption of a given strategy—i.e., intelligent docile (*id*), unintelligent docile *ud*, or non-docile *nd* (see below for further details)—would lead a given individual to better adaptation in a social environment. From this loose connection to biology comes the use of the word "fitness." The assumption is that more successful decision strategies are imitated and followed by others. If the search and use of information from social channels reveals to be a suitable and *successful decision strategy*, others may follow it.

A few words need to be spent in defining what a *successful decision strategy* is. On a very traditional perspective, this can be defined either as a process or as an outcome (March, 1994; Simon, 1979, 1997). As the words used suggest, a decision strategy is the process that the individual uses to arrive at a decision. This, in turn, involves individual *abilities*, *availability* and *access* to resources, together with an assessment of the nature of the decision to be made. A successful decision process is one that involves an *efficient* use of these elements, respectively a less intensive use of one's abilities, more available resources, and easy access to them so that the problem appears simpler. If we turn our attention to the outcome, a successful decision strategy (i.e., efficient, as defined above) also needs to show some results. In this sense, we may state it is effective. There is a vast literature on imitation processes that lead to bandwagon effects, i.e. the adoption of a practice, an idea, or a process due to its popularity (e.g., Abrahamson & Rosenkopf, 1997; David & Strang, 2006; Esposito, 2011; Fiol & O'Connor, 2003; Rosenkopf & Abrahamson, 1999; Staw & Epstein, 2000; Strang & Tuma, 1993). We claim that, when docility is perceived as a *successful decision strategy* it is more likely to spread and become popular because efficient and effective.

One way of looking at this statement is based on rational choice. Docility is adopted because it seems to be an efficient and effective way of dealing with decisions. This implies that individuals base their decisions—even cognitive strategies—on the basis of a rational evaluation of available alternatives, matched with their preferences, after having assessed actual and potential consequences of action (Simon, 1955; von Neumann & Morgenstern, 1944). However, there is another way of looking at this statement. We know that any judgement and decision is subject to biases and prejudices (Kahneman, 2003). We also know that most knowledge and understanding is socialized, in a way (Kunda, 1999). And we do understand that there are multiple layers of meaning, structured approximatively in the social circles each individuals is (or feels) part of (cfr. in this book Neumann & Cowley, 2016). Therefore, a rational evaluation is always relative to the conditions under which the individual is operating so that preferences change and adapt depending on resources (both social resources and artifacts Secchi, 2011). Also, the assessment of available alternatives may depend on how decision making proceeds and becomes tied to manipulations (Magnani, 2007). This leads to a slightly different reading of the statement, where *efficient* and *effective* do not necessarily refer to what is "rational" in a traditional sense, but refer to what makes sense given adaptive, complex, and emergent social and cognitive organizational conditions (Secchi, 2011).

If the use of docility leads to better decisions, then others may adopt a similar strategy and vice versa. If this is transposed to an organizational environment, we may hypothesize that people may start or continue to adopt successful strategies if they result effective and efficient. This is how "fitness" is understood in the context of this study.

9.1.1.2 Distributed Processes

Toward the end of his career, Simon gave the concept of "docility" some attention, probably in an attempt to direct the study of bounded rationality toward socially based mechanisms. This intuition can be matched with some of the developments in cognitive sciences that came to light in the mid-Nineties (Hutchins, 1995). The emphasis on the fact that decision makers reach out to other individuals when making decisions is one of the manifestations of our cognition being *distributed*. This is the idea that the cognitive process is not limited by what happens within the boundaries of the brain, instead it includes a complex and dynamic set of interactions between the brain and external resources (Clark, 2008; Clark & Chalmers, 1998; Clark, 2004). Docility is a behavioral representation of the use of socially distributed cognitive resources (Bardone & Secchi, 2009; Magnani, 2007; Magnani, Secchi, & Bardone, 2007; Secchi, 2009).

Bardone and I have argued elsewhere (Secchi, 2009; Secchi & Bardone, 2009) that the match between docility and the distributed nature of cognition makes it more palatable to human beings, especially when information is made extremely accessible through social channels. Thus, a behavior that is more tied to the way our cognition works may give more chances of success on the basis that it is more cognitively efficient. This is why, even though Simon wrote before distributed cognition came of age, the original model provides more chances of adaptation (in the fitness function) for individuals that show more docile dispositions. This read of the concept makes it even more up to date and forces us to think of how much of that model (Simon, 1993) acquires more insights in the light of recent developments in the field. In a study on Simon's legacy and the Carnegie School, in a quick and almost unnoticeable paragraph Gavetti, Levinthal, and Ocasio (2007) were able to make this link between bounded rationality and distributed cognition. This is to state that the interpretation proposed in this chapter is not too far from the mainstream.

9.1.1.3 Not Just Altruism

Some authors linked docility to "altruism" (Knudsen, 2003; Secchi & Bardone, 2009). An individual that makes decisions based on what other individuals around him or her suggest, recommend, advise needs to have a disposition to reciprocate (Khalil, 2004). The exchange of information involves an attitude toward the others such that individuals offer advice, for example, without expecting anything in return. Some others (Secchi, 2009) have argued that there is a range of prosocial behaviors that may be connected to individuals with varying levels of docility. In fact, this attention to others can be extended to, for example, cooperation, volunteering, extra-role behaviors, socially responsible actions (Secchi, 2009). If this assumption holds, the study of docility can be easily connected to aspects typical of organizational behavior studies, such as intrinsic and public service motivation, organizational citizenship behavior, social responsibility. In other words, it can be studied as the cognitive backbone that contributes to explain these behaviors.

In each and every one of these prosocial organizational behaviors, it is fair to assume that individuals sustain some costs of practicing them (Khalil, 2004; Knudsen, 2003). From a strict individualistic point of view, any behavior that is not oriented towards the self (even if it comes at a greater reward) is related to the expenditure of time, effort, and energy. Once again, the cost impacts on the fitness function of each individual in the organization, with those acting more pro-socially having also the highest negative impact on their chances of adaptation to the social environment (this concept is applied on a broader evolutionary context by Fehr & Fischbacher, 2003). This is reasonable if we assume that employees and managers need to step out of their way to help others, compatibly with their job requirements. This idea of the cost of docility (or docile behavior) is very much tied to the higher chances of adaptation reviewed above. Moreover, costs may be perceived to be high when the employee finds limited encouragement from the organization (Frey & Meier, 2004).

9.1.1.4 Range

The last argument presented here is that of an update to the original model. Simon used equations to model individual adaptation to the social environment (Simon, 1993). Although the model helps us understand what are the particular characteristics of the concept, it is fairly simple and shows a limited set of results. In addition to that, that model applied to a generic population, with little reference to the social system it refers to. An update to that model is needed to make it more realistic and contextualize it.

First, an ABM allows us to break the unrealistic (although implicit) assumption that each individual has an understanding of what is going on in the entire system (Secchi, 2015). This technique allows to model each agent in the system so that they only interact and know about what is closer to them. This is probably a more accurate representation of the idea of bounded rationality that Simon so strongly advocated (Simon, 1979, 1997). There is a limited *range* of interactions that each decision maker in the system has. Second, I do refer to organizations and make the model based on interactions rather than "survival." This provides a better way to analyze and interpret human behavior as it stems out of socially distributed cognitive processes.

Before moving on to the model, a few more notes on docility in organizations are probably needed. No empirical study on docility has shown its effective value for decision making in- or outside organizations, although this is the overall assumption of the concept. As complex and evolving social systems, organizations need "adaptable" individuals. Docility becomes a key concept for organizations in two substantial ways. First, it can be a mechanism through which individuals share information and build what can be thought of as a sense of community, belongingness, and comradeship (Secchi, 2011). Trust is probably one of the components of this aspect (Ossola, 2013). Second, organizations can support this way of socially distributing individual cognition, hence building what can be thought of as institutional conditions for a better cognitive fit between docile individuals and docile organizations (Secchi, 2011). An example of how these mechanisms are put in place is that of observing how docility works in teams (an application of Simon's docility is developed in Thomsen, 2016, cfr. in this book).

In short, the ABM is more complex than the original model, it gains in representativeness and richness of potential interpretations. With this in mind, the following section specifies how parameters are set and what defines the model.

9.2 The Model: Agents and Docility

Table 9.1 presents parameters and assumptions made to model docility in organizations. In the following pages each of these assumptions and parameters is explained. Most, if not all, of what is not explained in this section is consistent to what is in the original model. The reason for keeping this modeling effort similar to what originally proposed (e.g., Knudsen, 2003; Secchi & Bardone, 2009; Simon, 1993) is twofold. First, it makes comparisons more easily readable and, second, it also makes differences more apparent. What is meant here is that I have deliberately not modified the original model or, I have modified it the least possible to make it work as agent-based. Inevitably, there are differences that may make this model as similar as possible but obviously not the same. In fact, the agent-based "approach" to modeling adds complexity and builds the simulation bottom-up, making sense of interactions through emergence (Fioretti, 2013; Secchi, 2015).

9.2.1 Types of Individuals

Models of docile behavior published so far lean on the original equation developed by Simon (1993). Following Secchi and Bardone's (2009) interpretation, these are equations of fitness that docile and non-docile individuals show in a given community or environment. Depending on the extent to which these individuals exhibit prosocial behavior, there are three kinds of individuals: (a) docile and intelligent (*id*), (b) docile and unintelligent (*ud*), (c) non-docile (*nd*) (Simon, 1993). The docile individual can be accurate and discriminate with whom it is wise to provide/ask for recommendations, suggestions, advice; this is called *intelligent docile* or *id*. Instead, an individual may be extremely open to advice, recommendations, and suggestions independent of an assessment of others. This is a sort of inconsiderate docility and the portrayer is labelled *unintelligent docile*, or *ud*. Another way to characterize *ud* is when an individual leans solely on take-only (or passive) docility mechanisms. The third type is the *non-docile*, an individual that does not provide advice to other individuals but only tries to take advantage of those who give them instead. It is the prototype of selfishness and free-riding.

The success of each type of individual depends on how much the outcome of a "fitness" function outweighs the outcome of the "fitness" of the other categories in the system. Long-term success may take the form of either individuals switching to one of the other categories or attracting more individuals with characteristics similar to theirs in the system, community, or environment.

In order to be consistent with previous studies (Knudsen, 2003; Secchi, 2007, 2015; Secchi & Bardone, 2009; Simon, 1993) the model presented in this paper uses the original equations and their payoff/fitness to calculate the degree of success of each individual (agent) in the system. The equations were modified substituting the probability of meeting another individual based on their presence in the system with the *range* (see below). This way, individual fitness is calculated on the average fitness of the individuals around so that it is actual interactions that are considered.[1]

---

[1]The modified fitness equations are:

$$fI = fn + fd \cdot dI + faI \cdot qI \cdot cI + faU \cdot qU \cdot cU - c \cdot cI \tag{9.1}$$

Table 9.1 Parameter notations and explanation

Parameter	Values	Description
Cost of prosocial behavior	$[\mathbf{0.005}, 0.05, 0.5]$	Behavior that benefits other human beings is supposed to have a cost on the individual who provides it. Docility has its costs, that materialize every time prosocial behavior is displayed
Range of interaction	$[3, 6, 9, 12]$	The assumption here is that individuals only interact with other individuals given a certain "range of action." This means that the "fitness" or success an individual has is always relative to the local niche one is operating in
Docility impact	$[-0.1, -0.02, 0, \mathbf{0.02}, 0.1]$	There is a direct impact of docility on "fitness" and this gives a gain to individuals displaying docile behaviors. We theorize that the value is not always positive
Adaptation	ON	It assumes that individuals with the lowest "relative fitness" would adapt and become whatever is more suitable to achieve a better performance (closed dynamic system)

Note: Bold values are those tested in existing models (i.e., Secchi, 2007; Secchi & Bardone, 2009; Simon, 1993)

9.2.2 Costs of Prosocial Behavior

The first parameter shown in Table 9.1 is the *cost of prosocial behavior*. While other models consider it to be relatively cheap (i.e., 0.005), in the current ABM I ask what happens to docility when the costs raise significantly.

Some organizations may have climates (or even cultures) that do not favor or encourage prosocial behaviors, making them extremely costly (for example, when top executives do not set the standards; see Ormiston & Wong, 2013).

$$fS = fn + faI \cdot qI \cdot cI + faU \cdot qU \cdot cU \tag{9.2}$$

$$fU = fn + fd \cdot dU + faI \cdot qI \cdot cI + faU \cdot qU \cdot cU - c \cdot cU \tag{9.3}$$

where fI, fS, and fU are the net fitness of intelligent altruist, selfish, and unintelligent altruist individuals, respectively. The other symbols in the equations are: fn that is the natural fitness, common to everyone in the system; $fd \cdot dI$ and $fd \cdot dU$ are incremental fitness due to docility, multiplied by the coefficient for intelligent and unintelligent altruists; faI and faU are fitness gains from other altruists; [...] cI and cU are the extent to which I and U behave altruistically; c is the cost of altruism (Simon, 1993, pp. 157–158). In our ABM, qI and qU represent how many other intelligent and unintelligent docile individuals are in the specified *range*.

The two extremes, $C_{pb} = 0.005$ and $C_{pb} = 0.5$, represent conditions where prosocial behavior is welcome and made relatively cheap, and a situation where it is particularly costly, respectively. The mid-range value is taken to see whether differences emerge when there is no clear-cut condition to support one behavior or the other.

This set of values not only takes the original assumption on docility (0.005) but it tests what happens if actions become very costly. This is consistent with what discussed above and tests the boundary condition for docility to emerge in organizations that show relatively high and relatively low "tolerance" for it.

9.2.3 Range of Interaction

The second parameter refers to the *range of interactions* (Table 9.1). As stated in the table, the model makes more realistic assumptions when it considers how agents (decision makers; either employees or managers) interact. Individuals have limited interaction abilities, given their bounded rationality (Secchi, 2011; Simon, 1997). This means that they establish relationships with others (i.e., exchange information through social channels that are) in their range of possible operations. They cannot interact with the entire population, nor they would have the cognitive abilities to do so. This simple aspect was not modeled before although it seems to be more realistic and a closer representation of the way individuals interact with each other. However, even this aspect can be subject to some caveats. In fact, some research in neuroscience shows that individual brains are never "isolated" in the sense that they connect—mostly in an unconscious status—with others, setting the ground for social connections that can be much wider than the material and conscious ones (an example of these approaches is provided in this book Plikynas, Raudys, & Raudys, 2016).

The model presents four values for this parameter, i.e. $range\{3, 6, 9, 12\}$. The values are attributed given several pilot tests of this model and represent possible interactions with other agents that fall within the specified radius. The measurement unit is relative to the software used (i.e., NetLogo). Given that these are spatial parameters and that the simulation model attributes each agent's position in the organizational space stochastically, there is no way to know how many agents fall in *range* before the simulation starts. Also, the number changes as the simulation completes additional steps because agents move in the organizational space.

This element was not considered at all in the original model and it was probably one of the most significant limits to its generalizability. ABM helps to overcome those limitations by de-centering the model, making it more decision-maker centric than system- or equilibrium-centric.

9.2.4 Impact of Docility

There is an impact of being docile. This is what Table 9.1 labels as *docility impact* and is defined as the means through which docility affects "fitness" or the perception of a *successful decision strategy*. The model considers three extremes: (a) strong negative impact on individuals (−0.1), (b) no impact whatsoever (0), and (c) strong positive impact (0.1). These three values should show how much a better chance of social fitness is affected by what individuals gain from being docile. Of course, non-docile individuals are not affected by this change.

Although it has been emphasized that there are three values relevant to exploring the "boundary conditions" for docility to emerge and prosper (or fail) in an organization, there are other two intermediate values (i.e., −0.02 and 0.02). The positive value is the one in the original model that is considered in the ABM too. The other value is a reflection of the first, with a negative sign. These values are interesting in that they work the same way a control group works in a social experiment. In fact, they are benchmark values that may tell us something interesting in relation to where a given change happens (i.e., docility starts to be supported or not).

9.2.5 Adaptation

As anticipated above, the model presents adaptations to a decision making strategy that is deemed successful. It is assumed that individuals see what is the most suitable successful strategy and they adapt to it. However, this happens as a micro (or local) rather than at a macro (or global) and systemic level. Every agent in the system explores (sees) what the strategies of in-range connected agents are, and adjusts its own strategy on that basis. The agent with the highest fitness in the neighborhood is imitated by the others.

The choice of adaptation is not neutral. In fact, a viable alternative is what is called *expand* feature in an extended version of the model. In that mode, individuals in the model "reproduce" or "die." This is probably even closer to what Simon hypothesized in his model—he used a growth rate of 0.02. The former action (i.e., "reproduce") mimics the hiring or expansion process although it also assumes that the organization grows at some fixed semi-constant rate. The latter option for agents (i.e., "die") equals leaving the organization.

Now, the difference between the two approaches—i.e., the one used in this chapter, called *adapt*, and the other one featuring hiring and firing of employees, called *expand*—is also a difference in how we think of docility. Within the *adapt* mode, docility is an attitude that varies within individuals depending on contextual and situational variables. In this approach, we can technically tell it is a *state*. Instead, the approach *expand* characterizes docility as something that does not change nor adapt within an individual. The lack of fitness leads the individual to leave, due to incompatibility. This aligns docility to what is technically defined as a *trait* amongst applied psychology and organizational behavior scholars (for example in the study of mood George, 1991; Watson & Pennebaker, 1989). This somewhat deeper understanding of what docility is (state or trait?) may explain the choice made in this article more in detail, and provide more support to understand what was done in the simulation. From this approach, it is apparent that I abandoned the "genetic" (trait-based) approach used in most conceptualizations of docility, and made an attempt to tie it to a cognitive disposition with eventual links to behavior (Secchi, 2011). The purpose of this modification makes it more variable, let alone credible (for what I am trying to model, i.e. organizational cognition and behavior). Although this element is probably more realistic, it is also true that people leave and join organizations. For this reason, I see the *expand* mode as complementary to the *adapt*. However, only one was implemented in this chapter (adapt).

This is a significant innovation that this ABM brings to the original model since that one only allowed for individuals to multiply (to grow) in a given time period. In an organization, this can happen if we refer to new hires. But, it is not the most interesting process involving docility, given that adaptation can be more disruptive when it is contagious (e.g., Strang & Tuma, 1993).

9.2.6 Procedural Note and Expected Outcomes

The model is implemented in NetLogo 3D 4.1.3 (Wilensky, 1999) with agents appearing in the space (context, community, organization) at random and establishing relationships according to the rule above (i.e., *range of interaction*). Every condition, represented by a given value of a parameter, is tested all others being equal, i.e. *ceteris paribus*. This means that we are able to isolate what is the impact of that specific parameter value when other conditions do not vary.

To find the approximate impact of each value, every condition is run 30 times. This value was found using statistical power analysis (Liu, 2014). Assuming that the structure of the data analysis is similar to a factorial design, the formula for ANOVA was deemed appropriate (Secchi, 2014). A target power of $1 - \beta$ (power) $= 0.99$ was used because computer simulations are artificial systems and higher conditions can be met. I set *ES* (effect size) equal to 0.2, representing a small effect size (according to Cohen, 1988, 1992) to be conservative. A standard tolerance for Type-I error with $\alpha = 0.05$ was maintained. Finally, the groups are the total number of parameter combinations $groups = 3 \times 4 \times 5 = 60$. The number of runs that satisfy this condition is 25.07. Hence, the number 30 was chosen to avoid any risk of low power.

As already stated above, the design of the experiments is $3 \times 4 \times 5 = 60$, and that times the number of runs per condition (i.e., 30) gives 1,800 total runs for the model.

The starting number of the three types of individuals in the model is assumed constant at $N = 60$ for each type of individual. This is done to provide the same initial starting conditions and opportunities of interaction to all agents, independent of their type.

There is significant scope for this work to provide meaningful results and isolate conditions for docility to emerge, stabilize, or disappear. Whether docile attitudes depend on the (cognitive) cost of the behaviors that stem from it or it depends on the direct effects on performance (called "fitness" above) is yet to be defined. Findings showing that docility is somehow independent of these two conditions in particular would indicate that this concept is even stronger than what Simon and the other students of docility highlighted in previous studies.

9.3 Results

All calculations and figures are produced using *R*, an open source software for statistical analysis (R Core Team, 2013). Results are presented using co-plots per each type of individual (i.e., *id*, *ud*, and *nd*). The co-plots allow us to see what happens to the parameter we held constant when the other two parameters vary.

9.3.1 Negative Docility Impact

Figure 9.1 shows variations in the number of *id*s when the *impact* of docility is negative and equals −0.1. The co-plot shows the effect that the other two parameters (i.e., *range* of interaction and *cost* of prosocial behavior) have when this value is kept constant. The numbers in the horizontal axis are the steps of the runs, labelled *opportunities of interaction* because there may be new contacts among agents every step of the simulation model.

Figure 9.1 shows that, for negative values of how docility affects fitness, there always is a decrease in the number of *id*. No matter how strong, none of the other parameter values is capable of reverting the trend.

Figure 9.2 presents the number of *ud*, given the same conditions presented above for *id*. In most of the cases, a negative *impact* of docility on the chances to better fit in a social environment, the number of *ud* decreases. There are two combinations where this does not happen. When the *range* of interaction is particularly high and the *cost* of prosocial behavior is low, the number of this particular type of individual increases. And it does significantly so when the chance of interaction is particularly high (statistical tests are reported in the Appendix). In the four cases in the lower right sector of the conditional plot, the negative fitness level (i.e., impact) is less relevant than in the other two conditions.

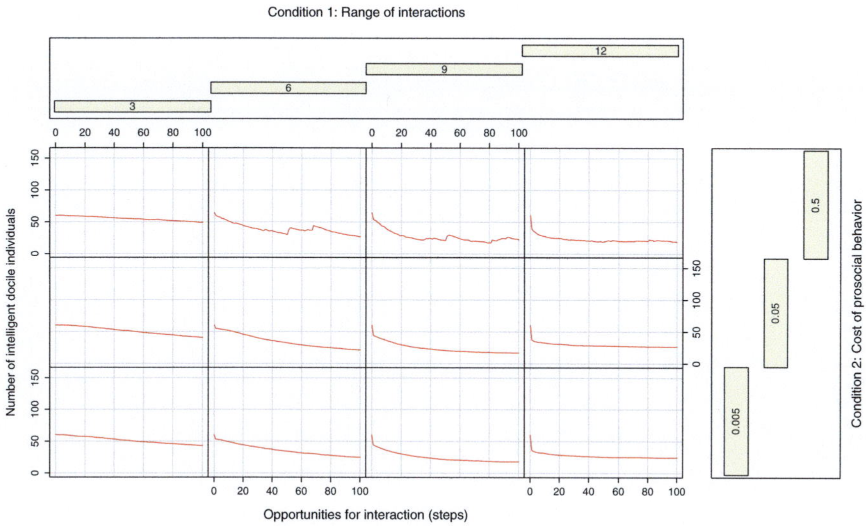

Fig. 9.1 Number of *id* for *impact* = −0.1, given *cost* and *range*

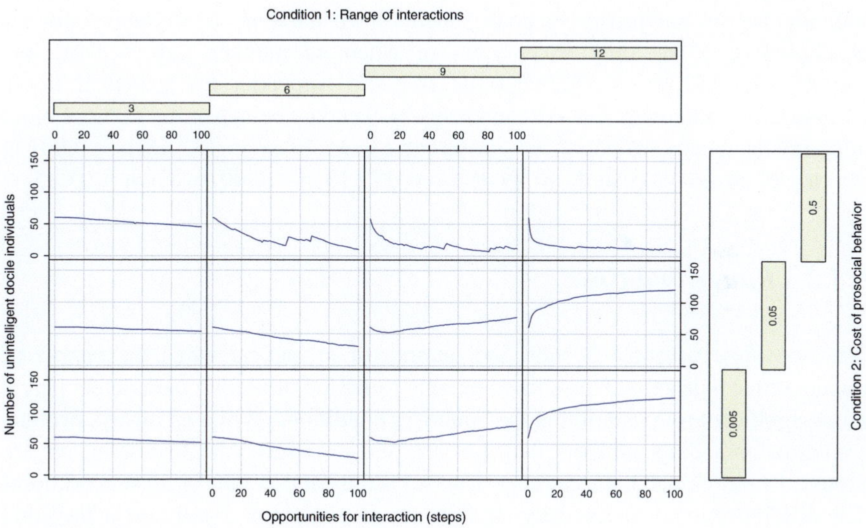

Fig. 9.2 Number of *ud* for *impact* = −0.1, given *cost* and *range*

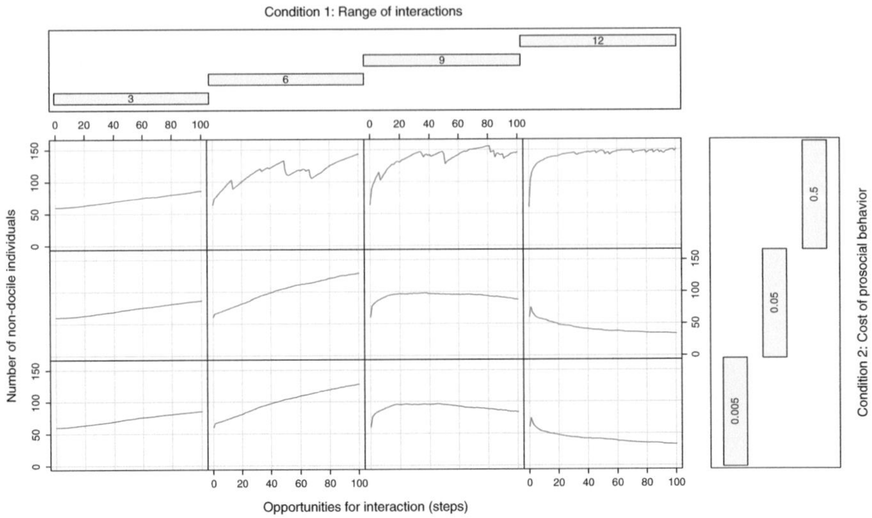

Fig. 9.3 Number of *nd* for *impact* $= -0.1$, given *cost* and *range*

As expected by looking at results presented so far, Fig. 9.3 shows that *nd* individuals grow and prosper in an organization when the *impact* of docile attitudes is discouraged. The only exceptions are when *nd* numbers are weakest, i.e. *range* = 12 and *cost* = [0.005, 0.05] (see the Appendix for statistical tests). The curves for relatively low *cost* and *range* = 9 end up being similar to those of *ud* although the means are statistically different: $t = 45.40, df = 182.68, p < 0.001$ in the case of *cost* = 0.05, and $t = 49.05, df = 177.13, p < 0.001$ when it is 0.005.

9.3.2 Range and Cost

The two Figs. 9.4 and 9.5 show the number of *id* and *ud* when the *impact* of docile attitudes is zero. This should be able to let the other two parameters play a more significant role in defining the boundary conditions. While *ud* always decline, sometimes reaching numbers that are very close to zero (the lowest means are around 13 individuals), the number of *id* stays almost constant in most conditions. The difference is not statistically significant when *range* = 3 and *cost* is 0.05 and 0.005: $t = -1.61, df = 197.71, p = 0.11$. There is a decrease in *id* numbers when the *cost* of prosocial behavior is high, but the numbers do not go down too much (e.g., ca. 40). The number of *id* increases significantly only when *costs* are in the mid and low range and chances of interactions are at the highest.

What happens to *nd* reflects what just reviewed for the other two types. There is a steady increase in numbers in most conditions although this is not always very strong (as opposed to Figs. 9.4 and 9.5) when the *cost* is mid and low. The decrease of *nd* (Fig. 9.5) that is compatible with the raise of *id* is not very steep, given that *ud* are those who suffer the most from this condition of zero impact Fig. 9.5.

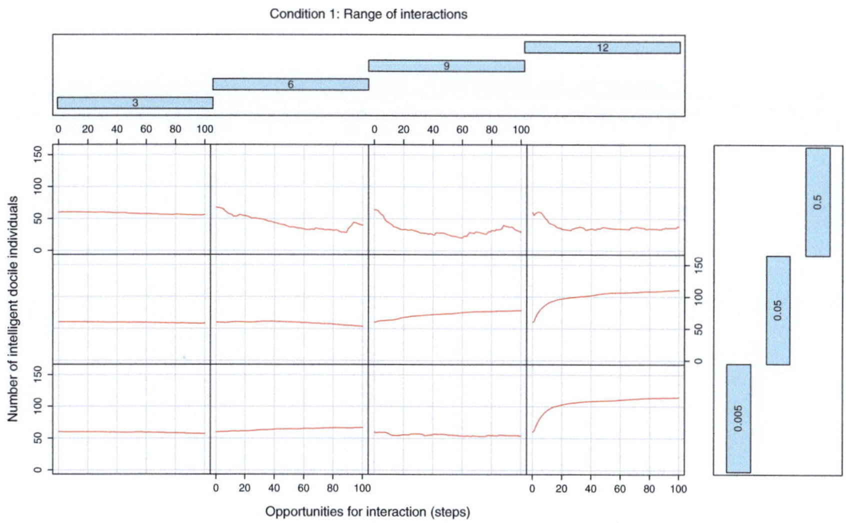

Fig. 9.4 Number of *id* for *impact* = 0, given *cost* and *range*

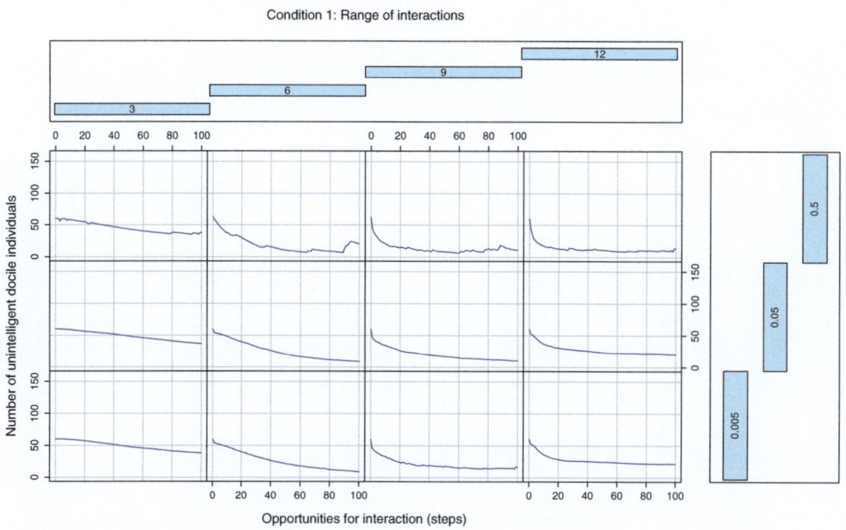

Fig. 9.5 Number of *ud* for *impact* = 0, given *cost* and *range*

9.3.3 The Docility Effect

The last set of conditions sees the *impact* of docility at 0.1, compared to the values attributed to the other parameters. Figure 9.7 shows that there is an increase in the number of *id* when the *cost* of prosocial behavior is in the low and mid range. The higher the *range* of interaction the more likely is that the *id* type is dominant.

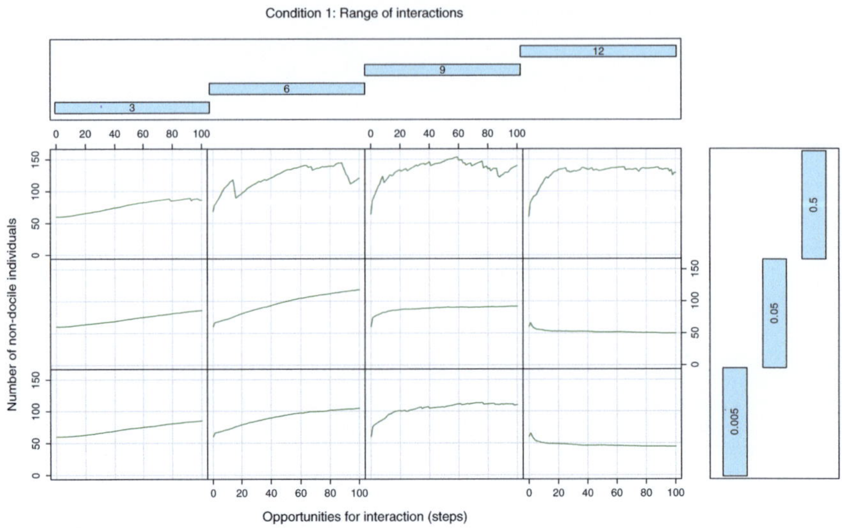

Fig. 9.6 Number of *nd* for *impact* = 0, given *cost* and *range*

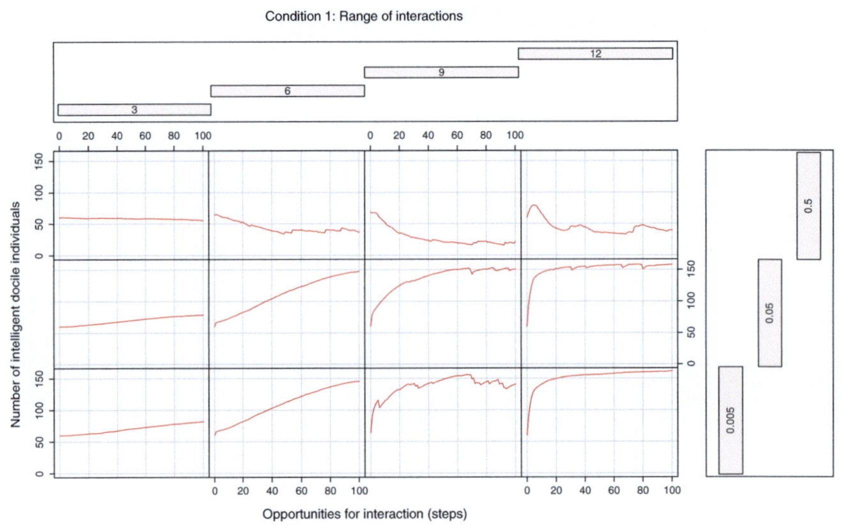

Fig. 9.7 Number of *id* for *impact* = 0.1, given *cost* and *range*

It is worth noting that the *cost* of prosocial behavior is particularly powerful for *id*s in that it has a strong impact in the spread of the attitude to the other types of individuals. The other type of docile individual, *ud*, never increases due to the high value of *impact* and its population in the organization reaches low values that suggest most of them switched to either *id* or *nd*, depending on when these are perceived as successful strategies, respectively.

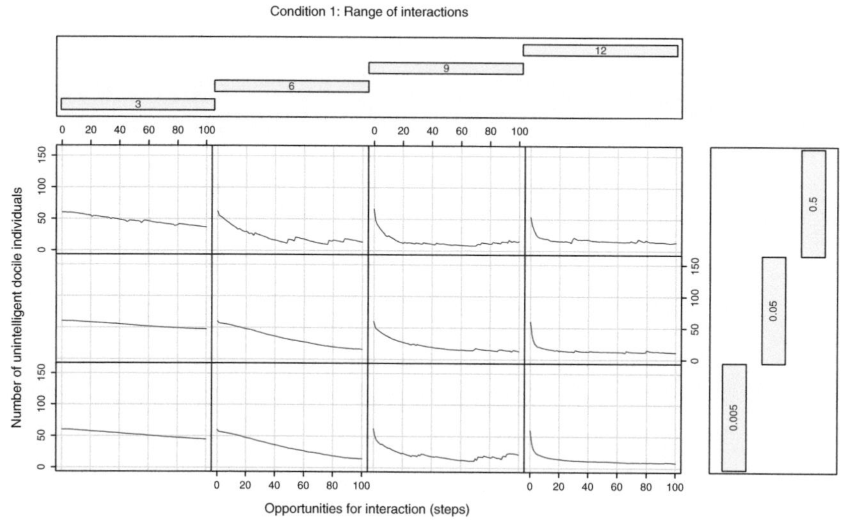

Fig. 9.8 Number of *ud* for *impact* = 0.1, given *cost* and *range*

Figure 9.9 represents increases or decreases in the population of *nd* individuals. As expected, when the *cost* of prosocial behavior is high, most of the other types switch to a non-docile type, independent of the *range* of interactions. As far as the other conditions are concerned, *nd* numbers decrease steadily when there is a sound and positive *impact* on social fitness from adopting docile attitudes. The conditions in the bottom left sections of Figs. 9.8 and 9.9 seem very similar (see the Appendix for statistical tests).

9.4 Implications and Conclusions

Some implications can be drawn from the results presented above. The simulation model has been entirely built on theoretical assumptions and it needs to be tested empirically (or validated, Fagiolo, Moneta, & Windrum, 2007; Moss, 2008). What I try to offer below are tentative implications, based solely on the simulation model results.

Previous studies isolated the elements that affect docility (Knudsen, 2003; Secchi & Bardone, 2009; Simon, 1993) but it is only with this ABM that we can estimate which element has a stronger impact on docile behaviors. It seems that docility prevails over other cognitive strategies when (a) the costs of prosocial behavior are not high, and (b) agents operate with higher ranges of interaction.

Results from simulated data show that the costs of prosocial behavior are extremely significant in understanding how docility emerges and becomes a prevalent cognitive attitude. In the previous pages, it was assumed that the cost of

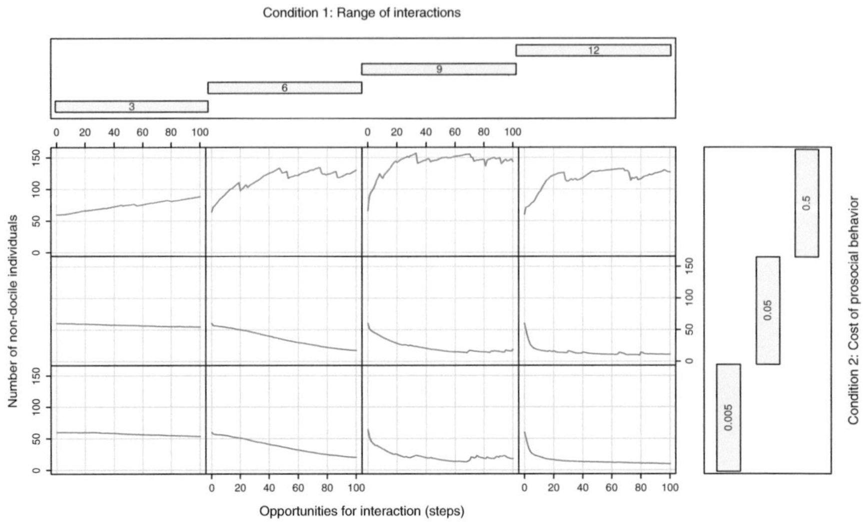

Fig. 9.9 Number of *nd* for *impact* = 0.1, given *cost* and *range*

prosocial behavior is "socially attributed," i.e. these are behaviors that an organization may encourage o discourage. This is then perceived by individuals in the organization and it may affect their attitudes and, ultimately, their behavior (Frey & Meier, 2004). Therefore, the burden of a high cost for behaving pro-socially makes individuals switch to *nd*. What exactly are these "costs" is an important area of enquiry that may reveal to be particularly helpful in moving this research forward.

When the *impact* of docility on fitness is positive unveils results that are probably similar to what we would have expected. However, in line with what written above, it is possible to draw the conclusion that cost is, by far, the most important variable in the equation, determining the emergence of the intelligent type among docile individuals. Even when the impact of docility is extremely positive, a high cost prevents individuals from turning into *id*. In fact, Fig. 9.7 shows that higher costs prevent *id* from being the dominant type, making *nd* always on the rise. It is worth noting that there is an interesting oscillatory pattern when the range of interaction is at its highest level that probably requires further exploration. Contrary to what emerged in previous studies, the *ud* is not very much an option when the contribution of docility to fitness is high and positive. Again, this is probably consistent with what is expected, however the model presented in this chapter tests this for the first time. Let me consider again the intriguing result on the increase of the *nd* type when costs are high and range is high, under the case of direct positive impact on fitness for docility. This points to the fact that, as already written above, the single parameter most important for docility to emerge is cost. This single finding is, per se, very significant and somehow new in docility research. This is the first time a study shows that the cost added to the fitness function is the one single most important factor affecting the emergence of docility.

Of course, there is the opposite effect when costs are in the low end. The most preferred strategy is that of the *id*, with some exceptions. One is that, when the impact of docility is negative then *nd* becomes the favorite strategy again. It seems that *nd* resembles a backup strategy, something agents use when conditions are not favorable or do not match their cognitive processes. This latter strategy is, in fact, much cheaper than the others as it involves free riding or other types of selfish behavior (Knudsen, 2003; Simon, 1993). The active-passive exchange that comes with docility involves costs and some benefits (better fit with the social environment). It may seem logical to expect that, when these two conditions are not met—i.e., costs are positive and contribution to fitness is negative—docility can never prosper. This is where results get interesting.

When the direct contribution of docility to fitness is negative, then *ud* individuals have better chances to succeed. There are two elements that can be pointed out in this case. First, docility is supported even when it is not "strategic," meaning that it contributes negatively to the chances of success in a social environment. This is probably related to the fact that the docile strategy of *ud* does not discriminate and, for this reason, they record a slightly lower impact of docility on their fitness compared to *id*s. It is as if quantity is preferred to quality of interactions, since this only happens when the interactions among agents are at the highest level (*range* $\geq$9). It seems that all it takes for a docile strategy to emerge (either *ud* or *id*) is that interactions are set at the highest level, independent of all the other conditions. This may be explained by the fact that, more than direct fitness benefits, docility contributes to the individual depending on interactions and social exchanges. Ultimately, docility is a social exchange mechanism. The higher the number of "social channels" (Secchi & Bardone, 2009; Simon, 1993) the more likely is that active-passive exchange of recommendations, advice, information are used to make decisions. This may happen passively, leading to bandwagons (e.g., Rosenkopf & Abrahamson, 1999), or more actively, leading to increased mindfulness (e.g., Secchi & Bardone, 2013), depending on high range of interaction and mid-low costs. Given these conditions, the direct impact of fitness seems to be irrelevant. Therefore, it may be a good organizational strategy to eliminate communication boundaries and share information freely. Again, this may be an effect of the quantity vs quality element that brings *ud* to succeed when the impact of docility is negative but it may eventually lead to more people switching to *id* if impact/fitness change. This is arguably a slow process, since it operates at a deeper level, making distributed cognition a favored element in how individuals perceive themselves as a good fit in a given social environment (Kunda, 1999).

There is another read for the emergence of *ud* when impact is negative. Non-docile individuals are described as selfish and their presence in the system seems to be somehow related to the negative impact that docility has on fitness for the other two types. In these cases, there is a fitness decrease when people are docile, and this makes *nd* the most widespread type at almost every configuration of the parameter. This is all fine and probably predictable. However, when individuals have the opportunity to interact with a larger number of individuals and the cost of being docile decreases, then things change. If docile behavior is relatively cheap, there is no reason why people should not perform it. Especially in the case of cost = 0.005, the incidence is so small that results show that individuals do not think of cost-related implications of their behavior. In this particular case, the fitness functions of docile and non-docile individuals are very similar. The cost is so small that it can be neglected although there still is a difference between the two functions. In fact, docile individuals have a decrease in fitness because they are docile and that is defined by impact being negative (0.1 in the example). The intelligent type is ruled out quickly while the unintelligent is not and it prospers. The explanation may be exactly the one implied above. The choice whether to be docile or not becomes irrelevant or, probably, almost mechanic. Under the circumstances of a social environment, the social being prefers docile thinking and behavior as a basic condition of existence. However, performing docility in an intelligent fashion seems to leave too much room to selfish individuals while having it to just "function" (i.e., as an *ud*) seems to be the default.

As stated above, *nd* agents always prevail when the costs of prosocial behaviors are high. Another element that can be brought in to explain this finding is that the environment (i.e., the organization) favors internal competition over cooperation. This may explain the switch to *nd* as a successful cognitive strategy; it is too costly to act pro-socially. There are examples of organizations that are known to make internal competition their functional basis. Most investment banks have not found the value of cooperation and are well known for a "dog-eat-dog" (the Hobbesian *homo homini lupus*) environment that causes high turnover and job dissatisfaction in the long run. Under this angle, the simulation seems a correct representation of what can be found in the real world.

Another occasion where the simulation brings in unexpected results is the case of zero *impact*. Under that condition, this time *id* flourish, surprisingly, when cost is low. Instead, *ud* are those who suffer the most: Why does this happen? Why has the result changed as opposed to the case when impact is negative? Is it how we would have expected it to happen? Was this clear from previous models? The answer to the last two questions is negative. Such a result is unexpected in relation to the findings discussed above (i.e., the case of negative impact) and also unexpected in relation to the original model. Previous models of docility postulate that there must be a positive impact on the fitness function in order for it to emerge in a population. This simulation shows that this is not always necessary, docility emerges also due to other circumstances. Specifically, it can be brought in by increased interactions among individuals and by its extremely low cost. This information was not available by running any of the previous models. Why is the *id* type increasing this time instead of *nd* or *ud*? I believe the explanation may be of the kind used above. Being docile does not bring immediate benefits to fitness (in terms of impact) nor it brings costs. Hence, the default is that of behaving in line with requirements of a social environment. This time there are no negative consequences of behaving this way so individuals can be almost strategic or be docile more tactically with the other individuals.

In short, the bounds for docility can be summarized as follows: (a) limited costs for prosocial behaviors (e.g., incentives, organizational support); (b) high range of interactions; (c) good fitness gains due to docility.

9.4.1 Ideas for Future Research and Concluding Remarks

The model can be expanded in many ways. By discussing about future research with this model, I also highlight some of the most striking limitations of the study. Before getting there, I would like to make a few statements on the justification of the use of ABM in the light of some of the results being foreseeable. The model was built to test "boundary" conditions that limit or enhance the presence of docility amongst organizational members. The use of agent-based simulations is supposed to bring in complexity and systemic effects to the model so that *emergent* phenomena can be observed. Most of the emergent aspects of the model presented here are in line with what one could expect before running the model (e.g., the impact of cost). However, some other aspects are not immediately clear or visible before the model is run (e.g., to what extent cost is effective, how "impact" affects the emergence of docility). The point here is that even in the case some results are not completely unexpected, the use of ABM is justified by the fact that it brings complexity and a "touch" of reality to the assumptions. The ABM community is always cheerful when a relatively simple model shows unexpected results. However, that should not be a criteria to judge the validity or the appropriateness of any given model. Sometimes, even reality goes as we expect it to go, given certain premises. Why shouldn't we expect models to behave in a similar fashion? In summary, this model is particularly tied to the original docility model and it attempts to test its limits. I believe what we found only in part supports the original claims that authors (Knudsen, 2003; Secchi & Bardone, 2009; Simon, 1993) made on docility, on the one hand, and specifies under what conditions those claims operate, on the other.

The ideas for future research presented below are divided in contributions to theory (first and second) and implications for practitioners (third and fourth). First, the structure of individual types can be completed by adding the fourth type to docile and intelligent, docile and unintelligent, non-docile and intelligent, and non-docile and unintelligent. An individual may free-ride or behave exploiting others however, some may do it in a more arrogant way that would ultimately upset other individuals. Some others may just do it as a strategy to survive.

Second, it is possible to allow agents to "come and go" at different times, depending on fitness. This implies that the model to compare with this "adaptation" model is the one that allows individuals to leave or join the organization. This is an important step to make the ABM more realistic. The best model possible would probably have both switching and mechanisms of firing/hiring.

Third, the impact and the cost can be modeled adding a parameter to represent how agents "perceive" them. This can be done with a value that remains stable and the same for everyone and then adding another value that would simulate a

Person-Organization fit (e.g., Edwards, 2008), i.e. the extent to which an individual values are in line with those of the organization. Another direction could be to posit the impact of docility on fitness as a dependent variable, letting it vary in relation to individual and organizational characteristics. The model presented here makes these assumptions too simplistic, taking directly from Simon's original equations. For example, the previous equations are based on a functional instrumental approach, where costs and extent of prosocial behavior define fitness. A different function (vector) can be defined adding variables more grounded in socio-cognitive and psychological tuning between the agent and the environment.

Fourth, organizations can also be analyzed as dissipative systems (Prigogine & Stengers, 1986) where docility can be thought of as a regulatory mechanism. A further step taken with the model would be that of analyzing how these socio-cognitive mechanisms affect dissipative structures (Stacey, 2003).

Finally, the ABM may allow agents to select those with whom to get in touch (and estimate fitness) instead of having a randomly generated procedure that makes the choice chance-based.

This chapter attempted to answer two questions: (1) Under what conditions is docility supported and/or encouraged? (2) What are the conditions under which other cognitive strategies emerge? These were addressed using an ABM that made Simon's model more complex and dynamic in an attempt to better represent reality. Simulated findings suggest that organizational support is key to docility and it should encourage it with incentives for individuals that embark in prosocial behavior. This implies that the community (the organization) may put some costs on those that behave pro-socially and this hinders the emergence or the increase of docile attitudes. The other condition that helps the emergence of docility is a relatively more flexible environment where individuals are allowed to interact more with each other. When these conditions are not met and in every case when costs of prosocial behavior are high, non-docile attitudes become prevalent.

Appendix

The following statistical tests were performed to circumstantiate results where the figures do not seem to provide a clear definite indication of what is happening.

Impact = –0.1

A *t*-test confirms that *ud* numbers are different when cost is at 0.05—$t = 33.38, df = 160.47, p < 0.001$—for $ud_{range=9}$ and $ud_{range=12}$. Another test shows similar results when *cost* is lowered to 0.005: $t = 32.95, df = 177.11, p < 0.001$.

The distribution of *nd* in the case of $range = 12$ and $cost = 0.05$ is significantly different from *ud*—$t = 45.40, df = 182.67, p < 0.001$—and from *id*—$t =$

$-13.94, df = 139.36, p < 0.001$—with $mean_{nd} = 42.14$, $mean_{id} = 28.89$, and $mean_{ud} = 108.96$. When *range*=12 and *cost*=0.005 *nd* are also significantly different from *ud*—$t = 49.04, df = 177.13, p < 0.001$—and from *id*—$t = -16.25, df = 152.71, p < 0.001$—with $mean_{nd} = 41.85$, $mean_{id} = 27.15$, and $mean_{ud} = 110.99$.

Impact = 0.1

A battery of *t*-tests show that results are significantly different when *range* = 3 and *cost* is either 0.05 or 0.005. In the former case, we have $t = -8.06, df = 136.19, p < 0.001$, with $mean_{ud} = 53.42$ and $mean_{nd} = 57.12$. In the latter case, the test is $t = -9.11, df = 139.85, p < 0.001$, with $mean_{ud} = 52.46$ and $mean_{nd} = 57.30$. This also implies that there is no significant difference in *ud* numbers under these conditions—$t = -0.65, df = 193.18, p = 0.52$. Some additional tests also show that there is no significant difference between *nd* and *ud* when *range* = 6 and *cost* = 0.05: $t = -1.33, df = 199.81, p = 0.18$, with $mean_{ud} = 33.27$ and $mean_{nd} = 35.73$. These two types follow a very similar pattern when *range* = 6 and *cost* = 0.05: $t = -1.33, df = 199.81, p = 0.18$.

References

Abrahamson, E., & Rosenkopf, L. (1997). Social network effects on the extent of innovation diffusion: A computer simulation. *Organization Science, 8*(3), 289–309.

Bardone, E. (2011). *Seeking chances. From biased rationality to distributed cognition*. Cognitive Systems Monographs (Vol. 13). New York: Springer.

Bardone, E., & Secchi, D. (2009). Distributed cognition: A research agenda for management. In M. A. Rahim (Ed.), *Current topics in management. Organizational behavior, performance, and effectiveness* (Vol. 14, pp. 183–207). New Brunswick, NJ: Transaction Publishers.

Bonaccio, S., & Dalal, R. S. (2006). Advice taking and decision-making: An integrative literature review, and implications for the organizational sciences. *Organizational Behavior and Human Decision Processes, 101*, 127–151.

Clark, A. (2008). *Supersizing the mind. Embodiment, action, and cognitive extension* (3rd ed.). New York: Oxford University Press.

Clark, A., & Chalmers, D. J. (1998). The extended mind. *Analysis, 58*, 7–19.

Clark, T. (2004). The fashion of management fashion: A surge too far? *Organization, 11*(2), 297–306.

Cohen, J. (1988). *Statistical power analysis for the behavioral sciences* (2nd ed.). Hillsdale, NJ: LEA.

Cohen, J. (1992). A power primer. *Psychological Bulletin, 112*, 155–159.

Dalal, R. S., & Bonaccio, S. (2010). What types of advice do decision-makers prefer? *Organizational Behavior and Human Decision Processes, 112*, 11–23.

David, R. J., & Strang, D. (2006). When fashion is fleeting: Transitory collective beliefs and the dynamics of TQM consulting. *Academy of Management Journal, 49*(2), 215–233.

Edwards, J. R. (2008). Person–environment fit in organizations: An assessment of theoretical progress. *Academy of Management Annals, 2*(1), 167–230.
Ellison, N. B., Steinfield, C., & Lampe, C. (2007). The benefits of Facebook "friends": Social capital and college students' use of online social networks sites. *Journal of Computer-Mediated Communication, 12*(4), 1143–1168.
Esposito, E. (2011). Originality through imitation: The rationality of fashion. *Organization Studies, 32*(5), 603–613.
Fagiolo, G., Moneta, A., & Windrum, P. (2007). A critical guide to empirical validation of agent-based models in economics: Methodologies, procedures, and open problems. *Computational Economics, 30*, 195–226.
Fehr, E., & Fischbacher, U. (2003). The nature of human altruism. *Nature, 425*(6960), 785.
Fiol, C. M., & O'Connor, E. J. (2003). Waking up! Mindfulness in the face of bandwagon. *Academy of Management Review, 28*(1), 54–70.
Fioretti, G. (2013). Agent-based simulation models in organization science. *Organizational Research Methods, 16*(2), 227–242.
Frey, B. F., & Meier, S. (2004). Pro-social behavior in a natural setting. *Journal of Economic Behavior and Organization, 54*, 65–88.
Gavetti, G., Levinthal, D., & Ocasio, W. (2007). Neo-carnegie: The carnegie school's past, present, and reconstructing for the future. *Organization Science, 18*(3), 523–536.
George, J. M. (1991). State or trait: Effects of positive mood on prosocial behaviors at work. *Journal of Applied Psychology, 76*(2), 299–307.
Gino, F., Brooks, A. W., & Schweitzer, M. E. (2012). Anxiety, advice, and the ability to discern: Feeling anxious motivates individuals to seek and use advice. *Journal of Personality and Social Psychology, 102*(3), 497–512.
Gino, F., & Moore, D. A. (2007). Effects of task difficulty on use of advice. *Journal of Behavioral Decision Making, 20*, 21–35.
Herath, D., Secchi, D., & Homberg, F. (2016). The effects of disorganization on goals and problem solving. In D. Secchi & M. Neumann (Eds.), *Agent-based simulation of organizational behavior. New frontiers of social science research*. New York: Springer.
Hutchins, E. (1995). *Cognition in the wild*. Cambridge, MA: MIT Press.
Kahneman, D. (2003). A perspective of judgement and choice. Mapping bounded rationality. *American Psychologist, 58*(9), 697–721.
Khalil, E. L. (2004). What is altruism? *Journal of Economic Psychology, 25*, 97–123.
Knudsen, T. (2003). Simon's selection theory: Why docility evolves to breed successful altruism. *Journal of Economic Psychology, 24*, 229–244.
Kunda, Z. (1999). *Social cognition. Making sense of people* (2nd ed.). Cambridge, MA: MIT Press.
Liu, X. S. (2014). *Statistical power analysis for the social and behavioral sciences*. New York: Routledge.
Magnani, L. (2007). *Morality in a technological world. Knowledge as a duty*. New York: Cambridge University Press.
Magnani, L., Secchi, D., & Bardone, E. (2007). The docile hacker: The open source model as a way of creating knowledge. In C. Schmidt (Ed.), *Proceedings from the International Conference on Computers and Philosophy 2006* (pp. 583–596). Laval, France: i-C&P.
March, J. G. (1994). *A primer on decision making*. New York: Free Press.
Miller, J. H., & Page, S. E. (2007). *Complex adaptive systems. An introduction to computational models of social life*. Princeton, NJ: Princeton University Press.
Miller, K. D., & Lin, S.-J. (2010). Different truths in different worlds. *Organization Science, 21*(1), 97–114.
Moss, S. (2008). Alternative approaches to the empirical validation of agent-based models. *Journal of Artificial Societies and Social Simulation, 11*(1), 5.
Neumann, M., & Cowley, S. J. (2016). Modelling social agency using diachronic cognition: Learning from the Mafia. In D. Secchi & M. Neumann (Eds.), *Agent-based simulation of organizational behavior. New Frontiers of social science research*. New York: Springer.

Ormiston, M., & Wong, E. M. (2013). License to ill: The effects of corporate social responsibility and CEO moral identity on corporate irresponsibility. *Personnel Psychology, 66*(4), 861–893.

Ossola, P. (2013). Trust as a mechanism to increase 'docility': A theoretical approach. *International Journal of Organization Theory and Behavior, 16*(4), 495–520.

Ou, C. X., Pavlou, P. A., & Davison, R. M. (2014). Swift guanxi in online marketplaces: The role of computer-mediated communication technologies. *MIS Quarterly, 38*(1), 209–230.

Plikynas, D., Raudys, A., & Raudys, S. (2016). Towards nonlocal field-like social interactions: Oscillating agent based conceptual and simulation framework. In D. Secchi & M. Neumann (Eds.), *Agent-based simulation of organizational behavior. New Frontiers of social science research*. New York: Springer.

Prigogine, I., & Stengers, I. (1986). *La nouvelle alliance*. Paris: Gallimard.

R Core Team. (2013). *R: A language and environment for statistical computing*. Vienna, Austria: R Foundation for Statistical Computing, http://www.r-project.org/ edition.

Rosenkopf, L., & Abrahamson, E. (1999). Modeling reputational and informational influences in threshold models of bandwagon innovation diffusion. *Computational and Mathematical Organization Theory, 5*(4), 361–384.

Ross, W. H., & Bohnert, D. (2010). The influence of social networking web sites on the evaluation of job candidates. *CyberPsychology and Behavior, 13*(3), 341–347.

Secchi, D. (2007). A theory of docile society: The role of altruism in human behavior. *Journal of the Academy of Business and Economics, 7*(2), 146–160.

Secchi, D. (2009). The cognitive side of social responsibility. *Journal of Business Ethics, 88*(3), 565–581.

Secchi, D. (2011). *Extendable rationality. Understanding decision making in organizations*. New York: Springer.

Secchi, D. (2014). *How many times should my simulation run? Power analysis for agent-based modeling*. In European Academy of Management Annual Conference, Valencia, Spain

Secchi, D. (2015). A case for agent-based model in organizational behavior and team research. *Team Performance Management, 21*(1/2), 37–50

Secchi, D., & Bardone, E. (2009). Super-docility in organizations. An evolutionary model. *International Journal of Organization Theory and Behavior, 12*(3), 339–379.

Secchi, D., & Bardone, E. (2013). Socially distributed cognition and intra-organizational bandwagons: Theoretical framework, model, and simulation. *International Journal of Organization Theory and Behavior, 16*(4), 521–572.

Simon, H. A. (1955). A behavioral theory of rational choice. *Quarterly Journal of Economics, 69*(1), 99–118.

Simon, H. A. (1979). Rational decision making in business organizations. *American Economic Review, 69*(4), 493–513.

Simon, H. A. (1990). A mechanism for social selection and successful altruism. *Science, 250*, 1665–1668.

Simon, H. A. (1993). Altruism and economics. *American Economic Review, 83*(2), 156–161.

Simon, H. A. (1997). *Administrative behavior* (4th ed.). New York: The Free Press.

Stacey, R. D. (2003). *Strategic management and organisational dynamics: The challenge of complexity*. Harlow: FT/Prentice Hall.

Staw, B. M., & Epstein, L. D. (2000). What bandwagons bring: Effects of popular management techniques on corporate performance, reputation, and CEO pay. *Administrative Science Quarterly, 45*, 523–556.

Strang, D., & Tuma, N. B. (1993). Spatial and temporal heterogeneity in diffusion. *American Journal of Sociology, 99*, 614–639.

Thomsen, S. E. (2016). How docility impacts team efficiency. An agent-based modeling approach. In D. Secchi & M. Neumann (Eds.), *Agent-based simulation of organizational behavior. New Frontiers of social science research*. New York: Springer.

von Neumann, J., & Morgenstern, O. (1944). *Theory of games and economic behavior*. Princeton, NJ: Princeton University Press.

Watson, D., & Pennebaker, J. W. (1989). Health complaints, stress, and distress: Exploring the central role of negative affectivity. *Psychological Review, 96*, 234–254.

Wilensky, U. (1999). *Netlogo*. Center for Connected Learning and Computer-Based Modeling. Evanston, IL: Northwestern University.

York, J. G., Sarasvathy, S. D., & Wicks, A. C. (2013). An entrepreneurial perspective on value creation in public-private ventures. *Academy of Management Review, 38*(2), 307–309.

Part III
Philosophical and Methodological Perspectives

Chapter 10
Intervening via Chance-Seeking

Emanuele Bardone

Abstract The main aim of this paper is to offer an epistemological discussion concerning a set of terms that can be useful for researchers when it comes to debating the predicaments related to the notion of intervention. Intervention is everything that a scientist or researcher does. More specifically, it is about what a researcher does with either an explicit or implicit intention to generate new hypotheses and views around a certain issue as well as to try to reach a better understanding of it. The set of terms that I am going to discuss in the paper will revolve around the notion of chance-seeking, which will help illustrate and stress the forward-looking dimension characterizing the notion of intervention.

Keywords Tinkering • Chance-seeking • Intervention • Phronesis • Abduction

10.1 Introduction

Richard Feynman once claimed that philosophy of science is about as useful for scientists as ornithology is to birds (Thagard, 2009). That is indeed, quite an interesting view. Whether one agrees with Feynman or not, I argue that such a statement addresses an important issue that is related to the role that philosophy of science may have for those who actually practice science and research.

One may argue that philosophy of science may help to clarify how certain terms are used, those notions that define the practice. Or, in some other case, it helps researchers reflect about certain methodological issues. So, a philosophical contribution can help discuss what we mean by terms like models and simulations. Or what kind of notion of causation is tacitly assumed, for example. In some other case we may discuss the ontological value of models. In this paper I decided not to touch upon any of these topics, but to address a broader issue that has to deal with the notion of *intervention*. In a nutshell, intervention can be defined as the *practical*

E. Bardone (✉)
Centre for Educational Technology, Institute of Education, University of Tartu, Tartu, Estonia
e-mail: bardone@ut.ee

D. Secchi, M. Neumann (eds.), *Agent-Based Simulation of Organizational Behavior*, DOI 10.1007/978-3-319-18153-0_10

side of science. It is not about theories, laws and the like—i.e. *what* researchers discover during research. It is about what researchers *do* in pursuing those theories, laws, etc.

However, in this paper I will not try to describe what researchers do, i.e. how they intervene. Nor will I try to provide a set of prescriptions about how to intervene. My aim is to offer a discussion concerning a set of terms that I find particularly useful when it comes to debating the predicaments related to intervention. I will not offer a discussion specifically related to intervention and agent-based modelling. Conversely, the discussion that I offer will (hopefully) furnish a kind of toolbox enabling the reader to get a handle on modelling as an intervention for herself/himself. That is, I will leave the reader the task to see how the discussion that I will develop on a quite abstract level can actually be applied to modelling and, more specifically, to agent-based modelling.

As I wrote before, intervention is everything that a scientist or researcher does. More specifically, it is about what a researcher does with either an explicit or implicit intention to generate new hypotheses and views around a certain issue as well as to try to reach a better understanding of it. In this regard, modelling can be considered as a form of intervention, which, in my view, does not specifically aim to prove or test hypotheses. Rather, it has the unique feature to expand our ability of *exploring* ways in which a phenomenon under investigation can be represented for further investigation. But what does the term "explore" mean in this specific context? What does it refer to in a concrete sense?

In my view, the term "explore" (and the like) suitably applies to intervention, because it captures an important feature, which is its *prospective*, *forward-looking* character. In order to clarify this I will start from the notion of abduction. Abduction has been referred to as the kind of "logic" that underlies scientific discovery and hypothesis generation. I will then move on and try to show how abduction is not the right candidate for illustrating the "logic" that, conversely, characterises intervention. I will point out that abduction is a valuable candidate when it comes to account for the way one may come up with a new hypothesis explaining a phenomenon under investigation. But it falls short when it comes to describing the tentative and prospective dimension characterising intervention. In the second part of the paper I will introduce the notion of chance-seeking in order to describe precisely this tentative, forward-looking dimension. More specifically, I will define chance-seeking as tinkering with chance events.

10.2 Abduction and Intervention

10.2.1 Abduction and Hypothesis Generation

More than a 100 years ago, Peirce (1992–1998) pointed to the concept of abduction in order to illustrate that the process of scientific discovery is not irrational and that a methodology of discovery is possible. Peirce interpreted abduction essentially as an "inferential" creative process for generating a new hypothesis.

Peirce helped clarify the notion of abduction by providing the following description:

> A fact, *C*, is observed.
> if *H* were true, *C* would be a matter of course.
> Hence, there is reason to suspect that *H* is true.

Abduction has a logical form (fallacious, if we model abduction by using classical syllogistic logic) distinct from deduction and induction. Within a syllogistic framework, abduction can be described as follows:

> All men are mortal,
> Socrates is mortal.
> Therefore, Socrates is a man.

As one can easily recognise, this is indeed a fallacious reasoning. And the reason is that Socrates can also be a cat, for instance. A cat is in fact mortal as well. Interestingly, the fallacious nature of this kind of reasoning is also what gives us the possibility to go beyond what we already know. Abduction is in fact an *ampliative* type of reasoning. That is, it potentially helps us enlarge our knowledge base—what we already know. If I say, as in deductive reasoning, that all men are mortal and Socrates is a man, then I can indeed derive the consequence that Socrates is mortal. However, that would be already present in the two premises. Conversely, in abduction the conclusion we derive from the two premises is in a way telling us something new, something that is not already implicitly stated in the premises.

Peirce's account adds an important detail to the picture. In an abduction the conclusion—which is a hypothesis—plays a specific function: it is selected or created, because it *explains* a given set of *known facts*. This is of capital importance, because it helps us see how an *explanatory hypothesis* can be generated. An explanatory hypothesis is generated, because it appears to be a good candidate to explain certain facts. So, if we go back to the previous example, the fact that Socrates is mortal *hints* at his being a man in a sense that the hypothesis that Socrates is a man (potentially) *explains* that he is mortal.

Magnani (2001, 2009) defines abduction as the process of inferring certain hypotheses that render some sentences plausible, that explain or discover some (eventually new) phenomenon or observation; it is the process of reasoning in which explanatory hypotheses are formed and evaluated. Gabbay and Woods labelled this conception of abduction the *AKM* model, as it stresses its explanatory dimension (Gabbay & Woods, 2005). According to Magnani (2001), there are two main epistemological meanings of the word abduction: (1) abduction that only generates "plausible" hypotheses ("selective" or "creative") and (2) abduction considered as inference "to the best explanation", which also evaluates explanatory hypotheses. An illustration from the field of medical knowledge is represented by the discovery of a new disease and its manifestations which can be considered as the result of a creative abductive inference.[1] Therefore, "creative" abduction deals with the whole field of the growth of scientific knowledge. This is irrelevant in medical diagnosis where instead the task is to "select" from an encyclopaedia of pre-stored diagnostic entities. We can call both inferences ampliative, selective and creative, because in both cases the reasoning involved amplifies, or goes beyond, the information incorporated in the premises (Magnani, 2001).

Abduction can fairly account for some crucial theoretical aspects of hypothesis generation as well as manipulative ones. Accordingly, Magnani (2001) distinguishes between two general abductions, *theoretical abduction* and *manipulative abduction*. Theoretical abduction illustrates much of what is important in creative abductive reasoning and in computational programs. It regards verbal/symbolic abductive inferences, but also all those inferential processes which are model-based and related to the exploitation of *internalised* models of diagrams, pictures, etc. In contrast to that, manipulative abduction accounts for those situations in which an explanatory hypothesis is formed "through doing". A simple example illustrating this point is the following. Suppose that we receive a birthday present. It is wrapped so that it is impossible to see what it is. As soon as we *sense* the pack, i.e. weigh, shake, rotate it, we come up with a number of guesses regarding what it may contain. If it is a hard, compact, modestly heavy "thing", then we may abduce that it is a book. The explanatory hypothesis is formulated very much in a distributed and embodied fashion, "through doing" as Magnani would put it. Which means that the clues that enable us to almost instantaneously guess that "yes, it's a book" mostly come from what we sense and perceive in the *here and now*, while we are playing with the package still unwrapped. Interestingly, other types of clues may indeed come into play, i.e. clues coming from *different time scales* (Hemmingsen, 2013; Torre, 2014; Vallée-Tourangeau & Cowley, 2013). For example, if the gift comes from a friend who is a book lover, then we may take that into consideration when we try to guess. This is a type of clue that does not come *directly* at the time of the interaction with the birthday present. It comes from our knowledge base.

Although in the study of abduction its manipulative dimension has been recognised, as I have just tried to show, it is not yet entirely clear how abduction can account for other aspects of hypothesis generation that are *not* related to coming up with an explanatory hypothesis—either it is done by relying on language, a model or through doing. To put it roughly: abduction is the kind of inference that produces an explanation for a given set of facts, clues or signs. But *where do those facts, clues and signs come from in the first place?* If we go back to the example of the birthday present, it is worth distinguishing between two different hypothetical activities. The first is the activity of guessing that, given certain clues, signs or facts, then it follows that things must be so, i.e., it must be a book. Abduction fairly accounts for this. The

[1] It is worth noting that different scholars have questioned the idea that abduction is exclusively explanatory, that is, it exclusively deals with the formation and evaluation of an explanatory hypothesis. For more information on this topic, see Gabbay and Woods (2005) and Magnani (2009, Ch. 2).

second activity specifically regards what we do, how we intervene, in my example, how we manipulate the birthday present. This second activity is still hypothetical, and yet of a different kind. Let us see why.

10.2.2 Intervention and Its Puzzles

As priorly mentioned, abduction operates on a set of known facts that function like clues or signs. It follows that the veracity of a conclusion also depends on the set of relevant clues or signs that it operates on. Which implies that the selection of such a set of relevant clues or signs is fundamental. This, indeed, opens up another and even more challenging aspect related to science and growth of scientific knowledge, which—I claim—has to do with *intervention*. As far as I am concerned here, intervention refers to two major elements. First of all, scientists are not passive observers: they always take part in the selection (and construction) of relevant facts. Besides, scientists inevitably have to face the burden of making boundary judgments, that is, to determine what is empirically relevant and what is not (Ulrich, 2000). Intervention is driven by one's understanding of the problem that he or she is actually facing.

However, and this is the second element, understanding is not formed and reached in a cognitive vacuum once and for all, but it is to a great extent—the result of reiterated interactions with the environment where the scientist operates. Agency as well as understanding is enriched in the interaction with external objects precisely because of the constant interaction going on between humans and their environment (see, for example, recent work done around this issue by Cowley & Vallée-Tourangeau, 2013; Perry, 2013; Steffensen, 2013). That is to say, the scientist's understanding is shaped and re-shaped through intervention.

This shaping and re-shaping of our understanding is particularly clear in the case of epistemic actions (or epistemic activities). According to Kirsh and Maglio (1994), epistemic actions are those actions that alter the representation of the task one is facing. Shaking a birthday present in order to guess what it contains is a perfect example of epistemic action. It prepares the basis for further investigation. Interestingly, an epistemic action may well be devoid of any particular understanding. This is brought to its extreme conclusion in the fictional dialogue between Gregory and Sherlock Holmes in the short story *Silver Blaze* by Sir Arthur Conan. In the dialogue Holmes is asked by Gregory—Scotland Yard detective—if there is something he would draw his attention to. Holmes points to the curious incident of the dog in the night-time. Actually, the dog did nothing. And that was exactly what Holmes was pointing to. That was the curious incident.

So, on the one hand, scientists are not passive observers, as they select and, to a certain extent, *construct* the relevant facts that they are going to factor. That is informed by the current understanding of the problem they are facing. On the other hand, it is precisely via intervening that scientists iteratively shape and re-shape their understanding of the problem.

An example illustrating this point is a fictional one and comes from the 1990 American film *Awakenings*. The film—based on Oliver Sack's autobiographical book *Awakenings*—tells the story of a neurologist called Malcolm Sayer, who at the end of the Sixties dealt with a number of patients with severe behavioural problems following the 1917–1928 epidemic of *encephalitis lethargica*. The epidemic left them catatonic. There is a crucial scene in the film, in which the doctor—portrayed by American actor Robin Williams—interviews one of those lethargic patients named Lucy. After a few unanswered questions, the doctor understands that there is very little to gain by trying to engage the lethargic patient, who seems not to respond to any stimuli coming from the outside world. So, out of courtesy, he takes the patient's glasses off to clean them, then puts them back and turns around from the patient to make a few notes on the typewriter on his desk. As he is finishing his notes, he hears that the patient has made a sudden movement. He turns back to her and sees that she is now bent over her feet holding her pair of glasses. The doctor is indeed puzzled, as he cannot explain how this could possibly happen with a catatonic patient. In order to further investigate he takes her glasses off again, brings her to the upright position, and puts the glasses on the floor expecting the patient to reproduce the same gesture as before. However, nothing happens. He then decides to have a second try. This time he takes the patient's glasses off and drops them. Surprisingly, the patient promptly reacts catching the glasses before they reach the floor.

This fictional example helps us see once again the distinction between two different types of hypothetical activities that I briefly referred to in the previous subsection. The doctor featured in the film does not know how to explain why the catatonic patient made the sudden movement that later puzzled him. He cannot make any *educated* guess to explain why the patient did what she did. Interestingly, his intervention can be viewed as a hypothetical activity—*epistemic*, as we saw from above, which is, however, of a different kind. In this case it is hypothetical in the sense that it is purely tentative, as the doctor *does not* know if what he is doing is useful or not. The term hypothesis refers to the fact that an action is taken without knowing what it will lead to. It is worth noting here that an intervention might be guided by some pre-conceptions that are explanatory in their nature. For instance, the doctor might have guessed that Lucy actually responded to a specific stimulus—the pair of glasses dropping on the floor. And that would have been the hypothesis guiding, or prompting, the intervention. If that would be the case, indeed, it would not anyway falsify the statement that intervention does not deal with explaining things, but exploring them (as I will show in the next section). Besides, the explanatory hypothesis guiding intervention is still a hypothesis to prove. Indeed, *in retrospection*—by looking backward—we know why the second attempt was the right one to make. But that is the case, precisely because we now know what the doctor was after. This is a very well-known fallacy called the narrative fallacy (Taleb, 2007).

To fully appreciate the tricky nature of this retrospective kind of thinking, I turn to a very simple example. Consider the following sentence:

> The Hundred Years' War began with England in control of the so-called English Channel and the North Sea.

This is a simple descriptive statement informing about the situation at the beginning of the war. And yet, as tricky as it may sound, it could not have been made at the time it refers to—the beginning of the war, a time in which nobody could know when the war could possibly end. Danto (1962) termed such statements "narrative" as one usually finds in them a reference to *a later point in time*. That is, they can only be said *after* the event they refer to comes to an end.

More generally, it seems that, if we want intervention to be rationally informed by some form of understanding, this can only be achieved in the light of those happenings that will follow an intervention. This somehow echoes the famous paradox that Polanyi (1962, p. 22) formulated in the following terms:

> To search for the solution of a problem is an absurdity. For either you know what you are looking for, and then there is no problem; or you do not know what you are looking for, and then you are not looking for anything and cannot expect to find anything.

It is not my aim here to discuss the paradox. It is sufficient to say that in my view the paradox emerges because we fail to fully understand the fundamental *tentativeness* and *looking-forwardness* of intervention, which, in turn, plays a pivotal role in any process dealing with discovery and creativity. But how to break it down? Can abduction help us?

10.2.3 Intervention and Its Logic

Above, I have argued that abduction is a powerful conceptual device to give an account of how an explanatory hypothesis is generated. Can we then employ the notion of abduction to clarify the tentative, forward-looking nature of intervention? Do explanation and intervention resort to the same underlying "logic"? My answer, as I have already hinted, is negative.

Consider now the following case. Suppose that John comes home and he sees that in the bathroom the light is on and the door is closed. He then guesses that his wife Beth is in the toilet. This is a very simple abduction. John infers that his wife is in the toilet from the two clues (or signs)—the light is on and the door is closed. The conclusion that John draws is explanatory, because it explains the presence of the two clues. Interestingly, the two clues are part of a specific set of signs that *jointly* appear and form what we may call a "symptomatology".

In this explanation there is also an important *causal* component to note. That is, John's conclusion can be taken as the *cause* explaining why the light is on in the toilet and the door is closed. Since we look backward to what has *already* happened, I claim that this kind of explanatory thinking is fundamentally *backward-looking*.

That is, it looks backward to those causes explaining why things are so. A final remark is that the conclusion that John reaches also has an important role in making him come to believe that a certain state of affairs is the case. That is, it deals with *belief formation*, as it makes him believe that something is the case.

Consider now another case. John comes home and, as soon as he steps in, he realises that he has lost his mobile phone and so all his contacts. He tells the story to his wife, who suggests that this might *mean* that he has to change something in his life. Here again we have a sign—the lost mobile phone along with all contacts—and a conclusion is drawn—John has to change something in his life. If we consider the inference made by Beth in the light of abduction, then we may be tempted to say that what she actually meant is that John has to change something in his life, *because* he lost the mobile phone.

However, one may interpret the second example in a quite different way. First of all, I may claim that the conclusion may not be taken as explanatory, rather, *exploratory*. This means that the conclusion that is drawn does not aim to explain the sign(s). Rather, John's wife takes the sign(s) as an opportunity or chance to explore the significance of a possible course of action.

So, in both cases we are dealing with a hypothetical activity. But the meaning that we give to the term hypothesis (and hypothetical) is different. In the first case the hypothetical activity is meant to claim that a state of affairs *is* the case (John's wife is in the bathroom). In science, for instance, this is very much the case of those experiments that are carried out to establish that a specific mechanism is at play. The experiment is meant to reproduce *in vitro* the phenomenon under investigation. Besides, the manipulation of the variables chosen is meant to show that the hypothesis formulated is the right one. In this specific case, as Magnani noted (Magnani, 2001, ch. 1), the notion of abduction accounts for the entire process of experimenting, which includes deductive as well as inductive elements besides the abductive ones.

In the second case the hypothetical activity is meant to explore, say, *a possible world*—a world whose intelligibility is for us still to come. That is, it does not aim to bring about some kind of definitive understanding about how things are in the *here and now*, but it aims to intervene in the world with a forward-looking, prospective intention, that is, to explore it.

Another important consideration to make is that in the second case the connection between sign(s) and conclusion is not causal, rather, it is *occasional*. Interestingly, if the light in the bathroom had been off, John would not have guessed that there is somebody in there. That is not the case in the second example. There is in fact no causal connection between losing a mobile phone and changing something in one's life. As I have just noted, the connection is *occasional*. That is, it may *suggest* a person to consider a course of action as somehow significant. So, John's wife may have suggested her husband to change something in his life independently from the event. Though, losing the mobile gave her *the chance* to do so. Moreover, Beth's conclusion is not meant to claim that a certain state of affairs is the case as in the first example. Her conclusion is not related to believing, but *intervening*. That is, it does not make us come to believe something, but it makes us come to *do* something.

There is a last consideration to make. As I have just noted, an explanation makes us believe that a state of affairs is the case. Conversely, when we intervene, we adopt a different attitude, which I would call "prospective" and "forward-looking". By that I mean that a course of action is taken in order to project us onto further opportunities, because we have not grasped something yet. This offers a completely different kind of justification. Usually, we tend to justify a specific course of action for what it leads us to. So, very often scientists have to *retrospectively* come up with justifications for actions they have already taken. In a way we come up with a valid explanation about why we did this or that, because we can see where this or that action eventually led to. In doing so we completely disregard the very simple fact that a certain course of action may have been taken as a mere attempt to get *somewhere*, that is, to simply get unstuck precisely as in the example from *Awakenings* that I presented above. For on a number of occasions, we select a course of action on the basis of the fact that *we hope* that it could lead us to further opportunities in a different direction. And that is a strategic choice that can never be rationally justified except retrospectively.

I will now summarise the main differences between these two types of "logic" that I, respectively, call *explanatory hypothesis* and *prospective hypothesis* in the following table.

Explanatory hypothesis	Prospective hypothesis
explanatory	exploratory
causal connection	occasional connection
believing	intervening
backward-looking	forward-looking
sign(s) as part of a symptomatology	sign(s) as chance

In this section I have argued that abduction provides a rich model illustrating how explanatory hypotheses are formed and evaluated. And yet it falls short when it comes to the investigation on the nature of intervention. I have tried to show why abduction fails to account for this forward-looking element characterising the phenomenon of intervention. In the next section, I will illustrate the notion of chance-seeking. What I am going to do is to try to shed light on the forward-looking nature of intervention. More specifically, I will try to single out a number of notions that seem to be coherent to the nature of intervention. So, I will leave more empirical considerations aside.

10.3 Intervention via Chance-Seeking

10.3.1 The Role of Chance Events

In the previous section I argued that intervention has its own "logic" that is different from the one underlying the selection or creation of explanatory hypotheses. When I presented the example of the lethargic patient, I argued that an explanatory hypothesis, about how things are, can be the basis for intervening in the world. More specifically, I pointed out that a pre-existing guess about why the patient picked up her glasses could in theory have guided the intervention process. And yet this would not be an argument supporting the idea that intervention can be reduced to an explanatory hypothetical activity. The reason is that, even when we rely on some pre-existing knowledge in the form of an explanatory hypothesis, that would count anyway as *chance*, that is, an opportunity that may be explored further. In this sense, I maintain that intervention has to deal with the exploitation of chances to one's advantage. In the remainder of this last section I will try to show that the fundamental forward-looking and prospective nature of intervention has to do with the way one may try to strategically utilise chance events to one's advantage, which is at the very core of the notion of chance-seeking.

One of the most popularised concepts related to investigating the role of chance events and, more generally, chance, is serendipity, which was popularised by Merton in his posthumous book *The Travels and Adventures of Serendipity* (Merton & Barber, 2006). Since then serendipity has increasingly become more and more popular, especially among historians and sociologists of science (see, for instance, de Rond & Morley, 2010). The term "serendipity" was actually coined more than two centuries ago by Horace Walpole in reference to making discoveries by accident and sagacity. He actually derived the expression from the Persian fairy tale "The Three Princes of Serendip". Serendip is an old name for Sri Lanka. Interestingly, The Century Dictionary defines the word "serendipper" as the one "who finds things unsought by merely dipping".

In the present usage, serendipity mainly refers to *unsought discoveries*. An interesting example is the invention of the Post-it note[2]. The Post-it note was invented by a gentlemen called Spencer Silver, who was at the time working at 3M, a company producing tapes and other forms of glue. Back then Silver was trying to develop a new adhesive, which had to be stronger than the ones already available on the market. After a few attempts Silver did not come up with a super-strong adhesive, but with one that was super-weak. This super-weak adhesive could stick to objects and at the same time it could easily be lifted off. The discovery was actually shelved for some time, until a colleague of Silver's, Arthur Fry, suggested that it could be used for bookmarking. Interestingly, Fry used to sing in the local

[2]http://web.mit.edu/invent/iow/frysilver.html.

church choir and he desperately needed something to keep his place in the hymnal without it falling out of the book every now and then. Silver's super-weak adhesive was the perfect solution to his problem.

The notion of serendipity acknowledges the role that is played by chance. However, I maintain that there is very little in that concept that helps us understand how we may come to use chance events strategically and, even more importantly, how we may handle situations that are fundamentally open to and thus affected by chance events. The idea of chance-seeking precisely tries to bridge this gap.

To introduce the notion of chance-seeking, the first thing to do is to demystify chance events. I posit that a chance event is nothing mysterious, as it can be defined as any event that falls outside of one's control, that is, an event that we *cannot anticipate*. For a chance conveys an opportunity as well as a risk for action (Ohsawa & McBurney, 2003), which appears to *potentially* have some strategic value in pursuing one's goal.

I argue that the strategic element of a chance event is intimately related to some sense of *meaningfulness* that is actually experienced by the subject. What appears meaningful is not that the chance event is perceived immediately relevant in relation to one's goal, i.e. it allows us to *directly* pursue our goal (Kay, 2011). Rather, its meaningfulness is perceived in relation to the fact that a chance event *may* help project the problem-solving process towards further chances. If we go back to the fictional example that I took from the film *Awakenings*, the doctor is actually trying out different options with some kind of *a sense of purposiveness*, which is, however, not accompanied by the actual ability of predicting (or understanding) what is going to happen (Chia & Holt, 2006). Conversely, it seems that, at least from a phenomenological point of view, he is open to *sensing the process*—a form of *ambulatory awareness*, which gives shape to knowledge *in the unfolding*, that is, *as he goes*, not before he goes (Ingold, 2001).

Indeed, the identification of what counts as a chance is subjective and contextual. That implies that its identification depends on several different factors specific to the single person on different time scales, including his or her knowledge, attitude, personality, and other more contingent and transitory factors like moods or feelings. I will come back to this issue in Sect. 10.3.4.

Having defined a chance as above, I now turn to the illustration of the idea of chance-seeking. It is worth noting that, in my view, chance-seeking does not deal with the prediction or anticipation of good chances, which by definition one cannot anticipate or predict. Conversely, I define chance-seeking as a form of intervention, which is characterised by the reliance on chance events and the amplification of their potential positive significance. Let us start with what I mean by "reliance on chance events".

10.3.2 Environmental Unanticipatedness as a Resource for Action

As mentioned above, a chance is related to our inability to guess and/or predict what is going to happen. It is important to note here that such an inability is not so much related to randomness as to *our inability to control.* So, a chance appears like a random event, simply because we cannot control the environment, and what is going on there. I claim that this inability may turn out to be a resource, which I propose to term "environmental unanticipatedness". The idea of environmental unanticipatedness posits that the environment plays an active role when we intervene, since we can rely on unanticipated and unexpected events, which, in turn, potentially open up the way to new pieces of information we would not be able to acquire otherwise. For instance, anomalies and falsifications are derived from environmental unanticipatedness, and they have been praised by several philosophers of science as a fundamental source of scientific knowledge (see Popper, 1959 and more recently Thagard, 2005 among many others).

Interestingly, we tend to assume that the distribution of cognition, and the subsequent extension of our ability to face and solve problems, can only regard the interaction with specific objects or tools, which, as a result, extend or shape specific cognitive abilities. However, little attention has been given precisely to situations in which it is the unanticipatedness of our ecology that turns out to be a formidable resource. Chinese general Sun Tzu in his The Art of War pointed out: "if we do not know what we need to know, then everything looks important". This means that under the condition of ignorance, we can only turn to our environment as a provider of unanticipated and potentially helpful events. In a way this is not so different from using a pen and paper to jot down some thought which otherwise would soon be gone. In both cases we lean on something external to us, something that we basically lack. For we must entrust ourselves to something we do not fully or partly own the way we own our brain.

There is, however, a crucial difference between environmental unanticipatedness and virtually all other forms in which cognition is distributed onto the environment: we turn to external objects, because we have a precise intent in mind. So, if we have to fix some thought, we look for a pencil and paper to prevent it from disappearing. In the case of environmental unanticipatedness, what we make use of is our ignorance. That is, we turn to environmental unanticipatedness, because we just do not know. In this sense environmental unanticipatedness is a major resource when we are facing an *impasse*, that is, a situation in which there are no known options that seem to be adequate to proceed with. Or, there are no options at all.

10.3.3 Chance-Seeking as Tinkering with Chance Events

As I mentioned above, chance-seeking is not limited to acknowledging the importance of chance events. In that respect, chance-seeking would not be different from serendipity. By contrast, chance-seeking aims to describe the amplification of the potential positive significance of chance events by taking advantage of what I called environmental unanticipatedness. By "potential positive significance" I mean that the amplification of a chance is not a random process. It is not, in other words, the same process as the flip of a coin. There is, I claim, some form of intentionality that is preserved. Indeed, the whole process of amplification is conjectural and it does not guarantee that the amplification will actually lead to the solution of a problem.

As I have noted above, the fact we cannot anticipate certain happenings in our ecology may turn out to be a resource when we cannot rely on a pre-determined course of action—a plan. When that is the case, we must adopt a forward-looking attitude. Interestingly, venturing into the unknown does not necessarily exclude purposiveness. If we cannot anticipate what is going to happen, we may try to amplify the positive potential of those chance encounters that happen to appear somehow meaningful to us. In doing so we do not proceed directly towards the endpoint of a problem-solving process, but *obliquely* (Chia, Holt, & Li, 2013; Kay, 2011).

This kind of process, which is at the heart of chance-seeking, can be characterised as a *deviation-amplifying mutual causal process*. This concept was introduced by Maruyama (1963) to refer to the fact that the outcome of a process is initiated by an insignificant or accidental "kick" and is then built upon its subsequent amplifications and so diverging from the initial condition. An example is the weathering of rock:

> A small crack in a rock collects some water. The water freezes and makes the crack larger. A larger crack collects more water, which makes the crack still larger. A sufficient amount of water then makes it possible for some small organisms to live in it. Accumulation of organic matter then makes it possible for a tree to start growing in the crack. The roots of the tree will then make the crack still larger.

The environmental feedback is so that deviations—in the form of unanticipated/unexpected events—are not counteracting our actions as in the case of following a predefined and planned course of action. Conversely, deviations become a source of mutual positive feedback, which exposes the agent to subsequent and potentially positive unanticipated events.

Once a chance is recognised, an action is taken to amplify potentials of positive significance. This is indeed entirely explorative and tentative, as argued above. The action taken on the basis of inevitably marginal, unassorted and apparently irrelevant resources may uncover new possibilities in terms of subsequent chances or novel observations. This process involves *iterative circularity*. Which means that the amplification of the positive potentials of chance encounters is a circular process, which comes to an end when a satisfying solution is reached, if it is reached Lawley and Tompkins (2008).

The whole process of chance amplification can be described in terms of *tinkering with chance events*. That is, what the chance-seeker does is to tinker with chance events. Tinkering—the English word for *Bricolage*—can de described by four key elements. (1) Tinkering is a resource-bound approach; (2) it is a non-ergodic process; (3) it leads to clumsy and yet workable solutions; (4) it does not require domain-specific knowledge.

Tinkering is a Resource-Bound Approach The process of tinkering on chance encounters is not driven by the existence of a plan, which, as I have shown above, would lead to the paradoxical conclusion that we would need to know beforehand what we are looking for. The absence of a plan is not however a necessary condition for action. We tend to think that purposiveness of action is necessarily linked to one's ability to predict what is going to happen next. However, that is the case in which a course of action is driven by a plan. We may still be purposive without being predictive, if we turn our attention to more immediate, marginal concerns, while renouncing addressing more general, systematic and apparently relevant ones. In this sense, tinkering allows latent strategies to emerge *non-deliberately* "through the exercise of local coping actions", as put by Chia and Holt (2009, p. 24). That implies, as noted by Lévi-Strauss (1962), to subordinate any course of (possible) action to the availability of resources as they arise, rather than doing the opposite, as in the case of a plan-driven process. That is, the chance-seeker as a tinkerer does not subordinate a course of action to making a list of resources one should necessarily have beforehand.

Tinkering is a Non-ergodic Process By definition, non-ergodicity regards all those processes that cannot be shaken free from their history (David, 2001; Garud, Kumaraswamy, & Karnøe, 2010). Turner (2007) expresses this idea pointing out that tinkering is immediate and contingent upon past events, *but with no view to the future*. In this respect, creative outcomes emerge by recombining pre-existing resources resonating with chance encounters, as noted above. It is worth noting here that those pre-existing resources are never the result of a linear process. Conversely, they are bound to contingent happenings. As Lévi-Strauss (1962) contributes, the resources one has are "the contingent result of all the occasions there have been to renew or enrich the stock or to maintain it with the remains of previous constructions or destructions".

Tinkering Leads to Clumsy and Yet Workable Solutions The third aspect is related to the kind of outcomes from tinkering. Since planning mostly relies on knowledge that necessarily must be held in stock before one starts, one may reasonably design for and aim at optimised solutions. In the case of tinkering with chance events, solutions are never optimised solutions, but always workable and provisional ones, which may serve more as a springboard to subsequent ones than as end-points with definitive results. Such workable solutions are quite like *kluges*—collections of ill-assorted parts put together to accomplish a specific purpose as it emerges (Marcus, 2009).

Tinkering Does Not Require Domain-Specific Knowledge There is a fourth element worth mentioning here and it is related to the kind of knowledge that the chance-seeker as a tinkerer makes use of. To think in terms of a plan to implement necessarily implies identifying the most suitable body of knowledge, which inevitably resorts to some kind of *expertise*. In the case of tinkering, it is not possible to identify beforehand the body of knowledge that will turn out to be relevant: one must act flexibly, and be ready to adjust his or her strategy according to contextual elements as they arise. In this sense, we may say that tinkering with chance events implies that "we only know what we know when we need to know it", as Snowden put it (Snowden, 2002, p. 110).

There is in this case a fundamental circularity to take into account: on the one hand, the chance-seeker can only make use of whatever comes in handy. On the other hand, what comes in handy is inevitably identified as such because of one's pre-existing skills and knowledge. So, we may say that the chance-seeker can employ certain skills and knowledge as long as they are useful for solving problems, once again, as they arise.

10.3.4 Chance-Seeking as a Phronetic Activity

Generally speaking, I argue that to tinker with chance events implies to be able to act in situations, which are inevitably particular and specific. Besides, they differ from each other the extent to which the solution for one situation may not be necessarily applied to others. The absence of certified knowledge—expertise—informing the process characterises all those cases in which the notion of *phronesis* acquires a fundamental epistemic value. The term phronesis was introduced by Aristotle and has indeed quite a long and important philosophical pedigree. As far as I am concerned here, phronesis refers to *practical wisdom*, that is, the capacity of making practical judgements. So, it deals more with practice rather than theory. Its domain of application is related to complex, variable matters. For it is not subjected to any form of scientific demonstration and precision.

I am now raising the notion of phronesis because it describes a specific aspect related to chance-seeking. To be more precise, it describes the chance-seeker. In discussing the concept, Dunne (1993) pays attention to an important distinction. Building on Aristotle's discussion, Dunne posits that *the capacity to make* is completely different from *the capacity to act*. The former implies the production or fabrication of something, which has its goal *in the product itself*. In this case, the maker can be considered a *detached executor*, who merely follows a predefined plan of specific steps to take in order to bring about a specific outcome. So, the maker stands outside the process taking care that the plan is successfully implemented. Chia and Holt (2009) add that the capacity of making is the source of purposeful change, which inevitably involves deliberate intervention.

Acting is rather different. According to Dunne, there is no predefined outcome to bring about. The agent is no longer a *detached executor*, but she takes part in a process, which does not terminate in anything tangible like an object or a tool, thus entirely separable from herself. Conversely, acting primarily implies the disclosure of the actor's individuality, identity, values, and aspirations so that the means and ends cannot be entirely separated. Phronesis precisely characterises acting. As Dunne put it, phronesis is

> acquired and deployed not in the making of any product [. . .]. It is personal knowledge in that, in the living of one's life, it characterises and expresses the kind of person that one is (Dunne, 1993, p. 244).

As far as we are concerned here, the notion of phronesis adds an important layer to what has been described so far. Chance-seeking is phronetic for three specific and yet related reasons. The first reason is that chance-seeking regards a person as a whole, let us say, it is individuating. The absence of a plan to follow, forces a person to step in and take responsibility for finding her/his own way of intervention, which is inevitably related to what comes in handy for him/her. For this involves some change in one's identity, as in the chance-seeking process a person arrives at disclosing something specific about themselves. Change is inevitable when the incorporation of something new—be it a new skill or a body of knowledge—may imply a part if not full re-definition of oneself. The last point is related to the fact that chance-seeking is appropriative. That means that a person does not simply use instruments and tools in some kind of habitual way as a mere means to an end. Conversely, she builds his/her own toolbox making it specifically his/her own. This may involve a certain degree of creativity, as there are no ready-made solutions, which may fit with needs that are specific to a person.

10.4 Conclusions

As I mentioned in the introduction to my article, intervention is a key concept to investigate by those who are interested in reaching a better understanding of science as a practice. If abduction has been proven as a solid concept to deal with the way an explanatory hypothesis is generated and tested, it falls short when it comes to providing an account related to what leads us to the formation of an explanatory hypothesis. I claimed that it is precisely here that the analysis of the notion of intervention along with its specific "logic" becomes salient.

I have tried to argue that a possible way to deal with intervention is to point at its fundamental prospective and forward-looking nature. In my view that is connected with the way we come to utilise chance events to our advantage. That is, the looking-forwardness and prospectiveness characterising intervention can be fruitfully addressed, if we acknowledge that chance events may come to play a pivotal role in the process of discovery. This does not mean the support of a sort of mindless account. Conversely, I have tried to point out how important it is to develop the proper vocabulary to deal with processes in which we have to confront and also be open to chance events, which I defined as any event that we cannot anticipate.

The idea of chance-seeking, which I presented in the second part of my article, is an attempt to find room for chance events in a way that our sense of purposiveness is not somehow lost—at least on a theoretical/conceptual level. I claimed that chance-seeking is a form of reliance on chance events. That is, we may come to benefit from what our environment can offer precisely in terms of chance events. The sense of purposiveness is then granted by the fact that one may actively try to amplify the positive significance of chance events in a way that new and potentially good opportunities for action may come out in due course, as the process unfolds.

Acknowledgements This research was supported by the Estonian Science Foundation and co-funded by the European Union through Marie Curie Actions, ERMOS72.

References

Chia, R., Holt, L. R., & Li, Y. (2013). In praise of strategic indirection: Towards a non-instrumental understanding of *phronesis* as practical wisdom. In M. Thompson & D. Bevan (Eds.), *Wise Management in Organisational Complexity* (pp. 57–67). New York: Palgrave.

Chia, R., & Holt, R. (2006). Strategy as practical coping: A heideggerian perspective. *Organization Studies, 27*, 635–55.

Chia, R., & Holt, R. (2009). *Strategy without design: The silent efficacy of indirect action.* Cambridge: Cambridge University Press.

Cowley, S., & Vallée-Tourangeau, F. (2013). Systemic cognition: Human artifice in life and language. In S. Cowley & F. Vallée-Tourangeau (Eds.), *Cognition beyond the brain. Computation, interactivity and human artifice* (pp. 255–273). Heidelberg/London: Springer.

Danto, A. (1962). Narrative sentences. *History and Theory, 2*(2), 146–179.

David, P. (2001) Path dependence, its critics and the quest for historical economics. In *Evolution and path dependence in economic ideas: Past and present* (pp. 15–40). Cheltenham: Edward Elgar.

de Rond, M., & Morley, I. (Eds.). (2010). *Serendipity: Fortune and the prepared mind.* Cambridge: Cambridge University Press.

Dunne, J. (1993) *Back to the rough ground.* Notre Dame: University of Notre Dame Press.

Gabbay, D., & Woods, J. (2005). The reach of abduction. In *A Practical Logic of Cognitive Systems* (Vol. 2). Amsterdam: North-Holland.

Garud, R., Kumaraswamy, A., & Karnøe, P. (2010). Path dependence or path creation? *Journal of Management Studies, 47*(4), 760–774.

Hemmingsen, B. (2013). The quick and the dead: On temporality and human agency. In S. Cowley & F. Vallée-Tourangeau (Eds.), *Cognition beyond the brain. Computation, interactivity and human artifice* (pp. 92–112). Heidelberg/London: Springer.

Ingold, T. (2001). *The perception of the environment: Essays in livelihood, dwelling and skill.* London: Routledge.

Kay, J. (2011). *Obliquity: Why our goals are best achieved indirectly*. London: Profile Books.

Kirsh, D., & Maglio, P. (1994). On distinguishing epistemic from pragmatic action. *Cognitive Science, 18*, 513–549.

Lawley, J., & Tompkins, P. (2008). Maximising serendipity: The art of recognising and fostering potential. http://www.cleanlanguage.co.uk/articles/articles/224/1/Maximising-Serendipity/Page1.html

Lévi-Strauss, C. (1962). *The savage mind*. Chicago: University of Chicago Press.

Magnani, L. (2001). *Abduction, reason, and science. Processes of discovery and explanation*. New York: Kluwer Academic/Plenum Publishers.

Magnani, L. (2009). *Abductive cognition. The epistemological and eco-cognitive dimensions of hypothetical reasoning*. Berlin/Heidelberg: Springer-Verlag.

Marcus, G. (2009). How does the mind work? Insights from biology. *Topics in Cognitive Science, 1*(1), 145–172.

Maruyama, M. (1963). The second cybernetics: Deviation-amplifying mutual causal processes. *American Scientist, 5*(2), 164–179.

Merton, R. K., & Barber, E. (2006). *The travels and adventures of serendipity: A study in sociological semantics and the sociology of science*. Princeton: Princeton University Press.

Ohsawa, Y., & McBurney, P. (Eds.). (2003). *Chance discovery*. Berlin: Springer.

Peirce, C. S. (1992–1998). *The essential peirce. Selected philosophical writings*. Bloomington/Indianapolis: Indiana University Press. vol. 1 (1867–1893), N. Houser & C. Kloesel (Eds.); vol. 2 (1893–1913), Peirce Edition Project.

Perry, M. (2013). Socially distributed cognition in loosely coupled systems. In S. Cowley & F. Vallée-Tourangeau (Eds.), *Cognition beyond the brain. Computation, interactivity and human artifice* (pp. 147–170). Heidelberg/London: Springer.

Polanyi, M. (1962). *The Tacit Dimension*. Chicago: University of Chicago Press.

Popper, K. (1959). *The logic of scientific discovery*. London: Hutchinson.

Snowden, D. (2002). Complex acts of knowing: Paradox and descriptive self-awareness. *Journal of Knowledge Management, 2*, 100–111.

Steffensen, S. (2013). Human interactivity: Problem-solving, solution-probing and verbal patterns in the wild. In S. Cowley & F. Vallée-Tourangeau (Eds.), *Cognition beyond the brain. Computation, interactivity and human artifice* (pp. 195–222). Heidelberg/London: Springer.

Taleb, N. (2007). *The Black Swan*. New York: Randon House.

Thagard, P. (2005). How to be a successful scientist. In M. E. Gorman, R. D. Tweney, D. C. Gooding & A. P. Kincannon (Eds.), *Scientific and technological thinking* (pp. 159–171). Mawah, NJ: Lawrence Erlbaum Associates.

Thagard, P. (2009). Why cognitive science needs philosophy and vice versa. *Topics in Cognitive Science, 1*(2), 237–254.

Torre, E. (2014). Digital inscriptions as material anchors for future action: Multi-scalar integration and dynamic systems. *Cybernetics and Human Knowing, 21*(1–2), 128–142.

Turner, J. S. (2007). *The Tinkerer's accomplice: How design emerges from life itself*. Cambridge, MA: Harvard University Press.

Ulrich, W. (2000). Reflective practice in the civil society: The contribution of critically systemic thinking. *Reflective Practice, 1*(2), 247–268.

Vallée-Tourangeau, F., & Cowley, S. (2013). Human thinking beyond the brain. In S. Cowley & F. Vallée-Tourangeau (Eds.), *Cognition beyond the brain. Computation, interactivity and human artifice* (pp. 1–11). Heidelberg/London: Springer.

Chapter 11
Exploring Social and Asocial Agency in Agent-Based Systems

Sabine Thürmel

Abstract Agent-based systems focus on the simulation of complex interactions and relationships of human and/or non-human agents. Social and asocial agency in agent-based systems depends on the conceptual engineering performed by computer scientists and application engineers. The perspective of multidimensional, gradual agency allows both agency (potentiality) and action (actuality) in socio-technical systems to be examined. A conceptual framework is presented which permits the phenomena of complex regulation of behavior and execution control in computer-mediated environments to be characterized. On this basis scenarios in which humans and non-human agents interact can be analyzed. Emergence in such systems may be described. Distributed action in the material reality can be compared to test-bed simulations. It is shown how the exploration of social and asocial agency in virtual environments may profit from work done in machine ethics.

Keywords Distributed agency • Multi-agent systems • Social computing systems

11.1 Introduction

Since the early 1990s computational science and engineering approaches have profited from agent-based models (ABM) and multi-agent systems (MAS) in general. ABM and MAS focus on the simulation of complex interactions and relationships of human and/or non-human agents. Natural scientists apply ABM to the study of complex adaptive systems in biology or many-particle physics. Engineers use MAS to realize distributed problem solving based on bionic or societal metaphors. Swarm intelligence systems (Dorigo, Maniezzo, & Colorni, 1996) or electronic auctioning systems (Woolridge, 2009) are a case in point. In silico experiments have been performed in the humanities too. Academics have applied ABM to study the evolution of norms (Muldoon et al., 2014), languages (Cowley, 2014) and to explore the impact of different social organization models on

S. Thürmel (✉)
Technische Universität München, Munich, Germany
e-mail: sabine@thuermel.de

D. Secchi, M. Neumann (eds.), *Agent-Based Simulation of Organizational Behavior*, DOI 10.1007/978-3-319-18153-0_11

settlement locations in ancient civilizations (Chliaoutakis & Chalkiadakis, 2014). Thus, agent-based simulators are well-established tools for gaining insights into the dynamics of complex systems, experimenting with behavioral variants and designing virtual and hybrid environments. Following Ferber (1999) ABM are regarded as a special variant of MAS employed for the simulation of complex distributed systems. MAS in general may not only be used for simulation but also for distributed problem solving. MAS systems are found in virtual worlds, in scenarios where robots collaborate, and as a novel approach to govern and control distributed processes in the real world.

This paper provides a short overview of the conceptual engineering currently performed when agent-based approaches are used in computational science and sociology. Following Floridi the task of the "philosophy of information" is "conceptual engineering, that is, the art of identifying conceptual problems and of designing, proposing, and evaluating explanatory solutions" (Floridi, 2011, p. 11). In our case, the conceptual problem is how to characterize agency and interagency between humans, robots, and software agents in such a way that all current forms of interplay can be analyzed. Moreover the approach should be flexible in order to allow future technical developments to be included. However, it should be as straightforward as possible. The proposed solution is a multidimensional gradual classification scheme which is presented in this paper.

The multidimensional gradual framework for agency and action enables the engineer, the socio-technograph, and the philosopher to evaluate agent-based behavior in socio-technical systems. Following Ropohl (1999) socio-technical systems are "action systems" where technical agents and humans interact in order to achieve pre-set goals. It is a rationalistic approach which intends to do justice to the broad capabilities of technical actors today. It does not pretend to capture the complexities of human organizations.

Agent-based systems are inspired by nature as well as by human coordination and collaboration. In the natural sciences they allow complex adaptive systems to be modeled as demonstrated in (Scheutz, Madey, & Boyd, 2005). In the humanities they are used to model and experiment with certain aspects of human agency, e.g. behavioral variants in joining in on standing ovations (Muldoon et al., 2014). In engineering they are deployed as a means to an end to provide embedded governance in smart energy grids (Wedde, Lehnhoff, Rehtanz, & Krause, 2008) or distributed health monitoring systems (Nealon & Moreno, 2003). Varieties in agent-based systems are outlined in Sect. 11.2.

The computer is employed both as a multipurpose machine and a unique medium. Since the computer is indifferent to the applications being run on it is an ideal multipurpose machine where formally specified programs may be executed. Section 11.3 is dedicated to describing the specific mediality of computing systems that is the relation between their specifications and runtime instantiations. Their potentiality and actuality is described based on Hubig's two-tiered presentation of technology in general as a medium (2006).

Floridi's "method of levels of abstraction" (2008) lets us focus on agential perspectives. A multidimensional gradual framework for agency and action is presented in Sect. 11.4. It may be applied to the role-based modeling of socio-technical systems and to the observation and interpretation of scenarios where humans and non-humans interact. Variants of agent-based systems may be studied and the benefits and limits of current approaches may be characterized.

In order to demonstrate that agent-based approaches are a complex tool in itself emergence of novel behavior and the potential for social and asocial behavior are briefly introduced in Sects. 11.5 and 11.6, respectively. This paper does not intend to present them in depth but relies on them to formulate a caveat when in trying to transfer the insights gained in the laboratory to real world scenarios: due to the nondeterministic nature of agent-based systems one must proceed with great care.

11.2 Varieties of Agent-Based Systems

The goal of the agent-oriented programming paradigm is the adequate and intuitive modeling and implementation of complex interactions and relationships. Software agents were introduced by Hewitt's Actor Model (Hewitt, Bishop, & Steiger, 1973). They were presented as encapsulated objects possessing an internal model and capabilities for communication which may be executed in parallel to others. Today a whole variety of definitions for software agents exist (Woolridge, 2009) but all of them include mechanisms to support persistence, autonomy, interactivity, and flexibility. Persistence refers to the fact that agents are permanent objects outliving the processes which created them. They can decide in an autonomous way when and how to pursue their (currently predefined) goals. They may interact both with other software agents and human users. Flexibility may be supported by specific learning strategies thus allowing the agents to adapt to their environment and especially to other agents.

MAS are suited to role-based modeling and simulation in such diverse fields as biology, economics, and sociology, (1) if the information and expertise is distributed in space and time, (2) if the relationships among the entities may be dynamically changed, and (3) if new organizational structures may arise and change over time. From a computer scientist's perspective using MAS may be a way to realize heuristics for NP-complete problems pursuing a distributed problem solving approach.

In the natural sciences agent-based systems are employed in diverse ways: While the classical biosciences intend to better understand life-as-we-know-it, engineering focuses on life-as-it-could-be. In 1987 the notion of artificial life (AL) was created at the first AL conference organized by Chris Langton. Today the field encompasses the in silico simulation of synthetic life (soft AL), multi-robot systems (hard AL), and biochemical systems (wet AL). The origin of life, evolutionary and ecological dynamics, and the social organization of virtual agents and robots are studied. In AL the focus is not so much on the single organism but on the population as a whole. Both digital evolution and self-organization are important research areas. The goal is to simulate life from the bottom up.

In engineering, bionic approaches such as swarm intelligence as well as societal models are adapted in order to implement collaborative approaches to distributed problem solving. Cooperation strategies provide new heuristics for decentralized planning and optimization (Eymann, 2003, p. 100). Both purely reactive and proactive approaches exist. MAS toolboxes provide a basis for crowd simulation as well as electronic market mechanisms. The latter may be deployed to coordinate emergency response services in disaster recovery systems (Jennings, 2010). MAS provide a basis to cyber-physical systems (CPS). While classical computer systems separate physical and virtual worlds, CPS observe their physical environment by sensors, process their information, and influence their environment with actuators while being connected by a communication layer. Agent-based CPS may be found in distributed rescue systems (Jennings, 2010), smart energy grids (Wedde et al., 2008) or distributed health monitoring systems (Nealon & Moreno, 2003). These systems are first simulated and intended to be deployed to control processes in the material world. In the latter case humans may be integrated for clarifying and/or deciding non-formalized conflicts in an ad hoc manner.

The humanities, social and political science, behavioral economics, and studies in law have discovered agent-based modeling too. Social and asocial agency has been studied by performing in silico experiments and comparing the results with real world behavior. ABM may provide a better fit than conventional economic models to model the "herding" among investors. Early-warning systems for the next financial crisis could be built based on ABM (Agents of Change, 2010). These early results may extend to other domains of behavioral economics. The emergence of social norms can be simulated (Muldoon et al., 2014). Even criminal behavior, deliberate misinterpretations of norms or negligence can be studied. Therefore it is hardly surprising that the Leibniz Center for Law at the University of Amsterdam had been looking—although in vain—for a specific Ph.D. candidate in legal engineering: He or she should be capable of developing new policies in tax evasion scenarios. These scenarios were planned to be based on ABM (Leibnizcenter for Law, 2011). Such a "social computing" approach does not only offer to model social behavior, it could also suggest ways to change it. Policies can be inscribed in semiotic or virtual devices. Constellations of inter-agency and distributed agency materialize.

While technographs such as Latour (2005) strive to observe and analyze the interactions without prejudices by "opening up black boxes" this paper advocates making use of computational science and engineering knowledge in order to enhance the understanding of socio-technical environments. If one understands the capabilities of technical agents due to being familiar with their design and their implementation the analysis is grounded in knowledge about their inner workings and not in observations alone. Such a twofold approach takes both the potential and the actuality of computer-mediated artifacts into account.

11.3 Potentiality and Actuality of Agent-Based Approaches

Virtuality in technologically induced contexts is best explained if Hubig's two-tiered presentation of technology in general as a medium (2006) is adopted. He distinguishes between the "potential sphere of the realization of potential ends" and the "actual sphere of realizing possible ends" (Hubig, 2010, p. 4). Applied to agent-based systems—or IT systems in general—it can be stated that their specification corresponds to the "potential sphere of the realization of potential ends" (Hubig, 2010, p. 4) and any run-time instantiation to a corresponding actual sphere. In other words: Due to their nature as computational artifacts, the potential of social computing systems becomes actual in a concrete instantiation. Their inherent potentiality is actualized during run-time. "A technical system constitutes a potentiality that only becomes a reality if and when the system is identified as relevant for agency and is embedded into concrete contexts of action" (Hubig, 2010, p. 3).

Since purely computational artifacts are intangible, i.e. existing in time but not in space, the situation becomes even more challenging: One and the same social computing program can be executed in experimental environments and in real-world interaction spaces. The demonstrator for the coordination of emergency response services may go live and coordinate human and non-human actors in genuine disaster recovery scenarios. With regard to its impact on the physical environment, it possesses a virtual actuality in the test-bed environment and a real actuality when it is employed in real time in order to control processes in the natural world.

In test-bed environments and real-time deployments, the potential of agent-based systems becomes actual. Thus, the "actual sphere of realizing possible ends" (Hubig, 2010, p. 4) can either be an experimental environment composed exclusively of software agents or a system running in real time. When MAS are used for distributed problem solving the overall objective is to automate processes as far as possible. Thus humans are integrated only if need arises, e.g. for solving potential conflicts in an ad hoc manner. Automatic collaborative routines or new practices for ad hoc collaboration are established. Novel, purely virtual or hybrid contexts realizing collective and distributed agency materialize.

In the following, the agency of technology is not considered a "pragmatic fiction" as it was by Rammert (2011). It is perceived as a (functional) abstraction corresponding to a level of abstraction (LoA) as defined by Floridi: A LoA "is a specific set of typed variables, intuitively representable as an interface, which establishes the scope and type of data that will be available as a resource for the generation of information" (Floridi, 2008, p. 320). For a detailed definition, see (Floridi, 2011, p. 46). A LoA presents an interface where the observed behavior—either in virtual actuality or real actuality—may be interpreted. Under a LoA, different observations may result due to the fact that social computing software can be executed in different run-time environments, e.g. in a test-bed in contrast to a real-time environment. Different LoAs correspond to different abstractions of one and the same behavior of computing systems in a certain run-time environment.

Different observations under one and the same LoA are possible if different versions of a program are run. This is the case when software agents are replaced by humans. Conceptual entities may also be interpreted at a chosen LoA. Note that different levels of abstraction may co-exist. Since levels of abstractions correspond to different perspectives, the system designer's LoA may be different from the sociologist's LoA or the legal engineer's LoA of one and the same social computing system. These LoAs are related but not necessarily identical. By choosing a certain LoA a theory commits itself to a certain interpretation of the object types (Floridi, 2008, p. 327) and their instantiations, e.g. the software agent types and their realizations.

In the design phase ideas guiding the modeling phase are often quite vague at first. In due course their concretization results in a conceptual model (Ruß, Müller, & Hesse, 2010) which is then specified as a software system. From the user's or observer's point of view during run-time the more that is known about the conceptual model the better its potential for (distributed) agency can be predicted, and the better the hybrid constellations of (collective) action, emerging at run-time, may be analyzed. Snapshots of technical agents in action may be complemented by a perspective on the system model. The philosophical benefit of this approach does not only lie in a reconstructive approach as intended by Latour (2005) and Rammert (2011) but also in the conceptual engineering of the activity space. Under a LoA for agency and action, activities may be observed as they unfold.

Using a multidimensional gradual agency concept such a LoA may be characterized in more detail. The classification scheme may already be used in the design phase, when a system based on different agent types is to be modeled. Moreover, the system may be analyzed and educated guesses about its future behavior can be made. Both the specifics of distinct systems and their commonalities may be compiled.

11.4 A Multidimensional Gradual Framework for Evaluating Socio-Technical Systems

A multidimensional gradual framework for agency and action is introduced in Thürmel's paper (2012) and expanded in her dissertation (2013). It is a classification scheme developed so that the potential for individual and joint action of technical agents may be characterized in an efficient way. It is based on as few dimensions as possible doing justice to their capabilities but at the same time demonstrating the width of the gap between humans and current technical agents. Moreover, suggestions are made how this gap could be closed in the future.

The multidimensional classification scheme may used to analyze in detail the role-based modeling of socio-technical systems and to the observation and interpretation of scenarios where humans and non-humans interact. In the following a short overview of the classification scheme is given: In order to demonstrate the potential for agency not only the activity levels of any entities but also their potential for adaptivity, interaction, personification of others, individual action, and conjoint action have to be taken into account.

The potential for individual action in technical agents such as individual software agents or individual robots depends on their activity level that is their potential for self-induced action and their potential for adapting to their environment. A hammer is just a passive tool unable to act. In contrast a (software) bid agent in high frequency bidding system proactively makes its bid without any human intervention and may even learn to adapt its strategy based on trading patterns and information available in the market.

The potential for conjoint action in MAS or multi-robot systems requires the capability for interaction. If plans and strategies are shared and labor is (re)distributed during execution the technical agents and the humans must attribute capabilities to others, treat them as some kind of person. Suitable distinctions must be made: a filter-agent must be treated in totally different way than an avatar if collaboration is to be successful.

In the following the different dimensions are presented in more detail: The activity level permits the characterization of individual behavior depending on the degree of the self-inducible activity potential. It starts with passive entities such as road bumpers or hammers. Reactivity, realized as simple feedback loops or other situated reactions, is the next level. Active entities permit individual selection between alternatives resulting in changes in the behavior. Pro-active ones allow self-reflective individual selection. The next level corresponds to the capability of setting one's own goals and pursuing them. These capabilities depend on an entity-internal system for information processing linking input to output. In the case of humans it equals a cognitive system connecting perception and action. For material artifacts or software agents an artificial "cognitive" system couples (sensor) input with (actuator) output. Based on such a system for (agent-internal) information processing the level of adaptivity may be defined. It characterizes the plasticity of the phenotype, i.e. the ability to change one's observable characteristics including any traits, which may be made visible by a technical procedure, in correspondence to changes in the environment. Models of adaptivity and their corresponding realizations range from totally rigid to simple conditioning up to impressive cognitive agency, i.e. the capability to learn from past experiences and to plan and act accordingly. A wide range of models co-exist allowing one to study and experiment with artificial "cognition in action." This dimension is important to all who define agency as situation-appropriate behavior and who deem the plasticity of the phenotype as an essential assumption of the conception of man. Based on activity levels and on being able to adapt in a "smart" way acting may be discerned from just behaving and the potential for individual action may be defined. A hammer is just a passive tool, a sensor-controlled power drill demonstrates reactive behavior. A robopet may display active behavior. An automatic bid agent or a car on auto-pilot may perform proactive actions.

Conjoint actions depend on interaction and the potential for personification. The potential for interaction, i.e. the coordination by means of communications, is the basis of most if not all social computing systems and approaches to distributed problem solving. It may range from uncommunicative, to hard-wired cooperation mechanisms, up to ad hoc cooperation.

The potential for the personification of others enables agents to integrate predicted effects of own and other actions. "Personification of non-humans is best understood as a strategy of dealing with the uncertainty about the identity of the other... Personifying other non-humans is a social reality today and a political necessity for the future" (Teubner, 2006, p. 497). Alluding to Dennett's intentional stance (Dennett, 1987) Rammert talks about "as-if intentionality" which humans must attribute to technical agents for goal-oriented interaction (Rammert, 2011, p. 19). I deem it more appropriate to focus on the capability for personification of others. Behavioral patterns may be explained based on the respective ability to perceive another agent as such. Thus a level of abstraction is found which focuses on agency and interaction and not on the ontological statuses of the involved agents. The personification of others lays the foundation for interactive planning, sharing strategies and for adapting actions. The personification of others in technical agents may lead to an interdisciplinary sort of conceptual engineering, Floridi had in mind, when named it "the art of identifying conceptual problems and of designing, proposing, and evaluating explanatory solutions" (Floridi, 2011, p. 11). The designers' and philosopher's task would be to define the concrete form of collaboration, the concrete level of abstraction one is interested in and the computer scientists' and engineers' task would be to realize such collaborative technical agents and their capabilities of personalization. One approach could be to focus on "shared cooperative activities" and "shared agency" in the sense of Bratman (1992, 2014): Mutual responsiveness, commitment to joint activity and commitment to mutual support form the basis of "shared cooperative activity" (Bratman, 1992). Examples include rational, self-governing groups formed in order to realize a joint project. Human groups of that kind display a so-called "modest sociality" (Bratman, 2014) which may be explained based on Bratman's notion of "shared agency" (2009, 2014). Such agency emerges from structures of interconnected planning agency. Practical rationality forms its core. Examples of such shared agency can be found in distributed health monitoring systems (Nealon & Moreno, 2003). These endeavors and similar research intend to support the vision of "smart health," i.e. patients' competent treatment to be offered by collaborating humans, robots, and software agents at any location while constantly monitoring the patients' health. Another example would be the collaboration of humans, robots, and software agents in "smart manufacturing" offering customized products in highly flexible production environments. The ad hoc coordination of activities in these environments would benefit from even a basic understanding of others and their capabilities for social interaction.

Today, this capability for personification is non-existent in most material and software agents. Some agents have more or less crude models of others, e.g. realized as so-called minimal models of the mind. A further qualitative level may be found in great apes which also have the potential for joint intentionality (Call & Tomasello, 2008). This provides the basis for topic-focused group decision making based on egoistical behavior. Understanding the other as an intentional agent allows even infants to participate in so-called shared actions (Tomasello, 2008). Understanding others as mental actors lays the basis for interacting intentionally and acting collectively (Tomasello, 2008). Currently there is quite a gap between non-human actors and human ones concerning their ability to interact intentionally. This strongly limits the scope of social computing systems when they are used to predict human behavior or if they are intended to engineer and simulate future environments.

The capabilities for individual action and conjoint action may be defined based on activity levels, the potential for adaptivity, interaction, and personification of others possessed by the involved actor(s). One option is the following: In order to stress the communalities between human and non-human agents, an agent counts as capable of acting (instead of just behaving), if the following conditions concerning its ontogenesis hold: "the individual actor [evolves] as a complex, adaptive system (CAS), which is capable of rule based information processing and based on that able to solve problems by way of adaptive behaviour in a dynamic process of constitution and emergence" (Kappelhoff, 2011, p. 320). Based on the actor's capability for joint intentionality respective of understanding the other as an intentional agent or even as a mental actor, the actor may be capable of joint action, shared or collective action. These levels show how the gap between non-human and human actors could eventually be closed.

Constellations of inter-agency and distributed agency in social computing systems or hybrid constellations, where humans, machines, and programs interact, may be described, examined, and analyzed using the classification scheme for agency and action introduced above. These constellations start with purely virtual systems like swarm intelligence systems and fixed instrumental relationships between humans and assistive software agents where certain tasks are delegated to artificial agents. They continue with flexible partnerships between humans and software agents. They range up to loosely coupled complex adaptive systems. The latter may model such diverse problem spaces as predator–prey relationships of natural ecologies, legal engineering scenarios, or disaster recovery systems. Their common ground and their differences may be discovered when the above outlined multidimensional, gradual conceptual framework for agency and action is applied. A subset of these social computing systems, namely those which may form part of the infrastructure of our world, provide a new form of "embedded governance." Their potential and limits may also be analyzed using the multidimensional agency concept.

Since MAS and most multi-robot systems are not centrally controlled but rely on some sort of distributed control based on self-organization where behavior on the meso- or macro-level emerges from the interaction of the individual agents the next section gives a short introduction to emergence in agent-based systems.

11.5 Emergence in Agent-Based Systems

Starting with Anderson's seminal paper "More is Different" (1972) a revival of the discussion on emergence has taken place: "Emergence, largely ignored just thirty years ago, has become one of the liveliest areas of research in both philosophy and science" (Bedau & Humphreys, 2008). In the current literature a wide variety of emergence concepts is discussed. Important distinctions are to be found between diachronic and synchronic emergence and between weak and strong emergence.

"Diachronic emergence is "horizontal" emergence evolved through time in which the structure from which the novel property emerges exists prior to the emergent." (Vintiadis, 2014, 2.ii). Concerning the novelty of a property, a pattern or a phenomenon in agent-based systems one may follow Darley (1994) and define that "true emergent phenomenon is one for which the optimal means of prediction is simulation." Thus emergence as "the arising of novel and coherent structures, patterns and properties during the process of self-organization in complex systems" (Goldstein, 1999, p. 49) seems appropriate when focusing on agent-based behavior in ABM and MAS. Diachronic emergence due to adaptive behavior in agent-based systems may occur on different levels: Adaptivity on system, i.e. macro-level, e.g. of whole organizations, on the meso-level, e.g. of groups of agents, and on the individual agent level. On all these levels interrelated dynamic processes of constitution and emergence may take place.

In simulation based on certain multi-layered models one may find synchronic emergence, too. In contrast to diachronic emergence "in synchronic emergence [...] the higher-level, emergent phenomena are simultaneously present with the lower-level phenomena from which they emerge" (Vintiadis, 2014, 2.ii). One example is:

> a multi-scale agent-based framework to model phenomena at different levels of organization even if the exact dependence and determination relations are not known. Such models provide insights into the inter-level dynamics of complex systems and might help scientists to discover and formulate equation-based models for multi-scale phenomena, which would otherwise be difficult (if not impossible) to detect (Scheutz et al., 2005).

This agent-based approach was employed in a four-level biological model used for the study of the effects of low-level synaptic and neuro-chemical processes on social interactions in bull frogs (Scheutz et al., 2005, p. 3). Such an approach displays not only diachronic emergence but it may also offer snapshots of synchronic emergence.

One may speak of weak emergence in a system if one focuses on the unpredictability or unexpectedness of a systemic property, a pattern or a phenomenon given its components (Vintiadis, 2014, 2.ii). It may be found in swarm intelligence systems or in agent-based systems investigating the emergence of social norms. In biological models of evolution emergence as unpredictability is judged to be a fundamental fact (e.g., Mayr, 2000, p. 403). In ABM of evolution emergence as unpredictability is a by-product of the in silico experiments and as such the validation of ABM is nontrivial. For some authors like Bedau (1997) the main characteristic of weak emergence is that "though macro-phenomena of complex systems are in principle ontologically and causally reducible to micro-phenomena, their reductive explanation is intractably complex, save by derivation through simulation of the system's microdynamics and external conditions" (Vintiadis, 2014, 2.ii). Thus weak emergence may be compatible with reduction. Therefore it may make sense to complement an ABM with a numerical one focusing on the system's view. Numerical methods based on nonlinear equation systems support the simulation of quantitative aspects of complex, discrete systems (Mainzer, 2007). In contrast, MAS (Woolridge, 2009) permit collective behavior to be modeled based on the local perspectives of individuals. Both approaches may complement each other. They can even be integrated to simulate both numerical, quantitative and qualitative, logical aspects, e.g. within one expressive temporal specification language (Bosse, Sharpanskykh, & Treur, 2008).

In strong emergence novelty means irreducibility and downward causation, i.e. that the emergent properties and laws supervene on their subvenient base. Whereas the so-called British emergentists in the nineteenth century were convinced that many cases of strong emergence exist (McLaughlin, 2008) today many scientists wonder whether examples (apart from consciousness) exist at all (Bedau & Humphreys, 2008).

In scenarios of distributed cognition where humans, software agents, and robots collaborate novel faculties may become manifest over time in a variant of weak emergence. Even the human controlling an avatar in a game may be affected. The relationship between player and avatar is a multi-faceted phenomenon since avatars simultaneously serve as characters in a simulated world, as a tool which extends the player's agency in the game activity and as props which can be used as a part of the player's presentation (Linderoth, 2005). Inspired by Mead (1934) and Blumer (1973) one could assume that the meaning of virtual objects, situations, and relationships result from the process of symbolic interaction and communication and that this participation in a virtual environment forms the virtual identity and influences the self. Mead distinguishes between three levels of role adoption in the process of identity formation: imitating role playing (play), rule-conforming cooperation (game), and universal cooperation and understanding. These levels can also be found in synthetic worlds which provide opportunities for role-playing, rule-governed games, involving cooperation and negotiation. Thus they allow for multiple virtual identities and new experiences in the virtual realm. On the other hand, they provide a basis for agency in virtual worlds offering novel experiences. These systems provoke us to ask questions about traditional categories such as "What kinds of relationships are appropriate to be had with machines?" (Turkle, 2010, p. 30) or more generally, how this technological progress will affect our interpersonal relationships (Turkle, 2011). Abstraction in mathematics does not challenge us in such a way.

11.6 The Potential for Social and Asocial Agency in Agent-Based Modeling

Agent-based approaches are especially suited to modeling and implementing open systems based on dynamically interacting entities pursuing individual potentially conflicting goals, without central control, using sophisticated approaches to communication and cooperation. This is exemplified in the ALADDIN project where a MAS toolbox was developed and employed to realize a demonstrator for the coordination of emergency response services in disaster management systems (Jennings, 2010). Agent-based systems are employed to simulate social norms (see, e.g., Savarimuthu & Cranefield, 2011). Current work focuses mostly on the detection of patterns in the behavior of crowds, like the phenomenon of standing ovations (Muldoon et al., 2014). The question arises under which circumstances the insights gained in the laboratory through social computing systems are transferable to real world scenarios.

In basic crowd simulation systems the pattern found in the simulations may be compared to the pattern found in real-world examples. In applications, where instrumental rationality is the sole basis of goal-oriented behavior such a transference is often possible. The most obvious case is that of agent-based CPS which are first simulated and then deployed to control processes in the material word. Examples include smart energy grids or distributed health monitoring systems. Even criminal behavior, deliberate misinterpretations of norms or negligence can be studied if it is based on bounded rationality.

Current MAS may be especially suited to modeling interacting egoists perceiving others only as social tools. This is due to the fact that current software agents resemble sociopaths rather than caring humans. This conviction is maintained, for example, by Noreen Herzfeld (2013) who cites M. E. Thomas' *Confessions of a Sociopath* (2013): "Remorse is alien to me… I am generally free of entangling and irrational emotions. I am strategic and canny, intelligent and confident, but I also struggle to react appropriately to other people's confusing and emotion-driven social cues."

The emotionality of humans is one indication that not all results gained in the laboratory via social computing systems are transferable to real world scenarios. Human capabilities and those of technical agents may differ widely. Their acts are based on different cognitive systems, different degrees of freedom and only partially overlapping spheres of experience. Current software agents possess at best synthesized emotions. Human drives and needs are (at least currently) alien to them.

Concerning commonalities and fundamental differences in unethical or illegal behavior in investigations into machine ethics and the treatment of artificial agents as legal subjects are very instructive. Books such as *The Law of Robots* (Pagallo, 2013) and *A Legal Theory for Autonomous Artificial Agents* (Chopra & White, 2011) demonstrate this. Chopra and White are convinced that "in principle artificial agents should be able to qualify for independent legal personality, since this is the closest legal analogue to the philosophical conception of a person" (Chopra & White,

2011, p. 182). In their view "artificial agents are more likely to be law-abiding than humans because of their superior capacity to recognize and remember legal rules" (Chopra & White, 2011, p. 166). If they do not abide the law "a realistic threat of punishment can be palpably weighed in the most mechanical of cost-benefit calculations" (Chopra & White, 2011, p. 168). Pagallo perceives the legal personhood of robots and their constitutional rights as an option only being relevant in the long term (Pagallo, 2013, p. 147). However, he discusses at length both human greediness, using robots as criminal accomplices, and artificial greediness. He states that "in certain fields of social interaction, 'intelligence' emerges from the rule of the game rather than individual choices" (Pagallo, 2013, p. 96). Moreover, investigations into potential ethical status of software agents have been undertaken (e.g., Moor, 2006) and propositions to teach "moral machines" to distinguish right from wrong have been developed (e.g., Wallach & Allen, 2008).

In order to clarify the state of the art in software agents' ethics Moor's distinctions between ethical-impact agents, implicit ethical agents, explicit ethical agents and full ethical agents may be employed (Moor, 2006). In social computing the three classes of lesser ethical agents may be found: software agents used as mere tools may have an ethical impact; electronic auctioning systems may be judged implicit ethical agents, if their "internal functions implicitly promote ethical behavior—or at least avoid unethical behavior" (Moor, 2006, p. 19); disaster management systems based on MAS systems (Jennings, 2010) may be exemplary explicit ethical agents if they "represent ethics explicitly, and then operate effectively on the basis of this knowledge" (Moor, 2006, p. 20). It is open to discussion whether any software agent will ever be a fully ethical agent which "can make explicit ethical judgments generally and is competent to reasonably justify them" (Moor, 2006). But the first variants of ethical (machine) behavior, i.e. proto-ethical systems, are already in place.

Analogous to this classification of ethical behavior displayed by software agents, a wide variety of amoral agents could be implemented. They could range from unethical impact agents or implicit unethical agents to explicit unethical agents, e.g. based on virtue ethics. They could be modeled for use in online games. Such games could provide sheer entertainment, edutainment or form part of the currently so popular serious games. The latter "have an explicit and carefully thought-out educational purpose and are not intended to be played primarily for amusement" (Abt, 1970, p. 6).

To conclude, ABM allow one to model a wide variety of asocial behavior. Yet when transferring the insights gained in the laboratory to real world scenarios, one must proceed with great care.

11.7 Conclusions and Future Directions

The proposed conceptual framework for agency and action offers a multidimensional gradual classification scheme for the observation and interpretation of scenarios where humans and non-humans interact. It may be applied to the analysis of the potential of social computing systems and their virtual and real actualizations. The above-introduced approach may be used both by the software engineer and the philosopher when role-based interaction in socio-technical systems is to be defined and analyzed during execution. Proto-ethical agency in social computing systems may be explored by adapting (Moor, 2006). Profiting from work done by Darwall (2006), the framework could be expanded in order to potentially attribute commitments to diverse socio-technical actors. Shared agency, a "planning theory of acting together" as defined by Bratman (2014), could be investigated in socio-technical contexts where technical elements are not mere tools but interaction partners.

References

Abt, C. (1970). *Serious games*. New York, NY: Viking.

Agents of Change. (2010). Agents of change. *The Economist*. http://www.economist.com/node/16636121/print. Accessed 30 Jan 2015.

Anderson, P. (1972). More is different: Broken symmetry and the nature of the hierarchical structure of science. *Science, 177*, 393–396.

Bedau, M. (1997). Weak emergence. In J. Tomberlin (Ed.), *Philosophical perspectives: Mind, causation and world* (Vol. 11, pp. 375–399). Malden, MA: Blackwell.

Bedau, M., & Humphreys, P. (2008). *Emergence: Contemporary readings in philosophy and science*. Cambridge, MA: MIT Press.

Blumer, H. (1973). Der methodologische Standort des symbolischen Interaktionismus. In Arbeitsgruppe Bielefelder Soziologen (Eds.), *Alltagswissen, Interaktion und gesellschaftliche Wirklichkeit, Bd. 1*. Reinbek bei Hamburg: Rowohlt.

Bosse, T., Sharpanskykh, A., & Treur, J. (2008). Integrating agent models and dynamical systems. In M. Baldoni, T. C. Son, M. van Riemsdijk, & M. Winikoff (Eds.), *Declarative agent languages and technologies V* (pp. 50–68). Heidelberg: Springer.

Bratman, M. (1992). Shared cooperative activity. *The Philosophical Review, 101*(2), 327–341.

Bratman, M. (2009). Modest sociality and the distinctiveness of intention. *Philosophical Studies, 144*, 149–165.

Bratman, M. (2014). *Shared agency: A planning theory of acting together*. Cambridge, MA: Harvard University Press.

Call, J., & Tomasello, M. (2008). Does the chimpanzee have a theory of mind? 30 years later. *Trends in Cognitive Sciences, 12*(5), 187–192.

Chliaoutakis, A., & Chalkiadakis, G. (2014). Utilizing agent-based modeling to gain new insights into the ancient Minoan civilization. In *Proceedings of the 2014 International Conference on Autonomous Agents and Multi-agent Systems* (pp. 1371–1372). Paris: International Foundation for Autonomous Agents and Multiagent Systems.

Chopra, S., & White, L. (2011). *A legal theory for autonomous artificial agents*. Ann Arbor: The University of Michigan Press.

Cowley, S. (2014). Cognition beyond the body: Looking differently at ABM. Invited lecture, *The Society for the Study of Artificial Intelligence and Simulation of Behavior (AISB)*. Workshop IV: Modeling Organizational Behavior and Social Agency, Bournemouth.

Darley, V. (1994). Emergent phenomena and complexity. In R. Brooks & P. Maes (Eds.), *Artificial Life IV: Proceedings of the Fourth International Workshop on the Synthesis and Simulation of Living Systems* (pp. 411–416). Cambridge: MIT Press.

Darwall, S. (2006). *The second person standpoint: Morality, respect and accountability*. Cambridge, MA: Harvard University Press.

Dennett, D. (1987). *The intentional stance*. Cambridge, MA: MIT Press.

Dorigo, M., Maniezzo, V., & Colorni, A. (1996). Ant system: Optimization by a colony of cooperating agents. *IEEE Transactions on Systems, Man, and Cybernetics – Part B, 26*(1), 29–41.

Eymann, T. (2003). *Digitale Geschäftsagenten*. Berlin: Springer.

Ferber, J. (1999). *Multi-agent system: An introduction to distributed artificial intelligence*. Harlow: Addison Wesley Longman.

Floridi, L. (2008). The method of levels of abstraction. *Minds and Machines, 18*(3), 303–329.

Floridi, L. (2011). *The philosophy of information*. Oxford: Oxford University Press.

Goldstein, J. (1999). Emergence as a construct: History and issues. *Emergence: Complexity and Organization, 1*(1), 49–72.

Herzfeld, N. (2013). *When the second person is not a person*. Presented at the Second Person Perspective Conference, Oxford, unpublished manuscript.

Hewitt, C., Bishop, P., & Steiger, R. (1973). A universal modular actor formalism for artificial intelligence. In *Proceedings of the 3rd International Joint Conference on Artificial Intelligence (IJCAI)* (pp. 235–245). Stanford.

Hubig, C. (2010). *Technik als Medium und "Technik" als Reflexionsbegriff*. Manuscript. http://www.philosophie.tu-darmstadt.de/institut/mitarbeiterinnen_1/professoren/a_hubig/download bereich/downloadsprofhubig.de.jsp. Accessed 30 Jan 2015.

Hubig, C. (2006). *Die Kunst des Möglichen I – Technikphilosophie als Reflexion der Medialität*. Bielefield: Transcript Verlag.

Jennings, N. (2010). *ALADDIN End of Project Report*. http://www.aladdinproject.org/wp-content/uploads/2011/02/finalreport.pdf. Accessed 30 Jan 2015.

Kappelhoff, P. (2011). Emergenz und Konstitution in Mehrebenenselektionsmodellen. In J. Greve & A. Schnabel (Eds.), *Emergenz – Zur Analyse und Erklärung komplexer Strukturen* (pp. 319–345). Berlin: suhrkamp taschenbuch wissenschaft.

Latour, B. (2005). *Reassembling the social: An introduction to actor-network-theory*. Oxford: Oxford University Press.

Leibnizcenter for Law. (2011). Multi-agent PhD position available. www.leibnitz.org/wp-content/uploads/2011/02/wervering.pdf. Accessed 30 July 2011.

Linderoth, J. (2005). Animated game pieces. Avatars as roles, tools and props. In *Aesthetics of Play Conference Online Proceedings*. http://www.aestheticsofplay.org/linderoth.php. Accessed 30 Jan 2015.

Mainzer, K. (2007). *Thinking in complexity. The complex dynamics of matter, mind, and mankind* (5th ed.). Heidelberg: Springer.

Mayr, E. (2000). *Das ist Biologie – Die Wissenschaft des Lebens*. Heidelberg: Spektrum Akademischer Verlag.

McLaughlin, B. (2008). The rise and fall of British emergentism. In M. Bedeau & P. Humphreys (Eds.), *Emergence: Contemporary readings in philosophy and science* (pp. 19–60). Cambridge, MA: MIT Press.

Mead, G. (1934). *Mind, self, and society from the standpoint of a social behaviourist*. Chicago, IL: The University of Chicago Press.

Moor, J. (2006). The nature, importance, and difficulty of machine ethics. *IEEE Intelligent Systems, 21*(4), 18–21.

Muldoon, R., Lisciandra, C., Bicchieri, C., Hartmann, S., & Sprenger, J. (2014). On the emergence of descriptive norms. *Politics, Philosophy & Economics, 13*(1), 3–22.

Nealon, J., & Moreno, A. (2003). Agent-based health care systems. In J. Nealon & A. Moreno (Eds.), *Applications of software agent technology in the health care domain* (pp. 3–18). Whitestein Series in Software Agent Technologies. Basel: Birkhäuser Verlag.

Pagallo, U. (2013). *The law of robots: Crimes, contracts, and torts*. Dordrecht: Springer.

Rammert, W. (2011). *Distributed agency and advanced technology or: How to analyse constellations of collective inter-agency*. The Technical University Technology Studies Working Papers, Berlin.

Ropohl, G. (1999). Philosophy of socio-technical systems. *Society for Philosophy and Technology, 4*(3). http://scholar.lib.vt.edu/ejournals/SPT/v4_n3html/ROPOHL. Accessed 20 Jan 2015.

Ruß, A., Müller, D., & Hesse, W. (2010). Metaphern für die Informatik und aus der Informatik. In M. Bölker, M. Gutmann, & W. Hesse (Eds.), *Menschenbilder und Metaphern im Informationszeitalter* (pp. 103–128). Berlin: LIT Verlag.

Savarimuthu, B., & Cranefield, S. (2011). Norm creation, spreading and emergence: A survey of simulation models of norms in multi-agent systems. *Multiagent and Grid Systems – An International Journal, 7*, 21–54.

Scheutz, M., Madey, G., & Boyd, S. (2005, April). tMANS – The Multi-Scale Agent-Based Networked Simulation for the study of multi-scale, multi-level biological and social phenomena. In *Proceedings of Spring Simulation Multiconference (SMC 05), Agent-Directed Simulation Symposium*. San Diego.

Teubner, G. (2006). Rights of non-humans? Electronic agents and animals as new actors. *Journal of Law and Society, 33*, 497–521.

Thomas, M. E. (2013). Confessions of a sociopath. *Psychology Today, 46*(3), 52–61.

Thürmel, S. (2012, July). A multi-dimensional agency concept for social computing systems. In G. Dodig-Crnkovic, A. Rotolo, G. Sartor, J. Simon, & C. Smith (Eds.), *Proceedings of the AISB/IACAP Word Congress Social Computing, Social Cognition, Social Networks and Multiagent Systems* (pp. 87–91). Birmingham.

Thürmel, S. (2013). *Die partizipative Wende: Ein multidimensionales, graduelles Konzept der Handlungsfähigkeit menschlicher und nichtmenschlicher Akteure*. Dissertation. Technische Universität München.

Tomasello, M. (2008). *Origins of human communication*. Cambridge, MA: MIT Press.

Turkle, S. (2010). In good company? On the threshold of robotic companions. In Y. Wilks (Ed.), *Close engagements with artificial companions: Key social, psychological, ethical and design issues* (pp. 24–34). Amsterdam: John Benjamins.

Turkle, S. (2011). *Alone together, why we expect more from technology and less from each other*. New York, NY: Basic Books.

Vintiadis, E. (2014). *Emergence*. Internet Encyclopedia of Philosophy. http://www.iep.utm.edu/emergenc. Accessed 30 Jan 2015.

Wallach, W., & Allen, C. (2008). *Moral Machines: Teaching Robots Right from Wrong*, New York: University of Oxford Press.

Wedde, H., Lehnhoff, S., Rehtanz, Chr., & Krause, O. (2008). Bottom-up self-organization of unpredictable demand and supply under decentralized power management. In *Proceedings of the 2nd IEEE International Conference on Self-Adaptation and Self-Organization (SASO'08)* (pp. 10–20). Venice: IEEE Press.

Woolridge, M. (2009). *An introduction to multi-agent systems* (2nd ed.). New York, NY: John Wiley & Sons.

Chapter 12
Towards Nonlocal Field-Like Social Interactions: Oscillating Agent Based Conceptual and Simulation Framework

D. Plikynas and S. Raudys

Abstract This chapter takes a multidisciplinary perspective to examine a fundamentally novel approach to the agency and field-based nonlocal organization of digitally interconnected social systems. The main theoretical cornerstone of the new modeling approach (OSIMAS—oscillation-based multi-agent system) is built on the premises of an agent as a coherent system of oscillations. In our approach, the theoretical assumptions of the oscillating agent model are backed up with experimental brain-imaging studies inspired by cognitive neuroscience (electroencephalography—EEG), which reveal people's states of mind in terms of the specific distribution of coherent brainwaves. Based on the premises of OSIMAS and our experimental findings, in this chapter we review our two different approaches to the construction of oscillating agent models: (1) phonons as vibrating quanta, and (2) quantum mechanical wave function. Both approaches are designated for the simulation of the oscillating agent model and subsequently field-like nonlocal social interactions. Some initial work-in-progress simulation results of stylized local and nonlocal excitation propagation in the social mediums are also provided in the final section.

Keywords Nonlocal social interactions • Oscillating agent model • Multi-agent system • Coherent oscillations • Cognitive neuroscience • Excitation propagation

12.1 Introduction

The mainstream agent-based modeling (ABM) research still employs Newtonian (mechanistic) type pair-to-pair-based interactions between agents. However, in modern digital societies we often observe simultaneously one-to-many, many-to-one, and many-to-many communication and broadcasting, which take place in a

---

D. Plikynas (✉) • S. Raudys
Research and Development Center, Kazimieras Simonavicius University, J. Basanaviciaus 29a, Vilnius, EU, Lithuania
e-mail: darius.plikynas@ksu.lt; sarunas.raudys@mif.vu.lt

D. Secchi, M. Neumann (eds.), *Agent-Based Simulation of Organizational Behavior*, DOI 10.1007/978-3-319-18153-0_12

virtual space of social and economic information networks (Jackson, 2010; Raudys, Plikynas, & Raudys, 2014).

Modern information and communication technologies enable a new type of agent, i.e. nonlocal agency, which is nonlocal in the sense of participation in global information, networks, where invoked information spreads over social networks in a field-like propagation fashion. That is, agents in the ordered social system (organization) act like mutually coherent information storage, transformation and retransmitting processes. In our understanding, synchronization between agents in complex organizations takes place largely not because of local peer-to-peer interactions, but because of the presence of nonlocal (contextual) information, which is being constantly interpreted and enacted by agents locally.

In our simplified version, agents can be interpreted as resonators, which are able to resonate to the specific frequency of contextual information and readapt their resonating (natural) frequencies. In this way we assume that a contextually orchestrated system of oscillating agents creates organized social behavior. However, practical modeling of such a point of view is facing conceptual lack of a multidisciplinary connecting paradigm, which could link fragmented research in the domains of artificial intelligence (AI), multi-agent systems (MAS), social networks, and neuroscience.

Multidisciplinary investigation of the oscillatory nature of agents and social mediums is also necessary in order to gain a deeper understanding of complex social phenomena. A closer look at applied social networks research reveals some related approaches, which deal—in one way or another—with simulations of the spread of field-like information in social networks. For instance, the spread of behavior in dynamic social networks (Zhang & Wu, 2011), spread of behavior in online social networks (Centola, 2010), urban traffic control with coordinating fields (Camurri, Mamei, & Zambonelli, 2007), mining social networks using wave propagation (Wang, Tao, Xie, & Yi, 2012), network models for the diffusion of innovations (Valente, 1996; Young, 2006), and virtual field-based simulation of complex social systems (Plikynas, 2010; Plikynas, Basinskas, Kumar, et al., 2014; Raudys et al., 2014). A number of other wave-like information-diffusion approaches have been introduced, such as gradient routing (GRAD), directed diffusion, co-fields at the TOTA Programming Model (Mamei & Zambonelli, 2006), and CONRO (Shen, Salemi, & Will, 2002).

In fact, almost all of these approaches are employed for various technological or robotic applications, and very few of them, like MMASS, agent-based computational demography (ABCD), or Agent-Based Computational Economics (Tesfatsion & Judd, 2006), are suitable for programmable simulations of rapidly changing social phenomena. For instance, Multilayered Multi-Agent Situated System (MMASS) is related to the simulation of artificial societies and social phenomena (Bandini, Manzoni, & Vizzari, 2004). In essence, MMASS specifies and manages a field emission–diffusion–perception mechanism, i.e. asynchronous and at-a-distance interaction among agents. Fields are emitted by agents according to their type and state, and they are propagated throughout the spatial structure of the environment according to their diffusion function, reaching and being eventually perceived by other spatially distant agents (Bandini, Manzoni, & Vizzari, 2006).

All these approaches, in one way or another, have encountered similar problems, i.e. the limitations of the currently prevailing direct peer-to-peer and local communication methods, which have been unable to incorporate the huge amounts of indirect (contextual) information that prevails in social networks. This is due to the associated complexity and intangibility of informal information, as well as the lack of foundational theory that could create a conceptual framework for the incorporation of implicit contextual information in a more natural way. Hence, there is a need to expand prevailing agent-based conceptual frameworks in such a way that allows the incorporation of nonlocal (contextual) interaction and exchange of information.

Hence, we had to enlarge our scope of investigation considerably, looking for answers in other fundamental research areas. Consequently, we found solid experimental proof of the agent's oscillatory nature in recent advances in neuroscience, i.e. in the research area of brain-activity mapping (Haan & Gunnar, 2011). In our approach the theoretical assumptions of the oscillating agent model are supported by experimental brain imaging studies (electroencephalography—EEG) inspired by cognitive neuroscience, which reveal people's states of mind in terms of specific distribution of coherent brainwaves. By and large, neuroscience methods allow the observation of individual and group-wide dynamics of states of mind in the making. This is of great interest for the social sciences, where an agent can be anything from states to socio-cultural organizations to the environment. Methodologically this boils down to the theoretical question of what is the basic unit for analyzing social systems among culture, organization, interactions, and the body.

Hopefully, with advances in neuroscience methods, some answers are emerging. With the increase of computing power, neuroscience methods have gone beyond the confines of research into individual brain and mind states. Hardware and software used for mapping and analyzing electromagnetic brain activations have enabled measurements of brain states not only individually, but also across groups of people in real time (Lindenberger, Li, Gruber, & Müller, 2009; Nummenmaa et al., 2012; Stevens et al., 2012). This research frontier has made room for emerging multidisciplinary research areas like field-theoretic modeling of consciousness (McFadden, 2002; Pessa & Vitiello, 2004; Thaheld, 2005; Travis & Arenander, 2006; Vitiello, 2001), social neuroscience, neuroeconomics, and group neurodynamics (Cacioppo & Decety, 2011).

By and large, in the context of social neuroscience, team neurodynamics and neuroeconomics research, brain activity is usually measured together with other methods of observing social structures—such as the observation of other real-time physiological measures (e.g., heart rate, respiration rate, etc.), behaviors, cognitive performance, or self-reported individual and group states of mind (Lindenberger et al., 2009; Lutz, Greischar, Rawlings, Ricard, & Davidson, 2004; Newandee & Reisman, 1996; Nummenmaa et al., 2012). In this way, social artifacts are compared with the appropriate brain states. Merging these methods provides additional insights revealing, for example, group leaders, roles, activity patterns, drowsiness, stress management, activity synchronization, social coherence, etc. Recently, plenty of new quantitative measures have been developed using group-wide brain-imaging techniques (Cacioppo, Berntson, & Decety, 2010; Haan & Gunnar, 2011). Ordinary qualitative social research methods are enriched with these accurate quantitative measures, which gives an entirely new dimension and strength to the research. In addition, the observation of brain activity using neuroscientific methods provides meaningful feedback for observing social structures (the behaviors, cognitive performance, or self-reported states of mind of individuals and groups). In short, neuroscience-based qualitative research methods provide entirely new niches for beneficial social-research approaches.

On the other hand, some perspicacious biologically inspired simulation approaches have emerged in the areas of computational (artificial) intelligence, agent-based and multi-agent systems research. In turn, these advances have laid the foundations for simulation methods oriented towards intelligent, ubiquitous, pervasive, amorphous, organic computing (Poslad, 2009; Servat & Drogoul, 2002), and field-based coordination research (Bandini et al., 2004, 2006; Mamei & Zambonelli, 2006).

Hence, common research trends in neuroscience, AI/MAS, and social networks are leading toward field-based representations of individual and collective mental and behavioral phenomena (Haven & Khrennikov, 2013).[1] Historically, a number of well-known scholars like William James (Perry, 1996), Emile Durkheim (Martin & McIntyre, 1994), and Carl Jung have argued that the unconscious level spans beyond individual consciousness, and can be shared by us all. The closest confirmations come from the fundamental sciences, e.g., quantum (Oppenheim & Wehner, 2010; Popescu & Rohrlich, 1994) and biological (Josephson & Pallikari-Viras, 1991; Thaheld, 2005) nonlocality experiments.[2]

All these theories and experiments, when taken together, seem to be pointing in an unusual direction by implying biological entanglement and nonlocality effects that take place between human brains (Orme-Johnson & Oates, 2009; Travis & Orme-Johnson, 1989).

For instance, from the perspective of a network economy, social networks are highly heterogeneous with many links and complex interrelations. Uncoupled and indirect interactions among agents require the ability to affect and perceive a broadcast information context. Therefore, there is a need to look for ways to model the information network as a virtual information field, where each network node receives pervasive (broadcasted) information-field values. Such an approach is targeted to enforce indirect and uncoupled (contextual) interactions among agents in order to represent contextual broadcasted information in a form locally accessible

---

[1]Field-based or oscillations-based terms can be used interchangeably in the presented context.

[2]In quantum physics, the property of nonlocality ("instantaneous action at a distance") is associated with the so-called quantum entanglement when physical properties such as position, momentum, spin, polarization, etc. of entangled particles are found to be appropriately correlated at a big distance. So that the quantum state of each particle cannot be described independently. Instead, a quantum state may be given for the system of particles as a whole. Recent evidences show that in the similar manner correlated states can be found between distant molecules and even cells (Josephson & Pallikari-Viras, 1991; Thaheld, 2005).

and immediately usable by network agents. In this regard, there is a clear need to develop a collective mind-field paradigm capable of objectively simulating some complex social cognitive and behavioral phenomena, such as herd effects, fluctuations in economic activity and demography, social clustering, economic convergence, etc.

These findings directed us to the conceptually novel idea that contextual implicit information is distributed in virtual fields and that these fields—although expressing global information—are locally (unconsciously) perceived by agents. Hence, we proposed a conceptual framework for the incorporation of nonlocal (implicit) information in the agent based simulation (ABS) platforms. In a sense, we proposed two major layers of self-organization: local explicit ABM_{LE} and global implicit ABM_{GI} levels[3]

$$\mathrm{ABM} = (1-\eta)\,\mathrm{ABM}_{\mathrm{LE}} + \eta\mathrm{ABM}_{\mathrm{GI}}, \tag{12.1}$$

where $0 \leq \eta \leq 1$ denotes the degree of nonlocality and

$$\begin{aligned} \mathrm{ABM} &= \mathrm{ABM}_{\mathrm{LE}}, \text{ then } \eta \to 0, \\ \mathrm{ABM} &= \mathrm{ABM}_{\mathrm{GI}}, \text{ then } \eta \to 1. \end{aligned}$$

Thus, starting with $\eta \to 0$ self-organization can be observed on the single-agent scale; on the intermediate level $0 < \eta < 1$ self-organization can be observed on the scale of groups and organizations of agents; and on the global level $\eta \to 1$ self-organization can be observed on the scale of a coherent society. By nonlocality we have denoted contextual distributed social cognitive processes that implement self-organization above the local agent level.

In short, the major insights of this chapter are derived from the novel oscillation-based multi-agent system (OSIMAS) social simulation paradigm. The major conceptual implications of the OSIMAS paradigm, which are presented in our earlier publications (Kezys & Plikynas, 2014; Plikynas, 2010; Plikynas, Basinskas, Kumar, et al., 2014; Plikynas, Basinskas, & Laukaitis, 2014), are essentially oriented to field-theoretic ways of modeling and simulating individual and collective mind states, whereas the major prospective practical applications of OSIMAS are targeted at the simulation of real social phenomena.[4] The major methodological tools

[3]In general, self-organization is interpreted as a global order or coordination that arises from spontaneous local interactions between components of an initially disordered system. The resulting organization is wholly distributed among all the components of the system. Hence, our proposed pervasive information field (PIF) concept can be interpreted in a similar manner, i.e. as a spontaneously evolving order or coordination of the components of a system. In the context of OSIMAS, these components of a social system are individual mind-fields. Hence, the term 'self-organization' implies global order or a coordination mechanism among individual mind-fields.

[4]The OSIMAS paradigm pertains to the idea that our conscious minds are a certain type of field. Such a view goes back at least as far as the insights of the gestalt psychologists of the early twentieth century. They emphasized the holistic nature of perception, which they claimed was more

suitable for appropriate simulations are within the area of agent-based and multi-agent systems (ABS and MAS, respectively) research.[5]

Hence, in this chapter we have presented a conceptual synopsis of the novel multidisciplinary paradigm with some references to our earlier publications. It is imperative to note that OSIMAS stems primarily from deductive reasoning, not from the empirical inductive reasoning that currently prevails in the mainstream natural sciences. However, we also succeeded in finding fundamental underpinning based on empirical observations.

The OSIMAS paradigm is still at an early stage of development, during which conceptual ideas are explored in order to find ways of expressing them in the modeling sense. However, a few practical applications in the social domain have recently begun to evolve, such as a group-wide neuroscientific approach to studying teamwork, research into the wave-like diffusion of information across social media, a recent study of oscillating agent-based multi-agent systems for adaptive portfolio management, etc. In years to come a much wider area of social applications, including organizational cases, will be explored using the OSIMAS paradigm.

This chapter is organized as follows. Section 12.2 briefly presents the oscillation-based paradigm and experimental validation framework. Section 12.3 reviews oscillating agent model construction using phonons and quantum mechanics approaches. Section 12.4 presents the results of local and nonlocal agent-based simulation of excitation propagation in social mediums. Finally, Sect. 12.5 draws concluding remarks.

12.2 Oscillation-Based Paradigm and Experimental Validation Framework

A review of the literature has revealed that adoption of the oscillations backed up field-like excitatory models is still slow in the agent-based modeling of social systems. There are still major unresolved problems due (1) to the complexity of the associated field-based modeling of implicit (nonlocal) self-organizing social systems, and (2) to the lack of a foundational theory which could provide the conceptual multidisciplinary research framework for the modeling and experimental validation.

---

akin to fields than to particles. Later, Karl Popper proposed that consciousness is a manifestation of an overarching force field in the brain that can integrate the diverse information held in distributed neurons. Only recently an understanding has emerged that this force field is actually generated by the bioelectromagnetic activity of neurons in the form of the conscious mind as an electromagnetic field. It is through this mechanism that humans acquired the capacity to become conscious agents who are able to influence the world (Malik, 2002).

[5]For instance, contextual (implicit) information spread using social media (e.g., propaganda, political campaigns, and information wars), network models of the diffusion of innovations, models of self-excitatory wave propagation in social media, etc.

Our research may contribute to the resolution of the above-mentioned problems via the earlier proposed (Plikynas, Basinskas, Kumar, et al., 2014) multidisciplinary research framework OSIMAS (oscillations-based multiagent system), where we have formulated a set of assumptions and postulates that lay the ground for the OSIMAS simulation paradigm.[6] OSIMAS assumptions are based on the integration of the multidisciplinary knowledge and designed to pave the ground for modeling nonlocal contextual environments in complex information-rich social networks, where not only intangible but also tangible natural resources and even social agents themselves can be simulated as oscillating processes (OAM) immersed in an all-pervasive contextual information field (PIF).

The OSIMAS paradigm is based on the key assumptions, which at least theoretically open up a new way for modeling and simulating emergent social properties as collective mind-field effects. To further clarify the OSIMAS paradigm and some fundamental insights we refer to our earlier publications (Plikynas, 2010; Plikynas, Basinskas & Laukaitis, 2014). Below, we briefly review our experimental framework, which is dedicated (1) to falsify some key assumptions of OSIMAS paradigm and (2) to provide further insights about agents' mind-field properties.

First, while formulating our experimental framework, we faced some challenging fundamental questions like how to bring human interaction, occurring in a complex social environment, under the scrutiny of laboratory testing and how to identify human interaction itself naming the most basic social communication artifacts to be measured. Obviously, human behavior shows only the tip of the iceberg and can only vaguely represent the states of individual and collective mind-fields. Hence, we had to search for a direct representation. That is how we got the idea of evaluating human (social agents) states using encephalographic (EEG) brain-wave activation patterns, i.e. spectra that directly indicate an agent oscillatory nature.

Admittedly, EEG, fMRI, MEG, and other modern neuroscience-based brain-imaging techniques are not blunt instruments for measuring states of human agents. On the contrary, these objective quantitative techniques are improving very quickly and some of the results from the research frontiers are already proving to be very impressive, i.e. not only various cognitive, emotional, and sensomotoric states, but also single thoughts can be depicted and recognized. For instance, the brain–machine interface (BMI) realizes communication between the brain and an external device (Lebedev & Nicolelis, 2006), neuroprosthetics applies brain communication to artificial limbs (Do, Wang, King, Chun, & Nenadic, 2013), and neuroscientists recently reported that direct communication between human brains is possible over extended distances through Internet transmission of EEG signals. These examples, along with many others, illustrate that brain-imaging techniques are no longer blunt instruments. They are precise tools for measuring the mind-brain states of human agents.

[6]The evolving multidisciplinary OSIMAS paradigm not only spans the breadth of several research domains, but also plunges through several levels of self-organized complexity, beginning with fundamental quantum, proceeding to the biological level and ending at a social level.

However, we must also admit that the scope of our EEG research was very limited due to the conceptual, experimental, and methodical constraints of the real-time group-wide EEG studies available. Therefore, during this initial stage of our EEG analyses we mostly employed data from individual EEG studies dealing with just few baseline states such as thinking, counting, dreaming, deep sleep, meditating, etc. Of course, these are just a few basic states. Admittedly, from the social—and particularly, psychological—perspectives there are more relevant emotional, cognitive, communicative, relaxing, action-response, sensomotoric, and other mind and physiological (heart rate, breathing rate, myographic data) states that need to be explored in the prospective group-wide studies.

Consequently, for the experimental validation of our proposed paradigm we have designed a three-stage experimental and simulation research framework which (1) starts with an investigation of the common features of benchmark individual mind-field states, (2) proceeds with estimates of the coherence and synchronicity measures for group-wide (collective) neurodynamics, and (3) ends with a simulation setup for the multiagent system (MAS) design, see Fig. 12.1.

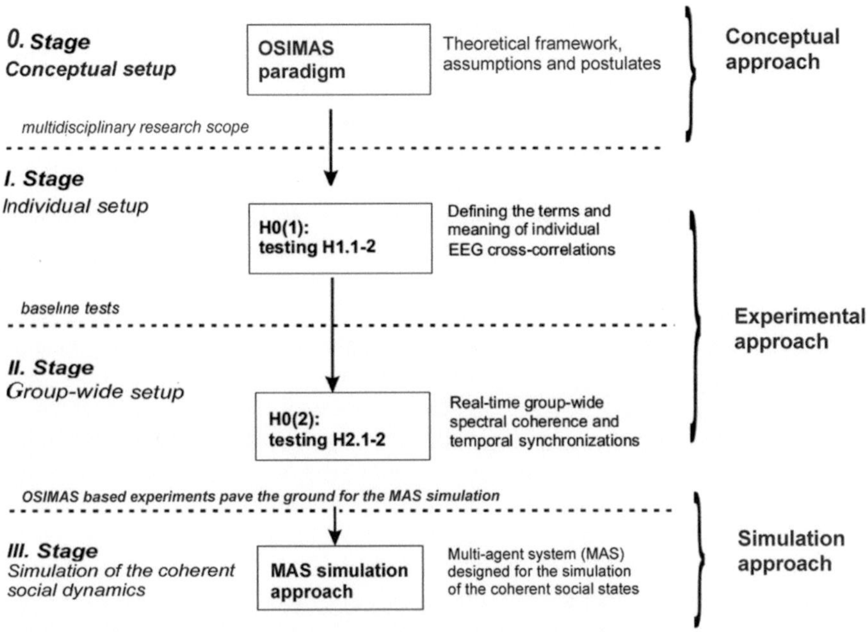

Fig. 12.1 Overall research framework: major research stages. Null hypothesis H0(1): temporally separated people doing the same mental or physical activities demonstrate a significant increase of cross-correlations in their brain-wave patterns and H0(2): a real-time spatially close, but mutually separated group of people demonstrates a statistically significant increase of the mutual synchronization in their brain-wave patterns during collectively coordinated or even uncoordinated, but mutually induced states

Some experimental EEG cases (see Stages 1 and 2 in Fig. 12.1) presented below illustrate observed cross-correlations of individual mind states. However, the main purpose of this section is not to present a thorough EEG-based experimental setup, analysis techniques, or statistical results. Some results are described in our earlier research papers (Kezys & Plikynas, 2014; Plikynas, Basinskas, Kumar, et al., 2014; Plikynas, Basinskas & Laukaitis, 2014).[7] In this review, however, our main focus is (1) to show some baseline EEG results (Stage 1) used to falsify the conceptual OSIMAS assumptions about the oscillatory nature of agents; and (2) based on the individual tests, to discuss the group-wide EEG experimental framework (Stage 2), which is designed to test cross-correlations of EEG signals between individuals within groups in real time.

The results of our findings are based on the EEG signals recorded from ten healthy volunteers (five women and five men, four of them were experienced yoga practitioners aged between 30 and 50, and the remainder were beginners) who were all asked to stay in five different mental states, each for a duration of 30 min. Between targeted states there were 5-min pauses for relaxation. For further reference, these states are denoted with numbers as follows: (1) meditation, (2) meditation with acoustic sound signals, (3) counting of sound signals, (4) thinking, and (5) thinking with acoustic sound signals (Plikynas, Basinskas, & Laukaitis, 2014).

We carried out a comparison between the different mental states by calculating the total differences (summing the activations in all EEG channels) for different brainwaves. To illustrate the observed differences, we also used a colored head-map representation in which the differences between the separate channels are not added up but are averaged out using spline interpolation over the 64 channels for a long time interval, see Fig. 12.2. This approach helps greatly to distinguish similar brain activations when both activation patterns are very different and tend to have rapidly changing dynamics.

Such a visualization of brainwave dynamics is very helpful for the recognition of group synchronization patterns for different persons, mind states, and frequency ranges. For the sake of clarity, we have added smaller head-maps (see Fig. 12.2) that show direct differences in brainwave activation patterns (for the chosen mind state) between pairs of people. If brainwave activations for a pair of people are dissimilar, the corresponding differences between activations produce a color and intensity-rich activation pattern in the difference head-map. In the opposite case, if the brainwave activations for a pair of people are similar, the corresponding difference map tends to be less rich with a low intensity of color. This approach helps greatly to distinguish similar brain activations when both activation patterns are very

[7]Our experimental findings are based on the EEG signals recorded using the BioSemi ActiveTwo Mk2 system with 64 channels. We used 64 channels in the BioSemi ActiveTwo Mk2 EEG measuring system. This system obtains and records high-quality (resolution LSB = 31.25 nV) and low-noise (total input noise for $Z_e < 10$ kΩ is 0.8 μV_{RMS}) electric local field potentials from the surface of the skull (Nunez & Srinivasan, 2005).

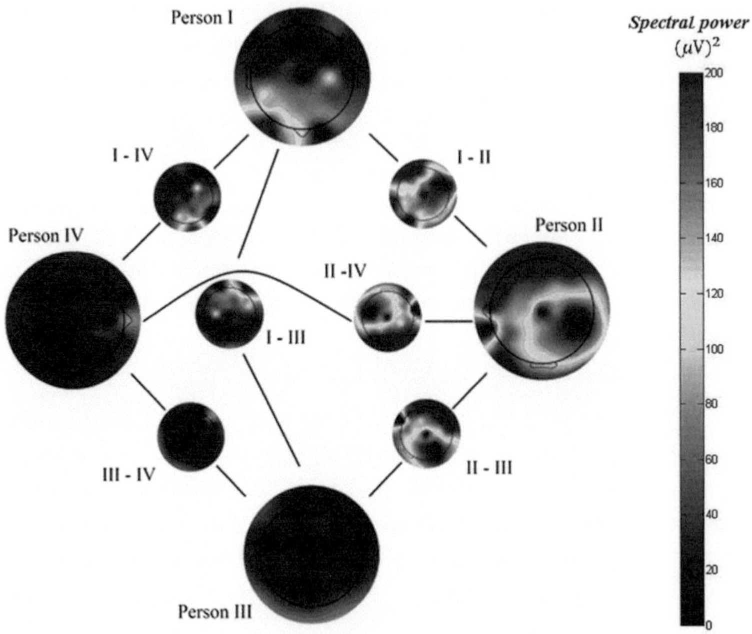

Fig. 12.2 Spectral power activation (alpha range) of brainwave dynamics illustrated for four persons in thinking state. Smaller diagrams and connecting lines indicate spectral power differences between respective persons

different and tend to have rapidly changing dynamics. Our proposed group-wide mind-field visualization approach extends well-known brain-imaging techniques (Nunez & Srinivasan, 2005). Therefore, we named it the group-wide mind-field imaging method—GMIM. For more samples, visit http://osimas-eeg.vva.lt/.

We observed that spectral power dynamics take place not only in the spatial sense, but also in the sense of the redistribution of brainwave energy over the spectral regions. This is particularly clear during the transitions between mind states, when the redistribution process of spectral power takes place between the spectral ranges Δ, Θ, α, β, and γ (Plikynas, Basinskas, Kumar, et al., 2014).[8]

The intrinsic spatial and spectral dynamics show that very complex processes are involved, which cannot be grasped by the average estimates. However, for the baseline testing we made average measurements of the spectral power distributions over the Δ, Θ, α, β, and γ frequency ranges for 10 people. See Fig. 12.3 for an illustration.

[8]We have included the γ frequency range in order to embrace whole brainwaves region reported in the literature. However, in some of our analyses we have used only Δ, Θ, α, and β brainwaves in order to eliminate the influence of Fourier boundary transformation conditions, where a high noise-to-signal ratio prevails.

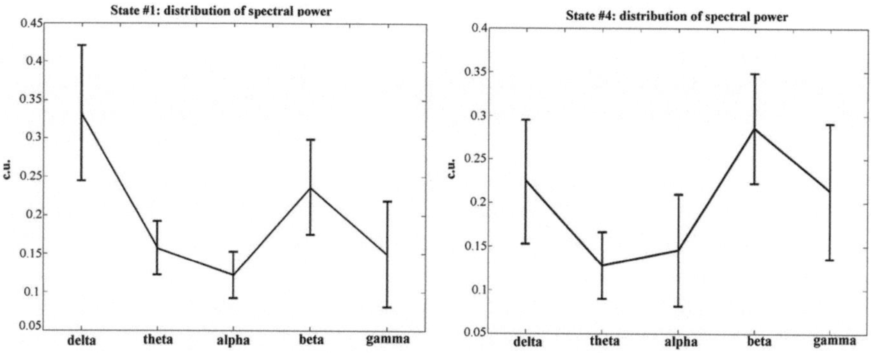

Fig. 12.3 Spectral power distribution results over Δ, Θ, α, β, and γ frequency ranges for the states #1 and 4 (averaged for all channels and all ten participants)

Table 12.1 Statistical estimates of average total spectral power (SP) fluctuations measured in c.u. for ten persons over 600 s in each mind state

	Statistical estimates of total spectral power (SP) dynamics, c.u.	
State no.	Mean SP	Standard deviation
1	4,053.8	969.2
2	3,908.8	1,157.1
3	4,294.4	810.5
4	4,078.4	1,011.5
5	3,944.8	1,257.1

These results illustrate that regardless of their highly dynamic nature, mind states can be distinguished in terms of relative spectral power distribution differences for the Δ, Θ, α, β, and γ brainwave activations. Despite the high standard deviation of the total spectral power distribution for the 0.05 significance level, our reiteration results clearly demonstrated that characteristic spectral power redistributions were taking place in the different mind states (Plikynas, Basinskas, Kumar, et al., 2014). See Table 12.1.

High variance has been reported in other research too (Nummenmaa et al., 2012; Standish, Kozak, Johnson, & Richards, 2004; Travis & Arenander, 2006). Observation of spectral power dynamics over the EEG channels in various spectral ranges clearly indicates spatial location as playing an important role (Plikynas, Basinskas & Laukaitis, 2014).

Let us recall that proposed individual EEG baseline tests were designed to test the basic conceptual OSIMAS assumption, that different states of social agents can be represented in terms of coherent oscillations. In fact, EEG experimental results revealed how the theoretically deduced idea of the agent as a system of coherent oscillations can find solid empirical backup in terms of coherent Δ, Θ, α, β, and γ brainwave oscillations, which uniquely describe agent's mind states.

In summary, we developed some simplified individual benchmark EEG tests. The main idea was to show that the conceptual premises of OSIMAS concerning the oscillations-based nature of human states have an empirical background. Some other very important implications from our EEG data analyses are: (1) basic human mind states can be recognized even from a few EEG channels (reductionist approach), (2) basic mind states have characteristic spectral power energy distribution patterns in well-known brainwave regions (delta, theta, alpha, beta, and gamma), (3) specific spectral power redistribution takes place during the transitions between different mind states.

Additionally, below we have included a basic overview of research into mind states, which shows that in contrast to the raw EEG signal, *intra-individual* quantitative electroencephalography (qEEG) parameters (such as spectral features including peak frequency and relative or absolute power spectrums in frequency bands) are highly reliable (usually more than 80 %) over minutes, months, and even years for the same subject mental state in the same registration conditions (Aguilar, Congedo, & Minguez, 2011; Fingelkurts, Fingelkurts, Ermolaev, & Kaplan, 2006; Thatcher, 2010).

However, the reliability of the qEEG parameters is highly dependent on the length of the EEG epoch for which the parameters are calculated, where epochs of 40–60 s in length are enough to demonstrate stable parameters (Gudmundsson, Runarsson, Sigurdsson, Eiriksdottir, & Johnsen, 2007). The reliability of qEEG is affected by intra-individual variability. Most (about 95 %) intra-individual variability in spectral parameters is usually captured within several minutes of recording time, while longer epochs may accumulate additional variability due to changes in vigilance. Although qEEG has great inter-individual variability, consistent qEEG norms have been found across cultures and ethnicities (Aguilar et al., 2011; Thatcher, 2010).

The above short review illustrates that basic mind states can be distinguished using individual EEG data. Hence, based on our individual EEG benchmark tests, we proposed a group-wide methodology for the recognition of collective interpersonal mind states (see an example on our website, http://osimas.ksu.lt/eeg/). In this way, we also suggested some benchmark group-wide methods and paved the way for the subsequent studies of real-time group-wide EEG settings.

After carrying out control baseline individual EEG tests, we also tested data from the group-wide simultaneous EEG measurements we obtained from the Advanced Brain Monitoring Company. In summary, we succeeded in recognizing individual basic mind states in this case, as well. However, our main goal was to find coherence and synchronicities between the basic mind states for different individuals in the real-time group setup. In this case, we had to analyze precisely synchronized EEG measurements and accurate signal phases for different people. However, our analyses showed that the signals did not meet these requirements due to the high noise-to-signal ratio. Hence, we obtained inconclusive results. This infers the conclusion that more precise experimental data and analyses are needed for the group-wide EEG settings. Fortunately, some other group-wide EEG studies have just begun to emerge from the perspective of real-time group-wide EEG measurement and analysis platforms in social domains (Likens, Amazeen, Stevens, Galloway, & Gorman, 2014; Stevens et al., 2012; Stevens & Galloway, 2014). From this perspective, we believe that group-wide EEG studies will be expanded and used for various social applications, e.g., teamwork, leadership, critical assignments, group management, and organizational studies.

Hence, the primary goal of our EEG data analyses was not to fine-tune methods for researching the neural correlates of mind states. We used neuroscience only as a tool to show an empirical way of representing conceptual oscillating-agent and mind-field OSIMAS ideas in terms of brainwave spectra measured in experiments. In this initial study we used just a few canonical examples of different mind and brain states. Hence, our goal was to show an experimental way to test major OSIMAS assumptions. We showed few EEG research cases as examples. However, it is beyond the scope of the current paper to provide in-depth EEG studies in order to validate statistically solid evidences. Further studies should follow in this regard. In the next research stage, our proposed approach can be applied to discern subtle individual and group-wide emotional, cognitive, and relaxation states in group-wide settings. We can only say that at this early stage our work-in-progress and other above-mentioned studies do not contradict the basic OSIMAS assumptions.

In the next section, based on the assumptions and experimental findings of OSIMAS, we provide some insights about the construction of an oscillating agent model (OAM), taking a phonons and quantum mechanical approach.

12.3 Oscillating Agent Model: Phonons and Quantum Mechanical Approach

According to OSIMAS, social agents are open processes, which are strongly influenced not only by internal states but also by external ones, i.e. not only the local environment, but also the regional and global environment. We stepped further ahead, claiming that each agent can be understood not only as an individual but also as a distributed cognitive system, which unconsciously internalizes and, therefore, shares social norms, behaviors and, more broadly, a cognitive environment (Secchi, 2011).

The abstraction of an oscillating agent as an environmentally distributed cognitive system can be implemented using proper oscillation-based modeling tools. For instance, such oscillation-based approaches can employ weakly coupled oscillators, wave packets, phonons, soliton waves, wave functions, etc. First, we will briefly review an adapted phonons model, which was designed (1) to represent each agent as a unique composition of oscillations, (2) to quantify the associated oscillatory energy, and (3) to propose an interchange mechanism between agents. For more details, we refer to our earlier paper (Plikynas, 2010). Below, we briefly present the key modeling ideas using the adapted phonons approach.[9]

In the proposed model, each agent acts like an elementary oscillator, which, depending on inner conditions, can absorb incoming wave spectra, transform them, and transmit them to the environment, i.e. to the pervasive information field (PIF). Hence, we are proposing an energy-information state space model for an agent and its systems, where information is coded using a pair of quantum numbers that denote energy transitions between states. That is, in such a model we adapt the principle of quantization of energy-information states to social agents, with an analogy to the rotational-vibrational states of the diatomic molecular model.

In the proposed approach not only there are allocated unique frequencies for nodes, resources and agents, but also superposed spectra are calculated for each node. Such spectrum includes all bands coming from all resources, agents, and other nodes. Bands don't overlap as they cover different spectral zones. In addition, we assume that all oscillations are transmitted instantaneously over the whole virtual space.

Nodes and resources are latent objects. They can only passively emit their own unique natural frequencies in the surrounding pervasive information field. Agents passively emit their unique identifying frequencies too, but essentially they are proactive, i.e. agents, depending on their behavioral rules (internal production instructions), are capable of absorbing incoming frequencies, transforming and emitting different frequencies. This interactive process is twofold: (1) automatic in the form of law, which holds whenever appropriate wave-like conditions are met and (2) personalized, i.e. it depends on the agent's individual behavioral patterns governed by the OAM (oscillating agent model) rules.

The agent's efficiency depends on his spectral coherence with the global criteria (e. g., market rules) which specify some spectrum measures like minimum internal energy (e.g., available capital etc.) needed for survival. Extremely coherent agents can be rewarded, while extremely incoherent agents (i.e., corresponding investment strategies in the financial application case) are removed from the simulation process.

In sum, a novel simulation paradigm offers some wave-like methods to transform multidimensional factor space (representing a multiplicity of phenomenal forms and interactions) into the most universal spectral coding system. In this way, not only the communication mechanism but also the social agents themselves can be simulated as oscillating processes. They are represented in the form of unique spectra.

To the authors' knowledge, there is no simulation in the social research field that focuses on the communication mechanisms in such a virtual setting. However, like all pioneering approaches, this approach needs thorough further investigation.

[9]A phonon is a quantum mechanical description of an elementary vibrational motion in which a lattice of atoms or molecules uniformly oscillates at a single (natural) frequency. A phonon represents an excited state in the quantum mechanical quantization of the modes of vibrations of elastic structures of interacting particles. The approach through phonons is appealing, because it is used to describe a collective excitation in a periodic, elastic arrangement of atoms (or molecules) or in our case—agents as coherent sets of oscillations.

The method presented above can be interpreted as an initial first "take" on the simulation of social phenomena using phonons-based approach. Next, we shortly introduce yet another field-based approach, i.e. the quantum mechanical agent model.

In the previous section, for the OAM construction we adapted phonons using the vibrating quanta approach, which is borrowed from classical physics. In this section we briefly discuss our earlier proposed neoclassical approach (Plikynas, 2015), which integrates the previously mentioned neuroscience findings with quantum physics.

In this case, we do exploit the fact that OSIMAS is close to the dynamic causal modeling (DCM) framework, which has been developed recently by the neuroimaging community to explain, using biophysical models, the non-invasive brain imaging data caused by neural processes (David, 2007). In DCM, the parameters of biophysical models are estimated from measured data and the evidence for each model is evaluated. This enables one to test different functional hypotheses (i.e., models) for a given data set. The goal is to show that these models can be adapted to get closer to the self-organized and dissipative dynamics of living systems, as covered by formal theories used in biology such as autopoiesis. Therefore, from the theoretical standpoint, the OAM approach gets close to the important autopoietic systems theoretical framework (Georgiev & Glazebrook, 2006).

Hence, we attempt to connect experimentally driven DCM and conceptually driven autopoietic systems theory. Based on the DCM framework we construct the OAM, which employs structural and dynamical effects using the quantum mechanical approach for modeling self-organized states' dynamics. From the other side, we use autopoietic theory to describe the dynamics of mind states' transformation processes, which through their interactions continuously regenerate and realize the network of processes (relations) that produced them (Maturana, 1980).

In neurodynamics, there are two classes of effects: dynamic effects and structural effects. The duration and form of the resulting dynamic effect depends on the dynamical stability of the system to perturbations of its states (i.e., how the system's trajectories change with the state). Structural effects depend on structural stability (i.e., how the system's trajectories change with the parameters). Systematic changes in the parameters can produce systematic changes in the response, even in the absence of input (David, 2007).

In the proposed OAM, we are looking how to address both classes of neurodynamic effects, i.e. dynamic and structural. Therefore, we use the quantum mechanical representation of self-organized mind states. In other words, the OAM simulates human basic mind states (BMS) dynamics and structural effects employing stylized oscillations-based representations of experimentally observed characteristic EEG power spectral density (PSD) distributions of brainwaves (Buzsaki, 2011; Plikynas, Basinskas, Kumar, et al., 2014) in delta, theta, alpha, beta, and gamma spectral ranges, see Fig. 12.3. We infer that PSD patterns can objectively identify BMS (Plikynas, 2015; Plikynas, Basinskas & Laukaitis, 2014).[10]

We elaborate further that the wave-like nature of coherent human mind-field states (BMS) can be approximated using the wave mechanics approach, i.e. wave function (also named as state function) and linear operators (Buzsaki, 2011; Haven & Khrennikov, 2013). This assumption is based not only on recent theories like Pribram's and Bohm's holonomic brain theory (Pribram, 1999) or Vitello's dissipative quantum model of brain (Pessa & Vitiello, 2004; Vitiello, 2001), but also on recent evidences, which show "warm quantum coherence" in plant photosynthesis, bird brain navigation, human sense of smell, and brain neurons' microtubules (Engel et al., 2007; O'Reilly & Olaya-Castro, 2014).

These evidences well corroborate the 20-year-old "Orch OR" (orchestrated objective reduction) theory of consciousness proposed by Stuart Hameroff and Sir Roger Penrose (Hameroff & Penrose, 2014). According to this theory and recent experimental evidences, EEG rhythms (brainwaves) derive from deeper level microtubule (protein polymers inside brain neurons) vibrations in the megahertz frequency range, which govern neuronal and synaptic function, and also connect brain processes to self-organizing processes in the fine scale (Georgiev & Glazebrook, 2006).[11] Hence, according to "Orch OR" theory, consciousness depends on biologically "orchestrated" coherent quantum processes in collections of microtubules within brain neurons. These quantum processes correlate with and regulate neuronal synaptic and membrane activity. Continuous Schrödinger evolution of each such process terminates in accordance with the specific Diósi–Penrose (DP) scheme of "objective reduction" ("OR") of the quantum state (Hameroff & Penrose, 2014). This orchestrated OR activity ("Orch OR") is taken to result in moments of conscious awareness and/or choice. The DP form of OR is related to the fundamentals of quantum mechanics.

In short, in our conceptual OAM model, following the Orch OR theory, we assumed that Schrödinger type of partial differential equation (Schrödinger, 1955) can be fitted for the description of the temporal evolution of mind-field states. It is important to notice that in the proposed OAM the wave function ψ can be derived via superposition of brainwaves (Plikynas, 2015). Hence, each BMS has a mind-field described by the composition of characteristic brainwaves (delta, theta, alpha, beta, and gamma), which via superposition produce brainwaves function. Hence,

[10]We chose these basic mind states (BMS)—sleeping, wakefulness, thinking, and resting. We make use of the fact that each BMS has characteristic brainwave pattern, which can be identified using power spectral density (PSD) distribution analyses (Müller et al., 2008; Plikynas, Basinskas, Kumar, et al., 2014).

[11]Despite a century of clinical use, the underlying origins of EEG rhythms have remained a mystery. However, microtubule quantum vibrations (e.g., in the megahertz frequency range) appear to interfere and produce much slower EEG "beat frequencies" in the range 4–70 Hz. Clinical trials of brief brain stimulation—aimed at microtubule resonances with megahertz mechanical vibrations using transcranial ultrasound—have shown reported improvements in people mood (Hameroff & Penrose, 2014).

filtered EEG spectrum produces our wave function. In this way, experiments meet the theory. We use state (wave) function to represent the probability amplitude of finding the system in some particular BMS.

An operator is transforming function acting on the characteristic BMS wave function. Consequently, agent "moves" from one basic mind state (BMS) to another. Similarly, like in the biophysical DCM, the parameters of transitions between states in the OAM model can be estimated from measured EEG data (David, 2007). This enables one to test different functional hypotheses (i.e., models) for a given data set.

In such a model it is quite natural that transitions of the mind-field in the state space starts from the initial BMS and proceed in a probabilistic and aperiodic manner to the other states, depending on the individual parameters of each agent. The driving factors for these transitions depend on marginal conditions described for the kinetic and potential energy with the help of the Hamiltonian operator, which controls the total energy of wave (state) function.

Following the OSIMAS paradigm (Plikynas, Basinskas, Kumar, et al., 2014) and other related research (Haven & Khrennikov, 2013; Orme-Johnson & Oates, 2009; Pessa & Vitiello, 2004), we foresee OAM as a building block for the construction of multi-agent systems that could lead to the explanation of collective coherent states (Nummenmaa et al., 2012; Pizzi, Fantasia, Gelain, & Rossetti, 2004; Standish et al., 2004; Stevens et al., 2012; Thaheld, 2005; Travis & Orme-Johnson, 1989). However, further empirical research is required so that the oscillation-based conclusive and experimentally proven social simulation theory can further evolve. For more details about the quantum mechanical approach, we refer to our articles (Plikynas, 2015; Plikynas, Basinskas & Laukaitis, 2014).

In the final section we briefly present another work-in-progress simulation approach, which uses thousands of simple neural networks (perceptrons) to model excitation propagation in artificial social mediums.

12.4 Agent-Based Simulation: Excitation Propagation in Social Mediums

In this section we briefly present some results of excitation propagation in social mediums composed of a multitude of state-changing agents modeled using neural networks (perceptrons). We propose a novel applied simulation scheme for a multi-agent automated trading system, which deals with self-excited oscillations arising in the chaotically changing financial markets. Our approach is based on the generation of a multitude of artificial self-excitatory investment agents, the fluctuating activity of which generates the volatile financial time series observed in the modern financial markets. Below, we have presented a short synopsis of our earlier research in this area. For more detailed information, please read the following: (Plikynas, Raudys, & Raudys, 2014; Raudys, 2001; Raudys et al., 2014).

We assume that a social medium is composed of a large number of mutually communicating human and computer-based agents that interchange novel information. Each agent (actor) can transmit and pick up signals from several local and non-local neighbors. In this way, our stylized agents assist in generating chaotic or coherent local and long-distance oscillations in a social investment medium. Modeling of lengthy high-dimensional chaotic time series allows investment strategy schemes to be developed that, to some extent, are robust to unexpected changes (crises) rarely observed in the real financial markets. In our novel scheme we make use of clustering time series to reduce dimensionality and employ algorithms based on an evolutionary artificial immune system approach to select typical time series employed for trading during short time intervals. The novel multi-agent system was tested with real-world everyday data for the period between 2003 and 2013, where a total of 20,000 investing strategies were considered. In an out-of-sample regime, the novel approach considerably outperformed benchmark trading strategies (Plikynas, Raudys & Raudys, 2014; Raudys et al., 2014). To test these and other simulation results, please visit our online virtual lab (V-lab) at http://vlab.vva.lt/, MEPSM1 model, login: Guest, Password: guest555). Below we briefly provide a few details about the model setup.

Similar to the cellular grid-based models, each node is summing input signals transmitted from local and nonlocal other nodes. In the nature-inspired model, however, magnitudes of the output signals and their release times depend on the sums of the accumulated inputs non-linearly. That is, each element of the grid is represented by a single layer perceptron, which has a number of inputs (say p) and uses weights (connection strengths between the nodes), $w_1, w_2, \ldots, w_p$ to calculate a weighted sum $\mathrm{arg} = \sum_{i=1}^{p} w_i x_i$, and produce an output, $o = f(\mathrm{arg})$, by using sigmoid *nonlinearity*, $f(\mathrm{arg}) = 1/(1 + \exp(-\mathrm{arg}))$, habitually used in artificial neural networks (Haykin, 1998; Raudys, 2001). We adopted this function for feasible needs

$$f_s(\mathrm{arg}) = \gamma/(1 + \exp(-\eta \times \mathrm{arg} - \theta)) \;\text{ if } \mathrm{arg} \geq \Delta^* \text{ and } f_s(\mathrm{arg}) = 0 \text{ otherwise} \tag{12.2}$$

where $\Delta^* \geq 0$ is an a priori defined sensitivity threshold. In simulations we used $\gamma = 1.333$, $\eta = 5$, $\gamma = 0.4$ and $\theta = -1.333$. The constants were selected to have the weights w_i, and outputs o, between 0 and 1.

After obtaining excitation signals the agent calculates the weighted sum and after some delay fires out transformed sum of input signals, $f_s(\Sigma_i w_i x_i)$, accumulated during two previous time periods. In our model, signal transfer time, t_{transf}, is discrete, 1, 2, …, m. This time depends on strength of accumulated output signal, o. For that reason, output's signal interval (0, 1) is split into m equal intervals, corresponding to time periods, 1, 2, …, m.

In our social medium model we have a "negative feed-back": *the larger is excitation signal, arg, the later the* jth *agent will fire out its output signal.* To define t_{transf}, we followed observations from cellular automata and differential equations based excitable medium models, see (Spach, 1997): "the longer is delay in transfer of the excitation, the greater the node-to-node strength of the signal." Minimal transmission time can be equal to 1, i.e. the cell does not transmit signal if $f(\text{arg}) < 1/m$. Minimal transmission time is affected also by a sensitivity threshold, $\Delta *$.

Both discrete time and the negative feed-back introduce stochastic (chaotic) components. Comparative experiments showed that utilization of fixed or variable time delays changes the characteristics of the model essentially. To speed up computer calculations, a look-up table was used to find $o = f(\text{arg})$. The use of the look-up table introduces additional stochastic component into the model. Accumulated signals are transferred only to non-excited neighbor agents.

An important parameter traditionally used in signal propagation models is *the refractory period*, t_{refr}, a number of elementary time periods, when after excitation, the node cannot be excited again. In our model's version, the refractory period is determined by saturation, sat_j of the jth agent after its excitation and the strength of potential new excitation, o_{new}. Just after excitation, $\text{sat}_j = o$. The saturation exponentially decreases with the time, t:

$$\text{sat}_j(t) = o \times \exp\left(-\alpha_{\text{refr}} \times (t - t_{\text{excitation}})\right). \tag{12.3}$$

When saturation falls below a threshold

$$\Delta^* - \beta \times \left(o_{\text{new}} - \Delta^*\right), \tag{12.4}$$

the refractory period terminates, and the jth agent can be excited by new excitation signal, o_{new}, if $o_{\text{new}} \geq \Delta *$. In above equations, $\alpha_{\text{refr}} = 1/(\text{refr} \times m)$, and β is a small positive constant. Parameter refr is an a priori determined time constant, *the refractory time parameter.* This parameter can be common for all agents or individual for each of them. Equation (12.4) shows that powerful excitations of neighboring agents, o_{new}, can shorten the refractory period a little bit. For simplicity sake, in experiments reported in this paper, $\beta = 0$.

To understand the main properties of the model more easily, we first present its simplified version, see Fig. 12.4. In order to ensure chaotic behavior of the agents, we introduced additional noise while determining the coordinates of the nodes and calculation of the nearest neighbors. The signal transmission starts from a central node, as shown by the arrows, see Fig. 12.4. In the model, each element of the grid is represented by a single-layer perceptron (SLP), with six inputs that use weights (connection strengths between the nodes) to calculate a weighted sum of inputs in each node. In the output of the nodes we have non-linear sigmoid activation functions that restrict outputs between 0 and 1. After the refractory period ends each unexcited node can be excited only in cases where the sum of input signals exceeds the a priori defined sensitivity threshold.

A new feature of the model is that the refractory period depends on the magnitude of the node's outputs. It makes the model's behavior similar to biology inspired excitable medium models that claim "the longer is delay in transfer of the excitation,

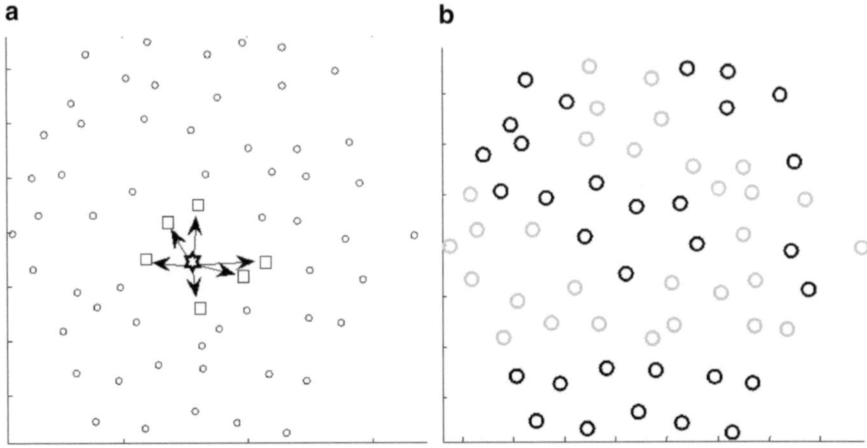

Fig. 12.4 (**a**) Hexagonal grid of information transmission distorted by injection of noise, (**b**) excitation wave after 15 propagation time moments (the *dark color* shows excited nodes, and *lighter colors* indicate cells still in the refractory period)

the greater the node-to-node strength of the signal." Reaction to the excitation signal and refractory periods are necessary, e.g. to verify obtained information or become familiar with it.

It is worth noting that the SLP is a nature-inspired model of information processing, and has several universal properties. For that reason, we can say that the excitable media model considered here is partially inspired by nature. The main media parameters are: N_y, a number of nodes in each edge of the hexagonal media, w_1, w_2, …, w_6, the connection weights, $\theta*$, the sensitivity threshold, and the rule and its parameters that determine the refractory period. To realize human-information agent-based social media, the parameters mentioned above can be common to a group of nodes or specific to each node, which represents an element of social community (in different applications it can be a human being, a group of individuals, an economy, a political unit, or even a network of information-processing and transmitting computers). Depending on the weights, initial excitation, excitation threshold, refractory period, etc., we obtained various excitation propagation patterns, see Fig. 12.5.

If the weights and initial excitation are small and the excitation threshold is too high (or very small), the wave propagation can cease. In intermediate situations, gaps (non-excited nodes) appear within a circle of excited nodes. If the refractory period is long, the gap is filled quickly by excitations from neighboring nodes. If the refractory period is brief, after the excitation the nodes can be excited without a lengthy delay. In such cases, the number of non-excited nodes increases quickly and the wave can start to propagate backwards. We observe such situations in the propagation patterns depictured in Fig. 12.5.

In summary, for the investment market behavior analysis it is important to understand how investors (people, organizations, algo-traders) react to information

Fig. 12.5 Three diverse wave-propagation patterns after 260 wave-propagation steps in three two-dimensional social medium spaces differing in refractory period and other model parameters

about new technological, political, economic, and environmental changes. In this way, we model investment markets as social excitatory systems composed from artificially created networking components, i.e. thousands of investing strategies (agents as perceptrons). Our main goal is to observe how such simple excitatory systems of mutually connected artificial agents (acting as investing strategies) get excited and how this excitement evolves in time in the simulated social media. Hence, we want to reproduce close to the real life simulation conditions for excitation propagation via excitatory mediums. Especially we are interested to observe conditions (parameter space and boundary conditions) under which news (e.g., novelty as excitement) not only spread or damp but also produce sustaining self-excited oscillations in the simulated medium, see provided references.

The implications of collective behavior modeling using the simulated agent-based social mediums have a paramount role to play to enable a better understanding of modern digitally interconnected social systems. This paper simulates behavior of only one out of many possible practical implications, i.e. automated trading systems in the investment sector. The proposed simulation approach provides a unique possibility to define ways to manage the core parameters of the digital network, which impede or enable observed local and non-local emergent complex automated trading phenomena depending on the characteristics of the simulated simple investing agents and their connections.

12.5 Concluding Remarks and Discussion

Presented multidisciplinary research introduces a conceptually novel approach towards agency, where an agent is understood as a process of mind-states dynamics. We put forward states of mind as a primary source for the agent's subsequent behavioral patterns. The novelty of our approach is based on the previously proposed OSIMAS paradigm (Plikynas, Basinskas, Kumar, et al., 2014), which lays down the conceptual foundations for the agent as a system of coherent oscillations. Based on recent advances in neuroscience, we performed a set of experimental EEG studies in order to make spectral analyses of the baseline individual EEG signals for various mind states (Plikynas, Basinskas & Laukaitis, 2014).

The proposed individual EEG baseline tests were designed to test the basic conceptual OSIMAS assumption, that different states of social agents can be represented in terms of coherent oscillations. In fact, EEG experimental results revealed how the theoretically deduced idea of agent as system of coherent oscillations can find empirical backup in terms of coherent Δ, Θ, α, β, and γ brainwave oscillations, which uniquely describe agent's mind states. In sum, we showed an experimental way to test major OSIMAS assumptions and presented a few EEG research cases as examples. However, it is beyond the scope of the current work to provide in-depth EEG studies in order to validate statistically solid evidences. Further studies should follow in this regard. We can only say that at this early stage our work-in-progress results do not contradict the basic OSIMAS assumptions.

Our studies revealed the possibility to model agents as people's mind states, i.e. in terms of specific distribution of coherent brainwaves. Therefore, we shed new light on complex social systems as coherent neurodynamic processes taking place in individual minds. Our work in progress outlines some general fundamental design principles of the field-theoretical view of the oscillating agent as well as of coherent social systems. Consequently, from the systems point of view, ordered social systems—by their own intrinsic nature—are interpreted as coherent brainwave activations.

Based on the premises and experimental findings of OSIMAS, we proposed two different approaches to construct an oscillating agent model: (1) phonons as vibrating quanta (Plikynas, 2010), and (2) quantum mechanical wave function (Plikynas, 2015). In the former case, an adapted phonon model was designed to (a) represent each agent as a unique composition of oscillations, (b) quantify associated oscillatory energy, and (c) realize the energy and information interchange mechanism between agents.

In addition, the quantum mechanical wave function approach provides yet another neoclassical method, integrating the previously mentioned findings of neuroscience with quantum physics. In this way we become close to the DCM framework and to the self-organized and dissipative dynamics of living systems, as covered by formal theories used in biology, such as autopoiesis. In short, both approaches provide a way to simulate the oscillating agent model and subsequently to realize field-like nonlocal (contextual) social interactions in the multi-agent settings.

We also provide some work-in-progress simulation results of local and nonlocal excitation propagation in social mediums (Raudys et al., 2014). Investigation of the oscillatory nature of social mediums and agents also plays a paramount role in understanding periodic and non-periodic fluctuations. Hence, our vision in the prospective research is to incorporate implicit information in the form of non-local (contextual) information, which, as in the case of natural laws (e.g., the laws of gravity, entropy, symmetry, energy conservation, etc.), would affect an entire system of social agents at once. Following such an analogy with natural laws, we assume that explicit local activities of social agents can be influenced by implicit (contextual or non-local) information. Each agent would respond to this contextual (non-local) information in a different way depending on individual characteristics. In this way, we envisage the concept of agent-based modeling through non-local levels of self-organization.

From a wider perspective, however, such modeling provides the means to simulate and investigate various sensitivities, fragilities, and contagion processes in different social mediums. In this way, via agent-based information-diffusion properties we can investigate complex social phenomena such as the spread of stock-market crashes, banking panics, currency crises, speculative oscillations (bubbles and crashes), financial contagion and recessionary effects, sovereign defaults, propaganda, information wars, etc. All these social effects are closely associated with social fragility, which moves together with the seasonal, production, political, business, financial, and other cycles.

The main contributions of the OSIMAS paradigm with respect to other conceptually related research approaches can be summarized as follows:

- OSIMAS provides a multidisciplinary connecting framework that links fragmented research in the domains of the above-mentioned neuroscience, artificial intelligence (AI), multi-agent systems (MAS), and social research;
- following DCM, OSIMAS provides a missing link between the fundamental field-theoretical approaches and experimental neuroscientific findings of individual and group-wide coherent brainwave oscillations;
- the proposed unique oscillating-agent and pervasive-information-field conceptual models (OAM and PIF, respectively) can extend and considerably deepen the other field-based approaches mentioned above, providing the necessary means for the simulation of coherent nonlocal and contextual interactions taking place in various social mediums.

However, we have also to name few evident drawbacks and limitations of the proposed OSIMAS paradigm:

- in a technical sense, it is hard to implement a group-wide EEG experimental OSIMAS validation setup (there are some organizational, equipment-synchronization and methodological issues);
- there is a lack of ready-to-use field-based methods and simulation platforms tailored to agent-based and MAS modeling;
- there is still a big gap between the observed complex social phenomena of distributed real cognitive systems and the results of simulated social modeling.

In general, the major limitations stem from the conceptual, experimental, and methodical constraints of the field-based approaches that are currently available. In this and in other papers, we have challenged these limitations, providing insights as well as new experimental and simulation approaches. Thus, like all pioneering approaches, this work in progress requires thorough further investigation. This study, however, provides some clear intermediate outlines with explanatory fundamental, experimental, and simulating guidelines.

Acknowledgments This research project is funded by the European Social Fund under the Global Grant measure (project No. VP1-3.1-SMM-07-K-01-137). We are grateful to the anonymous reviewers for their insightful comments, which have helped to improve this manuscript.

References

Aguilar, M., Congedo, M., & Minguez, J. (2011). A data-driven process for the development of an eyes-closed EEG normative database. In *Conference Proceedings: ... Annual International Conference of the IEEE Engineering in Medicine and Biology Society. IEEE Engineering in Medicine and Biology Society. Annual Conference, 2011* (pp. 7306–7309). doi:10.1109/IEMBS.2011.6091704.

Bandini, S., Manzoni, S., & Vizzari, G. (2004). Multi-agent approach to localization problems: The case of multilayered multi-agent situated system. *Web Intelligence and Agent Systems, 2*(3), 155–166.

Bandini, S., Manzoni, S., & Vizzari, G. (2006). Toward a platform for multi-layered multi-agent situated system (MMASS)-based simulations: Focusing on field diffusion. *Applied Artificial Intelligence, 20*(2-4), 327–351. doi:10.1080/08839510500484272.

Buzsaki, G. (2011). *Rhythms of the brain* (1st ed.). New York: Oxford University Press.

Cacioppo, J. T., Berntson, G. G., & Decety, J. (2010). Social neuroscience and its relationship to social psychology. *Social Cognition, 28*(6), 675–685.

Cacioppo, J. T., & Decety, J. (2011). Social neuroscience: Challenges and opportunities in the study of complex behavior. *Annals of the New York Academy of Sciences, 1224*(1), 162–173. doi:10.1111/j.1749-6632.2010.05858.x.

Camurri, M., Mamei, M., & Zambonelli, F. (2007). Urban traffic control with co-fields. In D. Weyns, H. V. D. Parunak, & F. Michel (Eds.), *Environments for multi-agent systems III* (pp. 239–253). Berlin, Heidelberg: Springer.

Centola, D. (2010). The spread of behavior in an online social network experiment. *Science, 329*(5996), 1194–1197. doi:10.1126/science.1185231.

David, O. (2007). Dynamic causal models and autopoietic systems. *Biological Research, 40*(4), 487–502. doi:10.4067/S0716-97602007000500010.

Do, A. H., Wang, P. T., King, C. E., Chun, S. N., & Nenadic, Z. (2013). Brain–computer interface controlled robotic gait orthosis. *Journal of NeuroEngineering and Rehabilitation, 10*(1), 111. doi:10.1186/1743-0003-10-111.

Engel, G. S., Calhoun, T. R., Read, E. L., Ahn, T.-K., Mančal, T., Cheng, Y.-C., et al. (2007). Evidence for wavelike energy transfer through quantum coherence in photosynthetic systems. *Nature, 446*(7137), 782–786. doi:10.1038/nature05678.

Fingelkurts, A. A., Fingelkurts, A. A., Ermolaev, V. A., & Kaplan, A. Y. (2006). Stability, reliability and consistency of the compositions of brain oscillations. *International Journal of Psychophysiology, 59*(2), 116–126. doi:10.1016/j.ijpsycho.2005.03.014.

Georgiev, D. D., & Glazebrook, J. F. (2006). Dissipationless waves for information transfer in neurobiology—Some implications. *Informatica, 30*, 221–232.

Gudmundsson, S., Runarsson, T. P., Sigurdsson, S., Eiriksdottir, G., & Johnsen, K. (2007). Reliability of quantitative EEG features. *Clinical Neurophysiology, 118*(10), 2162–2171. doi:10.1016/j.clinph.2007.06.018.

Haan, M. de, & Gunnar, M. R. (2011). *Handbook of developmental social neuroscience*. New York: Guilford Press.

Hameroff, S., & Penrose, R. (2014). Consciousness in the universe: A review of the "Orch OR" theory. *Physics of Life Reviews, 11*(1), 39–78. doi:10.1016/j.plrev.2013.08.002.

Haven, E., & Khrennikov, A. (2013). *Quantum social science*. New York: Cambridge University Press.

Haykin, S. (1998). Neural networks: A comprehensive foundation (2nd ed.). Upper Saddle River, NJ: Prentice Hall.

Jackson, M. O. (2010). *Social and economic networks*. Princeton, NJ: Princeton University Press.

Josephson, B. D., & Pallikari-Viras, F. (1991). Biological utilization of quantum nonlocality. *Foundations of Physics, 21*(2), 197–207. doi:10.1007/BF01889532.

Kezys, D., & Plikynas, D. (2014). Prognostication of human brain EEG signal dynamics using a refined coupled oscillator energy exchange model. *Neuroquantology, 12*(4), 337–349. doi: 10.14704/nq.2014.12.4.779.

Lebedev, M. A., & Nicolelis, M. A. L. (2006). Brain–machine interfaces: Past, present and future. *Trends in Neurosciences, 29*(9), 536–546. doi:10.1016/j.tins.2006.07.004.

Likens, A. D., Amazeen, P. G., Stevens, R., Galloway, T., & Gorman, J. C. (2014). Neural signatures of team coordination are revealed by multifractal analysis. *Social Neuroscience, 9*(3), 219–234. doi:10.1080/17470919.2014.882861.

Lindenberger, U., Li, S.-C., Gruber, W., & Müller, V. (2009). Brains swinging in concert: Cortical phase synchronization while playing guitar. *BMC Neuroscience, 10*(1), 22. doi:10.1186/1471-2202-10-22.

Lutz, A., Greischar, L. L., Rawlings, N. B., Ricard, M., & Davidson, R. J. (2004). Long-term meditators self-induce high-amplitude gamma synchrony during mental practice. *Proceedings of the National Academy of Sciences of the United States of America, 101*(46), 16369–16373. doi:10.1073/pnas.0407401101.

Malik, K. (2002). *Man, beast, and zombie: What science can and cannot tell us about human nature* (1st ed.). New Brunswick, NJ: Rutgers University Press.

Mamei, M., & Zambonelli, F. (2006). *Field-based coordination for pervasive multiagent systems*. Berlin: Springer Science & Business Media.

Martin, M., & McIntyre, L. C. (Eds.). (1994). *Readings in the philosophy of social science*. Cambridge, MA: A Bradford Book.

Maturana, H. R. (1980). *Autopoiesis and cognition: The realization of the living*. Berlin: Springer Science & Business Media.

McFadden, J. (2002). The conscious electromagnetic information (CEMI) field theory: The hard problem made easy? *Journal of Consciousness Studies, 9*(8), 45–60.

Müller, K.-R., Tangermann, M., Dornhege, G., Krauledat, M., Curio, G., & Blankertz, B. (2008). Machine learning for real-time single-trial EEG-analysis: From brain–computer interfacing to mental state monitoring. *Journal of Neuroscience Methods, 167*(1), 82–90. doi:10.1016/j.jneumeth.2007.09.022.

Newandee, D. A., & Reisman, S. S. (1996). Measurement of the electroencephalogram (EEG) coherence in group meditation. In *Bioengineering Conference, 1996., Proceedings of the 1996 IEEE Twenty-Second Annual Northeast* (pp. 95–96). doi:10.1109/NEBC.1996.503234.

Nummenmaa, L., Glerean, E., Viinikainen, M., Jääskeläinen, I. P., Hari, R., & Sams, M. (2012). Emotions promote social interaction by synchronizing brain activity across individuals. *Proceedings of the National Academy of Sciences of the United States of America, 109*(24), 9599–9604. doi:10.1073/pnas.1206095109.

Nunez, P. L., & Srinivasan, R. (2005). *Electric fields of the brain: The neurophysics of EEG* (2nd ed.). New York: Oxford University Press.

O'Reilly, E. J., & Olaya-Castro, A. (2014). Non-classicality of the molecular vibrations assisting exciton energy transfer at room temperature. *Nature Communications, 5*. doi:10.1038/ncomms4012.

Oppenheim, J., & Wehner, S. (2010). The uncertainty principle determines the nonlocality of quantum mechanics. *Science, 330*(6007), 1072–1074. doi:10.1126/science.1192065.

Orme-Johnson, D. W., & Oates, R. M. (2009). A field-theoretic view of consciousness: Reply to critics. *Journal Of Scientific Exploration, 23*(2), 139–166.

Perry, R. B. (1996). *The thought and character of William James*. Nashville: Vanderbilt University Press.

Pessa, E., & Vitiello, G. (2004). Quantum noise induced entanglement and chaos in the dissipative quantum model of brain. *International Journal of Modern Physics B, 18*(06), 841–858. doi:10.1142/S0217979204024045.

Pizzi, R., Fantasia, A., Gelain, F., & Rossetti, D. (2004). Non-local correlation between human neural networks on printed circuit board. In *Toward a science of consciousness conference*. Tucson, Arizona.

Plikynas, D. (2015). Oscillating agent model: Quantum approach. *NeuroQuantology, 13*(1), 20–34. doi:10.14704/nq.2015.13.1.796.

Plikynas, D. (2010). A virtual field-based conceptual framework for the simulation of complex social systems. *Journal of Systems Science and Complexity, 23*(2), 232–248. doi:10.1007/s11424-010-7239-1.

Plikynas, D., Basinskas, G., Kumar, P., Masteika, S., Kezys, D., & Laukaitis, A. (2014). Social systems in terms of coherent individual neurodynamics: Conceptual premises, experimental and simulation scope. *International Journal of General Systems, 43*(5), 434–469. doi:10.1080/03081079.2014.888552.

Plikynas, D., Basinskas, G., & Laukaitis, A. (2014). Towards oscillations-based simulation of social systems: A neurodynamic approach. *Connection Science, 0*(0), 1–24. doi:10.1080/09540091.2014.956293.

Plikynas, D., Raudys, A., & Raudys, S. (2014). Agent-based modelling of excitation propagation in social media groups. *Journal of Experimental & Theoretical Artificial Intelligence, 0*(0), 1–16. doi:10.1080/0952813X.2014.954631.

Popescu, S., & Rohrlich, D. (1994). Quantum nonlocality as an axiom. *Foundations of Physics, 24*(3), 379–385. doi:10.1007/BF02058098.

Poslad, S. (2009). *Ubiquitous computing: Smart devices, environments and interactions* (1st ed.). Chichester, UK: Wiley.

Pribram, K. H. (1999). Quantum holography: Is it relevant to brain function? *Information Sciences, 115*(1–4), 97–102. doi:10.1016/S0020-0255(98)10082-8.

Raudys, A., Plikynas, D., & Raudys, Š. (2014). Novel automated multi-agent investment system based on simulation of self-excitatory oscillations. *Transformations in Business & Economics, 13*(2), 42–59.

Raudys, S. (2001). *Statistical and neural classifiers: An integrated approach to design*. Berlin: Springer Science & Business Media.

Schrödinger, E. (1955). *WHAT IS LIFE? – The physical aspect of the living cell* (Fifth Printing ed.). Cambridge: Cambridge University Press.

Secchi, D. (2011). The "Docile" organization. In *Extendable rationality* (pp. 113–133). New York: Springer. Retrieved from http://link.springer.com/chapter/10.1007/978-1-4419-7542-3_9

Servat, D., & Drogoul, A. (2002). Combining amorphous computing and reactive agent-based systems: A paradigm for pervasive intelligence? In *Proceedings of the First International Joint Conference on Autonomous Agents and Multiagent Systems: Part 1* (pp. 441–448). New York, NY, USA: ACM. doi:10.1145/544741.544842.

Shen, W.-M., Salemi, B., & Will, P. (2002). Hormone-inspired adaptive communication and distributed control for CONRO self-reconfigurable robots. *IEEE Transactions on Robotics and Automation, 18*(5), 700–712. doi:10.1109/TRA.2002.804502.

Spach, M. S. (1997). Discontinuous cardiac conduction: Its origin in cellular connectivity with long-term adaptive changes that cause arrhythmias. In *Discontinuous conduction in the heart* (pp. 5–51). Armonk, NY: Futura Publ. Company, Inc.

Standish, L. J., Kozak, L., Johnson, L. C., & Richards, T. (2004). Electroencephalographic evidence of correlated event-related signals between the brains of spatially and sensory isolated human subjects. *Journal of Alternative and Complementary Medicine (New York, NY), 10*(2), 307–314. doi:10.1089/107555304323062293.

Stevens, R. H., & Galloway, T. L. (2014). Toward a quantitative description of the neurodynamic organizations of teams. *Social Neuroscience, 9*(2), 160–173. doi:10.1080/17470919.2014.883324.

Stevens, R., Galloway, T., Wang, P., Berka, C., Tan, V., Wohlgemuth, T., et al. (2012). Modeling the neurodynamic complexity of submarine navigation teams. *Computational and Mathematical Organization Theory, 19*(3), 346–369. doi:10.1007/s10588-012-9135-9.

Tesfatsion, L., & Judd, K. L. (Eds.). (2006). *Handbook of computational economics, volume 2: Agent-based computational economics* (1st ed.). Amsterdam; New York: North Holland.

Thaheld, F. H. (2005). An interdisciplinary approach to certain fundamental issues in the fields of physics and biology: Towards a unified theory. *Biosystems, 80*(1), 41–56. doi:10.1016/j.biosystems.2004.10.001.

Thatcher, R. W. (2010). Validity and reliability of quantitative electroencephalography. *Journal of Neurotherapy, 14*(2), 122–152. doi:10.1080/10874201003773500.

Travis, F. T., & Orme-Johnson, D. W. (1989). Field model of consciousness: EEG coherence changes as indicators of field effects. *International Journal of Neuroscience, 49*(3-4), 203–211. doi:10.3109/00207458909084826.

Travis, F., & Arenander, A. (2006). Cross-sectional and longitudinal study of effects of transcendental meditation practice on interhemispheric frontal asymmetry and frontal coherence. *The International Journal of Neuroscience, 116*(12), 1519–1538. doi:10.1080/00207450600575482.

Valente, T. W. (1996). Network models of the diffusion of innovations. *Computational & Mathematical Organization Theory, 2*(2), 163–164. doi:10.1007/BF00240425.

Vitiello, P. D. G. (2001). *My double unveiled: The dissipative quantum model of brain*. Amsterdam; Philadelphia, PA: John Benjamins Publishing Company.

Wang, X., Tao, H., Xie, Z., & Yi, D. (2012). Mining social networks using wave propagation. *Computational and Mathematical Organization Theory, 19*(4), 569–579. doi:10.1007/s10588-012-9142-x.

Young, H. P. (2006). The diffusion of innovations in social networks. In *The economy as an evolving complex system III: Current perspectives and future directions* (p. 267).

Zhang, Y., & Wu, Y. (2011). How behaviors spread in dynamic social networks. *Computational and Mathematical Organization Theory, 18*(4), 419–444. doi:10.1007/s10588-011-9105-7.

Chapter 13
Analytical Approaches to Agent-Based Models

Raffaello Seri

Abstract The aim of this article is to present an approach to the analysis of simple systems composed of a large number of units in interaction. Suppose to have a large number of agents belonging to a finite number of different groups: as the agents randomly interact with each other, they move from a group to another as a result of the interaction. The object of interest is the stochastic process describing the number of agents in each group. As this is generally intractable, it has been proposed in the literature to approximate it in several ways. We review these approximations and we illustrate them with reference to a version of the epidemic model. The tools presented in the paper should be considered as a complement rather than as a substitute of the classical analysis of ABMs through simulation.

Keywords Individual-based models • Markov processes • Differential equations • Diffusion approximation • Central limit theorem

13.1 Introduction

The aim of this paper is to provide an introduction to the approximation of a class of models that may be of some interest in the study of organizations.

The models we consider here describe the evolution over time of a population composed of similar individuals moving from one to another of d mutually exclusive categories. Models of this class are sometimes called *compartmental* (see, e.g., Matis & Kiffe, 2000) as they represent transitions of individuals between compartments. From another perspective, the models we consider belong to the class of *individual-based* models. Some authors consider individual-based and agent-based as synonyms (see, e.g., Railsback & Grimm, 2011), while others reserve the term individual-based for models in which rules of behavior are formulated in probabilistic terms at the individual level (see, e.g., Black & McKane, 2012, p. 338). This requires that some simplifying assumptions are needed in order to allow an

R. Seri (✉)
Dipartimento di Economia, Università degli Studi dell'Insubria,
Via Monte Generoso 71, 21100 Varese, Italy
e-mail: raffaello.seri@uninsubria.it

D. Secchi, M. Neumann (eds.), *Agent-Based Simulation of Organizational Behavior*, DOI 10.1007/978-3-319-18153-0_13

affordable analysis: usually each individual can be in only one of a finite number of states, and members of each state are supposed to be identical in every other respect.[1] These hypotheses are not necessary in agent-based models, in which the fact that the solution is obtained through simulation allows the researcher to consider more complex rules of behavior and continuous attributes. The price to pay for this freedom is that results thus obtained are only numerical. Even if we recognize these advantages of agent-based models, we claim that the techniques that we are going to present may still serve several purposes. First, in simplified contexts they could be seen as direct alternatives to the computer-intensive simulations of agent-based models. Second, they could be used as a preliminary step in the analysis of agent-based models, in order to obtain some hints concerning the behavior of the system. Third, they could serve as auxiliary simulation methods for parts of an agent-based simulation.

In practice, the models we consider are described by density dependent jump Markov processes with time homogeneous transition intensities (see, e.g., Kurtz, 1981, Chap. 8 and Ethier & Kurtz, 1986, Chap. 11). As the explicit analysis of these models may be daunting, we discuss some approximations that have been proposed in the literature. Their study has been pioneered by Feller (1951) and they have been developed by Norman (1968, 1972, 1974a, 1974b), Kurtz (1970, 1971, 1976, 1978, 1980, 1981, 1983) and Barbour (1972, 1974). Here we just consider the simplest situation, without any attempt to cover more advanced topics, such as spatial issues, age dependence, time inhomogeneity or dependence upon the whole past of the process. Moreover, we limit ourselves to introduce results already present in the literature.

We consider a series of models indexed by a number N, that can be the total population size, the area or the volume occupied by the population or any other indicator. For N large, the behavior of the model can be approximated by what happens in the limiting situation in which N is infinity. It turns out that this amounts to approximate these Markov processes through ordinary and stochastic differential equations. Clearly, the interest of the approximations is that the limiting behavior is simpler than what happens for finite N. These approximations have been used to describe abundances in biological populations (see the reviews in Pollett, 2001; Black & McKane, 2012), quantities of reactants in chemical reactions (see, e.g., Kurtz, 1972) and stochastic process algebra models in computer science (see, e.g., the introductory treatment in Bortolussi, Hillston, Latella, & Massink, 2013), among others. It is important to note here that the discrete time case is covered in Bortolussi et al. (2013, Sect. 2) and Challenger, Fanelli, and McKane (2014), while an alternative approach based on the so-called master equation can be found in Goutsias and Jenkinson (2013).

The theoretical results will be illustrated using an example of information spread in a fixed population. The model is simplistic in several respects. First, the structure of the model is the simplest possible, with only two compartments and a transition

[1] In the following models, discrete differences between individuals can be accounted for by adequately expanding the number of compartments and by varying the transition intensities.

between them. This is justified by the fact that the model has only an expository purpose. However, more reasonable models could be obtained, e.g., supposing that the population is stratified in several mutually exclusive groups, each one with a different exposure to the information and a different probability of passing it to someone else. Second, we suppose very simple interaction mechanisms between individuals in different states. Indeed, the present form, in which interaction terms are bilinear in the cardinalities of the two interacting subgroups, has a long history dating back at least to Lotka and Volterra (note that, while in Lotka, 1925, p. 89 and Volterra, 1962, pp. 119–120, the form of the interaction is justified as an approximation to the true one, in Volterra, 1931, p. 14 and, especially, in Volterra, 1962, pp. 9–10, pp. 119–120, a probabilistic interpretation is provided). However, more complex interactions can be considered, the price to pay being an increased complexity in the study of the system (by the way, the irrealistic form of interactions in the Lotka–Volterra model is the rationale that led Gause and Kolmogorov to introduce their variants of the predator-prey system, see, e.g., Sigmund, 2007). Third, the transition intensities between states are supposed to be time homogeneous, i.e. the rate at which individuals move between states does not depend explicitly upon time; moreover, the intensities do not depend upon the past of the process but only upon its present value. We maintain both hypotheses throughout the whole paper, but we remark that they can be relaxed using the results in Kurtz (1983). Fourth, the network modeling the agent interactions has no topological structure (see, e.g., Centola, 2010; Hirshman, Charles, & Carley, 2011; Zhang & Wu, 2012; Wang, Tao, Xie, & Yi, 2013; Plikynas & Masteika, 2014; however, see the Introduction in Collet, Dai Pra, & Sartori, 2010 for a justification of mean-field interactions without topological structure in social sciences).

Now we introduce the notation used in the following. The symbols $\mathbb{Z}$, $\mathbb{R}$, and $\mathbb{R}_+$ denote respectively the set of integer (positive and negative), real, and nonnegative real numbers. Vectors are always supposed to be column vectors and indicated with bold letters. For a vector $\mathbf{x}$, x_i denotes its i–th element and $|\mathbf{x}|$ is the sum of the absolute values of the elements of $\mathbf{x}$. The superscript T, as in $\mathbf{x}^{\mathsf{T}}$, indicates that the transpose of $\mathbf{x}$ is taken. Capital letters usually indicate random variables. Whenever needed, we will indicate derivatives of X with respect to time as $\dot{X}$, while we reserve the prime symbol (X', X'', X''') for indicating approximations of X. Differentials of a variable x are indicated as $\mathrm{d}x$ and derivatives of a function f with respect to an argument x are written as $\frac{\partial f}{\partial x}$. The quantities corresponding to finite values of N will be indexed, whenever possible, by a superscript (N).

As concerns the structure of the paper, in Sect. 13.2 we introduce the process specified in terms of transitions between compartments and of density dependent transition intensities. In Sect. 13.3 we present the first deterministic approximation through an ordinary differential equation. Section 13.4 contains two different stochastic results; the first one approximates directly the process with a stochastic differential equation (see Sect. 13.4.1), the second one shows that the scaled deviations of the original process from the deterministic process of Sect. 13.3 behaves for large N as a Gaussian process (see Sect. 13.4.2). At last, Appendix contains a non-technical discussion of the conditions under which the results hold.

13.2 The Original Process

We consider a process $\left\{\hat{\mathbf{X}}_t^{(N)}\right\}_{t\in\mathbb{R}_+}$ such that, for any instant of time $t \geq 0$, $\hat{\mathbf{X}}_t^{(N)}$ is a vector of size d with integer coordinates; more formally, we say that $\hat{\mathbf{X}}_t^{(N)}$ takes its values in $\mathbb{Z}^d$. Each coordinate of the vector $\hat{\mathbf{X}}_t^{(N)}$ corresponds univocally to one of the possible states or compartments of the model, and its value measures the number of individuals in that state in time t. The process moves in continuous time from a point of $\mathbb{Z}^d$, say $\mathbf{k}$, occupied in t, to another point, say $\mathbf{k}+\boldsymbol{\ell}$, occupied in $t+s$, with $s > 0$. As already explained in the introduction, the process $\left\{\hat{\mathbf{X}}_t^{(N)}\right\}_{t\in\mathbb{R}_+}$ is indexed by a number N, that can be integer (e.g., the size of the population) or real (e.g., the area in which the population dwells).

Exercise 1 (News Diffusion Model). The model that we are going to analyze is (a version of) the simple epidemic model. Consider the spread of a piece of news in a population of N individuals. Let $\hat{S}_t$ and $\hat{I}_t$ be, respectively, the number of susceptibles (people that have not yet been reached by the news) and infected (i.e. people that have been reached by the news) at time t. Clearly, $\hat{S}_t + \hat{I}_t = N$ for any $t > 0$. Therefore, $\left[\hat{S}_t, \hat{I}_t\right]^\top$ will be equal to $\mathbf{k} = [k_1, k_2]^\top$ with $k_1 + k_2 = N$ and $0 \leq k_1 \leq N$. No other values are allowed for $\left[\hat{S}_t, \hat{I}_t\right]^\top$. On the other hand, $\left[\hat{S}_{t+s}, \hat{I}_{t+s}\right]^\top$ takes the value $\mathbf{k}+\boldsymbol{\ell}$. Two facts should be clear. First, the first element of $\boldsymbol{\ell}$ should be negative while the second should be positive, as people can become aware of the news but cannot do the reverse. Second, all values of $\boldsymbol{\ell}$ should be of the form $\boldsymbol{\ell} = [-\ell, +\ell]^\top$, otherwise the elements of $\mathbf{k}+\boldsymbol{\ell}$ fail to sum to N. □

We suppose that $\left\{\hat{\mathbf{X}}_t^{(N)}\right\}_{t\in\mathbb{R}_+}$ is a *Markov process*, i.e. a stochastic process whose state in $t+s$ depends on the past before t only through the state occupied in t (see, e.g., Ethier & Kurtz, 1986, Sect. 4.1 or Karlin & Taylor, 1975, Chap. 4, for definitions). A Markov process can be described by its *transition probability*, i.e. the probability that the process $\left\{\hat{\mathbf{X}}_t^{(N)}\right\}_{t\in\mathbb{R}_+}$ starting from the value $\mathbf{k}$ in t reaches the value $\mathbf{k}+\boldsymbol{\ell}$ in $t+s$:

$$\mathbb{P}\left\{\hat{\mathbf{X}}_{t+s}^{(N)} = \mathbf{k}+\boldsymbol{\ell} \,\middle|\, \hat{\mathbf{X}}_t^{(N)} = \mathbf{k}\right\},$$

for any $t \geq 0$ and $s > 0$, and where $\mathbf{k}$ and $\boldsymbol{\ell}$ should in general respect some constraints. In the following, it will be particularly useful to consider what happens when $s = \mathrm{d}t$. In this case, we introduce the so-called *transition intensities* $q_{\mathbf{k},\mathbf{k}+\boldsymbol{\ell}}^{(N)}$ for $\mathbf{k}, \boldsymbol{\ell} \in \mathbb{Z}^d$, namely the quantities defined as:

$$\mathbb{P}\left\{\hat{\mathbf{X}}_{t+\mathrm{d}t}^{(N)} = \mathbf{k}+\boldsymbol{\ell} \,\middle|\, \hat{\mathbf{X}}_t^{(N)} = \mathbf{k}\right\} = q_{\mathbf{k},\mathbf{k}+\boldsymbol{\ell}}^{(N)} \cdot \mathrm{d}t + o(\mathrm{d}t)$$

or

$$\lim_{dt\downarrow 0} \frac{\mathbb{P}\left\{\hat{\mathbf{X}}_{t+dt}^{(N)} = \mathbf{k} + \boldsymbol{\ell} \,\middle|\, \hat{\mathbf{X}}_t^{(N)} = \mathbf{k}\right\}}{dt} = q_{\mathbf{k},\mathbf{k}+\boldsymbol{\ell}}^{(N)}.$$

Therefore, a transition intensity in t is the limit, as $s \downarrow 0$, of the transition probability between t and $t + s$ divided by the length of the time period s. It measures the instantaneous probability that a jump of size $\boldsymbol{\ell}$ takes place immediately after t, for a process starting from $\mathbf{k}$ in t. It is often the case that transition intensities are null for large values of $|\boldsymbol{\ell}|$ and for some combinations of $\mathbf{k}$ and $\boldsymbol{\ell}$. As these intensities do not depend on t, the transition probabilities are called *time homogeneous* or *stationary*.

In the following we will further suppose that $\left\{\hat{\mathbf{X}}_t^{(N)}\right\}_{t\in\mathbb{R}_+}$ is *density dependent* (see Ethier & Kurtz, 1986, Chap. 11 for definition and examples), i.e. that its transition intensities $q_{\mathbf{k},\mathbf{k}+\boldsymbol{\ell}}^{(N)}$ depend on $\mathbf{k}$ only through the ratio $\mathbf{k}/N$. In particular, this means that the transition intensity between the states $\mathbf{k}$ and $\mathbf{k} + \boldsymbol{\ell}$ takes the following form:

$$q_{\mathbf{k},\mathbf{k}+\boldsymbol{\ell}}^{(N)} = N \cdot \beta_{\boldsymbol{\ell}}\left(\frac{\mathbf{k}}{N}\right)$$

for a function $\beta_{\boldsymbol{\ell}}$ indexed by the jump size $\boldsymbol{\ell}$, with $\mathbf{k}, \boldsymbol{\ell} \in \mathbb{Z}^d$. The requirement of density dependence implies that the transition intensity increases proportionally to the index N and depends on the state of the process $\mathbf{k}$ only through its density $\mathbf{k}/N$. Because of density dependence, we are led to consider $\left\{\mathbf{X}_t^{(N)}\right\}_{t\in\mathbb{R}_+}$, defined by $\mathbf{X}_t^{(N)} = \hat{\mathbf{X}}_t^{(N)}/N$. In this case, we have:

$$\lim_{dt\downarrow 0} \frac{\mathbb{P}\left\{\mathbf{X}_{t+dt}^{(N)} = \frac{\mathbf{k}}{N} + \frac{\boldsymbol{\ell}}{N} \,\middle|\, \mathbf{X}_t^{(N)} = \frac{\mathbf{k}}{N}\right\}}{dt} = N \cdot \beta_{\boldsymbol{\ell}}\left(\frac{\mathbf{k}}{N}\right). \tag{13.1}$$

Exercise 2 (News Diffusion Model—Continued). In each infinitesimal interval dt, the number of contacts between susceptibles and infected can be assumed to be proportional to $\hat{S}_t \cdot \hat{I}_t$. The probability that two or more contacts take place in dt is $o(dt)$. When such a contact takes place, we suppose that the probability that the news is transmitted from the infected to the susceptible is fixed and independent of everything else. Let $\hat{\mathbf{X}}_t^{(N)} = \left[\hat{S}_t, \hat{I}_t\right]^{\mathsf{T}}$. Therefore:

$$\mathbb{P}\left\{\begin{bmatrix}\hat{S}_{t+dt}\\ \hat{I}_{t+dt}\end{bmatrix} = \begin{bmatrix}\hat{s}_t - 1\\ \hat{i}_t + 1\end{bmatrix} \,\middle|\, \begin{bmatrix}\hat{S}_t\\ \hat{I}_t\end{bmatrix} = \begin{bmatrix}\hat{s}_t\\ \hat{i}_t\end{bmatrix}\right\} = p \cdot \frac{\hat{s}_t \cdot \hat{i}_t}{N} \cdot dt + o(dt).$$

In dt values of $\boldsymbol{\ell}$ different from $\boldsymbol{\ell} = [-1,+1]^{\mathsf{T}}$ yield transitions of such a low probability to be $o(\mathrm{d}t)$. This means that:

$$\beta_{[-1,+1]^{\mathsf{T}}}\left([x_1, x_2]^{\mathsf{T}}\right) = p \cdot x_1 x_2.$$

This simple example lends itself to a further remark. As $\hat{S}_t + \hat{I}_t = N$ and N is fixed, $\hat{S}_t$ is known when $\hat{I}_t$ is and we can also identify $\hat{\mathbf{X}}_t^{(N)} = \hat{I}_t$. In this case $\mathbf{k} = k$ with $0 \leq k \leq N$ and $\boldsymbol{\ell} = 1$:

$$\mathbb{P}\left\{\hat{I}_{t+\mathrm{d}t} = \hat{\imath}_t + 1 \,\middle|\, \hat{I}_t = \hat{\imath}_t\right\} = p \cdot \frac{\left(N - \hat{\imath}_t\right)\hat{\imath}_t}{N} \cdot \mathrm{d}t + o(\mathrm{d}t), \qquad (13.2)$$

while other values of $\boldsymbol{\ell}$ yield 0 (or $o(\mathrm{d}t)$) transition intensities. In the following we will use the definitions $S_t = \hat{S}_t/N$ and $I_t = \hat{I}_t/N$. Equation (13.2) becomes:

$$\mathbb{P}\left\{I_{t+\mathrm{d}t} = i_t + \frac{1}{N} | I_t = i_t\right\} = N \cdot p \cdot (1 - i_t)\, i_t \cdot \mathrm{d}t + o(\mathrm{d}t),$$

where $\beta_1(x) = p \cdot x(1-x)$. In Fig. 13.1, a trajectory of $\left\{\hat{I}_t\right\}_{t\in\mathbb{R}_+}$ and $\{I_t\}_{t\in\mathbb{R}_+}$ with $p = 0.01, N = 20$ and $\hat{I}_0 = 2$, is reproduced as a step function. □

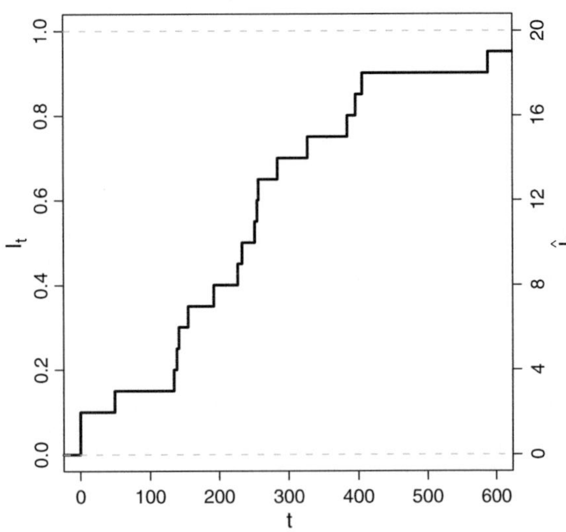

Fig. 13.1 Graph of a trajectory of $\left\{\hat{I}_t\right\}_{t\in\mathbb{R}_+}$ and $\{I_t\}_{t\in\mathbb{R}_+}$ with $p = 0.01$, $N = 20$ and $\hat{I}_0 = 2$

Now we try to understand heuristically what happens to $\mathbf{X}^{(N)}_{t+\mathrm{d}t} - \mathbf{X}^{(N)}_t$ when N diverges. Equation (13.1) leads to:

$$\mathbb{P}\left\{\mathbf{X}^{(N)}_{t+\mathrm{d}t} = \frac{\mathbf{k}}{N} + \frac{\boldsymbol{\ell}}{N} \middle| \mathbf{X}^{(N)}_t = \frac{\mathbf{k}}{N}\right\} = \mathbb{P}\left\{\mathbf{X}^{(N)}_{t+\mathrm{d}t} - \mathbf{X}^{(N)}_t = \frac{\boldsymbol{\ell}}{N} \middle| \mathbf{X}^{(N)}_t = \frac{\mathbf{k}}{N}\right\}$$
$$\simeq N \cdot \beta_{\boldsymbol{\ell}}\left(\frac{\mathbf{k}}{N}\right) \cdot \mathrm{d}t.$$

This means that, for any $\boldsymbol{\ell} \in \mathbb{Z}^d$, the random variable $\mathbf{X}^{(N)}_{t+\mathrm{d}t} - \mathbf{X}^{(N)}_t$ will take the value $\frac{\boldsymbol{\ell}}{N}$ with probability approximately equal to $N \cdot \beta_{\boldsymbol{\ell}}\left(\frac{\mathbf{k}}{N}\right) \cdot \mathrm{d}t$. Therefore its mean and variance are approximately:

$$\mathbb{E}\left[\mathbf{X}^{(N)}_{t+\mathrm{d}t} - \mathbf{X}^{(N)}_t \middle| \mathbf{X}^{(N)}_t = \frac{\mathbf{k}}{N}\right] \simeq \sum_{\boldsymbol{\ell}} \frac{\boldsymbol{\ell}}{N} \cdot N \cdot \beta_{\boldsymbol{\ell}}\left(\frac{\mathbf{k}}{N}\right) \cdot \mathrm{d}t = \sum_{\boldsymbol{\ell}} \boldsymbol{\ell} \cdot \beta_{\boldsymbol{\ell}}\left(\frac{\mathbf{k}}{N}\right) \cdot \mathrm{d}t$$

and:

$$\mathbb{V}\left[\mathbf{X}^{(N)}_{t+\mathrm{d}t} - \mathbf{X}^{(N)}_t \middle| \mathbf{X}^{(N)}_t = \frac{\mathbf{k}}{N}\right] \simeq \sum_{\boldsymbol{\ell}} \frac{\boldsymbol{\ell}\boldsymbol{\ell}^{\mathsf{T}}}{N^2} \cdot N \cdot \beta_{\boldsymbol{\ell}}\left(\frac{\mathbf{k}}{N}\right) \cdot \mathrm{d}t = \frac{1}{N} \cdot \sum_{\boldsymbol{\ell}} \boldsymbol{\ell}\boldsymbol{\ell}^{\mathsf{T}} \cdot \beta_{\boldsymbol{\ell}}\left(\frac{\mathbf{k}}{N}\right) \cdot \mathrm{d}t.$$

This shows that, when $\mathbf{X}^{(N)}_t = \mathbf{x}$, $\mathbf{X}^{(N)}_{t+\mathrm{d}t} - \mathbf{X}^{(N)}_t$ approximately behaves, on average, as $\sum_{\boldsymbol{\ell}} \boldsymbol{\ell} \cdot \beta_{\boldsymbol{\ell}}(\mathbf{x}) \cdot \mathrm{d}t$, and that the variance of $\mathbf{X}^{(N)}_{t+\mathrm{d}t} - \mathbf{X}^{(N)}_t$ around its mean decreases as N^{-1}. This means that, when N is very large, $\mathbf{X}^{(N)}_{t+\mathrm{d}t} - \mathbf{X}^{(N)}_t$ is well approximated by $\sum_{\boldsymbol{\ell}} \boldsymbol{\ell} \cdot \beta_{\boldsymbol{\ell}}(\mathbf{x}) \cdot \mathrm{d}t$, a fact that is the object of Sect. 13.3. Moreover, in Sect. 13.4, we will show that also the deviation between $\mathbf{X}^{(N)}_{t+\mathrm{d}t} - \mathbf{X}^{(N)}_t$ and $\sum_{\boldsymbol{\ell}} \boldsymbol{\ell} \cdot \beta_{\boldsymbol{\ell}}(\mathbf{x}) \cdot \mathrm{d}t$ can be studied and used to improve the previous approximation.

13.3 The Deterministic Limit

In this section we show that, when N is large enough, $\left\{\mathbf{X}^{(N)}_t\right\}_{t\in\mathbb{R}_+}$ can be approximated by a deterministic process $\{\mathbf{X}'_t\}_{t\in\mathbb{R}_+}$ (see Appendix for conditions).

Define the function:

$$\mathbf{f}(\mathbf{x}) := \sum_{\boldsymbol{\ell}} \boldsymbol{\ell} \cdot \beta_{\boldsymbol{\ell}}(\mathbf{x})$$

where the sum is extended over all possible values of $\boldsymbol{\ell}$. As $N \to \infty$, under some additional conditions that will be detailed in Appendix, $\left\{\mathbf{X}^{(N)}_t\right\}_{t\in\mathbb{R}_+}$ converges to the deterministic process $\{\mathbf{X}'_t\}_{t\in\mathbb{R}_+}$ defined by:

$$\mathbf{X}'_t = \mathbf{X}'_0 + \int_0^t \mathbf{f}\left(\mathbf{X}'_s\right) \mathrm{d}s, \qquad t \geq 0.$$

Now, using this formula for $\mathbf{X}'_{t+\mathrm{d}t}$ and $\mathbf{X}'_t$, this process can be written as:

$$\begin{aligned}
\mathbf{X}'_{t+\mathrm{d}t} - \mathbf{X}'_t &= \int_0^{t+\mathrm{d}t} \mathbf{f}\left(\mathbf{X}'_s\right) \mathrm{d}s - \int_0^t \mathbf{f}\left(\mathbf{X}'_s\right) \mathrm{d}s \\
&= \int_t^{t+\mathrm{d}t} \mathbf{f}\left(\mathbf{X}'_s\right) \mathrm{d}s = \mathbf{f}\left(\mathbf{X}'_t\right) \mathrm{d}t, \quad t \geq 0,
\end{aligned}$$

or, using the equality $\frac{\mathbf{X}'_{t+\mathrm{d}t} - \mathbf{X}'_t}{\mathrm{d}t} = \dot{\mathbf{X}}'_t$, equivalently as:

$$\dot{\mathbf{X}}'_t = \mathbf{f}\left(\mathbf{X}'_t\right), \qquad t \geq 0$$

or:

$$\mathrm{d}\mathbf{X}'_t = \mathbf{f}\left(\mathbf{X}'_t\right) \cdot \mathrm{d}t, \qquad t \geq 0. \tag{13.3}$$

Exercise 3 (News Diffusion Model—Continued). In the first version of the news diffusion model (see Exercise 2):

$$\mathbf{f}(\mathbf{x}) = \sum_{\ell} \boldsymbol{\ell} \cdot \beta_{\ell}(\mathbf{x}) = \begin{bmatrix} -1 \\ +1 \end{bmatrix} \cdot p \cdot x_1 x_2$$

and:

$$\begin{bmatrix} \dot{S}'_t \\ \dot{I}'_t \end{bmatrix} = \begin{bmatrix} -p \cdot S'_t I'_t \\ +p \cdot S'_t I'_t \end{bmatrix}, \qquad t \geq 0.$$

In the second rewriting of the model (see Exercise 2), we get:

$$f(x) = \sum_{\ell} \ell \cdot \beta_{\ell}(x) = p \cdot x(1-x).$$

Therefore, the corresponding differential equation is:

$$\dot{I}'_t = p \cdot I'_t \left(1 - I'_t\right), \qquad t \geq 0$$

or

$$\mathrm{d}I'_t = p \cdot I'_t \left(1 - I'_t\right) \mathrm{d}t, \qquad t \geq 0. \tag{13.4}$$

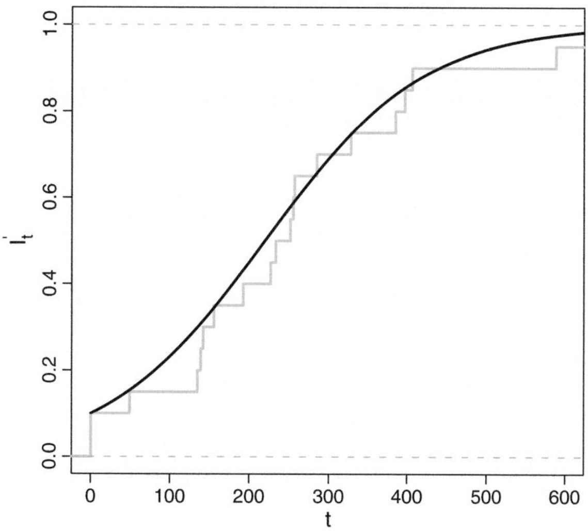

Fig. 13.2 Graph of $\{I'_t\}_{t\in\mathbb{R}_+}$ (in *black*) over a trajectory of $\{I_t\}_{t\in\mathbb{R}_+}$ (in *grey*)

It is possible to see that the two models are indeed the same. By the way, this model has a closed form solution. Supposing that $I'_0 = i_0$, the solution is:

$$I'_t = \frac{\exp(p \cdot t)}{\frac{1-i_0}{i_0} + \exp(p \cdot t)}.$$

When $t = 0$, we have $I'_0 = i_0$ while, when $t \to \infty$, $\lim_{t\to\infty} I'_t = 1$. Moreover, the curve $t \mapsto I'_t$ is increasing. In Fig. 13.2, the deterministic approximation $\{I'_t\}_{t\in\mathbb{R}_+}$, corresponding to $p = 0.01$ and $i_0 = 0.1$, is reproduced in black over the previous trajectory of $\{I_t\}_{t\in\mathbb{R}_+}$, in grey. In Fig. 13.3, the difference between the trajectory of the original process and its deterministic approximation, $\{I_t - I'_t\}_{t\in\mathbb{R}_+}$, is displayed. □

As shown in the figures, the process $\left\{\mathbf{X}_t^{(N)}\right\}_{t\in\mathbb{R}_+}$ deviates from its deterministic approximation $\{\mathbf{X}'_t\}_{t\in\mathbb{R}_+}$. The new stochastic process $\left\{\mathbf{X}_t^{(N)} - \mathbf{X}'_t\right\}_{t\in\mathbb{R}_+}$ is characterized by fluctuations that decrease when N increases. In particular, it can be shown that:[2]

$$\mathbf{X}_t^{(N)} = \mathbf{X}'_t + O_{\mathbb{P}}\left(\frac{1}{\sqrt{N}}\right). \tag{13.5}$$

[2] We write that $X_n = O_{\mathbb{P}}(a_n)$ where n is an index diverging to infinity if, for any $\varepsilon > 0$, there exists a finite $M > 0$ such that $\mathbb{P}(|X_n/a_n| > M) < \varepsilon$ for any n large enough.

Fig. 13.3 Graph of a trajectory of $\{I_t - I'_t\}_{t\in\mathbb{R}_+}$

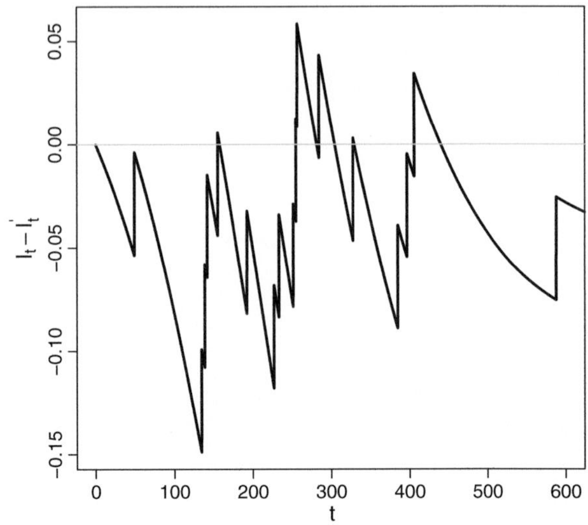

In terms of the original process, we have:

$$\hat{\mathbf{X}}_t^{(N)} = N \cdot \mathbf{X}'_t + O_{\mathbb{P}}\left(\sqrt{N}\right).$$

In the next section we will see that the $O_{\mathbb{P}}\left(\frac{1}{\sqrt{N}}\right)$ term in (13.5) provides a refinement to this approximation.

13.4 The Stochastic Limit

The previous result states that, when N is large enough, the process $\left\{\mathbf{X}_t^{(N)}\right\}_{t\in\mathbb{R}_+}$ converges to a deterministic process $\{\mathbf{X}'_t\}_{t\in\mathbb{R}_+}$ expressed as a differential equation. The results that we are going to present in this section describe the fluctuations of the process $\left\{\mathbf{X}_t^{(N)} - \mathbf{X}'_t\right\}_{t\in\mathbb{R}_+}$ for large values of N.

In the literature on approximations for density dependent Markov processes, two different kinds of stochastic results are considered. In the first one, often called *diffusion approximation*, $\left\{\mathbf{X}_t^{(N)}\right\}_{t\in\mathbb{R}_+}$ is directly approximated through a diffusion. In the second one, one approximates the process $\left\{\mathbf{V}_t^{(N)}\right\}_{t\in\mathbb{R}_+}$, where:

$$\mathbf{V}_t^{(N)} := \sqrt{N}\left(\mathbf{X}_t^{(N)} - \mathbf{X}'_t\right),$$

given by the scaled fluctuations of the stochastic process $\left\{\mathbf{X}_t^{(N)}\right\}_{t\in\mathbb{R}_+}$ around the deterministic evolution $\{\mathbf{X}'_t\}_{t\in\mathbb{R}_+}$, through a Gaussian process $\{\mathbf{V}_t\}_{t\in\mathbb{R}_+}$. This goes under the name of *Central Limit Theorem approximation*.

13.4.1 The Diffusion Approximation

Let us start from the diffusion approximation. In this case, $\left\{\mathbf{X}_t^{(N)}\right\}_{t\in\mathbb{R}_+}$ is approximated by the Gaussian process $\{\mathbf{X}''_t\}_{t\in\mathbb{R}_+}$ (see Appendix for conditions) described by the following stochastic differential equation (SDE) or Itô diffusion:[3]

$$\mathrm{d}\mathbf{X}''_t = \mathbf{f}\left(\mathbf{X}''_t\right)\mathrm{d}t + \frac{1}{\sqrt{N}}\sum_{\boldsymbol{\ell}} \boldsymbol{\ell}\cdot\sqrt{\beta_{\boldsymbol{\ell}}\left(\mathbf{X}''_t\right)}\cdot\mathrm{d}W_{\boldsymbol{\ell},t}, \qquad t\geq 0,$$

where the processes $\{W_{\boldsymbol{\ell},t}\}_{t\in\mathbb{R}_+}$ are independent Brownian motions, each one associated with a value of $\boldsymbol{\ell}$. Remark that $\sum_{\boldsymbol{\ell}} \boldsymbol{\ell}\cdot\sqrt{\beta_{\boldsymbol{\ell}}(\mathbf{x})}\cdot\mathrm{d}W_{\boldsymbol{\ell},t}$ is a Gaussian random vector with $\mathbf{0}$ mean and variance:

$$\mathbb{V}\left(\sum_{\boldsymbol{\ell}} \boldsymbol{\ell}\cdot\sqrt{\beta_{\boldsymbol{\ell}}(\mathbf{x})}\cdot\mathrm{d}W_{\boldsymbol{\ell},t}\,|\mathbf{x}\right) = \mathrm{d}t\cdot\sum_{\boldsymbol{\ell}} \boldsymbol{\ell}\boldsymbol{\ell}^{\mathsf{T}}\cdot\beta_{\boldsymbol{\ell}}(\mathbf{x})\,. \tag{13.6}$$

The limit of the process $\{\mathbf{X}''_t\}_{t\in\mathbb{R}_+}$ for large N is exactly $\{\mathbf{X}'_t\}_{t\in\mathbb{R}_+}$.

In integral terms, the process can be written as:

$$\mathbf{X}''_t = \mathbf{X}''_0 + \int_0^t \mathbf{f}\left(\mathbf{X}''_s\right)\mathrm{d}s + \frac{1}{\sqrt{N}}\sum_{\boldsymbol{\ell}} \boldsymbol{\ell}\cdot\int_0^t \sqrt{\beta_{\boldsymbol{\ell}}\left(\mathbf{X}''_s\right)}\cdot\mathrm{d}W_{\boldsymbol{\ell},s}, \qquad t\geq 0.$$

Exercise 4 (News Diffusion Model—Continued). The diffusion equation is:

$$\mathrm{d}I''_t = p\cdot I''_t\left(1-I''_t\right)\mathrm{d}t + \frac{1}{\sqrt{N}}\cdot\sqrt{p\cdot I''_t\left(1-I''_t\right)}\cdot\mathrm{d}W_t, \quad t\geq 0.$$

The stochastic part of the equation has variance:

$$\mathbb{V}\left(\frac{1}{\sqrt{N}}\cdot\sqrt{p\cdot i_t\left(1-i_t\right)}\cdot\mathrm{d}W_t\,|i_t\right) = \frac{1}{N}\cdot p\cdot i_t\left(1-i_t\right)\cdot\mathrm{d}t.$$

[3] We follow here the Kunrei-shiki romanization convention, instead of the more common Hepburn romanization Itō, because Itô himself used the first one in several publications.

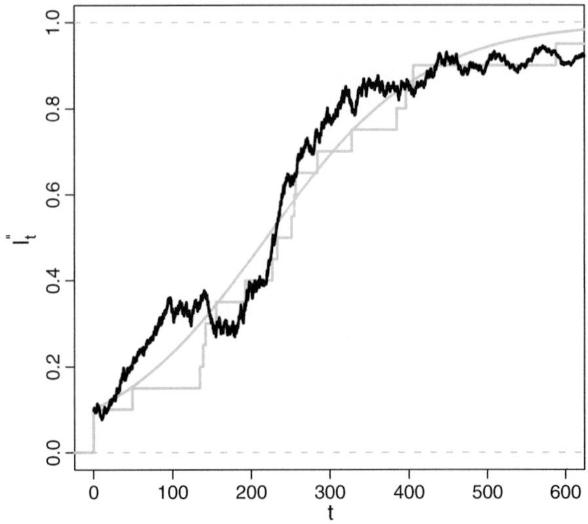

Fig. 13.4 Graph of a trajectory of $\{I''_t\}_{t\in\mathbb{R}_+}$ (in *black*), over $\{I'_t\}_{t\in\mathbb{R}_+}$ and a trajectory of $\{I_t\}_{t\in\mathbb{R}_+}$ (both in *grey*)

This implies that the process is heteroskedastic, i.e. its variance depends on t. In Fig. 13.4, we reproduce a trajectory of $\{I''_t\}_{t\in\mathbb{R}_+}$, in black, over the deterministic approximation $\{I'_t\}_{t\in\mathbb{R}_+}$ and the previous trajectory of $\{I_t\}_{t\in\mathbb{R}_+}$, both in grey. From the graph there seems to be no particular similarity between $\{I''_t\}_{t\in\mathbb{R}_+}$ and $\{I_t\}_{t\in\mathbb{R}_+}$: we will pursue this point at the end of Sect. 13.4.2, showing that, for large enough N, the paths $\{I''_t\}_{t\in\mathbb{R}_+}$ and $\{I_t\}_{t\in\mathbb{R}_+}$ look similar in distribution. □

As concerns the precision of the approximation, for any process $\{\mathbf{X}_t\}_{t\in\mathbb{R}_+}$ it is possible to find a process $\{\mathbf{X}''_t\}_{t\in\mathbb{R}_+}$ such that (see Appendix for references):

$$\mathbf{X}_t^{(N)} = \mathbf{X}''_t + O\left(\frac{\ln N}{N}\right).$$

13.4.2 *The Central Limit Theorem Approximation*

As briefly explained above, this result considers the process $\left\{\mathbf{V}_t^{(N)}\right\}_{t\in\mathbb{R}_+}$, where:

$$\mathbf{V}_t^{(N)} := \sqrt{N}\left(\mathbf{X}_t^{(N)} - \mathbf{X}'_t\right).$$

By (13.5), we expect $\mathbf{V}_t^{(N)}$ to be $O_{\mathbb{P}}(1)$.

Consider $\partial\mathbf{f}$, the matrix of partial derivatives of $\mathbf{f}$, defined as:

$$[\partial\mathbf{f}(\mathbf{x})]_{i,j} = \frac{\partial f_i(\mathbf{x})}{\partial x_j}$$

where f_i is the i–th element of the vector of functions $\mathbf{f}$ and x_j is the j–th element of $\mathbf{x}$. We define a Gaussian process $\{\mathbf{V}_t\}_{t\in\mathbb{R}_+}$ through the SDE:

$$\mathrm{d}\mathbf{V}_t = \partial\mathbf{f}\left(\mathbf{X}'_t\right)\cdot\mathbf{V}_t\mathrm{d}t + \sum_{\boldsymbol{\ell}}\boldsymbol{\ell}\cdot\sqrt{\beta_{\boldsymbol{\ell}}\left(\mathbf{X}'_t\right)}\cdot\mathrm{d}W_{\boldsymbol{\ell},t}, \qquad t\geq 0, \tag{13.7}$$

where the processes $\{W_{\boldsymbol{\ell},t}\}_{t\in\mathbb{R}_+}$ are independent Brownian motions, each one associated with a value of $\boldsymbol{\ell}$. Remark that $\left\{\mathbf{X}'_t\right\}_{t\in\mathbb{R}_+}$ is deterministic and therefore, in this SDE, both the drift and the diffusion coefficients are known in advance.

Under certain regularity conditions (see Appendix), we have:

$$\mathbf{V}_t^{(N)} \to_{\mathcal{D}} \mathbf{V}_t, \quad t\geq 0, \tag{13.8}$$

where the subscript on the arrow denotes convergence in distribution. This means that the fluctuations of $\left\{\mathbf{X}_t^{(N)}\right\}_{t\in\mathbb{R}_+}$ around $\left\{\mathbf{X}'_t\right\}_{t\in\mathbb{R}_+}$, opportunely scaled, behave as the Gaussian process $\{\mathbf{V}_t\}_{t\in\mathbb{R}_+}$.

Exercise 5 (News Diffusion Model—Continued). We get:

$$\partial f(x) = p(1-2x).$$

Therefore, the corresponding diffusion equation is:

$$\begin{aligned}\mathrm{d}V_t &= \partial f\left(I'_t\right)\cdot V_t\mathrm{d}t + \sqrt{\beta_1\left(I'_t\right)}\cdot\mathrm{d}W_t \\ &= p\left(1-2I'_t\right)\cdot V_t\mathrm{d}t + \sqrt{p\cdot I'_t\left(1-I'_t\right)}\cdot\mathrm{d}W_t.\end{aligned} \tag{13.9}$$

In Fig. 13.5, a trajectory $\{V_t\}_{t\in\mathbb{R}_+}$, in black, is plotted against the trajectory of $\left\{V_t^{(N)}\right\}_{t\in\mathbb{R}_+} = \left\{\sqrt{N}\cdot\left(I_t - I'_t\right)\right\}_{t\in\mathbb{R}_+}$, in grey, already displayed in Fig. 13.3 with a different scaling. □

Now, from the definition $\mathbf{V}_t^{(N)} := \sqrt{N}\left(\mathbf{X}_t^{(N)} - \mathbf{X}'_t\right)$ and the approximate result $\mathbf{V}_t^{(N)} \simeq \mathbf{V}_t$, valid in distribution for large N, we get:

$$\sqrt{N}\left(\mathbf{X}_t^{(N)} - \mathbf{X}'_t\right) \simeq \mathbf{V}_t,$$

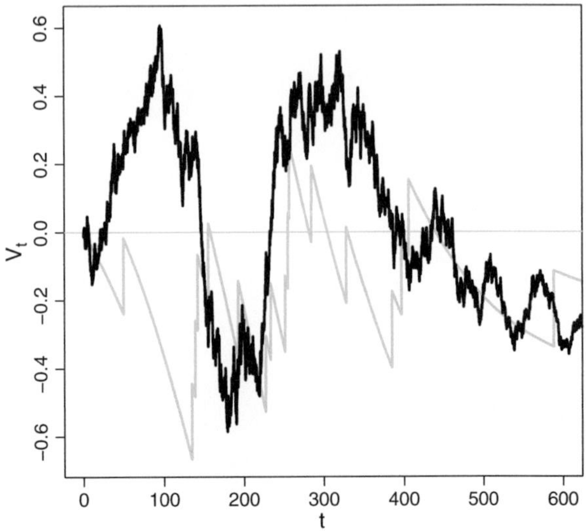

Fig. 13.5 Graph of a trajectory of $\{V_t\}_{t\in\mathbb{R}_+}$ (in *black*) and of one of $\left\{\sqrt{N}\cdot\left(I_t-I_t'\right)\right\}_{t\in\mathbb{R}_+}$ (in *grey*)

$$\mathbf{X}_t^{(N)} \simeq \mathbf{X}_t' + \frac{1}{\sqrt{N}}\cdot\mathbf{V}_t. \tag{13.10}$$

The right-hand side of the last line leads us to consider the process $\{\mathbf{X}_t'''\}_{t\in\mathbb{R}_+}$, defined through the equality $\mathbf{X}_t''' := \mathbf{X}_t' + \frac{1}{\sqrt{N}}\cdot\mathbf{V}_t$. This process is an approximation to $\left\{\mathbf{X}_t^{(N)}\right\}_{t\in\mathbb{R}_+}$. In differential terms, $\{\mathbf{X}_t'''\}_{t\in\mathbb{R}_+}$ is defined by:

$$\begin{aligned}
\mathrm{d}\mathbf{X}_t''' &= \mathrm{d}\mathbf{X}_t' + \frac{1}{\sqrt{N}}\cdot\mathrm{d}\mathbf{V}_t \\
&= \mathbf{f}\left(\mathbf{X}_t'\right)\cdot\mathrm{d}t + \frac{1}{\sqrt{N}}\cdot\partial\mathbf{f}\left(\mathbf{X}_t'\right)\cdot\mathbf{V}_t\cdot\mathrm{d}t + \frac{1}{\sqrt{N}}\cdot\sum_{\ell}\boldsymbol{\ell}\cdot\sqrt{\beta_\ell\left(\mathbf{X}_t'\right)}\cdot\mathrm{d}W_{\ell,t}, \qquad t\geq 0
\end{aligned}$$

where we have used (13.3) and (13.7). The replacement $\mathbf{V}_t = \sqrt{N}\cdot\left(\mathbf{X}_t'''-\mathbf{X}_t'\right)$ leads us to:

$$\begin{aligned}
\mathrm{d}\mathbf{X}_t''' &= \left\{\mathbf{f}\left(\mathbf{X}_t'\right) + \frac{1}{\sqrt{N}}\cdot\partial\mathbf{f}\left(\mathbf{X}_t'\right)\cdot\mathbf{V}_t\right\}\cdot\mathrm{d}t + \frac{1}{\sqrt{N}}\cdot\sum_{\ell}\boldsymbol{\ell}\cdot\sqrt{\beta_\ell\left(\mathbf{X}_t'\right)}\cdot\mathrm{d}W_{\ell,t} \\
&= \left\{\mathbf{f}\left(\mathbf{X}_t'\right) + \partial\mathbf{f}\left(\mathbf{X}_t'\right)\cdot\left[\mathbf{X}_t'''-\mathbf{X}_t'\right]\right\}\cdot\mathrm{d}t + \frac{1}{\sqrt{N}}\cdot\sum_{\ell}\boldsymbol{\ell}\cdot\sqrt{\beta_\ell\left(\mathbf{X}_t'\right)}\cdot\mathrm{d}W_{\ell,t}, \qquad t\geq 0.
\end{aligned}$$

The differences with respect to $\{\mathbf{X}_t''\}_{t\in\mathbb{R}_+}$ are the more complex form of the drift coefficient and the fact that the diffusion coefficient depends on the process

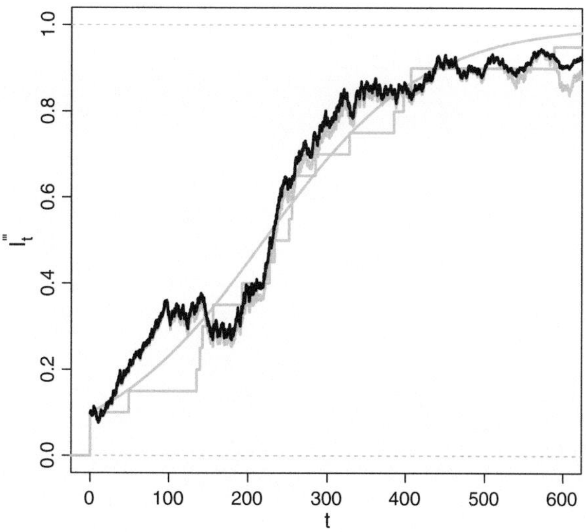

Fig. 13.6 Graph of a trajectory of $\{I_t'''\}_{t\in\mathbb{R}_+}$ (in *black*), over trajectories of $\{I_t''\}_{t\in\mathbb{R}_+}$, $\{I_t\}_{t\in\mathbb{R}_+}$ and over $\{I_t'\}_{t\in\mathbb{R}_+}$ (all in *grey*)

$\{\mathbf{X}_t'\}_{t\in\mathbb{R}_+}$. As this process is a deterministic function of t, the diffusion coefficient behaves as if a forcing is applied.

Exercise 6 (News Diffusion Model—Continued). Starting from (13.10) and replacing in it the formulas (13.4) and (13.9) for $\mathrm{d}I_t'$ and $\mathrm{d}V_t$, we get:

$$\begin{aligned}
\mathrm{d}I_t''' &= \mathrm{d}I_t' + \frac{1}{\sqrt{N}}\cdot \mathrm{d}V_t \\
&= p\cdot I_t'\left(1-I_t'\right)\mathrm{d}t + \frac{1}{\sqrt{N}}\cdot\left\{p\left(1-2I_t'\right)\cdot V_t\mathrm{d}t + \sqrt{p\cdot I_t'\left(1-I_t'\right)}\cdot \mathrm{d}W_t\right\} \\
&= p\cdot\left\{\left(1-2I_t'\right)\cdot I_t''' + \left(I_t'\right)^2\right\}\cdot \mathrm{d}t + \frac{1}{\sqrt{N}}\cdot\sqrt{p\cdot I_t'\left(1-I_t'\right)}\cdot \mathrm{d}W_t, \quad t\geq 0.
\end{aligned}$$

In Fig. 13.6, we plot a trajectory of $\{I_t'''\}_{t\in\mathbb{R}_+}$, in black, over the previous trajectories of $\{I_t''\}_{t\in\mathbb{R}_+}$, $\{I_t\}_{t\in\mathbb{R}_+}$ and over $\{I_t'\}_{t\in\mathbb{R}_+}$, all in grey. In order to ensure comparability, both $\{I_t'''\}_{t\in\mathbb{R}_+}$ and $\{I_t''\}_{t\in\mathbb{R}_+}$ have been based on the same Brownian motion path $\{W_t\}_{t\in\mathbb{R}_+}$. □

There is little to choose between $\{\mathbf{X}_t''\}_{t\in\mathbb{R}_+}$ and $\{\mathbf{X}_t'''\}_{t\in\mathbb{R}_+}$ as concerns the precision of the approximation. Indeed, for any process $\left\{\mathbf{V}_t^{(N)}\right\}_{t\in\mathbb{R}_+}$ it is possible to find a process $\{\mathbf{V}_t\}_{t\in\mathbb{R}_+}$ such that (see Appendix for references):

$$\sqrt{N}\cdot\left(\mathbf{X}_t^{(N)}-\mathbf{X}_t'\right) = \mathbf{V}_t + O\left(\frac{\ln N}{\sqrt{N}}\right).$$

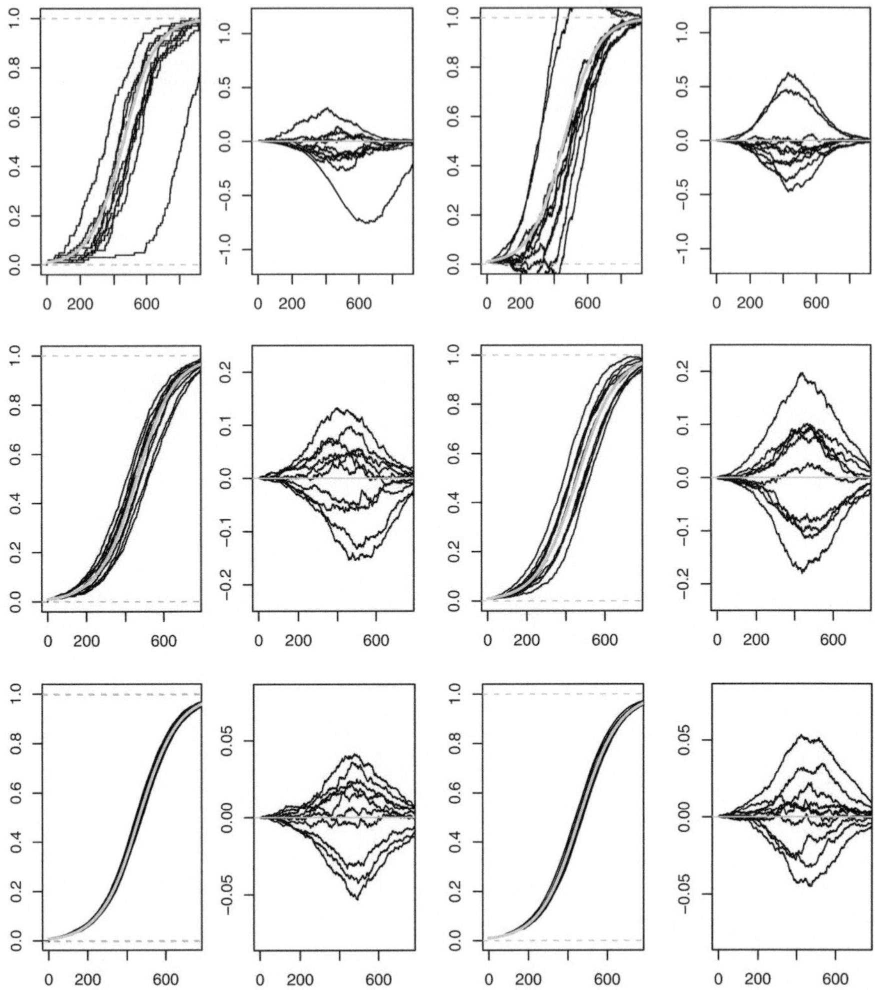

Fig. 13.7 Plot of 10 paths of $\{I_t\}_{t\in\mathbb{R}_+}$, $\{I_t - I'_t\}_{t\in\mathbb{R}_+}$, $\{I'''_t\}_{t\in\mathbb{R}_+}$ and $\{I'''_t - I'_t\}_{t\in\mathbb{R}_+}$ (in columns, from *left to right*) for $N = 100, 1{,}000, 10{,}000$ (in rows, from *top to bottom*)

This implies that, for any process $\{\mathbf{X}_t\}_{t\in\mathbb{R}_+}$ it is possible to find a process $\{\mathbf{X}'''_t\}_{t\in\mathbb{R}_+}$ such that:

$$\mathbf{X}_t^{(N)} = \mathbf{X}'''_t + O\left(\frac{\ln N}{N}\right).$$

Exercise 7 (News Diffusion Model—Continued). In Fig. 13.7, we, respectively, represent some paths of $\{I_t\}_{t\in\mathbb{R}_+}$, $\{I_t - I'_t\}_{t\in\mathbb{R}_+}$, $\{I'''_t\}_{t\in\mathbb{R}_+}$ and $\{I'''_t - I'_t\}_{t\in\mathbb{R}_+}$, for three values of N. The parameters are $p = 0.01$ and $i_0 = 0.01$ for all the graphs.

Each row corresponds to a different value of N, namely, from top to bottom, 100, 1,000, and 10,000. The first column contains the graphs of 10 realizations of $\{I_t\}_{t\in\mathbb{R}_+}$, in black, as well as the curve $\{I'_t\}_{t\in\mathbb{R}_+}$, in grey. The second column illustrates the behavior of $\{I_t - I'_t\}_{t\in\mathbb{R}_+}$, displaying the deviations between each one of the 10 paths of the previous column and the deterministic approximation $\{I'_t\}_{t\in\mathbb{R}_+}$. The third column contains 10 realizations of the central limit theorem approximation $\{I'''_t\}_{t\in\mathbb{R}_+}$, in black, and the curve $\{I'_t\}_{t\in\mathbb{R}_+}$, in grey. The fourth column contains the differences $\{I'''_t - I'_t\}_{t\in\mathbb{R}_+}$. We do not plot $\{I''_t\}_{t\in\mathbb{R}_+}$ because the graphs in which this process replaces $\{I'''_t\}_{t\in\mathbb{R}_+}$ are undistinguishable with respect to these ones. The rationale of the graph is that the processes in the third (fourth) column should be approximations of the ones in the first (second) column. We have depicted several realizations in each subplot, because the approximation holds only in distribution and, as such, one realization would be insufficient to illustrate how its quality increases when passing from small N (i.e., the first row) to large N (i.e., the third row). Indeed, it is apparent from the graph that, for $N = 100$, the agreement between the distribution of the centered point process $\{I_t - I'_t\}_{t\in\mathbb{R}_+}$ and that of the Gaussian process $\{I'''_t - I'_t\}_{t\in\mathbb{R}_+}$ is not particularly good; this fact is witnessed by the different appearance of the curves $\{I_t\}_{t\in\mathbb{R}_+}$ and $\{I'''_t\}_{t\in\mathbb{R}_+}$. For $N = 1{,}000$, the agreement is clearly much better, while for $N = 10{,}000$ the two sets of curves are indistinguishable. □

13.5 Conclusions

In this paper, we have presented some probabilistic results that can be useful to approximate analytically a class of intrinsically stochastic individual- or agent-based models. With respect to classical agent-based models whose behavior is studied through simulation, the present approach is not able to deal with arbitrarily complex rules of behavior and often requires simplified assumptions. However, we believe that the methods presented here can still be helpful in the analysis of models customarily approached through simulation. Up to our knowledge, the most lucid example of this interaction is the analysis, performed in Galán and Izquierdo (2005), of the Norms and Metanorms models introduced in Axelrod (1986). This example shows how much insight can be gained when the mathematical approach is used as a supplement of simulations.

Appendix: Technical Conditions

In this appendix, we discuss the technical conditions under which the results stated above hold true.

As concerns the deterministic approximation of Sect. 13.3, we follow Theorem 8.1 in Kurtz (1981) (similar results are Theorem 3.1 in Norman, 1968; Theorem (3.1) in Kurtz, 1970; Theorem 8.1.1 in Norman, 1972; Theorem (2.1) in Kurtz, 1976; Theorem 2.2 in Kurtz, 1978; Theorem (2.16) in Kurtz, 1980; Theorem 2.1 in Chap. 11 in Ethier & Kurtz, 1986).

Let $K \subset E$ be a bounded and closed (i.e., compact) set. The first condition requires that, for each K:

$$\sum_{\boldsymbol{\ell}} |\boldsymbol{\ell}| \cdot \sup_{\mathbf{x} \in K} \beta_{\boldsymbol{\ell}}(\mathbf{x}) < \infty.$$

The second condition requires that, for any K, there exists M_K such that:

$$|\mathbf{f}(\mathbf{x}) - \mathbf{f}(\mathbf{y})| \leq M_K \cdot |\mathbf{x} - \mathbf{y}|, \quad \mathbf{x}, \mathbf{y} \in K.$$

At last, we require that the initial condition of the original process converges to the one of the deterministic one, i.e. $\lim_{N \to \infty} \mathbf{X}_0^{(N)} = \mathbf{x}_0$. By the way, under these conditions, the convergence of $\left\{\mathbf{X}_t^{(N)}\right\}_{t \in \mathbb{R}_+}$ to $\{\mathbf{X}'_t\}_{t \in \mathbb{R}_+}$ is uniform for t belonging to bounded subsets of $\mathbb{R}_+$.

Exercise 8 (News Diffusion Model—Continued). Consider the epidemic model seen in Exercise 1 in the second rewriting. Using the fact that $x \in [0, 1]$, it is possible to see that $x(1-x) \leq \frac{1}{4}$. Therefore, we have:

$$\sum_{\ell} |\ell| \cdot \sup_{x \in K} \beta_{\ell}(x) = p \cdot \sup_{x \in K} x(1-x) \leq \frac{p}{4} < \infty.$$

As concerns the second hypothesis, we have:

$$\begin{aligned}
|f(x) - f(y)| &= p \cdot |x(1-x) - y(1-y)| \\
&\leq p \cdot \sup_{z \in [x,y]} \left| \frac{\partial [z(1-z)]}{\partial z} \right| \cdot |x - y| \\
&= p \cdot \sup_{z \in [x,y]} |1 - 2z| \cdot |x - y| \leq p \cdot |x - y|
\end{aligned}$$

where the second step derives from the mean value theorem. At last, we have supposed that $I_0 = i_0$ so that the initial condition is trivially verified. □

The diffusion approximation of Sect. 13.4.1 holds under the following conditions (this is Theorem 8.4 in Kurtz, 1981; see Theorem (3.13) in Kurtz, 1976; Theorem 3.3 in Kurtz, 1978; Theorem 2.1 in Kurtz, 1983; Theorem 3.1 in Chap. 11 in Ethier & Kurtz, 1986 for alternative or more general conditions):

- for any index $\boldsymbol{\ell}$ but a finite number, $\beta_{\boldsymbol{\ell}}(\mathbf{x}) \equiv 0$;
- for any index $\boldsymbol{\ell}$, $\overline{\beta}_{\boldsymbol{\ell}} = \sup_{\mathbf{x}} \beta_{\boldsymbol{\ell}}(\mathbf{x}) < +\infty$;

- there exists $M > 0$ such that:

$$|\beta_{\boldsymbol{\ell}}(\mathbf{x}) - \beta_{\boldsymbol{\ell}}(\mathbf{y})| \leq M \cdot \overline{\beta}_{\boldsymbol{\ell}} \cdot |\mathbf{x} - \mathbf{y}| ;$$

- there exists $M > 0$ such that:

$$|\mathbf{f}(\mathbf{x}) - \mathbf{f}(\mathbf{y})| \leq M \cdot |\mathbf{x} - \mathbf{y}| .$$

The rate on the approximation of $\{\mathbf{X}_t\}_{t\in\mathbb{R}_+}$ through $\{\mathbf{X}''_t\}_{t\in\mathbb{R}_+}$ at the end of Sect. 13.4.1 can be found in Theorem (3.13) in Kurtz (1976), Theorem 3.3 in Kurtz (1978), Theorem 8.4 in Kurtz (1981) and Theorem 3.1 in Chap. 11 in Ethier and Kurtz (1986). By the way, the coupling is uniform over bounded intervals of the real line.

Exercise 9 (News Diffusion Model—Continued). There exists only one index ℓ, i.e. $\ell = 1$, for which $\beta_\ell \not\equiv 0$. For this index, $\overline{\beta}_1 = p \cdot \sup_{x\in[0,1]} x(1-x) = p/4 < +\infty$. Now, from Exercise 8:

$$|\beta_1(x) - \beta_1(y)| \leq p \cdot |x - y| ,$$

i.e. one can take $M = 4$. On the other hand, always from Exercise 8:

$$|f(x) - f(y)| = |\beta_1(x) - \beta_1(y)| \leq p \cdot |x - y| ,$$

i.e. one can take $M = p$. Therefore, any $M \geq \max\{4, p\}$ respects the conditions.

□

The convergence in Sect. 13.4.2 holds under the following conditions (these are the ones stated in Theorem 8.2 in Kurtz, 1981; for related results, see Theorem 1.1 in Norman, 1968; Theorem (3.5) in Kurtz, 1971; Theorem 8.1.1 in Norman, 1972; Theorem 1 in Barbour, 1974; Theorem (2.3) in Kurtz, 1976; Theorem 2 in Allain, 1976a; Theorem 4.4 in Kurtz, 1978; Theorem 2.2 in Kurtz, 1983; Theorem 2.3 in Chap. 11 in Ethier & Kurtz, 1986):

- for each bounded closed set K, we have:

$$\sum_{\boldsymbol{\ell}} |\boldsymbol{\ell}|^2 \sup_{\mathbf{x}\in K} \beta_{\boldsymbol{\ell}}(\mathbf{x}) < \infty;$$

- the functions $\partial\mathbf{f}$ and $\beta_{\boldsymbol{\ell}}$, for each $\boldsymbol{\ell}$, are continuous;
- the initial conditions converge in such a way that $\lim_{N\to\infty} \sqrt{N}\left|\mathbf{X}_0^{(N)} - \mathbf{x}_0\right| = \mathbf{0}$.

Versions of this result holding uniformly for $t > 0$ have been stated in Theorem 3.2 (ii) in Norman (1974b), Theorem 1 in Norman (1974a), Theorem (2.7) in Kurtz (1976) and Theorem 8.5 in Kurtz (1981). Berry–Esséen-type theorems can be found in Theorem 1 in Barbour (1974), Theorem (2.5) in Kurtz (1976), Allain (1976b), Corollary 4.5 in Kurtz (1978) and Chapters 5 and 6 in Alm (1978).

The rate on the approximation of $\{\mathbf{X}_t\}_{t\in\mathbb{R}_+}$ through $\{\mathbf{X}_t'''\}_{t\in\mathbb{R}_+}$ at the end of Sect. 13.4.2 is uniform over bounded subsets of the real line and can be found in Theorem 4.4 in Kurtz (1978) and in Theorem 3.2 and following remarks in Chap. 11 in Ethier and Kurtz (1986).

Exercise 10 (News Diffusion Model—Continued). Reasoning as in Exercise 8, we have:

$$\sum_{\ell} |\ell|^2 \cdot \sup_{x\in K} \beta_\ell(x) \leq \frac{p}{4} < \infty.$$

As concerns $\partial f(x) = p \cdot (1-2x)$ and $\beta_1(x) = p \cdot x(1-x)$, they are clearly continuous. □

References

Allain, M.-F. (1976). Approximation par un processus de diffusion des oscillations, autour d'une valeur moyenne, d'une suite de processus de Markov de saut pur. *Comptes rendus de l'Académie des sciences Paris Séries A-B, 282*(16), Aiii, A891–A894.

Allain, M.-F. (1976). Étude de la vitesse de convergence d'une suite de processus de Markov de saut pur. *Comptes rendus de l'Académie des sciences Paris Séries A-B, 282*(17), Aiii, A1015–A1018.

Alm, S. E. (1978). On the rate of convergence in diffusion approximation of jump Markov processes. Report 8, Uppsala University, Department of Mathematics.

Axelrod, R. (1986). An evolutionary approach to norms. *American Political Science Review, 80*(4), 1095–1111.

Barbour, A. D. (1972). The principle of the diffusion of arbitrary constants. *Journal of Applied Probability, 9*, 519–541.

Barbour, A. D. (1974). On a functional central limit theorem for Markov population processes. *Advances in Applied Probability, 6*, 21–39.

Black, A. J., & McKane, A. J. (2012). Stochastic formulation of ecological models and their applications. *Trends in Ecology & Evolution, 27*(6), 337–345.

Bortolussi, L., Hillston, J., Latella, D., & M. Massink (2013). Continuous approximation of collective system behaviour: A tutorial. *Performance Evaluation, 70*, 317–349.

Centola, D. (2010). The spread of behavior in an online social network experiment. *Science, 329*(5996), 1194–1197.

Challenger, J. D., Fanelli, D., & McKane, A. J. (2014). The theory of individual based discrete-time processes. *The Journal of Statistical Physics, 156*(1), 131–155.

Collet, F., Dai Pra, P., & Sartori, E. (2010). A simple mean field model for social interactions: Dynamics, fluctuations, criticality. *The Journal of Statistical Physics, 139*(5), 820–858.

Ethier, S. N., & Kurtz, T. G. (1986). *Markov processes. Characterization and convergence.* Wiley Series in Probability and Mathematical Statistics: Probability and Mathematical Statistics. New York: John Wiley & Sons, Inc.

Feller, W. (1951). Diffusion processes in genetics. In J. Neyman (Ed.), *Proceedings of the Second Berkeley Symposium on Mathematical Statistics and Probability* (pp. 227–246). Berkeley: University of California Press.

Galán, J. M., & Izquierdo, L. R. (2005). Appearances can be deceiving: Lessons learned re-implementing Axelrod's 'evolutionary approach to norms'. *Journal of Artificial Societies and Social Simulation, 8*(3), 2.

Goutsias, J., & Jenkinson G. (2013). Markovian dynamics on complex reaction networks. *Physics Reports, 529*(2), 199–264.

Hirshman, B. R., Charles, J. St., & Carley, K. M. (2011). Leaving us in tiers: can homophily be used to generate tiering effects? *Computational & Mathematical Organization Theory, 17*(4), 318–343.

Karlin, S., & Taylor, H. M. (1975). *A first course in stochastic processes*, 2nd ed. New York/London: Academic Press.

Kurtz, T. G. (1970). Solutions of ordinary differential equations as limits of pure jump Markov processes. *Journal of Applied Probability, 7*, 49–58.

Kurtz, T. G. (1971). Limit theorems for sequences of jump Markov processes approximating ordinary differential processes. *Journal of Applied Probability, 8*, 344–356.

Kurtz, T. G. (1972). The relationship between stochastic and deterministic models for chemical reactions. *The Journal of Chemical Physics, 57*(7), 2976–2978.

Kurtz, T. G. (1976). Limit theorems and diffusion approximations for density dependent Markov chains. *Mathematical Programming Studies, 5*, 67–78. Stochastic systems: Modeling, identification and optimization, I (Proc. Sympos., Univ. Kentucky, Lexington).

Kurtz, T. G. (1977/1978). Strong approximation theorems for density dependent Markov chains. *Stochastic Processes and their Applications, 6*(3), 223–240.

Kurtz, T. G. (1980). Relationships between stochastic and deterministic population models. In *Biological growth and spread (Proc. Conf., Heidelberg, 1979)*. Lecture Notes in Biomathematics (Vol. 38, pp. 449–467). Berlin/New York: Springer.

Kurtz, T. G. (1981). *Approximation of population processes*. CBMS-NSF Regional Conference Series in Applied Mathematics (Vol. 36). Philadelphia: Society for Industrial and Applied Mathematics (SIAM).

Kurtz, T. G. (1983). Gaussian approximations for Markov chains and counting processes. In *Proceedings of the 44th session of the International Statistical Institute, Vol. 1 (Madrid, 1983)* (Vol. 50, pp. 361–376). With a discussion in Vol. 3, pp. 237–248.

Lotka, A. J. (1925). *Elements of Physical Biology*. Baltimore: Williams & Wilkins Company.

Matis, J. H., & Kiffe, T. R. (2000). *Stochastic Population Models: A Compartmental Perspective*. Lecture Notes in Statistics. New York: Springer.

Norman, M. F. (1968). Slow learning. *British Journal of Mathematical and Statistical Psychology, 21*, 141–159.

Norman, M. F. (1972). *Markov processes and learning models*. Mathematics in Science and Engineering (Vol. 84). New York/London: Academic Press.

Norman, M. F. (1974a). A central limit theorem for Markov processes that move by small steps. *The Annals of Probability, 2*, 1065–1074.

Norman, M. F. (1974b). Markovian learning processes. *SIAM Review, 16*, 143–162.

Plikynas, D., & Masteika, S. (2014). Agent-based nonlocal social systems: Neurodynamic oscillations approach. In G. Meiselwitz (Ed.), *Social Computing and Social Media. Lecture Notes in Computer Science* (Vol. 8531, pp. 253–264). New York: Springer International Publishing.

Pollett, P. K. (2001). Diffusion approximations for ecological models. In F. Ghassemi, P. Whetton, R. Little & M. Littleboy (Eds.), *MODSIM 2001 International Congress on Modelling and Simulation* (pp. 843–848). Townsville: Modelling and Simulation Society of Australia and New Zealand Inc.

Railsback, S. F., & Grimm, V. (2011). *Agent-based and individual-based modeling: A practical introduction*. Princeton: Princeton University Press.

Sigmund, K. (2007). Kolmogorov and population dynamics. In *Kolmogorov's heritage in mathematics* (pp. 177–186). Berlin: Springer.

Volterra, V. (1931). *Leçons sur la théorie mathématique de la lutte pour la vie*. Cahiers scientifiques, Fascicule VII. Paris: Gauthier-Villars.

Volterra, V. (1962). *Opere matematiche. Memorie e Note. Volume quinto: 1926–1940*. Accademia nazionale dei Lincei.

Wang, X., Tao, H., Xie, Z., & Yi, D. (2013). Mining social networks using wave propagation. *Computational & Mathematical Organization Theory, 19*(4), 569–579.

Zhang, Y., & Wu, Y. (2012). How behaviors spread in dynamic social networks. *Computational & Mathematical Organization Theory, 18*(4), 419–444.

Part IV
Macro Aspects of Organizational Behavior

Chapter 14
Modeling Social Agency Using Diachronic Cognition: Learning from the Mafia

Martin Neumann and Stephen J. Cowley

Abstract Human cognition is *diachronic* in that concerted bodily activity links behavior to values that co-evolve with socio-culture: slow historical processes become interlaced with interaction. In principle, therefore, diachronic processes can be placed at the heart of a future socio-cognitive science. In showing how this can be done, we use evidence regarding the historical persistence of Cosa Nostra. In Sicily, the slow processes of a cultural ecosystem, self-maintaining practices, prompt agents to self-configure and make decisions that sustain the mafia. Culture is insinuated into cognitively complex agents who rely on *immergence*. Having explored how Cosa Nostra self-maintained, we offer a methodology for studying such processes. Agent-based simulation serves to pursue how time-scales are integrated, behavioral patterns sedimented and the effects these have on decision making. Accordingly, we offer a model of cognitively complex agents: these self-configure *beliefs, intentions, and desires* as they engage with social organizations whose rewards demand impersonal conformity. For Cosa Nostra to survive, the ecosystemic power of values like omertà must be sustained as self-configured agents decide how to act. We conclude that effective socio-cognitive modeling offers much to the field of organizational cognition and, above all, the study and management of organizational change.

Keywords Organizational cognition • Distributed language • Organizational change • Distributed cognition • Agent-based modeling • Immergence • Diachronic cognition

M. Neumann (✉)
Institute for Information Systems in Business and Public Administration, University of Koblenz, Koblenz, Germany
e-mail: maneumann@uni-koblenz.de

S.J. Cowley
Department of Language and Communication, Centre for Human Interactivity (CHI), Research Cluster for Cognition, Management and Communication (COMAC), University of Southern Denmark, Slagelse, Denmark
e-mail: cowley@sdu.dk

D. Secchi, M. Neumann (eds.), *Agent-Based Simulation of Organizational Behavior*, DOI 10.1007/978-3-319-18153-0_14

14.1 Human Modes of Organizing

Recent cognitive science is faced with increasing recognition of the significance of social embedding. In this paper we argue that diachronic cognition is fundamental for socio-cognitive science. In illustration, we turn to agent based simulation for building models that throw new light on the Sicilian Cosa Nostra. As maintained by Vico's principle of *verum factum*—truth is verified by creation—modeling permits the experimental investigation of theoretical concepts. This is possible because, using engineering, one program can be embedded in another. In cognitive models, this idea is often used to explore how a world is "represented." However, once one abandons eighteenth century philosophy, one can use the same idea to pursue, not just neural function, but how agents connect actions within embedded systems. Accordingly, we emphasize, not how the social emerges, but rather the *immergent* processes that drive complex agents to use organizations as they self-configure. Due weight thus falls on how history becomes enmeshed in human cognition. There are good reasons for pursuing this view. First, humans are born into linguistic worlds and, thus, learn from connecting the rapid scales of lived experience with slow ones depending on the slow evolution of external resources. Given their ontogenies, humans both resemble and contrast with social insects. While like bees in drawing on intra-group coordination, human agency is *also* extended by social and historical organizing. People are not totally reliant on factually observable resources—they also draw on what is called *society*. This is Durkheim's insight: the social can be used to ground the social. Addressing what is often seen as a paradox, one can link developmental psychology with distributed views of language and cognition to dissolve the seeming paradox. Pursuing this, in a previous paper (Neumann & Cowley, 2013), individual rationality is traced to a developmental history that builds on the micro-events of lived co-action. Over time, human agents become users of the resources of reason, language and, most fundamentally, the *products* of cultural evolution (Hollan, Hutchins, & Kirsh, 2000).

Enduring cultural products are necessary to diachronic cognition. Not only do they shape the cultural ecologies within which human lives unfold but they self-maintain as biological agents sustain the social world. For example, modern humans use numbers: we trace this to a flow of Shannon information that contributes to cultural ecosystems (Hutchins, 2014) as groups and individuals draw on the archeology of mathematics. Around 3000 BC, mathematical inscriptions that invoked counting (beyond three as in pre-literate cultures) co-evolved with organization and trade between human groups (Damerow, 1988, 2007). As a result, number enables people to use cultural products to perform otherwise impossible tasks. Such events exemplify diachronic cognition in that ecosystemic constraints transform body–world interaction. Maths based intelligence thus depends on interlacing natural abilities with cultural products that enable people to hone skills. We use the term *immergence* (Conte, Andrighetto, & Campennì, 2014) to describe how culture transforms human actors. Further, the argument applies wherever humans adapt to organizational constraints. While "society" is an abstract concept, we use organizations in dealing with mundane circumstances at the tax office or with an employer. Organization dominates life chances when, for example, a person comes to be unemployed. While all such modes of engagement depend on immergent processes, criminal organizations offer an especially powerful example. The Sicilian Mafia gives powerful insights into the process because it depends on informal conspiracy. Indeed, Cosa Nostra serves to clarify how modes of organization shape human agency: it represents a rare example of spontaneous evolution of a professional organization (Mintzberg, 1979) whose persistence is entirely sustained by the "immergent."

The paper begins by using the concept of diachronic cognition to reframe cognitive science with respect to the socio-cognitive domain of human life. After motivating the study of Cosa Nostra as an exemplar of social process, we sketch historical links between intra-organizational evolution and the socio-cultural environment. This provides the foundation for developing a model of agent rules that can be used in an experimental tool which serves to pursues the interweaving of cognitive times scales.

14.2 Cognition: History and Time

Until the 1990s, cognitive science associated the mind closely with the brain. This led to a focus on real-time processes and issues such as whether cognition was general and/or modular and symbolic and/or probabilistic. As in philosophical tradition, individual "cognitive systems" were taken to be causal: giving the work of Descartes, Hume and Kant a twentieth century gloss, mind was said to "supervene" on the brain. Computational models offered support to the credo that the world experienced is also "represented." Further since computing allows software packages to be embedded within one another, the model led to theoretical innovation. By positing that the mind's software supervenes on the brain's hardware it was posited, for example, that semantic interpretation interfaces with a grammatical system and, given embedding, allows problem solving based on mental models. In the heyday of classic cognitive science, therefore, social phenomena became marginal—communication was seen as rendering public what was within the mind. Cognition was traced to processes occurring between the ears that shaped both social and the non-social decision making. In Susan Hurley's (1998) image, the classic view invokes an input–output sandwich filled by mental process.

Today, it is increasingly acknowledged that what people remember, feel and say draw on concurrent action, perceiving and scaffolding of various kinds. Real-world cognition such as flying a plane can only be understood in relation to how people manage what happens in the cockpit, a very specific "cultural ecosystem" (Hutchins, 2014). By implication, cultural embedding transforms how cognition comes to be "embodied." To clarify this, it is useful to contrast mild, medium, and strong embodiment. Applied to Shapiro's (2011) work, in its mild form, the body drives conceptualization—processing uses individual experience and metaphor. On the medium view, action and perception play a constitutive role in cognition. Thus, one can argue that mind is extended or, more modestly, that artifacts are "unexpectedly" important. Finally, strong views aim to replace representation (and inner content) by appeal to the ecology of living. On methodological grounds, cognition is traced to a history of agent-environment dynamics (Chemero, 2009). Regardless of whether one appeals to conceptualization, scaffolding, or a history of agent-environment dynamics, there is no doubting that much depends on *how* information flows from beyond the body. For philosophical reasons, the cognitive sandwich underplays the bidirectionality of agent-world coupling. In linguistics, for example, people not only use hearing to modulate action but can shadow speaking in extremely rapid scales (Cummins, 2003). Far from needing to be planned, speech can be co-constructed (see, Thibault, 2011). In bringing multi-scalar complexity to social agency, we use examples such as how flying draws on actions in the cockpit (Hutchins, 1995a): as agents interlace their doings, they make effective use of an especially designed environment. While bodies enable coordination (and, perhaps, experience-based simulation), much depends on how decision making has been learned and scaffolded. Far from being organism-centered, many relevant processes depend on simplex tricks that allow environments to be partly shared. While ants and bees offer eusocial examples, cooperation is also crucial to elephants, meerkats, and humans. Indeed, homo sapiens live in a constructed or "cultural" world where they realize values (and norms) that connect historically derived institutions with a verbal domain. Human cognition depends on a niche or, for Steffensen and Fill (2014), how history extends the ecology.

Interest in how temporality contributes to cognition has long been central to ecological psychology. Alongside this tradition, the early 1990s saw a burgeoning of interest in work that drew on re-readings of Vygotsky. This shared activity theory, situated cognition and a focus on communities of practice. For our purposes, however, its most important outcome was a blend of ethnography and cognitive science that served in the study of navigation practice. In seminal work Hutchins (1995b) developed an ethnographic Ph.D. on navigation by Micronesian islanders into a way of modeling how cognition played out as members of the US navy brought a ship into port. In functional terms, he showed that the task of "navigating at sea" could be realized in highly contrasting ways. The Micronesians honed their observational powers while appealing to the myth that travelling from island to island depends on the arrival of the destination; in the US navy, by contrast, comparable outcomes drew on naval discipline, mathematics, and technology. This came to be known as *socially distributed cognition*. As with all good theories, the root ideas are simple: (1) culture and its artifacts function as an ecosystem that, when appropriately managed in lived time, is partly constitutive of human cognitive process; (2) expertise encompasses both the capacity to devise plans based on goal directed action and more intuitive ways of acting. Cognition involves complex decision making that link the actions of cultural agents with what they can do with available resources. Given both embodiment (including brains) and historical resources, cultural ecosystems enable human beings to animate distributed systems. In a classic publication, Hollan et al. (2000) characterize the approach in relation to axioms that can be paraphrased:

- Cognitive processes may be distributed across members of a social group.
- Cognitive processes may involve coordination between internal and external (material or environmental) structure.

Not only are the axioms widely accepted in cognitive science but they have been used in many settings. Further, as soon as cognitive processes are seen to criss-cross between agents and the world, any neurocentric approach loses its luster. One begins to ask about mechanisms and, specifically, how cognitive needs are constituted by a history of living in a cognitive ecology. Once one does this, special weight falls on a third axiom.

- Processes may be distributed through time in such a way that the products of earlier events can transform the nature of later events.

The claim pinpoints the core of diachronic cognition. In human life, decision-making is both situated and also non-local. A classic example is that of transactive memory which, as Kirchhoff (2013) notes, enables people to remember more together than they could have done alone. Together, using structures from many scales, they create a coherent and dynamic shared pattern—far from relying on linear causes, the parties call on impersonal aspects of the world (above all, the rich experience of language activity). For Kirchhoff, collective remembering results from "diachronic process constitution" where individuals reach beyond their own experience by talking in ways that create an ordered and co-ordinated pattern. However, diachronic processes are far from exotic. While uses of a historically derived number system may provide the simplest case, their peculiarity becomes clearer as applied to, say, reading or using diagrams. In such cases, a single person links thinking and learning with possible construals, perspectives and, crucially, how patterns should (and should not) be used. Lacking space to pursue how cultural products function, we stress one logical consequence.[1] Since earlier events are partly constitutive of later ones, there is a need for models that can reach beyond situated experience. While complex processes are amenable to synchronic *description*, this overlooks the bodily activity that meshes individual experience with that of other people. This has an important consequence:

- Processes distributed through time enable people manage to accomplish cognitive tasks through lived bodily processes and, inseparably, use of technological and other collective resources.

[1]Cowley (2014) highlights the question of how people use impersonal experience in terms of what he terms the integration problem. In illustration, he describes how one person solves the river problem by moving back and forth between more personal and impersonal modes or acting.

Human cognition and language spread in time; embodiment brings its multi-scalar nature to the lived present as people cooperate in cognitive projects. In well-worn terms, people depend on organizing and organizations—they manage temporality to reach beyond on lived time. Pursuing this opens up new horizons in the study of social agency by focusing on slow processes influence cognitive outcomes. In taking this diachronic view, we address an aspect of human social agency that comes to the fore in organized social environments. Human interaction is guided not only by socio-cultural norms but also by how people participate in (multiple) groups. Investigation of human society thus pursues how cultural artifacts and organizations exploit meso-scale material and interactional change. Pursuing this, we model on how cultural evolution influences real-time co-action: using agent-based modeling (ABM), we focus on not only the doings of social agents but also how people adapt to the changing properties of cultural ecosystems.

14.3 Criminal Organizations as a Social Laboratory

In showing how the organizational structure of the cultural ecosystem shapes human interactivity, we turn to the case of criminal organizations. These provide a test bed for investigating how time scales impact on each other as a result of the strong evolutionary pressures that operate on illegal organizations. Being illegal demands covert practices (Erickson, 1981; Simmel, 1908) that have to adapt quickly. By contrast, legal organizations rely on state protection through courts that enforce the rule of law. While enforcement of employee motivation cannot be guaranteed purely by the rule of law, a state monopoly of violence nonetheless offers some stability. Outside the law, commitment of its members to an illegal organization is more precarious: much depends on the individual commitment of the organization's members, a bond that may ultimately be driven by fear. Not only is this an evolutionary challenge to the stability of criminal organizations but these operate in a social environment that is characterized by fear of prosecution. As a consequence, many criminal groups fail to establish enduring structures: they are destroyed by the police or break up after a short life. Often, they are replaced by new organizations that serve demand in illegal markets such as, say, drugs or weapons. In other terms, whilst the constant generation of new organizations provides a large pool for evolutionary variation, the social environment provides high selection pressure. Thus criminal organizations evolve rapidly. This makes them an illustrative test-case of how social agency is shaped by organizational behavior. Organizational stability is highly improbable. Only a few criminal organizations have established lasting structures. Examples include the Chinese Triads which are said to have persisted for about three centuries and the Sicilian Cosa Nostra which dates back more than a century. Also some terrorist organizations such as the IRA or ETA have had lifetimes that have lasted for decades. These characteristics of covert organizations endow long-lasting criminal organizations with special interest: The lack of a juridical "backup" enables studying how diachronic cognition leads to the spontaneous evolution of organizations that extend human agency. Far from being designed or planned, enduring criminal organizations are highly reliant on immergent process. In consequence the axioms outlined above which characterize diachronic cognition can be reworked as follows:

- Cognitive processes may be distributed across members of a social group, namely the members of the criminal organization.
- However, persistence of these organizations can only be secured by some kind of tie between the legal world and the internal illegal domain. Thus, cognitive processes involve coordination between group internal and external structure.
- Moreover, adoption of the organization to the socio-cultural environment is a result of its history and evolution. Thus, processes are distributed through time in such a way that the products of earlier events can transform the nature of later events.
- However, organizational stability must be enacted in real-time. Thus it holds that processes distributed through time enable people manage to accomplish cognitive tasks through lived bodily processes and their real-time equivalents.

To exemplify this thesis, the case of Cosa Nostra is especially informative in that, as far as is known, it is more highly organized than Mafia type organizations such as Camorra (Dickie, 2011; La Spina, 2005; Scaglione, 2011). Next, we consider both the internal operation of its organizational structures and conditions provided by the social environment. This enables us to emphasize that the conditions for the establishment of enduring organizational structures draws on a co-evolutionary link between organizational and socio-cultural time scales. For this reason Cosa Nostra offers an example that serves to clarify how historical process influences human cognition: a Mafiosi's life connects situated events with the slow scales of cultural change.

14.4 Evolution of Cosa Nostra

While exact dating remains unclear (Gambetta, 2000) the origins of Cosa Nostra can be traced back to the first decades of the nineteenth century (Dickie, 2005; Hess, 1970; Hobsbawm, 1959). It seems to be related to early plantation of citrus fruits (Dickie, 2005) and how these enabled new proto-capitalist landlords move from their rural farms to live in cities. In a declining feudal society, however, the state was too weak to establish the rule of law. More or less structured bands of bandits proliferated and threatened property. For this reason, the landlords sometimes chose to defend their interests by using personnel to perpetrate acts of violence. These became known as *Mafiosi*. These persons undertook violence not only to secure the landlord's property but also for their own ends. However, landlords offered political protection to Mafiosi and thus nurtured a stable (long-lasting) kind of Mafia authority. Indeed, it was in the interest of these influential power brokers to favor protectors of property by allowing them to remain above criminal prosecution.

A first detailed study of the relations between landlords, aristocrats, working class people and criminals who protected the landlords' country estates was drafted by Ermanno Sangiorgi, police chief of Palermo around 1900. This followed, among other events, an 1893 scandal caused by the murder of Emanuele Notarbartolo, Mayor of Palermo (Dickie, 2005). The trial became a nation-wide affair that featured delayed proceedings and obstructions. Eventually, the person who had allegedly hired the hit-men was discharged on formal grounds. People and criminals gradually established a silent agreement as Mafiosi reasserted a monopoly of violence in "their" territory. The emergence of the Mafia thus drew on a social structure where the state had failed to exert a monopoly of violence (Franchetti, 1877).

Early scholars (Hess, 1970; Hobsbawm, 1959) described the Mafia as a cultural phenomenon. On their view, becoming a Mafioso led to being recognized as standing above the law. If somebody was known or rumored to have committed a crime that was not prosecuted (or convicted), most likely because of political contacts, the person's reputation became that of a Mafioso (Hess, 1970). However, in the 1980s, the state witness, Tommaso Buscetta, made clear that Cosa Nostra had a rich organizational structure (Dickie, 2005; Paoli, 2003). Mafiosi were not only criminals with good connections to political representatives but the mafia functioned as an organization. Specifically, individuals acted in the name of the organization and were committed to certain organizational rules. This brings home the fact that, far from acting as lone individuals, the individual is connected with the social at a mediating level of organizational life.

Cosa Nostra is a criminal organization whose history extends far beyond any individual lifetime. In the 1950s Cosa Nostra established the so-called "cupola" which co-ordinated drug trafficking between Sicilian and US-American Mafiosi. Organizational growth led to increasingly organized activities. Whereas the cupola began as a high-ranking Mafia boss committee who sought resolve clan conflicts, its authority remained precarious in that it relied on voluntary commitment. When the so-called first Mafia war (1962/1963) broke out, the cupola failed to prevent the escalation of violence. It is thought, that after an unsuccessful drug deal, the cupola's members set out to establish who was responsible. Though they cleared the prime suspect, he was nevertheless killed by rival Mafiosi. This undermined the cupola's authority (i.e., the monopoly of violence) and set off a cycle of retaliation. It took several years and eruptions of violence before Cosa Nostra was able to re-consolidate. In the 1970s an interprovincial commission set out to re-establish authority by establishing co-ordination between the different regions in Siciliy. The interprovincial commission was established at the initiative of Giuseppe Calderone who became its first secretary. However, in 1978 he was killed by rival clans and, in the 1980s, a second Mafia war broke out.

For our purposes, what this shows is that Mafioso action is subject to constant tension between organizational structure and individual interests. Arlacchi (1993) describes Cosa Nostra's intra-organizational structure as a Hobbesian society where, though organizational norms and rules of conduct exist, they are subject to constant manipulation. Although trust is precarious, organizational structure attains a degree of stability as organizational memory offers a way of re-stabilizing norms after a crisis.[2] Importantly, growth generates a need for innovation and, eventually, hierarchical organization that separates trust in persons from trust in the organization. While Mafiosi frequently distrust each other, they may nonetheless trust the organization. Next, we use the case of Bernardo Provenzano to exemplify how organizational norms function in a Hobbesian environment. We use his role as Boss from 1995 until his arrest in 2006 to illustrate how formal structure can be enacted.

14.4.1 Enaction of Organizational Norms

Provenzano went underground in 1963 and did not appear in public until his arrest in 2006. For this whole period, however, he remained an active, high-ranking member of Cosa Nostra and, in 1995, he became the Mafia's main boss. Whereas former boss, Toto Riina, had enforced authoritative leadership through aggressive and violent public display, Provenzano adopted a more democratic leadership style. Externally, he ensured that Cosa Nostra operated less violently and, by so doing, stayed in the shadows. Internally, not only did he manage the organization by setting broad guidelines but, in addition, he directed fine grained orders about, for example, how much extortion to request and how to resolve conflicts when undertaking executions (Ulreich, 2010). While living underground, he continued to act as leader. Thus, shortly before his arrest, even his lawyer asserted, as many believed, that Provenzano had long been dead. So how did he run the organization? For one thing, he innovated by communicating orders via so-called "pizzini," small pieces of paper. Only very few persons (allegedly 3) were able to collect these pieces of paper through direct contact. Their cryptic messages sometimes took the form of prosaic riddles, bible citations or other pieces of coded text. Accordingly, the British newspaper "the Sun" described him, literally, as the "codefather." This archaic communication undermined modern intelligence technology such as wiretapping while nevertheless permitting fine control of Cosa Nostra.

This brief summary reveals a number of insights: first, it is a professional organization which is characterized by formal positions which can be occupied by different persons (Blau, 1977). Toto Riina had been replaced by Bernado Provenzano. The positions are characterized by certain duties such as giving and executing commands. These positions describe a functional configuration (Mintzberg, 1979). There exists a strategic top management, as exemplified by Provenzano's strategic orientation. This is professionally implemented by a middle level management and

[2] Studies in legal companies revealed that trust is an essential component in work performance (Colquitt et al., 2012). However, these studies take the existence of the organization and roles such as supervisor and subordinate (which can be attributed to a social system) as given and investigate, e.g., the effect of justice on trust (which can be attributed to a human system). In contrast, in the covert organization the concepts of organizational memory and roles are an abstraction from enacted relationships. The concept of trust is fundamental for concepts such as roles.

the Cosa Nostra's soldiers who do the basic work. Thus to a certain degree Cosa Nostra can be described as a bureaucratic organization (Weber, 1972). Nevertheless, the covert nature of the organization requires adjustment. Rather than relying on codified rules, typical for bureaucratic organizations, this method of exerting leadership requires pre-conditions. An Italian inquisitor described Cosa Nostra as a living brain (Dickie, 2005). This calls for a comprehension of the processes of lived *realization* of organizational structure beyond an examination of the structures itself. In other terms, Cosa Nostra developed a system of distributed cognition that was needed, first, because the pizzinis had to recognized and understood as the Boss's authentic messages. Provenzano thus successfully communicated with addressees. Further, while hidden from the police, he lacked any means of ensuring that his commands had been obeyed. While he had once been known as a brutal assassin, killing disobedient subordinates had ceased to be a viable mode of conflict resolution. To kill with his bare hands became difficult if not impossible—it would compromise his incognito. Loyalty to his leadership thus had to use symbolic power based on reputation. Nevertheless, his leadership remained unquestioned. This demanded organizational structure whereby his individual actions could be concerted with those of the organization's members in order to guarantee the structure's precarious stability. Provenzano's position as boss was necessarily embedded in a web of social relations guided by rules of conduct. Indeed, the system of relations which constituted the organization of Cosa Nostra effectively reacted to triggers from and proactively manipulated the environment. For instance, the policy of reduced violence and acting in the shadows was an effective reaction to prosecution pressure in the 1990s prompted by the extreme violence exhibited during the leadership of Toto Riina. Conversely, proactive manipulation of the environment is exemplified by how Cosa Nostra conducted extortion. Further, sensitive reaction to environmental triggers and proactive manipulation of the world show the adaptive flexibility of a cognitive system. Thus the web of relations that constitute Cosa Nostra enfolds a cognitive organization whose capacity for control cannot be attributed to an individual actor. In this sense, Cosa Nostra encompasses a system of distributed cognition.

14.4.2 Socio-Cultural Embedding of the Organization

Provenzano's leadership exemplifies how interactions enact internal norms of organizational structure. Norms regulating organizational behavior operate in a slower time scale than spontaneous interaction. Further, the concerted actions that sustained Bernado Provenzano's power necessitated construal in relation to the much slower time scales that sustain organizational norms. These interactions could never have been realized without being "sedimented" in action routines. In short, the example shows how, through Provenzano, the slow time scale was realized as meaningful lived action. Next, we offer an overview of conditions in the Sicilian environment to show how the organization of Cosa Nostra is nested within a particular cultural ecosystem or, given the power of diachrony, an environment that ensures the co-evolution of culture and organization. The case of Cosa Nostra is especially apposite because, in the first place, it exemplifies co-evolutionary malfunction (see Fioretti, 2015; this volume). Second, it is striking for two reasons. On the one hand, a criminal organization operates in the shadows, hidden from state prosecution; on the other, the organization's effectiveness builds on a public reputation. Remaining covert is thus dependent on ensuring a certain level of complicity. This exemplifies the power of immergent processes, i.e. a social norm to respect the Mafia, even in the presence of criminal law. This effect shows that the time scale of the organizational norms can only be realized when it is embedded in the even slower long-term scales of a socio-cultural heritage. Extending the Neo-institutionalist emphasis of the impact of institutional setting on organizational practice (Scott, 2001; Senge, 2011), we now offer a brief summary of the discourse on its cultural characteristics. Then, with reference to the Mafia, we show how both institutions and organizations are best seen as *processes* rather than objects.

Cosa Nostra has been traced back to the early nineteenth century. However, the nesting of the organization in society drew on preconditions that have been called a culture of distrust (Gambetta, 2000; Putnam, 1993). The claim has led to much debate about differences in the economic performance and state efficiency in North and South Italy. For Putnam (1993), Southern Italy and, in particular, Sicily is characterized by "amoral familism." On this view, people seek to maximize short-term advantages of a nuclear family over civic engagement. This derives from the assumption that others will do the same. In a harsh social environment, this can be a rational survival strategy. However, familism generates an overall situation that traps people in a mutual non-cooperative equilibrium of general distrust (Gambetta, 2000). The distrust favors the cultural norm of so-called "omertà." In the first place, omertà demands silence in relation to all state authorities. However, it is also characterized by the attitude that a man is bound to defend his own honor, do justice and undertake revenge (Sterling, 1990) and, in this way, challenges the state monopoly of legitimate violence. The lack of state authority is triggered by an "iron circle of oligarchy" (Franchetti, 1877) going back to the beginning of the nineteenth century. The iron circle is characterized by short-term self-interest of a ruling southern elite who strive to secure their position of dominance by manipulating state government (Huysseune, 2003). In relation to the population, the authority of the ruling elite is secured by clientelism where followers are offered job opportunities in the state bureaucracy. Thus, state institutions become ineffective both because of incompetence and because the importance of administrative duties is subordinated to that of political arrangements. While much debated whether or not Putnam was correct to trace this to cultural circumstances (Huysseune, 2003), there is no doubt that culture exerts a major influence. Indeed, Putnam refers back to the absolute monarchy of Frederick II in the thirteenth century. In response, critics argue that Italian unification (1860/1861) was a more powerful influence. Referring to Tocqueville, Gambetta (2000) prefers to trace the origins of this cultural heritage to the sixteenth century Spanish occupation when the conquerors used a strategy of *divide et impera* to maintain control. Sicilians were thus unable to rely on fairness or protection by the law. The unpredictability of sanctions generates uncertainty in agreements (Gambetta, 2000). In turn, relations to strangers, e.g. trading come to be secured by criminal clientelism which reinforces the norm of "omertà" and the general distrust of civic society. Gambetta (2000) illustrates this argument with the story of a coachman selling a blind horse under the protection of a Mafioso who facilitates the deal.

We now turn to the enaction of cultural heritage in the temporality of the present. The example shows how cultural background gives rise to sedimented practices that continue to shape individual preferences. While Gambetta's story goes back to the mid-nineteenth century, the following example of Rita Atria dates from 1992. The fate of the teenage girl was widely discussed even beyond Italy (Reski, 1994); indeed, the events triggered an Anti-Mafia movement and a degree of cultural change in Sicily. Rita, daughter of a Mafioso, lived in Partanna, a small town south of Palermo. Her father (a Mafioso himself) was killed by the Mafia when she was 11 and, when she was 17, her elder brother met the same fate. After this killing, Rita decided to violate the norm of omertà by cooperating with the police. This had severe consequences for the teenager because, above all, her mother valued Mafia loyalty more highly than she did her daughter. As Reski (1994) documents, she wanted to kill Rita and, recognizing her danger, the daughter arranged to be transferred to a secret place in Rome. Her police confident was Paolo Borsellino who, together with Giovanni Falcone, had been the main instigator of state prosecution of the Mafia in the 1980s. At that time, Falcone had already been assassinated. Soon after Rita came to Rome, Borsellino was also killed by the Mafia; alone and in despair, she committed suicide. Her funeral became an Anti-Mafia demonstration for activists across Sicily who celebrated her as a heroine in the fight against organized crime. However, in Partanna nobody seemed to know her; her mother did not attend the funeral and a few weeks later she even destroyed her grave (Reski, 1994). In this example, the norm of omertà shaped concrete action of a kind that embeds criminal organization in society. Specifically, remaining silent in relation to state representatives (given familism loyalty is owed only to close social contacts) meets a criminal organization's need to operate covertly. The case brings home how social and organizational norms are able to co-function. Destroying a daughter's grave is a symbolic way of showing loyalty to the Mafia; it shows the long-term scale of cultural norms. Even if motivated by self-protection, the case enacts Sicilian history. A background of norms permeates individual decision-making and action. The tragic events of Rita's life both show and reinforce historically derived norms: in individual lives, slow scales can be realized in the fast. Note that like the realization of organizational structures (as described at the example of Provenzano) this concrete realization of the institutional setting (such the act of destroying a grave) must be described as a process.

14.5 Lessons for Modeling

We began by outlining a new direction for cognitive science. Next, using the case of Cosa Nostra, we showed that cognition extends beyond brain-bound cognitive processes as it draws on the norms of a socio-cognitive domain. Human actors depend on a diachronic entanglement of time scales. In contrast to the classic view that actions in the fast time scales of autonomous agents shape emergent properties and slow events, a socio-cognitive science will *also* bring into account how the slow impacts on the fast. Moreover, organizational and cultural time scales vary with regard to the dynamics of change. The next section will demonstrate that agent-based modeling (ABM) provides a basis for developing models that meet such challenges.

The basic principle of ABM is that multiple autonomous software entities—agents—interact with each other in an environment according to a given set of internal rules. Because the rules are internal and not determined by a global system supervisor they are deemed "autonomous." During simulation, agents generate new states of the overall system. Such models have usually been used to simulate how macro-social phenomena can be generated by the interaction of autonomous individuals. These show that relatively simple micro level properties can generate social macro level complexity (Epstein, 2006; Squazzoni, 2012) that characterizes complex configurations of actors engaged in overlapping and interlocking patterns of relationships (Martinás, Matika, & Srbljinović, 2012). The key insight is characterized by the catchword of *emergence*. While a scientific definition of this term as an explanatory principle in social complexity research is an ambitious task (Neumann, 2006; Sawyer, 2005), emergence characterizes an explanation from the micro to the macro, i.e. how interaction of autonomous agents generate a social phenomenon. On this view, autonomous agents are basic, the explanans, whereas the result of interaction is the explanandum. The direction of flow from fast to slow time scales is in line with classic cognitive science: Individual short-term preferences generate stable macro patterns on the social level. However, in recent work in computational social science, increasing attention has been given to the agent's complexity. New emphasis falls on the fact that computational representation of social processes calls for modeling that can show not only micro to the macro but its recursive workings. This process is characterized as *immergence* (Conte et al., 2014). Immergent processes can be defined as those where information flows from the social domain and back to the mind of the actor. This calls for cognitively complex agents. This view of agent-based modeling provides a repository of potential mechanisms that enable the slow to influence the fast. Thus the ABM approach offers an interdisciplinary view of the interlacing of structures across time. A key insight in dissecting diachronic cognition is that agent-based modeling allows software objects to be embedded in each other. In a future socio-cognitive science, models can use an architecture whereby a cultural ecosystem (e.g., a cockpit, Sicilian society or a family) specifies mechanisms whereby slow organizational processes give rise to (and are transformed by) changing medium and fast scale activity by embedded agents. Following Cohen (1961) the style of modeling that we apply is thus "analytic": Cohen describes the purpose of analytic models as being that of capturing (unknown) mechanisms that give rise to the behavior of a known phenomenon. We aim to identify potential mechanisms which give rise to diachronic cognition, namely how the systemic properties of an organization in a cultural ecosystem can be enacted in the temporality of the present.

14.5.1 Intra-Agent Processes: A Computational Socio-Cognitive Theory of Social Agency

Cognitive complexity needs to be represented in intra-agent processes. Accordingly, Fig. 14.1 offers a view of how culturally entrenched social agents can be represented in ABM. This highly abstract representation provides an overview of the system. Using Cosa Nostra, it shows how individual action in the temporality of the present draws on diachronic cognition. In the model, individual preferences express self-interest, as well as organizational and social norms: As for the precarious authority of the cupola and the breakdown of its monopoly of violence in Cosa Nostra organization, Mafiosi constantly balance self-interest with obedience to organizational norms. This is Arlacchi's (1993) Hobbesian society. However, self-interested action is also directed as organizational preconditions shape meaningful action. Thus, as shown by the riddles, bible citations and indirect hints in pizzini that characterize Provenzano's leadership, actions that demand an impersonal code of conduct where sense is ascribed to carefully concerted action. However, this style of enacting organizational structure depends on the *omertà* of a particular cultural ecosystem. The norm's power to influence individual preferences appears in the example of a mother who destroys her daughter's grave. In Fig. 14.1, therefore, cognition falls into three packages. Individual preferences represent the rapid scale of personal desires studied by cognitive science and social-psychology. The package of intra-organizational norms shows a life-cycle of organizational behavior that is independent of actors who, in real time, enact the organization's structures. The domain is, of course, the focus of organizational theories. The package of social norms represents slow historical scales of evolution traced in, for example, theories of cultural memory. The small squares in these packages represent concrete tags to be explained later. The dashed lines between the packages represent a flow of information that regulates how the parameters of each package dispose the others. Far from using causal relations, culturally embedded actors exploit slower socio-cultural time scales (Steiner & Stewart, 2009) as constraints. In terms of a socio-cognitive science, the faster time scales are both constrained by and enabled by the slower. For reasons of simplification we concentrate on the direction from the slow to the fast. For current purposes no weight is given to the reverse flow from, e.g. organizational to social norms. This is indicated by the light dotted lines. For instance, organizational norms, e.g. in investment banks can impact on the whole society by changing, say, a social culture of collective solidarity represented by the welfare state into one that welcomes neo-liberal individualism.

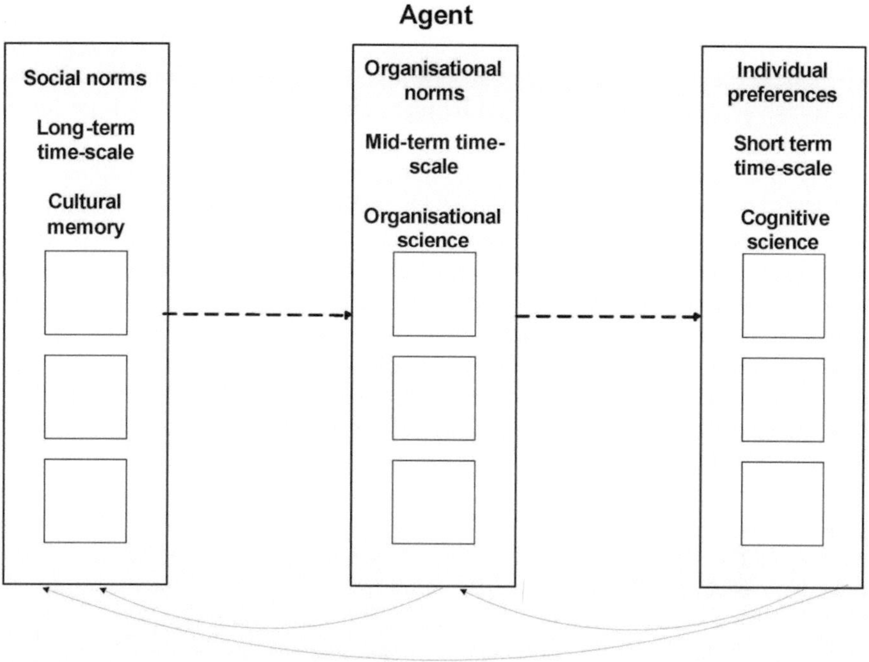

Fig. 14.1 Integration of diverse time scales

While Fig. 14.1 shows the architecture of a culturally entrenched social agent, Fig. 14.2 zooms into details of the agents' decision process. As in classic Belief, Decision, Intention (BDI) architectures, decisions are triggered by desires. However, if cognition is diachronic, it is necessary to rethink how entrenched social agents act to self-configure their desires. Far from being created from scratch, desires self-differentiate as individual preferences draw on social and organizational norms; they arise as an agent's actual actions are constrained-and-enabled in the time scales of impersonal processes. The classic element of individual preferences represents individual contingencies such as a preference for chocolate. The other elements of social and organizational norms explicitly represent how individual desires are self-configured as a result of interactions in a socio-cultural environment. For example, certain agents might desire intensely to preserve honor. While being an individual preference, this desire is conditioned by (and partly results from) the socio-cultural environment. Representation of multi-layered desires can be realized by applying central concepts of a tag based modeling approach (Holland, 1993; Shutters & Hales, 2013). In so doing, desires are represented here as tags or features that are attached to agents. These are observable by other agents and can thus represent social cues in interactions. They resemble "flags" or banners that mark social attitudes such as identities or belonging to a certain social group. Computational models represent these in an abstract manner as, for example, bit strings—a tag may look like {00} or {01}. Without having any direct implication for behavior, as indicators, they can be perceived by other agents. Interaction can thus be restricted to options arising in encountering agents with compatible tags. In the graphic the multi-layered desires are represented by tags of various kinds that indicate social and organizational norms and personal preferences. Crucially, in contrast to classical models of normative agents, impersonal norms immerge into the desire components. In contrast to obligation or permission which might be executed in order to conform to norms by, say, preserving personal honor, in this model it generates personal satisfaction. It functions as a self-determined action (Deci & Ryan, 2000). This is but one example how the space of possible actions and preferences is shaped by embedding in a social environment.

In zooming further into the desires component, Fig. 14.3 illustrates internal organization. As in Fig. 14.1, this incorporates information flow from longer time scales to faster ones. The information provides constraints from enduring time scales that set options on faster time scales. Organizational norms need to be compatible with the background of social norms just as individual desires need to be compatible with the frame of organizational norms. For instance, the norm of *omertà*, entrenched on a long-term time scale of socio-cultural norms, specifies a possible option for enaction of organizational norms like silent transfer of Provenzano's pizzini. In turn, organizational norms provide a maneuvering space for individual desires that holds when, and only when, an individual represents the organization. Although people act in different roles, it would cause cognitive dissonance if, for instance an investment banker participated in the Attack movement (or some anti-capitalistic social movement) and returned to his office the next day or, indeed, if a Mafioso participated in Anti-Mafia movements during leisure time. While the pentiti (i.e., principal witnesses) show that people can quit such an organization, this is a break with a former life (and roles). All these elements go into specification of the

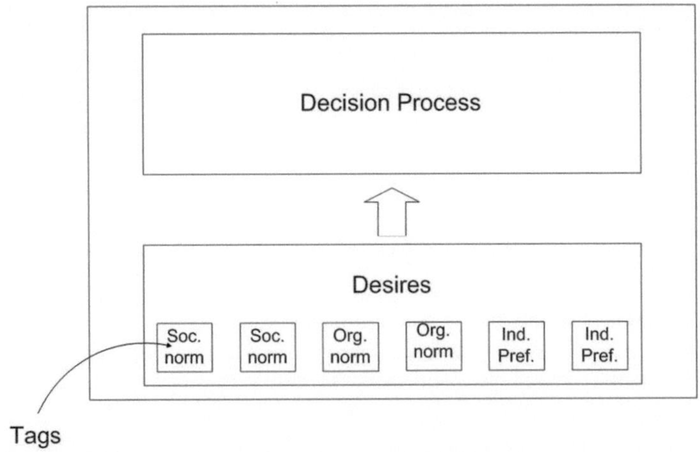

Fig. 14.2 The decision process of social agents

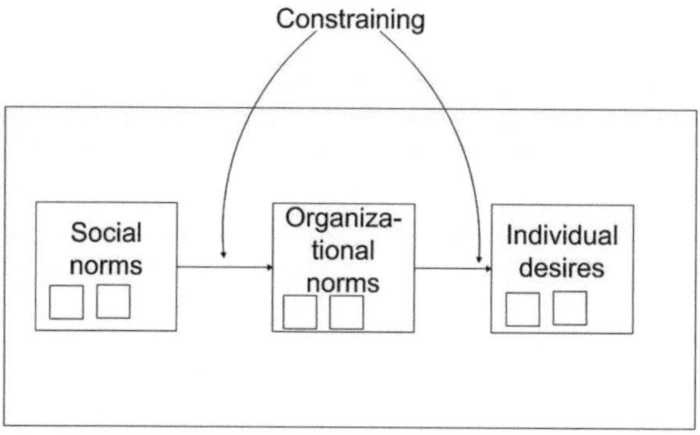

Fig. 14.3 The complexity of the desires of social agents

individual desires that frame the decision process for real-time action. Crucially, different time-scales are enacted in real-time.

A computational realization of how social constraints are incorporated can draw on the example of Xenitidou, Emde, Villard, Lotzmann, and Troitzsch (2014). This involves a number of characters, representing tags. The characters can be, for instance, instantiations of special characters such as #, *, $, etc., as well as alphabetical characters, such as A, B, C, etc., or number such as 2, 8, etc. Thus they are characters of different kind. This can then provide the basis for a grammar for rules. The scheme of social and organizational norms and individual desires could then have a form such as:

$$\{\#, \mathrm{A}, 3, \mathrm{T}\} \rightarrow \{\mathrm{X}, \$, 5\} \rightarrow \{7, *, \mathrm{Z}\}$$

In this example the first box represents social norms, the second, organizational norms and the third, individual preferences. The grammar is a constraint that the type of characters with which a box ends can determine the type of character with which the next box needs to start. In other words, a letter has to follow a letter, a number has to follow number, and a special character has to follow a special character. In this example, the T, as the last character of the social norms box determines that the box for organizational norms has to start with an alphabetic character, in this case realized by the X. This grammar for rules to determine the sequences of characters can be interpreted as representing the various constraints. For instance, the letters might stand for traditional norms (e.g., *omertà*), and numbers for physical action. In case of the mother destroying the grave of her daughter, Rita Atria, the T might stand for the demand to banish her daughter. A demand for symbolic physical action, represented, for instance, by the number 5, might be executed by 7, representing the action of destroying the grave.

14.5.2 Inter-Agent Processes: Diachronic Co-evolution

The next question to address us is that of how impersonal tags become incorporated into the agent. Since this depends on inter-agent processes, their design is essential to the co-evolution of a distributed cognitive system. The spread of tags in a population can be pictures as like to infection processes or fashion. Applying a tag based modeling approach leads to co-evolution of the multi-agent system. In fact, tags are a robust concept in evolutionary modeling (Edmonds, 2006; Shutters & Hales, 2013) and have been used to model various evolutionary processes (Edmonds, 2006; Edmonds & Hales, 2005; Hales, 2008; Holland, 1993; Riolo, 1997). Evolution is typically realized by differential reproduction of agents with more or less successful tags. Figure 14.4 illustrates how this concept is utilized for modeling distributed cognition in diachronic systems.

Whereas the large circle represents the environment, e.g. Palermo or Sicily, the small one shows the organization of Cosa Nostra as it operates in the environment. The big squares represent agents, the small, grey ones tags. Obviously, the representation is merely schematic. More importantly, recruitment of new members of the organization depends on the degree of fit between the tags of a potential new member and those favored by the organization. However, social evolution is not viewed as in classic tag models. In this setting, the objective is to model how agents adopt tags in a socio-cultural environment. Thus, agents do not die and reproduce differentially as in classical tag models. Rather, the incorporation of new tags by agents can be compared to epidemic processes or fashion. Agents adopt new tags if

Fig. 14.4 Schematic representation of the concept for modeling inter-agent processes

they repeatedly come into contact with other agents that possess compatible tags. If these agents continuously possess a further tag that an agent lacks, it may adopt this tag. Likewise it may abandon tags if these never appear in social contacts with other agents with a compatible tag set. In consequence, different tags spread differently across in the agent population. Thus tags serve as objects on their own or, in other terms, reproduce in the fertile environment. Continuing the infection analogy, while tags do not themselves act, they are legitimately seen as utilizing agents' as a medium for executing action. On the one hand, this represents cognitive complexity. On the other hand, the distributed aspect of cognition is represented by the reproduction of tags in social contacts between agents which provide a compatible tag set.

A framework of inter-agent processes serves to represent the co-evolution of social and organizational norms. For instance, whereas *omertà* can be represented by one tag, another (incompatible) tag might represent a norm to cooperate with state authorities. Spreading of the norm of *omertà* might have the effect of generating agents whose tags were compatible with both recruitment to a secret organization and allowing the secret organization to endure. This normative setting fosters enaction of the organizational structure in the absence of law by a formally representing a system of distributed cognition. Representation in a computational model thus provides a means to investigate diverging time scales experimentally with reference to how tags spread in the agent population. It becomes possible to examine how tags representing social norms foster the spread of tags, representing organizational norms. This generates a multi-layered co-evolution of socio-cultural norms. The different time scales in which tags spread in the cultural ecosystem and within the organization provides a measure of change. The manner in which slow time scales of spreading of tags in the society constraints internal change of the tag set in the organization provides a mechanism of diachronic cognition.

14.6 Outlook: Modeling Diachronic Cognition

The paper's contribution can be summarized around three main headings. First, it offers a new theoretical view of diachronic cognition. Second, it offers methodological insights for the design of agent-based simulation. And, third, it has practical implications for organization studies.

1. Theoretically the paper presents a view of diachronic cognition. The concept is clarified by empirical analysis of action and decision making in Cosa Nostra, an organization that is nested in the social environment of Sicilian culture. The analysis reveals a type of social agency, in which individual decision making is both enabled and constrained by social and organizational norms. The model of intra-agent processes demonstrates a mechanism whereby the impersonal impacts on the individual agent's decision making. In diachronic cognition different layers of historical contingency are enacted in the temporality

of the present. The model of inter-agent processes helps explicate the nature of different time scales: specifically, these represent how the dynamics of change become interlaced and how this leads to differing effects. The model specifies mechanisms of the dynamics of change by the dynamics of the spreading of tags. This mechanism allows for assessment of differences between time scales by comparing differences in the dynamics of tag change.

2. The methodological conclusion to be drawn from an architecture used in modeling actors in the world of the Mafia is that there is a need to represent cognitive complexity. This demands (at least) two dimensions: on the one hand, the agent's decision making and desires demand intra-agent complexity. However, in contrast to classic BDI models of autonomous agents, we focus on how the impersonal impacts on individual desires. Whereas a classic BDI account makes desires and intentions private properties that serve to preserve agent autonomy, our model allows for (partial) *immergence* of desires. Desires, wishes, and motivations draw, in part, on impersonal socio-cultural and organization norms and values. Rather than posit only that interaction of autonomous agents generates macro-phenomena, we thus emphasize how slow scales impact on the fast. This framework allows social agency to arise when agents live in—and as part of—the social world. Further, agent complexity demands that the cognitive system be allowed to spread beyond the individual agent. Decision making uses processes that are distributed among agents: it arises in acting on an environment while reacting to its triggers. By defining a cognitive system as the unit which drives decision-making, it extends beyond the agent. Admittedly, our inter-agent processes are merely rudimentary in that they leave aside how, in the first instance, the impersonal comes into being. That remains a question for the future; however, the simple model allows impersonal elements to be incorporated in the individual agents and thus affect intra-agent processes.
3. Lessons for studying organizational behavior can be drawn from considering how slow socio-cultural environment constrains mid-term organizational time scales. In the model of inter-agent processes the dynamics that spread change in the structure of a set of tags within the organization is constrained by the shape of the tag set in the whole environment. This provides insights for change management in the study of organizational behavior. Whereas the model focuses on endogenous change, it also provides a framework for investigating conditions for success and failure of externally induced change.

References

Arlacchi, P. (1993). *Mafia von innen – Das Leben des Don Antonino Calderone*. Frankfurt a.M.: S. Fischer Verlag.

Blau, P. (1977). A macrosociological theory of social structure. *American Journal of Sociology, 83*(1), 26–54.

Chemero, A. (2009). *Radical embodied cognitive science*. Cambridge, MA: MIT Press.

Cohen, K. J. (1961). Two approaches to computer simulation. *The Journal of the Academy of Management, 4*(1), 43–49.
Conte, R., Andrighetto, G., & Campennì, M. (2014). *Minding norms. Mechanisms and dynamics of social order in agent societies*. Oxford: Oxford University Press.
Colquitt, J., LePine, J., Piccolo, R. & Zapata, C. (2012). Explaining the Justice-Performance Relationship: Trust as Exchange Deepener or Trust as Uncertainty Reducer? *Journal of Applied Psychology, 97*(1), 1–15.
Cowley, S. J. (2014). The integration problem: Interlacing language, action and perception. *Cybernetics and Human Knowing, 21*(1-2), 53–65.
Cummins, F. (2003). Practice and performance in speech produced synchronously. *Journal of Phonetics, 31*(2), 139–148.
Damerow, P. (1988). Individual development and cultural evolution of arithmetical thinking. In S. Strauss (Ed.), *Ontogeny, phylogeny, and historical development* (pp. 125–152). Norwood, NJ: Ablex Publication Corp.
Damerow, P. (2007). The material culture of calculation: A theoretical framework for a historical epistemology of the concept of number. In U. Gellert & E. Jablonka (Eds.), *Mathematisation and demathematisation: Social, philosophical and educational ramifications* (pp. 19–56). Rotterdam: Sense Publication.
Deci, E., & Ryan, R. (2000). The "What" and "Why" of goal pursuits: Human needs and the self-determination of behavior. *Psychological Inquiry, 11*(4), 227–268.
Dickie, J. (2005). *Cosa Nostra. Die Geschichte der Mafia*. Frankfurt a.M.: Fischer.
Dickie, J. (2011). *Mafia brotherhoods. Camorra, mafia, 'ndranghetta: The rise of the honoured societies*. London: Sceptre.
Edmonds, B. (2006). The emergence of symbiotic groups resulting from skill-differentiation and tags. *JASSS, 9*(1). http://jasss.soc.surrey.ac.uk/9/1/10.html.
Edmonds, B., & Hales, D. (2005). Applying a socially inspired technique (tags) to improve cooperation in P2P networks. *IEEE Transactions on Systems, Man, and Cybernetics – Part A: Systems and Humans, 25*(3), 385–395.
Epstein, J. (2006). *Generative social science. Studies in agent-based computational modeling*. Princeton: Princeton University Press.
Erickson, B. (1981). Secret societies and social structure. *Social Forces, 60*, 188–210.
Fioretti, G. (2015). Emergent organizations. In D. Secchi & M. Neumann (Eds.), *Agent-based simulation of organizational behavior: New frontiers of social science research*. New York: Springer (this volume).
Franchetti, L. (1877). *Condizioni politiche e amministrative della Sicilia*. G. Barbèra.
Gambetta, D. (2000). Mafia: The price of distrust. In D. Gambetta (Ed.), *Trust: Making and breaking cooperative relations* (pp. 158–175). Oxford: Department of Sociology, University of Oxford (electronic edition).
Hales, D. (2008). Understanding tag systems by comparing tag models. In B. Edmonds, K. G. Troitzsch, & C. Iglesias (Eds.), *Social simulation: Technologies, advances and new discoveries* (pp. 68–80). Hershey: IGI.
Hess, H. (1970). *Mafia. ZentraleHerrschaft und lokale Gegenmacht*. Tübingen: Mohr.
Hobsbawm, E. (1959). *Primitive rebels: Studies in archaic forms of social movement in the 19th and 20th centuries*. Manchester: University Press.
Hollan, J., Hutchins, E., & Kirsh, D. (2000). Distributed cognition: Toward a new foundation for human-computer interaction research. *ACM Transactions on Computer-Human Interaction (TOCHI), 7*(2), 174–196.
Holland, J. (1993). *The effect of labels (tags) on social interaction*. SFI Working Paper: 1993-10-064.
Hurley, S. (1998). *Consciousness in action*. London: Harvard University Press.
Hutchins, E. (1995a). How a cockpit remembers its speeds. *Cognitive Science, 19*(3), 265–288.
Hutchins, E. (1995b). *Cognition in the wild*. Cambridge, MA: MIT Press.
Hutchins, E. (2014). The cultural ecosystem of human cognition. *Philosophical Psychology, 27*(1), 34–49.

Huysseune, M. (2003). Institutions and their impact on social capital and civic culture: The case of Italy. In M. Hooge & D. Stolle (Eds.), *Generating social capital: Civil society and institutions in comparative perspective* (pp. 211–239). New York: Palgrave.
Kirchhoff, M. D. (2013). Extended cognition & the causal constitutive fallacy: In search for a diachronic and dynamical conception of constitution. *Philosophy and Phenomenological Research*. doi:10.1111/phpr.12039.
La Spina, A. (2005). *Mafia, legalità debole e sviluppo del Mezzogiorno*. Bologna: il Mulino.
Martinás, K., Matika, D., & Srbljinović, A. (2012). Preface. In K. Martinás, D. Matika, & A. Srbljinović (Eds.), *Complex societal dynamics security challenges and opportunities* (pp. i–xiv). Amsterdam: IOS Press.
Mintzberg, H. (1979). *The structuring of organizations*. Hemel Hempstead/Englewood Cliffs, NJ: Prentice Hall.
Neumann, M. (2006). Emergence as an explanatory principle in artificial societies. Reflections on the bottom-up approach to social theory. In F. Squazzoni (Ed.), *Epistemological aspects of computer simulation in the social sciences* (pp. 69–88). Berlin: Springer.
Neumann, M., & Cowley, S. J. (2013). Human agency and the resources of reason. In S. J. Cowley & F. Vallee-Tourangeau (Eds.), *Cognition beyond the brain* (pp. 13–30). Berlin: Springer.
Paoli, L. (2003). *Mafia brotherhoods. Organized crime, Italian style*. Oxford: Oxford University Press.
Putnam, R. (1993). *Making democracy work: Civic traditions in modern Italy*. Princeton: Princeton University Press.
Reski, P. (1994). *Rita Atria. Eine Frau gegen die Mafia*. Hamburg: Hoffmann & Campe.
Riolo, R. (1997). *The effects of tag-mediated selection of partners in evolving populations playing the iterated prisoner's dilemma*. Santa Fe Institute Working Paper, 97-02-016.
Sawyer, K. (2005). *Social emergence. Societies as complex systems*. Cambridge: Cambridge University Press.
Scaglione, A. (2011). *Reti Mafiose. Cosa Nostra e Camorra: organizzazioni criminali a confronto*. Milano: FrancoAngeli.
Scott, R. (2001). *Institutions and organizations*. Thousand Oaks: Sage.
Senge, K. (2011). *Das Neue am Neo-Institutionalismus. Der Neo-Institutionalismus im Kontext der Organizationswissenschaft*. Wiesbaden: VS-Verlag.
Shapiro, L. A. (2011). *Embodied cognition*. London: Routledge.
Shutters, S., & Hales, D. (2013). Tag-mediated altruism is contingent on how cheaters are defined. *JASSS, 16*(1). http://jasss.soc.surrey.ac.uk/16/1/4.html.
Simmel, G. (1908). Das Geheimnis und die geheime Gesellschaft. In G. Simmel (Ed.), *Soziologie. Untersuchungen über die Formen der Vergesellschaftung* (pp. 256–304). Leipzig: Duncker& Humblot.
Squazzoni, F. (2012). *Agent-based computational sociology*. Chichester: Wiley.
Steffensen, S. V., & Fill, A. (2014). Ecolinguistics: The state of the art and future horizons. *Language Sciences, 41*, 6–25.
Steiner, P., & Stewart, J. (2009). From autonomy to heteronomy (and back). The enaction of social life. *Phenomenology and Cognitive Science, 8*, 527–550. doi:10.1007/s11097-009-9139-1.
Sterling, C. (1990). *Die Mafia. Der Griff nach der Macht*. Bern: Octopus.
Thibault, P. J. (2011). First-order languaging dynamics and second-order language: The distributed language view. *Ecological Psychology, 23*(3), 210–245.
Ulreich, S. (2010). Der Pate und die Pizzini. Sueddeutsche Zeitung 19. Marz 2010. http://www.sueddeutsche.de/panorama/mafia-prozess-der-pate-und-die-pizzini-1.920864. Accessed 6 Jan 2014.
Weber, M. (1972). *Wirtschaft und Gesellschaft*. Tübingen: Mohr.
Xenitidou, M., Emde, R., Villard, J., Lotzmann, U., & Troitzsch, K. G. (2014). Demonstrating the theory: The case of Wikipedia. In M. Campennì, R. Conte, & G. Andrighetto (Eds.), *Minding norms. Mechanisms and dynamics of social order in agent societies* (pp. 127–152). New York: Oxford University Press.

Chapter 15
Water Controversies Between Conflict and Cooperation: Agent-Based Models for Non-traditional Security

Stefania Paladini

Abstract In the last decade, a lot of attention has been increasingly devoted to ABMs (Agent-Based Models), facilitated also by the availability of computational power and open-source platforms. ABMs are thus becoming especially popular in social and political sciences for modelling complex situations with multiple actors that can evolve in highly unpredictable scenarios, due to a series of endogenous and exogenous variables often difficult to identify and even less to measure and predict. Conflicts and wars often qualify as ones. The aim of the present paper is to apply ABMs to analyse the complex issues arising from dam development on the Mekong River and the endless controversies this development has provoked since the 1960s, making it one of the most pressing non-traditional security issues in the region. It will preliminary examine the challenges of implementing ABMs to complex real-world situation like the ones into exam and which preliminary steps and theoretical considerations are necessary before the formulation of a definitive model. Finally, it will provide indications the state of the work in progress on the model created for this case-study, a few preliminary conclusions about its effectiveness, and some notes for future development.

Keywords Water security • River management • Shared resources • Non-traditional security • Mekong River

15.1 ABM in Social Sciences and Conflict Studies

In the last decade ABMs (Agent-Based Models) have become increasingly popular and their application has spread to virtually all natural and social sciences, facilitated also by the availability of computational power and open-source platforms.

S. Paladini (✉)
University of Coventry, Coventry, UK
e-mail: Stefania.Paladini@coventry.ac.uk

D. Secchi, M. Neumann (eds.), *Agent-Based Simulation of Organizational Behavior*, DOI 10.1007/978-3-319-18153-0_15

ABMs are now considered as "a third way of doing science, and could augment traditional deductive and inductive reasoning as discovery methods." (Axelrod, 1997; North & Macal, 2007), constituting the tool of choice for some economics and finance applications, such as firms' behaviour and stock markets (Tesfatsion, 2003).

ABMs are also well represented in social and political sciences for modelling complex situations with multiple actors that can evolve in highly unpredictable scenarios, due to a series of endogenous and exogenous variables often difficult to identify and even less to measure and predict. This is what security studies are essentially about, and conflicts and wars especially qualify as ones: this is why ABM can be a good approach. Therefore it's not surprising that this area of research has seen a series of studies addressing particular aspects of it (Epstein, 2002; Kustov, 2012; Yilmaz, Oren, & Ghasem-Aghaee, 2006).

The literature also shows that ABMs present a series of advantages for social sciences compared to other, more traditional approaches (Hassani-Mahmooei & Parris, 2012). For the present study, the most important one is the fact that ABMs successfully address the shortcoming of unrealistic approaches such as the perfect rationality of the agents (Axtell, Axelrod, Epstein, & Cohen, 1995), explain adaptive behaviours where the past is not necessarily predictive of the future (Axtell, 2000) and model with the necessary flexibility the relation environment–humans (Li & Liu, 2008). In this article the author has decided to apply agent-based modelling analysis to a well-known case in the non-traditional security issue contest, the area of water conflicts, one of the more relevant issues in environmental security.

Environmental security has attracted in the last two decades a lot of attention in the academic literature even if, historically, it has been one of the first to be identified as a non-traditional security issue (Buzan & Wæver, 2003; Deudney & Matthew, 1999), and as such well documented in the environmental geopolitical literature (Elliot, 2002). There are plenty of studies that clearly show the way environmental aspects might affect international relations, and they usually deal not only with the obvious economic side effects but also with new, recent threats.

A series of alternative paradigms can be identified in international relations on this regard, and they are here briefly recalled for clarity. The dominant one, generally called *environmental security studies*, specifically addresses environment as a source, direct or indirect, of acute conflicts. Scarcity is here regarded as the fundamental problem, together with the related aspect of the access to resources. Evidence suggests that it leads to conflicts, but in a nonlinear and at times tortuous way (Gleditsch, Wallensteen, Eriksson, Sollenberg, & Strand, 2002). Linkage of environmental concerns with fights on the territory exists (Klare, 2001), and competition and control over critical natural resources will be the guiding principles behind the use of military force in the twenty-first century. Kaplan (2000) also suggested a sort of Malthusian theory, linking the causes of conflicts with general resource shortages, and so does the Toronto School, with Homer–Dixon as team leader. The main thesis of Homer-Dixon focuses on the structural incapability of the state to manage environmental scarcity (1994, 2000).

There are, however, alternative approaches, that collectively go under the term of *critical environmental security studies*, represented, for instance, by Deudney, Dalby, Elliott, which follow the definition of Krause and Williams in 1997. In all of them, environmental security consists of two key elements, the first one being the relationship between environmental degradation and conflict (traditional security concern) and the second one represented by the relationship between environmental problems and social welfare (non-traditional area of concern).

Both involve the allocation of shared resources—potential causes of conflicts—the capacity of managing threats—crucial in this case the role of NGOs—and the increasing economic cost of environmental degradation, that could harm the growth of poor countries. More appropriate referents of security are the biosphere and the individual, together linked by the concept of human security (Dalby, 2002).

In this study, while both have been taken into consideration, the preference goes to the second paradigm, given the importance of environmental degradation of the Mekong Basin, analysed in the following sections, for the security of communities living in the area first and on the whole more in general.

Another distinction needs to be done taking into consideration more specifically the resource under contention. Non-renewable resources (essentially oil and minerals) have a quite specific character and propensity to fuel conflicts (Le Billon, 2001). Disputes on strategic, but renewable resources, such as freshwater, wood, arable land and fisheries, on the other hand, are in general less prone to violent confrontation (Theisen, 2008). And yet, water represents a special case nonetheless, and this is the reason why it has singled out for specific analysis in the next section.

15.2 Water as Object of Security: The Case of Mekong Dams

Water as object of security is nothing new, and there is a consolidated doctrine in international relations, regarding it as a threat in a traditional, military-oriented way, as well as a long and highly informative history of conflicts and tensions over water resources, the use of water systems as weapons during wars, and the targeting of water systems during conflicts caused by other factors. However, it has to be recognised that water resources have rarely been the sole source of violent conflicts (Eriksson, Wallensteen, & Sollenberg, 2003). In some cases, what have been defined (Yoffe & Wolf, 1999) as "water wars" were in fact some kind of conflict over something else. However, even if water is, per se, not a major cause of conflicts, nevertheless the lack of good political relations and sustainable economic development could undermine the security of a region. The existing literature on water disputes has generally related the likelihood of conflict to the perception of the value of the resources in contention (Diehl, 1991); the more vital the resource, the more likely the conflict. In approximately 260 different river systems existing worldwide, there have been quite a lot of conflicts crossing national boundaries and becoming regional security issues. Gleick (1993, 1998, 2008) has listed many possibilities of water-related conflicts, and among them:

- State and non-state parties fighting over water supplies or access to water supplies (control dispute).
- Nations' use of water resources or water systems as a weapon during a military action (military tool). It is important here to notice that water-ways can also be used as tools of war, i.e., water can be used as a delivery vehicle to carry destructive agents, throughout the ecosystem, to human and animal populations, where destructive agents can equally include microbiological agents (bioterrorism) or toxic chemicals.
- State and non-state parties' use of water resources or water systems for political goals (political tool).
- Non-state parties' use of water resources or water systems as a target or tool for violence or coercion (terrorism).
- Nations' use of water systems as a target for military action (military target).
- State and non-state disputes over water resources or water systems in the context of economic development (development disputes).
- Military and terrorist actions, which can target critical infrastructures and that are now of particular concern to security experts and those who are responsible for managing water resources and water systems.

Looking now specifically to Asia, the most extensive inhabited continent and area of large basins, as well as the region with some of the zones most densely populated in the world, it's not surprising that renewable resources represent a critical issue. Water stress has been long identified as one of the continent's most serious problems. Asia has the world's lowest per capita availability of freshwater, reflecting both natural and complex socio-political causes (Smith & Gross, 2003). In some cases, stress has become scarcity, leading to conflicts of different gravity over water. For this article, a specific case-study has been selected for analysis and it is related to dams development on the Mekong River.

There are two reasons why this specific case has been singled out for investigation here.

The first one is related to the endless controversies dam constructions have provoked since the 1960s, making it one of the most pressing non-traditional security issues in the region and a threat to the environment and the ethnic minorities of the riparian countries (Goh, 2001; Paladini, 2006). As a matter of fact, the Mekong Basin summarises all environmental problems, not only of the riparian countries but also of the whole region—a telling story about the unintended effects of industrial development in terms of water pollution, depletion of fisheries, and deterioration of the territory. The impressive dam programme has moreover created issues at all levels, including for trans-boundary security in the region.

Second, it represents one of the most significant regional case studies over shared resources. It's easy to see why—given the time span the controversies have been going on (half a century by now), the importance of the river (12th in the world and 7th in Asia) and its relevance for the livelihood of the riparian states. Therefore it constitutes a good example of the way a single issue can be relevant for different aspects of security—environmental, human, economic—making its analysis and its management especially challenging (Emmers, 2004). Moreover, its case differs from other of the same kind—distinct from example from the Colorado river and the disputes between Singapore and Malaysia on water supply contracts.

It is not possible here to provide more than a brief summary of the Mekong long and tormented history, for reasons of space. Some references have been provided at this purpose. Here it is just important to mention a few points. Dams on Mekong began in the 1960s, after the establishment in 1957 of the first trans-boundary control body, the Mekong Committee, with the aim at "promoting, coordinating, supervising and controlling the planning and investigation of water resources development projects in the Lower Mekong Basin." Among the projects completed in this period, the ones on the Mekong tributaries in Northeast Thailand and, in 1968, the big Nam Ngum Dam, which was the first one to be completed in Laos. The agreement was to sell power to Thai Egat, the Electricity Generating Authority of Thailand, according to a pattern that will be replicated in the near future, like the huge Xayaburi Dam currently in construction in Northern Laos,[1] and already highly controversial. Further on, the determination of Thailand—pushed by internal NGOs-driven opposition to dams—to search for energy beyond its borders, and the exclusion of some countries led to a disintegration of Mekong Committee in 1978, which was replaced in 1995 by the Mekong River Commission (MRC). Apart a decade's stop due to the Vietnam War, the dam development continued unabated all along. In April 2004, the Mekong River Commission formulated a four-nation strategy and programme for the development of navigation on the Lower Mekong. The programme, endorsed by the MRC member states of Cambodia, Lao PDR, Thailand and Vietnam, was consisting of five components, covering socio-economic planning, establishment of a legal and operational framework, enhancement of human and environmental safety, regional coordination of information, and institutional development. The programme was also supported by the regional integration initiatives being promoted by the Association of Southeast Asian Nations (ASEAN) and by the Asian Development Bank with its GMS Programme (more importantly including China among its members, which is not the case with the MRC). Nevertheless, this kind of initiatives has not radically changed the general trend yet, and the countries have been going on unilaterally as before, contributing to intricate the knots even more. An example is provided, in the case of Thailand, by one of the most controversial dam projects ever planned for the Mekong River, Pak Mun Dam, which has created huge environmental problems.

[1] http://www.internationalrivers.org/campaigns/xayaburi-dam.

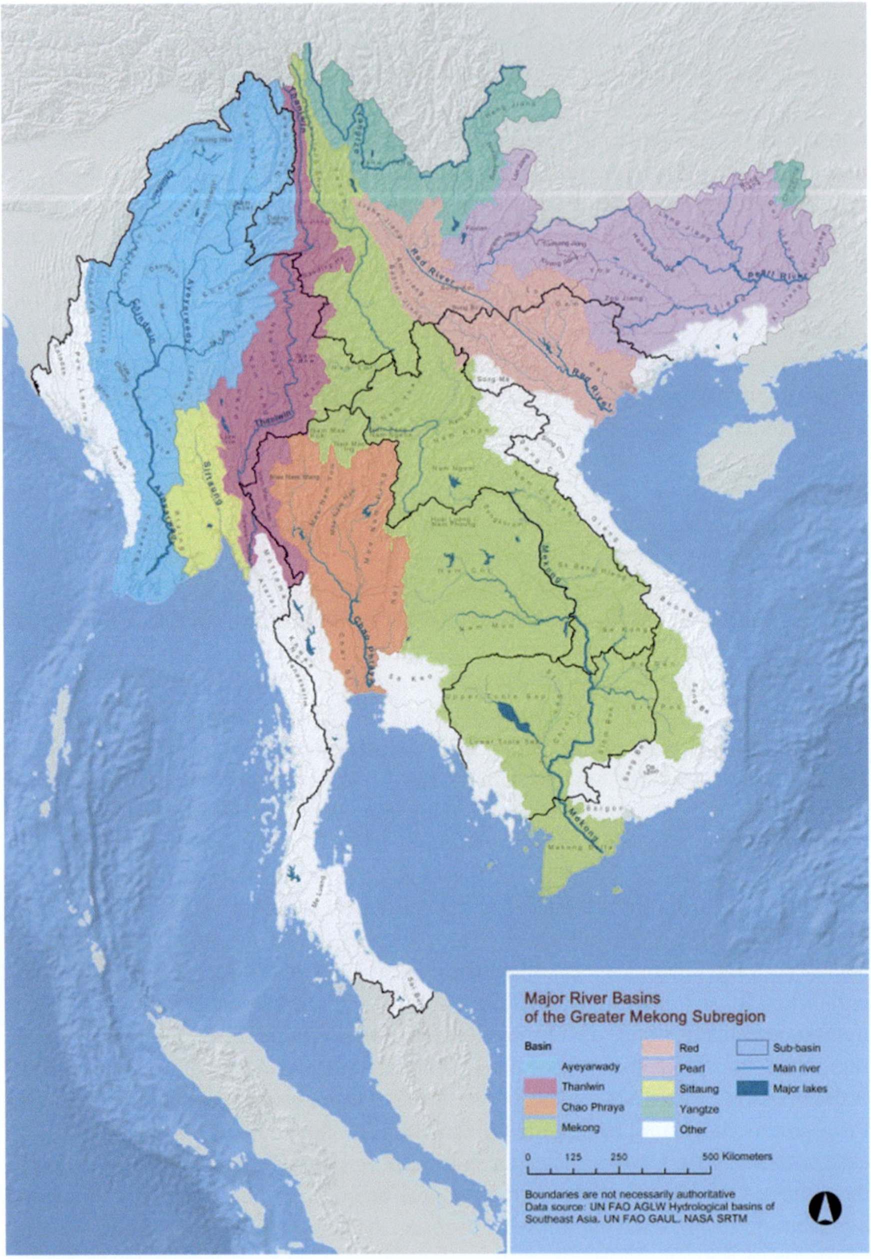

The second reason for the choice of the Mekong basin as area of analysis is instead related to the interest such a complex situation can present for an ABM perspective, and the unique suitability of ABM application to these specific areas of studies.

Conflict study is a discipline constantly in evolution, often borrowing and adapting tools from a series of different disciplines. ABM is a relatively new field of analysis in this context, and very promising indeed, as the following sections will try to illustrate.

15.3 The Model

There are at least two ways in which an ABM can be usefully adopted in international relation and conflict studies in general, and in the specific case of the Mekong River conundrum, and fare comparatively better than other methods.

First of all, in terms of interpretation: a model adopting an agent-based approach can help identify the most critical aspects in this complex issue, often related but not always directly interacting among themselves. That is, the modelling and simulation results can shed light on the social and political dynamics. But its usefulness is not limited to the analytics.

ABMs are far more than just technological tools to use computer to simulate reality and they can identify characters and properties from collective behaviours (Ferber, 1999)—otherwise defined as emerging behaviours. These kinds of behaviours represent a typical activity in complex systems modelling (Bar-Yam, 1997) and agent-based models are the best tools for analysing complex systems like the Mekong Basin (Hassas, Serugendo, & Phan, 2007). This predictive facet is what rates ABM comparatively better than other methods, especially some of more traditional quantitative approaches, such as vulnerability indices (Briguglio et al., 1999; Paladini, 2012) and multivariate statistics (Chander, 1996) which are deemed effective for their interpretation but not equally suited for prediction.

Going into more technical details in terms of feasibility, there are a series of additional reasons that make ABMs suitable to represent complex situations like conflicts on renewable resources. Based on a checklist from Macal and North (2005), a series of parameters has been identified as a benchmark and this specific model has been checked against it. The results have been fully satisfactory, and they are here summarised for reason of space. In synthesis, agents in the Mekong River Basin act on decisions and present behaviours that can be defined discretely, with possibility to adapt and change when necessity arises, and to learn through dynamic strategic relationships with other agents. The fact that this interaction has a clear spatial component—the Mekong Basin—adds an additional interest in the use of the model. Also, ABMs seem particularly apt in situations where the past is no predictor of the future—like the last 50 years of the Mekong River management prove quite effectively. In order to construct a suitable model to be used in this case, an ABM iterative approach already experimented in social science and ecology will be used here, since many of the issues considered there are similar. Also, environment represents here, as in Grimm and Railsback (2005), one of the key factors.

(The Modelling Cycle, Volker and Railsback, 2005)

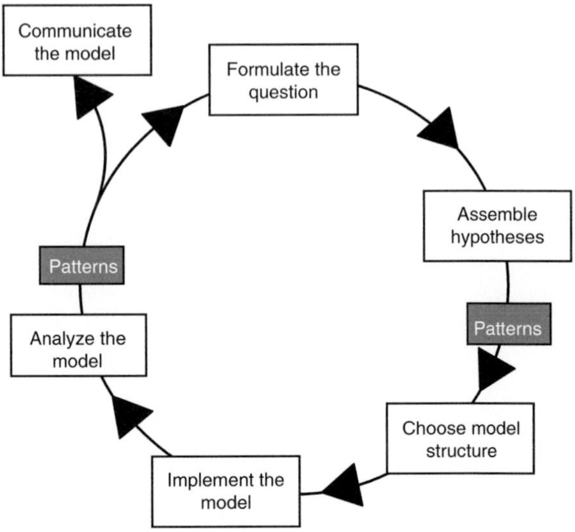

These are the five steps, broken down for convenience:

1. *Formulate the question.* The first and most important point is to define a clear research question for this model: this sometimes can be tricky, especially when dealing with complex situations with many different categories of agent and not clear-cut win/lose situations.

   Here it could be expressed as follows: What are the best strategies for handling the Mekong Basin in terms of dam development? Here "best" is what maximises gains for the widest number of agents and reduce the likelihood of conflict.
2. *Assemble hypotheses for essential processes and structures.* This is a critical step, since it has to deal with the identification of what is fundamental and must be incorporated in the model and what can be left for future analysis. It is often wise to start with an initial, maybe oversimplified but working model, and then to add layers of complexity and additional factors, instead than the other way around. Thus a choice has been made here of not making any initial distinction in what represent a gain for the different kind of agents, and just assuming that what is a gain for one is also a gain for another (even though in reality this is not necessarily true). In terms of definition, gain is anything that increases welfare of agents.
3. *Choose scales, entities, state variables, processes, and parameters.* This step covers the actual details of the model as it will be programmed by the software. In this specific case, it will include the agents themselves, their characters, the spatial dimension where they will move into—see the GIS paragraph in the

next section—the kind of objects that are included in the model, and a set of constraints.

4. *Implement the model.* This is the actual implementation of the model, using one of the many software programmes available for it. This is the technical part, and while sometimes daunting, it is in a way the easiest one, because it only requires software knowledge and enough time to get the programmes and the routines right. (More about the specific software used in this model on the next section.)
5. *Analyse, test, and revise the model.* This is what actually comes after the initial implementation of the models, i.e. running it a few times, debugging it, and testing how it behaves. Once it yields a satisfactory performance there are two questions that need to be asked. The first is what can be learnt from it. The second is how it can be improved for further accuracy, and therefore adding into it lessons learned from practice. While this phase has not yet been reached in the present case—the author is still in phase 4—it is expected that parameters and alternative algorithms will be changed and/or modified to improve the model.

After having dealt with the theoretical approach, some other crucial decisions needed to be made in order to build a working model.

The first one is related to the construction of the various agents that will populate this system, and which characteristics they will have to present. An agent here can be defined as "a set of properties that must characterize an entity to effectively call it an agent, and in particular autonomy (the possibility to operate without intervention by humans, and a certain degree of control over its own state), social ability (the possibility to interact employing some kind of agent communication language), reactivity (the possibility to perceive an environment in which it is situated and respond to perceived changes) and pro-activeness (the possibility to take the initiative, starting some activity according to internal goals rather than as a reaction to an external stimulus)".

This is what has been defined a weak notion of agency (Wooldridge & Jennings, 1995) and something more specific and/or differently characterised can be imagined. Other conceptions of agents also involve a series of other parameters, such as mobility—i.e. the ability of an agent to move around an electronic network, veracity and rationality (Galliers, 1988) and benevolence (Rosenschein & Genesereth, 1985). While these last mentioned characteristics can add substantially to the model, here a choice has been made to keep to a simpler, i.e. weaker, notion of agent, as for the reasons explained when discussing the theoretical approach above.

Having a closer look at the agents identified for this model, they are, as it can be expected, a rather heterogeneous set, including governments, NGOs (national and international), industries, local communities, ethnic minorities, international bodies.

Therefore, they will have to display different aims, different sets of goals and different behaviours—even if the notion of gain has been kept to one for the reasons explained. It is also to be expected that even the same category of agents—i.e. states—will behave in a different way from the others depending on what is at stake in a specific situation. Therefore, nationality has to be taken into account as a factor adding a specification. Another issue refers to the relations among agents of different level—for example state/sub-state actors. More precisely, the fact that one agent can have the capability to affect the prerogatives and actions of another— as in the case of governments with, say, individuals—has to be taken into account when designing the behavioural rules that make agents interact.

In some cases, especially in complex scenarios, their identifications and hierarchies among them can be complicated—as it is to be expected in this case. A model has to be something that can represent reality, but still being easier to analyse than reality, and yet meaningful. Something too sophisticated won't work, and yet hyper-simplification won't be realistic and of any interpretative value.

In the literature, distinction has been made (Brooks, 1986) between horizontal architectures and hierarchies in the agents that populate the model. More precisely, no priorities are associated with any specific layers and vertical, where a system of priorities is instead put in place. For this initial model, only horizontal structures have been used, in order to keep the functioning as simple as possible, even if it's expected that hierarchies will be later inserted, to better reflect the real-world dynamics.

After the identifications of the agents themselves, a second step is needed, and it is the definition of behaviours and a set of rules that are essential to articulate the way the agent will have to function. For reasons of space, a discussion about the characterisation of the agent behaviours used here in terms of deliberative/cognitive and reactive (Bandini, Manzoni, & Vizzari, 2009) has been omitted. It is only the case to observe that the agents included here are generally cognitive agents, capable of reflection and memories of past experience, and modelled according to the well-known BDI triad (Belief, Desire, Intention; Rao & Georgeff, 1991).[2]

Finally, it has to be taken into account that there are conflicting interests from a plethora of agents, but they cannot always be modelled in a linear way. Furthermore, this dialectic is dynamic and might change radically over time—in some case even rapidly. In fact, the same two agents can be in conflict in one occasion and cooperating in another, and there are few examples that it has happened on a regular basis in some situations (see, for instance, the case of the Xayaburi Dam in Laos, outlined in the previous section).

In cases like the one singled out, these are the agents that often can be seeing switching side and engaged in cooperation or conflict depending on the case:

1) Upper Mekong vs Lower Mekong countries
2) GMS vs MRC (the two international management bodies where some but not all the states are members)
3) Industries (National and International) vs Local Communities
4) Government(s) vs NGOs vs other interest groups

---

[2]It is just the case to observe here that not necessarily all agent behaviours might be included in this category. There are a few instances where an agent can simply be a taker, and react to an external action. An example could be, for example, the reaction of the local ethnic communities to a displacement order from the government to leave space to dam development. There are also a few examples in the past and, while reactions have been sometimes violent against it. They have not necessarily been expressed by the agents who have been targeted in the first place (i.e., communities), but by others (e.g., NGOs).

5) National governments vs International bodies

All these issues have to be reflected in the model, in order to be able to determine in which occasions these agents are going to cooperate and when instead are going to be antagonistic and working into a different set of alliances.

Generally speaking there are two ways this can happen. First, inserting a probability function, or at least stochastic variables that randomise behaviour. Second, inserting an event that makes the relation evolve when this event happens for whatever reason. Both are possible and they have their advantages and disadvantages.

When working with the modelisation of conflicts, there are a series of issues that need to be addressed, and that are not exclusively related to ABMs, even though they are still relevant and worth a discussion here, especially in terms of ABM approaches, in order to give them a working solution. But it is to be stressed that they represent a more general problem, and the choices made at this regard can be extended, at least theoretically, to other models as well.

The first one if the causal link between the role of water stress and onset of conflict. This has been briefly mentioned at the beginning, when discussing the literature about resources and conflict. This aspects worth mentioning since it affects directly the validation of the ABM adopted here—i.e., make sure that the right model has been built to represent the underlined reality of the conflict.

This identification can prove to be extremely problematic, because it refers to what is recorded as conflict. This is a well-known issue, and it is linked to the database of conflicts for water disputes and to what defines a conflict in principle, far more controversial than it might look *prima facie* (Paladini, 2012). Using different conflicts datasets can yield very different results, and debate exists about what variables should be used at all to study conflicts in the field human security (Sambanis, 2004; Sarkees, 2000). None of the usual databases deals with the specific causes of conflicts, not even the PRIO Armed Conflict Dataset which is one of the most widely used conflict datasets and where a war event is identified as one causing more than 1,000 casualties.[3] This issue is of relevance here, because if a definition of what constitutes a conflict has not been agreed at the onset, the identification of what leads to conflict becomes vague. Therefore, a precise choice had to be made at the beginning. While a final decision has not been made so far, the author's preference is for a classification not linked to war casualties, considered more suitable for non-traditional security.

Moreover, at the level of state agents, another problem in case of water conflicts is represented by the presence of the so-called fuzzy boundaries and the measurement of relative hydropower, where "shared basins do predict an increased propensity for conflict in a multivariate analysis" (Gleditsch, Furlong, Hegre, Lacina, & Owen, 2006, p. 362). Getting to model boundaries in an appropriate manner can prove

[3]In the Uppsala dataset, often adopted in alternative, an armed conflict is coded normally as one involving at least 25 deaths.

extremely complex, and a solution has not been identified so far. It is expected that the solution presented by Gleditsch in his articles, with the provision of matrix of possibilities, will be also adopted in this specific case.

The final aspect regarding the modalities of interaction among agents and the cooperation-conflict (discrete/continuum passing through *neutrality*, as coded in Goldstein, 1992) dynamics regards instead the problems of verification of the model itself, to make sure that it works correctly in the diverse situations represented and that the rules that regulate these shifts are tested and functioning as expected.

Finally, there are some disadvantages, compared to more traditional quantitative tools, that any ABM adopted in social sciences in general, and in conflict studies more specifically, entails. The first and most obvious is the complexity of the modelling itself, often requiring lengthy simulations and repetitive testing to fine-tune a suitable, valid, and working model. Whilst nobody denies that all quantitative methods present challenges, ABMs, for their relative novelty in conflict studies and the initial difficulties of writing working routines, present additional challenges.

Another difficulty, strictly related to the first one, resided in the availability of primary data to construct agent behaviours in a suitable way. While in the specific case of the Mekong Basin the author had the opportunity of conducting field work, this is not necessarily true for all conflict situations, and can limit the adoption of the model in similar cases.

15.4 Modelisation, Testing and Some Preliminary Conclusions: Ideas for Future Works

As mentioned in the introduction, the present study is to be considered a work in progress. The routines have been written and runs have started but they are still in their early test and the whole model has yet to be fully proved as effective, even if some early considerations can be made at this stage, based on some preliminary results.

An essential step has been the selection of the software to write and testing the model itself. A series of different programming tools have been considered, including Netlogo, Swarm and Starlogo. At the end, the most suitable software has been identified in the suite REPAST (REcursive Porous Agent Simulation Toolkit) toolkit, originally developed by Sallach, Collier and others (Collier et al., 2008) at the University of Chicago in 2000. It is one of the most used open-source platforms, originally developed in Java but that can accommodate other programming languages (like C++) and easily combines with other tools such as R

(North, Collier, & Vos, 2006), together with allowing the use of several layers. The version used here is Repast Symphony 2.0, the most recent.[4]

One of the main reasons to adopt Repast has been its suitability in being linked to statistical tools and to Geographic Information System platforms as well, an essential characteristic. Talking about tools used in this area, GeoTools (GeoTools—The Open Source Java GIS Toolkit), an Open Geospatial Consortium (OGC) compliant library and a precious support for Environmental Systems Research Institute (ESRI) shape files—the ones common in use by ARCGIS among others, and a range of raster data files. While this specific dimension has not been inserted yet in the simulation conducted so far, for the lack of updated figures and maps, it will be included in later trials, and it is expected to play a major role in the model.

There are two strategic choices that have been made since the beginning. The first one is related to the model itself, and to the opportunity to leave it as wide as possible. This is because the present study represents a specific case of a more general investigation about different scenarios in water-security, which will form the object of future works.

The second, important choice was instead related to what has been modelled as an agent. Here, the selection has been made in the sense of identifying each real-world agent as a software agent in the simulation. The author is aware that other approaches can be feasible, and that, for example, an alternative is represented by a scenario where agents in the model do not correspond to agents in the real world. Dams, rivers, boundaries, and even conflicts can be modelled as agents. However, this has been considered not suitable because of the political component. The author has assumed here that all agents have a political objective and/or motivation for their behaviours, and this makes the inclusion of different types of agents not consistent with this assumption.

It maybe too early to present a clear set of statements about the results. However, even at this initial stage, there are some conclusions that can be drawn and that provide some kind of confirmation about the capability of the model to meet the originally intended outcomes.

The first one was whether an agent-based construct could efficiently model in a suitable and flexible way complex behaviours of the different agents in water management settings like the case into exam, where there are conflicting interests, decade-long issues and even long-term consequences, and several constraints. Preliminary results have given a positive response in this direction, even if interpretation looked easier to achieve than prediction of future or emerging behaviours.

Another key question was, as mentioned before, the overall suitability of the model to predict likely outcomes. Is cooperation more frequent than conflict, as the literature in water management cases seems to suggest (Humphreys, 2005). At the state, there is no clear evidence in one sense or another in the early runs of this simplified model. Even the action of "dam construction" does not seem per

[4]The REPAST Suite, including past versions, libraries and the source code, is available from the online repositories at http://repast.sourceforge.net/ (Repast—The Repast Suite). Repast uses a "new BSD"-style license, which includes third-party libraries with their own licenses.

se to automatically provoke conflicts (even if this is statistically the most common outcome in the reality of Mekong Basin over more than 50 years and linked to the hydropower equilibrium among states existing in the region; Bakker, 1999).

A third point here is that's not clear at the present which are the variables and pre-existing conditions that produce an outcome instead of another. It can be hypothesised that it depends on the presence in the area of more than one ethnic group and of conflicting interests, but this has not been modelled so far.

In addition to what said, there are some general considerations to be made, affecting the effectiveness of the model. First of all, there is the philosophical and methodological issue of the empirical validation, something all scholars adopting ABM in a way or another will be eventually forced to consider (Windrum, Fagiolo, & Moneta, 2007). This will be done when the model has been fully tested, and it will be included in future studies.

Talking about validation, modelling turtles[5] and inputting a set of modalities of interactions present also some important questions, mainly the evaluation of how well the simulation does the job here: this is not trivial, in order to estimate the predictive value of the model. A solution would be to first test it on a past situation, where the outcome is already known, measure outcomes and whenever possible running statistical tests over the different results.

Another issue, more practical, regards the consequences over the civil unrests caused by the displacement due to the dams—one of the most frequent outcomes—and the way they can be modelled, and in a certain extent, predicted by the model. In India and China together, large dams could have already displaced between 26–58 million people between 1950 and 1990 (Paladini, 2006). In the case of Mekong, the direct adverse impacts of dams have fallen disproportionately on rural dwellers, subsistence farmers and indigenous peoples. A flood of displaced people is not in the interest of anybody, and it can make the level of tension among riparian countries rise dramatically, in an environment already ridden with ethnic conflicts and competition over scarce resources. There is no need for a section of the model to make realistic predictions on this point. Another problem is faced by the presence of a plethora of different ethnic groups, which normally live in the trans-boundary areas where dams are established. This is especially the case of the Upper-Mekong basin—Myanmar and Thailand—and it is evident that the model will have to be properly configured should this aspect have to be taken into due account.

Then, and as a conclusion, future scenarios can be proposed and tested in future revisions of this model, which reflect what is deemed more or less likely to happen in the reality of the Mekong Basin management. They directly relate to the research question outlined above, namely, what are the best strategies for handling the Mekong Basin in terms of dam development, and the likelihood of their outcome.

A first possibility can be the ratification of main international agreements regulating the trans-boundary impacts of dams—as the 1997 United Nations Convention

[5]Turtles refer here to the way agents are called and modelled in REPAST Symphony that has been used in this model construction.

on the Non-Navigational Uses of International Watercourses, as a way to promote stability and foster dialogue among states. So far, none of the Mekong Area countries has ratified the agreement yet, and this will represent a game changer—in reality as in the model. Another is the negotiation and signing of equitable basin agreements, which should be agreed also including those parts of civil society directly affected from them. Here the information sharing process, which should assure a system of early-time notification and agreement among states before starting any project involving dam construction and operation. At the end, flexibility is the overall key to water governance—as every time adjustments are required on the making and when is important to make amendments to past mistakes.

The best solution—even though not the most likely—would be, of course, the establishment of an independent international forum of high profile in charge to solve water disputes around the world. Other strategies, aiming at fostering cooperation as the institution of a basin management organisation, the involvement of civil societies in the decision process and a careful planning process highly acceptable by all the parts involved, will have to be strongly promoted as well.

ABM model will test these alternative scenarios and their success in promote cooperation over conflict, even if at this stage is too early to make any prediction in terms of likelihood and effectiveness.

References

Axelrod, R. (1997). Advancing the art of simulation in the social sciences. In R. Conte, R. Hegselmann, & P. Terna (Eds.), *Simulating social phenomena* (pp. 21–40). Berlin: Springer.

Axtell, R. (2000). *Why agents? On the varied motivations for agent computing in the social sciences* (Working Paper 17). Washington DC: Center on Social and Economic Dynamics, Brookings Institution.

Axtell, R., Axelrod, R., Epstein, J. M., & Cohen, M. D. (1995). *Aligning simulation models: A case study and results* (Working Papers 95-07-065). Santa Fe Institute.

Bakker, K. (1999). The politics of hydropower: Developing the Mekong. *Political Geography, 18*, 209–232.

Bandini, S., Manzoni, S., & Vizzari, G. (2009). Agent based modeling and simulation: An informatics perspective. *Journal of Artificial Societies and Social Simulation, 12*(4), 4. http://jasss.soc.surrey.ac.uk/12/4/4.html.

Bar-Yam, Y. (1997). *Dynamics of complex systems*. Reading, MA: Addison Wesley.

Briguglio, L., Kaly, U., McLeod, H., Schmall, S., Pratt, C., & Pal, R. (1999). *Environmental vulnerability index (EVI) to summarise national environmental vulnerability profiles* (Technical Report 275, p. 1). Fiji: SOPAC.

Brooks, R. A. (1986). A robust layered control system for a mobile robot. *IEEE Journal of Robotics and Automation, 2*, 14–23.

Buzan, B., & Wæver, O. (2003). *Regions and powers: The structure of international security*. Cambridge, UK: Cambridge University Press.

Chander, R. (1996). *Measurement of the vulnerability of small states*. London, UK: Commonwealth Secretariat.

Collier, Paul, A. Hoeffler, & D. Rohner (2008, August). *Beyond greed and grievance: Feasibility and civil war.* In Oxford Economic Papers 61: (pp. 1–27).

Dalby, S. (2002). *Security and ecology in the age of globalization* (ECSP Report, Issue 8) (Summer).

Deudney, D., & Matthew, R. A. (1999). *Contested grounds: Security and conflict in the new environmental politics*. Albany: Albany State University of New York Press.
Diehl, P. (1991). Geography and war: A review and assessment of the empirical literature. *International Interactions, 17*(1), 11–27.
Elliot, L. (2002). *Regional environmental security: Pursuing a non-traditional approach* (Non-traditional security issues). Singapore: Institute of Defence and Strategic Studies.
Emmers, R. (2004). *Non traditional security in South-East Asia Pacific: The dynamics of securitisation*. Singapore: Eastern Universities Press.
Epstein, J. M. (2002). Modelling civil violence: An agent-based computational approach. *Proceedings of the National Academy of Sciences of the United States of America, 99*(Suppl 3), 724–750.
Eriksson, M., Wallensteen, P., & Sollenberg, M. (2003). Armed conflict 1989–2002. *Journal of Peace Research, 40*(5), 593–607.
Ferber, J. (1999). *Multi-agent systems*. Reading: Addison-Wesley.
Galliers, J. R. (1988). A strategic framework for multi-agent cooperative dialogue. In: *Proceedings of the Eighth European Conference on Artificial Intelligence* (ECAI-88), pp. 415–420, Munich, Germany.
Gleditsch, N. P., Furlong, K., Hegre, H., Lacina, B., & Owen, T. (2006). Conflicts over shared rivers: Resource scarcity or fuzzy boundaries? *Political Geography, 25*(4), 361–382.
Gleditsch, N. P., Wallensteen, P., Eriksson, M., Sollenberg, M., & Strand, H. (2002). Armed conflict 1946–2001: A new dataset. *Journal of Peace Research, 39*(5), 615–637.
Gleick, P. H. (1993). Water and conflict: Fresh water resources and international security. *International Security, 11*(1), 79–112.
Gleick, P. H. (2008). Water conflict chronology, Pacific Institute website, http://www.worldwater.org/conflictchronology.pdf.
Gleick, P. H. (1998). *The world's water 1998–1999: The Biennial Report on freshwater resources*. Washington, DC: Island Press.
Goh, E. (2001). The hydro-politics of the Mekong River Basin: Regional cooperation and environmental security. In K. Boutin & A. Tan (Eds.), *Non-traditional security issues in Southeast Asia* (pp. 468–506). Singapore: Institute of Defence and Strategic Studies, Nanyang Technological University.
Goldstein, J. (1992). A conflict-cooperation scale for WEIS events data. *Journal of Conflict Resolution, 36*(2), 369–385.
Hassani-Mahmooei, B., & Parris, B. W. (2012). *Why might climate change not cause conflict? An agent-based computational response*. Online at http://mpra.ub.uni-muenchen.de/44918/1/MPRA_paper_44918.pdf.
Hassas, S., Serugendo, G. D. M., & Phan, D. (2007). *Multi-agents for modelling complex systems* (MA4CS).
Homer-Dixon, T. (1994). Environmental scarcities and violent conflict: Evidence from cases. *International Security, 19*(1), 5–40.
Homer-Dixon, T. (2000). *Environment, scarcity and violence*. Princeton: Princeton University Press.
Humphreys, M. (2005). Natural resources, conflict, and conflict resolution: Uncovering the mechanisms. *Journal of Conflict Resolution 49* (August 2005): 508–537.
Kaplan, R. (2000). *The coming anarchy: Shattering the dreams of the post cold war*. New York: Random House.
Klare, M. (2001, May 1). The new geography of conflict. *Foreign Affairs*. Available online at http://www.foreignaffairs.com/articles/57030/michael-t-klare/the-new-geography-of-conflict.
Kustov, A. (2012). *Modeling Ethnic Conflict*. Online at https://www.princeton.edu/politics/about/file-repository/public/Kustov.pdf.
Le Billon, P. (2001). The political ecology of war: Natural resources and armed conflicts. *Political Geography, 20*(5), 561–584.

Li, X., & Liu, X. (2008). Embedding sustainable development strategies in agent-based models for use as a planning tool. *International Journal of Geographical Information Science, 22*(1), 21–45.

Macal, C., & North, M. (2005). Tutorial on agent-based modeling and simulation. In M. E. Kuhl, N. M. Steiger, F. B. Armstrong, & J. A. Joines (Eds.), *Proceedings 2005 Winter Simulation Conference*, Orlando, FL, December 4–7, pp. 2–15. Available at http://www.informs-sim.org/wsc05papers/002.pdf.

North, M., Collier, N., & Vos, J. (2006). Experiences in creating three implementations of the repast agent modeling toolkit. *ACM Transactions on Modeling and Computer Simulation, 16*(1), 1–25.

North, M. J., & Macal, C. M. (2007). *Managing business complexity: Discovering strategic solutions with agent-based modeling and simulation.* Oxford, UK: Oxford University Press.

Paladini, S. (2006). Mekong: il fiume delle controversie [The controversial river: Mekong]. *Rivista Giuridica Dell'ambiente [Environmental Law Review], 21*(6), 210–225 (Torino: Giuffre' Editore).

Paladini, S. (2012). Evaluating water security in the Asia-Pacific: New approaches by vulnerability indices. *Eurasian Geography and Economics, 52*(6), 1–32.

Rao, A., & Georgeff, M. (1991). Modeling rational agents within a BDI-architecture. In: *Proceedings of Knowledge Representation and Reasoning.*

Rosenschein, J. S, & Genesereth, M. R. (1985). Deals among rational agents. In: *Proceedings of the Ninth International Joint Conference on Artificial Intelligence* (IJCAI-85), pp. 91–99, Los Angeles.

Sambanis, N. (2004). What is civil war? Conceptual and empirical complexities of an operational definition. *Journal of Conflict Resolution, 48*(6), 814–858.

Sarkees, M. R. (2000). The correlates of war data on war: An update to 1997. *Conflict Management and Peace Science, 18*(1), 123–144.

Smith, P., & Gross, C. H. (2003). Water and conflict in Asia? In D. E. Lorey (Ed.), *Global environmental challenges of the twenty-first century: Resources, consumption, and sustainable solutions.* Wilmington, DE: SR Books.

Tesfatsion, L. (2003). Agent-based computational economics: Modeling economies as complex adaptive systems. *Information Sciences, 149*(4), 262–268.

Theisen, O. M. (2008). Blood and soil? Resource scarcity and internal armed conflict revisited. *Journal of Peace Research, 45*(6), 801–818.

Volker, G., & Railsback, S. F. (2005). *Individual-based modeling and ecology.* Princeton: Princeton University Press.

Windrum, P., Fagiolo, G., & Moneta, A. (2007). Empirical validation of agent-based models: Alternatives and prospects. *Journal of Artificial Societies and Social Simulation, 10*(2), 8. http://jasss.soc.surrey.ac.uk/10/2/8.html.

Wooldridge, M. J., & Jennings, N. R. (1995). Intelligent agents: Theory and practice. *The Knowledge Engineering Review, 10*, 115–152. Available at http://eprints.soton.ac.uk/252102/4/publisher_download.pdf.

Yilmaz, L., Oren, T. I., & Ghasem-Aghaee, N. (2006). Simulation-based problem-solving environments for conflict studies. *Simulation & Gaming, 37*, 534–556.

Yoffe, S. B., & Wolf, A. T. (1999). Water, conflict, and cooperation: Geographical perspectives. *Cambridge Review of International Affairs, 12*(2), 197–213.

Chapter 16
Open Innovation Networks and the Role of Intermediaries: An Agent-Based Simulation

Enrico Secchi

Abstract This paper builds an agent-based simulation model that illustrates the dynamics of an open innovation (OI) network of firms in search of a technological development partnership. The model simulates an environment populated by innovation seekers and innovation providers. Each of these agents (firms) has half of the final product and has to decide whether to develop the rest internally or seek a partner that developed the other half of the product. Moreover, this paper explores the effects on the innovation network dynamics of the presence of intermediaries that act as brokers between innovation seekers and innovation providers. The results suggest that innovation providers are on average better off when they establish partnerships, especially when their number is limited and intermediaries are present in the market. The model shows that the presence of intermediaries makes the market more efficient by lowering costs of all firms in the network, whether they use an intermediary or not.

Keywords Open Innovation • Network Dynamics • Innovation Brokers • Innovation Market

16.1 Introduction

In the last 15 years, the landscape of innovation has changed radically: technology evolves faster than ever and companies are faced with a continuously increasing amount of uncertainty. In the current competitive environment, constant innovation seems to be at the same time indispensable and extremely expensive to attain. Therefore, many firms are experimenting with a variety of ways to increase their ability to innovate by creating synergies between their internal processes and external knowledge sources. To this end, many organizations started employing a set of practices that have been synthesized by Henry Chesbrough (Chesbroug, 2003c; Chesbrough, Vanhaverbeke, & West, 2006) with the expression *open innovation*

E. Secchi (✉)
Lecturer in Supply Chain Management, University College Dublin Carysfort Avenue, Blackrock, Co Dublin, Ireland
e-mail: esecchi@uvic.ca

D. Secchi, M. Neumann (eds.), *Agent-Based Simulation of Organizational Behavior*, DOI 10.1007/978-3-319-18153-0_16

(OI), defined as "the use of purposive inflows and outflows of knowledge to accelerate internal innovation, and to expand the markets for external use of innovation, respectively" (Chesbrough et al., 2006, p. 1). The transformations that this practices are collectively generating imply, Chesbrough argues, a paradigm shift in the way the problem of innovation is perceived and managed both by organizations and by end users (Chesbrough, 2003c; Kuhn, 1970). This shift is becoming more visible as several environmental factors make it increasingly difficult for companies to rely solely on internal innovation sources and to protect their intellectual property. On the one hand, increased workers' mobility, exposure to security breaches, and uncertainty of intellectual property regulations across countries make it more difficult for innovative firms to contain their knowledge within organizational boundaries for extended periods of time. On the other hand, new technologies and increased communication capabilities dramatically increase the availability of unused ideas that can find a profitable way to market. Thus, for many companies in highly innovative markets the switch to an OI strategy is a necessity rather than a choice.

Recognizing the relevance of this phenomenon, many scholars examined several different aspects of open innovation and the body of research is growing constantly (Chesbrough et al., 2006; West & Gallagher, 2006). Gianiodis, Ellis, and Secchi (2010) offered a comprehensive literature on the subject, centered around a classification of different strategies that firms can employ in the networks of firms arising from OI practices. Some firms act as *innovation seekers* and take the role of technology buyers, building their competitive strategy around the search of innovative solutions outside of their boundaries. For example, several software companies devolve some of their employees to participate full time in the open source community; similarly, many pharmaceutical companies procure new technologies by acquiring smaller companies which developed them (Dahlander & Wallin, 2006; Higgins & Rodriguez, 2006).

On the opposite side of the spectrum, we find firms that act as *innovation providers* and focus their efforts in offering an innovative concept or solution to other companies. Many high tech firms are born around a single innovative idea or technology, but do not have the infrastructure to embed it in a product and to bring it to market. Such companies need to establish partnerships to create appropriate channels to commercialize their technologies. Alternatively they can sell or license their innovations to technology seekers (Christensen, Olesen, & Kjær, 2005). Some firms, termed *open innovators*, act both as innovation takers and providers. These firms thrive on the continuous exchange of knowledge through their boundaries, and proactively stimulate inflows and outflows of innovative ideas with their environment.

The creation of a thriving market for innovations created the ideal space for the development of firms that facilitate exchanges by lowering transaction costs between seekers and providers. Such *innovation intermediaries* act as innovation brokers, by having on one side the innovation seeker and on the other a pool of innovation providers with the capabilities to solve the seekers' problems (Saur-Amaral & Amaral, 2010; Terwiesch & Xu, 2008). The peculiarity of these companies is that they are a genuine new product of the open innovation phenomenon, and they could not exist without other kinds of players in the open innovation network. Although some companies are starting to get a strong presence in the market for innovation (e.g., Innocentive, Yet2.com, Nine Sigma), innovation scholars have yet to develop a systematic theory of their effects on technology markets and how their presence changes the behavior of firms involved in Open Innovation. This paper contributes to filling this literature gap by developing a simulation model of an open innovation network, which can be used to explore the behavior of the agents involved under different circumstances.

The paper is organized as follows. The next section provides a literature review and the theoretical background for the development of the simulation model. Section 16.3 presents the development and implementation of the model, while Sect. 16.4 discusses the output analysis and its implications. Finally, Sect. 16.5 provides some conclusions and directions for future research.

16.2 Literature Review

16.2.1 Open Innovation

The theoretical construct of OI was first conceptualized by Chesbrough (2003c) as a way to denote a change in how research and development (R&D) practices were habitually conducted in a variety of industries. The traditional paradigm of innovation in the industrial era was epitomized by large research facilities established by major industrial companies (such as Xerox PARC or AT&T Bell Labs). The role of these R&D units was to generate a large amount of innovative technologies, only a small number of which was successfully commercialized by the parent company. This approach to innovation was based on the premise that the same organization took care of the whole process of innovation and development, from idea generation to research to commercialization (Chesbrough, 2003c, p. XX). This meant that a large number of innovations never reached the market, generating a substantial loss of efficiency in the innovation process. Conversely, the absence of an innovation market meant that the solution to a firm's technological problem could be lying in the closed-off archives of another company.

Things started to change in the decades around the turn of the century, as many conditions that enabled companies to pay a high price to develop their own technologies started to deteriorate. First, the costs of maintaining large R&D departments increased because of higher costs for highly skilled labor and because the nature of research itself changed, requiring more expensive technologies (Chesbrough, 2003c). Moreover, innovation cycles are constantly shortening, significantly reducing the payoffs of new technologies while at the same time requiring larger investments to keep up with the increased pace (Fine, 1998). At the same time, it became more and more difficult to retain a company's research personnel. The trend towards mobility of skilled labor means that companies have to provide more attractive hiring and retention packages and that, when they lose a researcher, they face the risk of their knowledge being transferred to a competitor (de Vrande, Lemmens, & Vanhaverbeke, 2006). Simultaneously, the expansion of venture capital market gave small companies with innovative ideas the possibility to develop and license out their technologies, while at the same time providing a possible outlet for unused ideas in large R&D centers (Bray & Lee, 2000).

Taken together, these factors led to a change in how companies approached technology development and commercialization. Companies in search of innovative solutions started to look outside their boundaries to universities, start-ups, and even their customers (Bray & Lee, 2000; Hippel, 2005; Perkmann & Walsh, 2007); and companies in possession of unused technologies started to consider licensing them out in the open market as well as through the creation of spin-offs and joint ventures (Chesbrough, 2003b; Hansen, Mors, & Lovas, 2005). This new, open innovation strategy changed the way firms and researchers considered the issues relating to innovation and intellectual property management.

As pointed out by Huizingh (2011), several practices of OI are not unique to this time in history or to the modern corporation. Indeed, even the most closed-off organization engaged to some degree in practices aimed at acquiring external knowledge or leveraging internal unused resources. In the modern industrial era, spin-offs, mergers, and acquisitions have been some of the most commonly employed strategies. Even further back, several productive sectors have, throughout history, benefited from the creation of communities that served the function of diffusing technological advances (Carbonara, 2004). However, the pervasiveness of such practices in recent times is unprecedented. The forces of globalization and the lowering of communication costs have effectively created a global market for innovations, which allowed firms to incorporate Open Innovation practices systemically in their operating strategy to an extent that was not previously possible.

16.2.2 Strategic Roles in Innovation Networks

Companies that systematically engage in open practices as a way to shape their innovation strategy are said to employ an open innovation strategy, defined as "a business model that is designed to purposefully allow and facilitate knowledge and technology transfers across organizational boundaries." (Gianiodis et al., 2010, p. 554). That is, such firms make the permeability of their organizational boundaries part of their overall strategy, rather than a one-time solution to a problem. With the increase in open-source software and user innovation communities, open innovation as the default mode of operation is becoming increasingly commonplace, originating a web of relationships revolving around innovation markets and exchanges (Gianiodis et al., 2010; West & Gallagher, 2006).

Firms that participate in open innovation networks can assume different roles, based on the types of knowledge flows that they decide to put at the center of their business model (Cowan, Jonard, & Zimmermann, 2007). Gianiodis et al. (2010) have proposed that firms in an open innovation network can assume the roles of Innovation Seeker, Innovation Provider, Open Innovator, or Intermediary. An innovation seeker is a firm that looks for technological solutions to its innovation problems outside its boundaries (instead of relying on an internal development effort). Innovation providers are companies that possess a technology or the ability to develop an innovative solution to a problem and are willing to offer it in the open market. Open innovators are companies that act as both seekers and providers, such as the large technology giants of the twentieth century, who had a significant amount of unused patents as they had unsolved problems (Chesbrough, 2003a). Finally, innovation intermediaries are a category of companies that emerged in order to facilitate the exchanges among seekers and providers and that act as a technology broker as well as a facilitator between the interested parties (Fleming and Waguespack, 2007; Howells, 2006). Formally, an innovation intermediary is defined as "an organization or body that acts as an agent or broker on any aspect of the innovation process between two or more parties." (Howells, 2006, p. 720).

Although intermediaries often take on multiple roles and expand their activities beyond the simple brokerage role of connecting seekers and providers, in the present study we are interested in what Howells (2006) refers to as intermediaries that fulfill the function of "diffusion and technology transfer" (p. 716). In this capacity, intermediaries have been argued to make the market more transparent by lowering information requirements for firms. By adopting a resource based view (Barney, 1991), a number of theoretical and case studies indicated that firms benefit from the vetting of potential partners by the intermediary, reducing the uncertainty about the partners' potential to bring resources that can lead to a competitive advantage (Hargadon & Sutton, 1997; Katzy, Turgut, Holzmann, & Sailer, 2013; Lee, Park, Yoon, & Park, 2010; Winch & Courtney 2007). Our forcus on the brokerage role is supported by literature suggesting that the role of intermediaries is more important in the creation and development phases (Janssen, Bouwman, van Buuren, & Haaker, 2014).

The implication of most of the studies is that intermediaries make markets more efficient (Tietze & Herstatt, 2009), and therefore lead to a lower cost incurred by participants in finding a suitable partner. Similarly, it can be argued that, by lowering search costs and facilitating the search for better partners, intermediaries will help in "clearing the market" more effectively, therefore resulting in higher utility for the network members, leading to the following research questions:

Research Question 1 (RQ1). Does the presence of intermediaries increase average utility for the network participants?

Research Question 2 (RQ2). Does the presence of intermediaries make the market more efficient?

Finally, although previous literature has discussed the effects of the presence of intermediaries in the market as well as their different typologies and characteristics, there is a lack of indications concerning when it is beneficial for firms in an innovation network to perform their search through an intermediary. Therefore, the last research question that this paper explores is:

Research Question 3 (RQ3). Under what conditions should an innovation seeker use an intermediary in its search?

16.3 Model

This paper develops a simulation of the interactions among firms involved in an innovation network using Agent Based Modeling (ABM). This modeling strategy is appropriate for the development of a theory of open innovation networks by helping in both refining the conceptualization and definition of constructs, and in developing empirically testable propositions (Davis, Eisenhardt, & Bingham, 2007; Fioretti, 2013).The dynamics of network formation are often too complex for closed-form mathematical modeling and, therefore, computational techniques such as ABM represent a valid alternative (Gilbert, 2008). In the study of Open Innovation, ABM has been used to examine the consequences of the decision to open innovate and the outcomes of engaging in flexible versus stable partnerships (Almirall & Casadesus-Masanell, 2010), but not to examine the relationships among multiple firms in a network.

16.3.1 Modeling Strategy

The network model described in this paper is loosely based on the concept of a "fitness landscape," which originated in evolutionary biology (Kauffman, 1993; Wright, 1931) and has been successfully applied to the study of technological innovation (Almirall & Casadesus-Masanell, 1997; Kauffman, Lobo, & Macready, 2000; Levinthal, 1997). A fitness landscape is defined as "a multidimensional space in which each attribute (gene) of an organism is represented by a dimension of the space and a final dimension indicates the fitness level of the organism." (Levinthal, 1997, p. 935). Each organism's position in this landscape is characterized by a set of genes and each of the genes can assume a specified set of values, indicating which allele is present in the agent's genome. Each agent is therefore described by an array of N scalars $A = \{a_1, \ldots, a_N\}$. Each combination of genes is associated to a specific "fitness" value, therefore associating the position in the space that a specific configuration of genes occupies to a fitness that is usually used to determine the ability of the organism to survive. If each organism possesses N genes and each gene can assume the values $\{0,1\}$—i.e., it can be switched on or off—, the fitness landscape is constituted by 2^N combinations, each with its own fitness value. The landscapes generated by this category of models are often referred to as "rugged," thus indicating the presence of local peaks that are likely to attract the optimization efforts of the agents (Levinthal, 1997).

This approach can be employed, with some modifications, to represent products in a product space. I follow the approach of Almirall and Casadesus-Masanell (2010) to adapting fitness landscape to the study of innovation dynamics. Each product (similarly to organisms in a fitness landscape) possesses a set of N features (analogous to genes), represented by a scalar. Each combination of features is associated with a predetermined utility level—which is analogous to fitness.

The utility level represents the willingness to pay of a firm's consumers for the product, and therefore is a representation of expected revenues. In this paper, each product possesses in two possible ways, and each is represented by a binary variable. The landscape is generated by randomly assigning a utility value to each of the 2^N combinations of features; for simplicity, we assume that the utility landscape is fixed and does not change over time. The utility value is scale-free and is represented by a continuous value within the [0, 1] interval. It is worthwhile noting that assigning utilities at random to each combination of features implies that the utility value of each feature is dependent on the configuration of the other $N - 1$ features in the product. In other words, the resulting utility value from changing the configuration of one feature will depend on the values of the other features.

Each product can be decomposed into two subsystems, each composed of $N/2 = 3$ features which we term α and β. The final, N-features product is therefore represented by an $< \alpha, \beta >$ array that concatenates the features of each sub-product. In this simulation, there are two types of agents, seekers and providers, each possessing only a sub-system of the total product α or β, respectively. The product needs to be complete in order to be of any utility. The goal of each agent is to search for a match that maximizes the utility of the final product, given time and cost constraints. The agents are randomly distributed in a two-dimensional space and perform a search of their surrounding to identify agents of the complementary type to complete their product. The details on the search and on the decision criteria on when to stop the search are described in the following Sect. 16.3.2. For the moment, it suffices to say that agents pay a fixed cost of search for every period in which they are looking for a partner.

It should be noted that the agents perform a local search in their two-dimensional space but that, because of the random assignment of utilities to different product configurations, the random distribution of the agents in the simulation space, and the fact that the agents are assigned a random set of features for their subsystem, the search of the agents is local with respect to their two-dimensional simulation space but cannot be considered local with respect to the product space (the multidimensional space defined by the string of product features). This means that when a seeker S_i gains information on the utility that it would derive from a provider P_i, this knowledge will not yield any information on the utility that would be given by partnering with a provider P_j that occupies a position in the agent space that is adjacent to P_i.

I use this basic model structure to answer the research questions posed in Sect. 16.2.2 by exploring the search behavior of the agents in the simulation space and the outcomes of their search. At this stage of the model development, it has been decided not to model intermediaries as separate agents, in order to be able to build a solid foundation before making the model more complex. When agents use an intermediary, they increase their search space and they pay a fixed cost at the beginning of their search.

16.3.2 Model Implementation

The model has been implemented using the software NetLogo 5.0.5. This section explains the mechanics of its implementation. The model goes through an initialization phase, which creates the agents and the simulation space, and then into an active simulation phase, which models the agents' behavior.

First, the model defines the types (or "breeds" in netlogo terminology) of agents, and the variables associated with them. Seekers and Providers both have variables indicating:

- What features of the product they possess, expressed as an array of three binary variables.
- Their current utility level.
- Length of their current relationship.
- Total cumulative cost.
- Total number of moves.
- Radius of their search space.
- A binary variable indicating whether they decided to use an intermediary.

Some general variables are also defined, that keep track of the environment and set specific values for environmental parameters, such as the number of agents of each type, used to simulate the level of scarcity of innovation markets. The setup procedure initializes all variables and assigns utility values to each combination of six product features. Each agent is also assigned a "fall-back" utility that represents the utility that it would get if it decided to develop the product in-house. If intermediaries are included in the scenario, each agent has a 50 % probability of deciding to use an intermediary, in which case a fixed amount gets added to their search cost and their search space increases.

After the setup phase, the program starts simulating the environment by setting the time period variable to $t = t + 1$ and calling a set of subroutines that determine the agents' behaviors. Each time period, the program goes through the following steps:

1. The program checks if the condition for stopping the simulation has been met. The condition is that every agent in the simulation has either found a partnership or decided to develop the product in-house.
2. Each agent checks if any of the condition to stop the search are met. The condition is that the agent created a link with an agent of the complementary kind for more than a predetermined number s (user defined) of time periods or that the agent has not found a suitable partner for the same number s of periods.
3. Each agent moves in a random direction.
4. Each agent examines the agents of the complementary kind within a radius r to evaluate the utility that would result from a partnership.
5. If an agent finds a higher utility than the one of the product that it holds at the moment, it establishes a new relationship.

In every period, the agents repeat the random move and the search, and if they find a better relationship they establish a new one; otherwise, they stay in their current situation. If a relationship lasts for a specified amount of time, then the agents settle. If agents don't find a partner that improves their starting utility, they set for their fall-back utility, which represents the utility that they get for developing the whole product in-house. For each turn that an agent is engaged in active search, it pays a search cost associated with its movement. Finally, when intermediaries are present in the market, each agent can choose to increase its search space by a factor of i (user defined) at the beginning of the simulation. The last part of the code deals with the computation of summary statistics ("reporters" in NetLogo terminology).

To answer the research questions proposed in Sect. 16.2, I ran different scenarios that simulate different types of environment. The scenarios have been created manipulating the number of providers (to reproduce different levels of scarcity in technological innovation) and whether intermediaries were present in the simulated environment. The number of innovation providers was set at one hundred, two hundreds, or five hundreds, while the number of innovation seekers was left unchanged at five hundreds. When the option of using an intermediary was available, the agents were assigned randomly to work using an intermediary or not. The length of relationship (s) required to settle has been set to 10 periods and the search space when using an intermediary (i) has been set to 5. The next section will discuss the results of the simulation.

16.4 Results

Each scenario has been run 2,000 times to test the effect of different conditions on the utility and search cost of different types of agents. The Appendix (Table A.1) reports a detailed summary of the simulation outcomes; all differences in utility and cost are significant ($p < 0.05$). In the rest of this section I will examine the more interesting results as they pertain to answering the research questions advanced in Sect. 16.2.

First, the simulation answers some questions about the general effect of entering into a partnership as well as the effect that the presence of intermediaries has on the market. The left side of Fig. 16.1 shows that the presence of intermediaries does not significantly contribute to the average utility of seekers when the market for innovation is thin, that is, when seekers significantly outnumber providers. Conversely, the right part of Fig. 16.1 shows that providers always benefit from the presence of intermediaries across every scenario. When the market is evenly matched, both seekers and providers achieve a higher utility when intermediaries are present. However, Fig. 16.4 shows that when the market for innovation is not developed, the presence of intermediaries does not create benefits for all seekers in the network, but only for those who decide to use them and end up finding a suitable partner. On the other hand, the mere presence of intermediaries in the market greatly helps providers by clearing the market more efficiently and hence making it easier

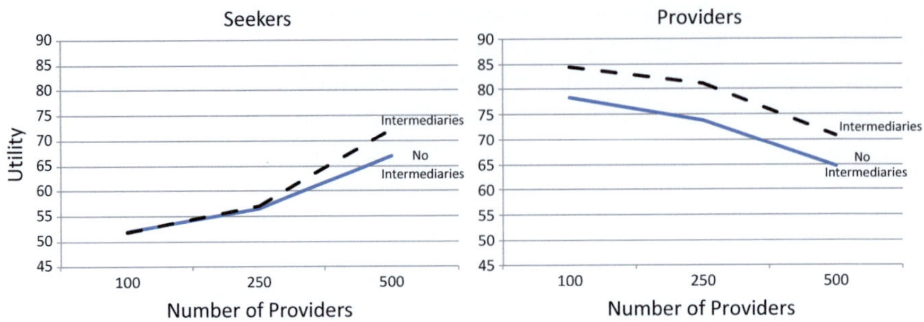

Fig. 16.1 Average utility across scenarios

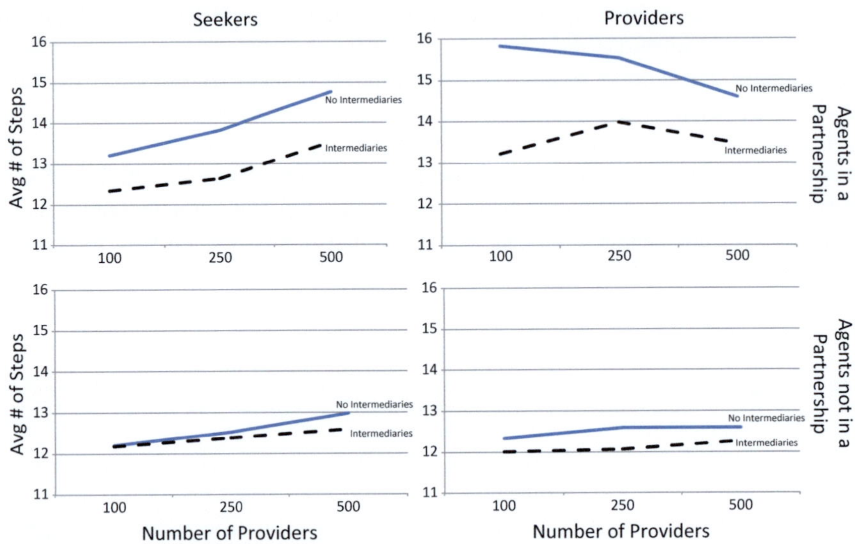

Fig. 16.2 Average cost across scenarios

for them to find higher-utility partners, whether they use an intermediary or not. Therefore, the answer to RQ1 is that intermediaries result in generalized benefits only for providers.

Figure 16.2 reports the effect of the presence of intermediaries on the search costs of the agents, as measured by the average number of steps taken before the search comes to a stop and the agent settles in the current partnership (or lack thereof). All agents that end up in a partnership experience a substantial reduction of their search costs when intermediaries are present: it is interesting to note that this reduction is experienced by agents whether they used the intermediary themselves or not. Although the benefits of intermediaries did not materialize in the utility levels for seekers in an unbalanced market, it does significantly impact the efficiency with which they can perform their search. The effect is markedly higher for agents that end up in a partnership going all the way to almost zero for seekers not in a partnership when the market for innovation is extremely scarce (i.e., when there are only 100 providers per 500 seekers). These results suggest that, in agreement with the findings of previous literature, the presence of intermediaries makes the market more efficient (therefore answering RQ2). In addition, my results indicate that when the market is thin it is much more difficult for providers to find a partner than it is for seekers. This result runs counter to the common wisdom, which suggests that when innovation is scarce, the seekers would be the ones benefiting more from better-organized markets. However, on closer inspection this finding adequately reflects the situation present in the closed innovation system: when the market for innovation is not developed, most of the seekers end up developing their product fully in house, therefore making more difficult for providers to find a buyer for their technologies. Although this state of affairs has always been interpreted under the light of an attempt by firms to protect their intellectual property, we show that a similar behavior emerges even when all legal and patent protection concerns are removed from the scenario.

As expected, Fig. 16.3 shows that, when the market for innovation is thin, providers consistently achieve higher levels of utility than seekers, whether they end up in a partnership or not. Similarly, we see that agents that enter into a partnership achieve higher utility levels than agents that do not. Figure 16.3 also shows that the presence of intermediaries always results in higher utility for providers but results in higher utility for seekers only when the market is even.

Figure 16.4 shows in more detail the results of the scenarios in which intermediaries are present. When intermediaries are available, seekers that used them achieved

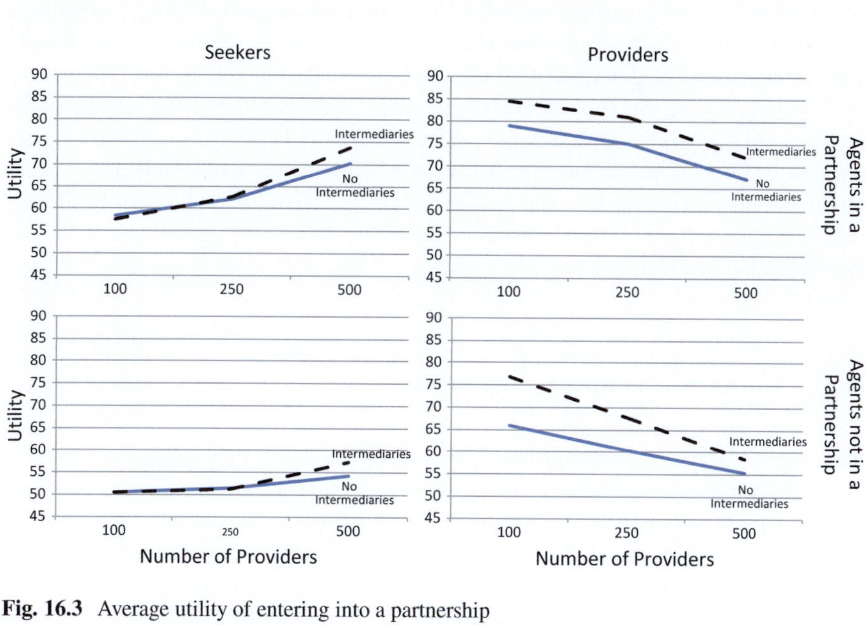

Fig. 16.3 Average utility of entering into a partnership

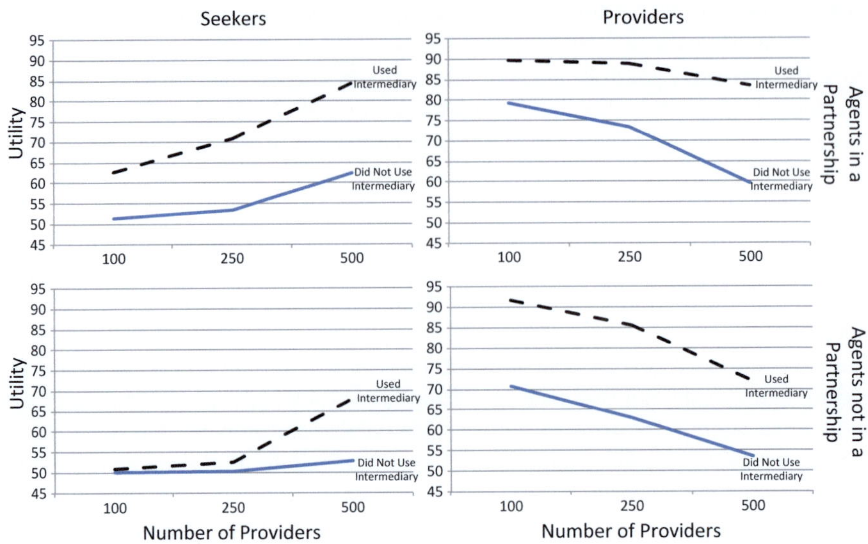

Fig. 16.4 Average utility of using an intermediary

higher levels of utility in thin innovation markets compared to seekers that did not use them, but only when they found a suitable partner. If no suitable partnership was found, using the intermediary only constitutes a cost without a benefit. Innovation seekers in a thin market face the possible reward of higher utility if they use an intermediary to find a partner, but risk to incur in a substantially higher cost without any benefit if they do not find a partner. On the other hand, providers always benefit from using an intermediary, whether they end up in a partnership or not. The answer for RQ3 is therefore that providers always benefit from using an intermediary but the situation for seekers is more complex. Seekers always benefit from intermediaries when the market is balanced (a very rare condition in the real world); in all other situations, however, they face the possibility of a substantial gain in utility (if they end up finding a partner) or a substantial cost with no benefit if they end up having to develop the product in-house.

16.5 Conclusions and Limitations

This paper develops an agent-based model of an open innovation network, in which different types of firms (innovation seekers and providers) look for suitable partnerships to solve their innovation problem. The simulation also explores the effect of innovation intermediaries (i.e., firms that facilitate the partnership search of the agents) on the functioning of the innovation network. Given the relevance of intermediaries in modern innovation markets, their inclusion in the model creates the potential to significantly contribute to the current debate (Hargadon & Sutton, 1997; Howells, 2006).

First and foremost, the model shows that intermediaries always make the search process more efficient by their mere presence in the market. Average cost of search is reduced for every agent in the network, regardless of the fact that they use an intermediary themselves or not. This result highlights the fundamental role that intermediaries can play in the creation and development of open innovation networks and therefore lends support to the systemic attempt of several governments to expand the role of firm incubators to technology brokerage between firms and research institutions.

As a counterbalancing point, intermediaries do not uniformly increase the utility of all agents. Seekers do not all gain similar increases in utility when intermediaries are present. On the other hand, providers always benefit, therefore lending more support to the role of stimulus that the presence of intermediaries can have on innovation. The last part of the analysis (Fig. 16.4) shows that the choice of using an intermediary for innovation seekers is not a simple one, when the market for innovations is not balanced. On the one hand, they stand to gain large increments in utility if they were to find a partner through an intermediary, because they are likely to find a much better match than they would have without brokerage. On the other hand, they risk to pay the increase search cost needed to use an intermediary and still not find a partner, therefore incurring in a cost without benefits.

This paper shows that the dynamics of innovation networks can become complex even with agents acting according to simple behavioral rules. Nevertheless, some clear indications emerge from the model. Providers are always better off using intermediaries in their transactions, while seekers have to consider the characteristics of the market as well as their own internal capabilities.

Like any research effort, the model presented in this paper has several limitations which chart the way for further developments. The first problem with the current implementation is that agents stop their search when one of the following criteria is met: (a) they have not switched relationship status (from one partner to another or from non-partnership to a partnership) in a specified number of time periods; (b) a pre-specified threshold level of utility has been met. These criteria are arbitrary and do not take in consideration cost when deciding their satisfactory level of utility. The first enhancement of the model would be to include an analytically derived stopping criterion.

Second, in the current implementation the seekers and the providers get the same payoff from the same set of features (i.e., in a partnership, seeker and provider get the same utility level). It would be more realistic to hypothesize that the partners gain a different utility from the transaction. Additionally, the payoff should be made stochastic in order to provide a more realistic scenario. The agents would therefore only be able to choose partners based on an expected utility rather than a deterministic one.

Third, a major simplification of this model is that Intermediaries have not been modeled as a separate type of agents. Therefore, an important step in creating a more realistic model would be to introduce them as decision makers in the model and to examine the effects of different strategies.

Finally, several parameters in this model (such as cost of search and utility) have been assigned arbitrary values not grounded in empirical data. Although this strategy is useful in assessing the general dynamics of the system, the model needs better calibration of its parameters to become meaningful in providing guidelines in the real world.

Appendix

See Table A.1.

Table A.1 Results of the simulation runs ($N = 2{,}000$ per scenario)

				Scenarios with no intermediaries			Scenarios with intermediaries		
P/S[a]	Measure[b]	P/NP[c]	I/NI[d]	100	250	500	100	250	500
P	Count	P	N/A	96.1	229.7	395.2	100.0	249.6	456.8
P	Percent	P	N/A	96 %	92 %	79 %	100 %	100 %	91 %
S	Utility	N/A	N/A	52.03	56.44	66.93	51.86	56.98	72.38
P	Utility	N/A	N/A	78.45	73.77	64.68	84.51	81.05	70.81
S	Utility	P	N/A	58.39	62.20	70.22	57.47	62.73	73.76
S	Utility	NP	N/A	50.52	51.54	54.40	50.46	51.24	57.38
P	Utility	P	N/A	78.94	74.91	67.11	84.51	81.07	71.94
P	Utility	NP	N/A	65.98	60.49	55.39	76.73	67.67	58.46
S	# Moves	P	N/A	13.21	13.81	14.77	12.33	12.62	13.53
S	# Moves	NP	N/A	12.20	12.51	12.97	12.17	12.39	12.58
P	# Moves	P	N/A	15.82	15.53	14.59	13.21	13.97	13.47
P	# Moves	NP	N/A	12.33	12.58	12.59	12.00	12.06	12.26
S	Utility	P	I				62.50	70.78	84.28
S	Utility	NP	I				50.88	52.49	68.06
P	Utility	P	I				89.72	88.89	83.43
P	Utility	NP	I				91.63	85.63	71.88
S	Utility	P	NI				51.27	53.46	62.46
S	Utility	NP	NI				50.07	50.19	52.74
P	Utility	P	NI				79.31	73.23	59.44
P	Utility	NP	NI				70.77	62.92	53.51

[a]Seekers (S) or providers (P)
[b]Measure for which the Average is Reported
[c]Agents ending up in a partnership (P) or not (NP)
[d]Agents used an intermediary (I) or not (NI)

References

Almirall, E., & Casadesus-Masanell, R. (2010). Open versus closed innovation: A model of discovery and divergence. *Academy of management review, 35*(1), 27–47.

Barney, J. (1991). Firm resources and sustained competitive advantage. *Journal of Management 17*(1), 99–120.

Bray, M.J., & Lee, J.N. (2000). University revenues from technology transfer licensing fees vs. equity positions. *Journal of Business Venturing, 15*(5–6), 385–392.

Carbonara, N. (2004). Innovation processes within geographical clusters: A cognitive approach. *Technovation, 24*(1), 17–28.

Chesbrough, H.W. (2003a). The era of open innovation. *Sloan Management Review, 44*(3), 35–41.

Chesbrough, H.W. (2003b). The governance and performance of xerox's technology spin-off companies. *Research Policy, 32*(3), 403–421.

Chesbroug, H.W. (2003c). *Open innovation: The new imperative for creating and profiting from technology*. Boston: Harvard Business School Press.

Chesbrough, H.W., Vanhaverbeke, W., & West, J. (2006). *Open innovation: Researching a new paradigm*. Oxford: Oxford University Press.

Christensen, J.F., Olesen, M.H., & Kjær, J.S. (2005). The industrial dynamics of open innovation—Evidence from the transformation of consumer electronics. *Research Policy, 34*(10), 1533–1549.

Cowan, R., Jonard, N., Zimmermann, J.B. (2007). Bilateral collaboration and the emergence of innovation networks. *Management Science, 53*(7), 1051–1067.

Dahlander, L., & Wallin, M.W. (2006). A man on the inside: Unlocking communities as complementary assets. *Research Policy, 35*(8), 1243–1259

Davis, J.P., Eisenhardt, K.M., & Bingham, C.B. (2007). Developing theory through simulation methods. *Academy of Management Review, 32*(2), 480.

de Vrande, V.V., Lemmens, C., & Vanhaverbeke, W. (2006). Choosing governance modes for external technology sourcing. *R&D Management, 36*(3), 347–363.

Fine, C.H. (1998). *Clockspeed: Winning industry control in the age of temporary advantage*. New York: Basic Books

Fioretti, G. (2013). Agent-based simulation models in organization science. *Organizational Research Methods, 16*(2), 227–242.

Fleming, L., Waguespack, D.M. (2007). Brokerage, boundary spanning, and leadership in open innovation communities. *Organization Science, 18*(2), 165–180.

Gianiodis, P.T., Ellis, S.C., & Secchi, E. (2010). Advancing a typology of open innovation. *International Journal of Innovation Management, 14*(04), 531–572.

Gilbert, G.N. (2008). *Agent-based models*. NewYork: Sage Publications, Inc.

Hansen, M.T., Mors, M.L., & Lovas, B. (2005). Knowledge sharing in organizations: Multiple networks, multiple phases. *Academy of Management Journal, 48*(5), 776.

Hargadon, A., & Sutton, R.I. (1997). Technology brokering and innovation in a product development firm. *Administrative Science Quarterly, 42*(4), 716–749.

Higgins, M.J., & Rodriguez, D. (2006). The outsourcing of r&d through acquisitions in the pharmaceutical industry. *Journal of Financial Economics, 80*(2), 351–383.

Hippel, E.A.V. (2005). *Democratizing innovation*. Cambridge: MIT Press.

Howells, J. (2006). Intermediation and the role of intermediaries in innovation. *Research Policy, 35*(5), 715–728.

Huizingh, E. (2011). Open innovation: State of the art and future perspectives. *Technovation, 31*(1), 2–9.

Janssen, W., Bouwman, H., van Buuren, R., & Haaker, T. (2014). An organizational competence model for innovation intermediaries. *European Journal of Innovation Management, 17*(1), 2–24.

Katzy, B., Turgut, E., Holzmann, T., & Sailer, K. (2013). Innovation intermediaries: A process view on open innovation coordination. *Technology Analysis & Strategic Management, 25*(3), 295–309.

Kauffman, S., Lobo, J., & Macready, W.G. (2000). Optimal search on a technology landscape. *Journal of Economic Behavior & Organization, 43*(2), 141–166.

Kauffman, S.A. (1993). *The origins of order: Self organization and selection in evolution*. Oxford: Oxford University Press.

Kuhn, T.S. (1970). *The structure of scientific revolutions*. Chicago: University of Chicago Press Chicago.

Lee, S., Park, G., Yoon, B., & Park, J. (2010). Open innovation in smes—An intermediated network model. *Research Policy, 39*(2), 290–300.

Levinthal, D.A. (1997). Adaptation on rugged landscapes. *Management Science, 43*(7), 934–950.

Perkmann, M., & Walsh, K. (2007). University–industry relationships and open innovation: Towards a research agenda. *International Journal of Management Reviews, 9*(4), 259–280.

Saur-Amaral, I., & Amaral, P. (2010). Contract innovation organisations in action: Doing collaborative new product development outside the firm. *International Journal of Technology Intelligence and Planning, 6*(1), 42–62.

Terwiesch, C., & Xu, Y. (2008). Innovation contests, open innovation, and multiagent problem solving. *Management Science, 54*(9), 1529–1543.

Tietze, F., & Herstatt, C. (2009). *Intermediaries and innovation: Why they emerge and how they facilitate ip transactions on the markets for technology*. Tech. rep., Working Papers/Technologie-und Innovationsmanagement, Technische Universität Hamburg-Harburg

West, J., & Gallagher, S. (2006). Challenges of open innovation: The paradox of firm investment in open-source software. *R&D Management, 36*(3), 319–331.

Winch, G.M., & Courtney, R. (2007). The organization of innovation brokers: An international review. *Technology Analysis & Strategic Management, 19(6)*, 747–763.

Wright, S. (1931). Evolution in mendelian populations. *Genetics, 16*(2), 97.

Index

D. Secchi, M. Neumann (eds.), *Agent-Based Simulation of Organizational Behavior*, DOI 10.1007/978-3-319-18153-0

MIX
Papier aus verantwortungsvollen Quellen
Paper from responsible sources
FSC® C105338

FSC
www.fsc.org

If you have any concerns about our products,
you can contact us on
ProductSafety@springernature.com

In case Publisher is established outside the EU,
the EU authorized representative is:
Springer Nature Customer Service Center GmbH
Europaplatz 3, 69115 Heidelberg, Germany

Printed by Libri Plureos GmbH
in Hamburg, Germany